THE RABIN MEMOIRS

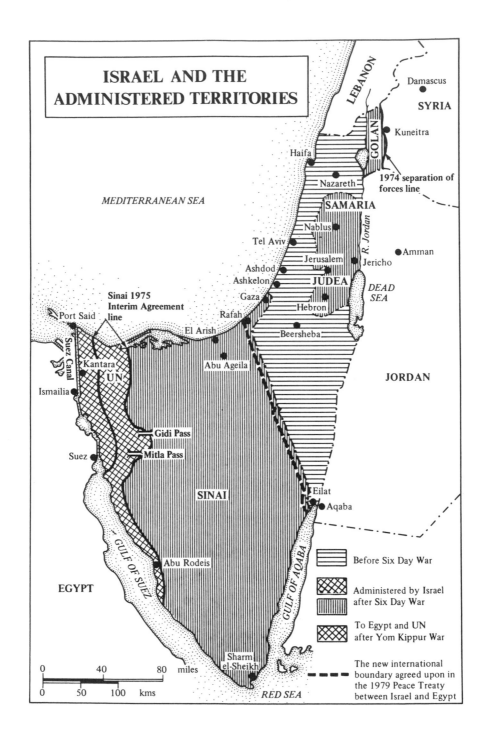

ISRAEL AND THE
ADMINISTERED TERRITORIES

LEBANON

Damascus

SYRIA

Kuneitra

GOLAN

Haifa

1974 separation of
forces line

Nazareth

MEDITERRANEAN SEA

SAMARIA

Nablus

R. Jordan

Tel Aviv

Jerusalem

Amman

Jericho

Ashdod

JUDEA

DEAD
SEA

Ashkelon

Sinai 1975
Interim Agreement
line

Gaza

Hebron

Port Said

Rafah

El Arish

Beersheba

Kantara

Abu Ageila

JORDAN

Suez Canal

UN

Ismailia

Gidi Pass

Mitla Pass

Suez

Eilat

SINAI

Aqaba

GULF OF SUEZ

GULF OF AQABA

Abu Rodeis

Before Six Day War

EGYPT

Administered by Israel
after Six Day War

To Egypt and UN
after Yom Kippur War

0   40   80   miles

Sharm
el-Sheikh

0   50   100   kms

RED SEA

The new international
boundary agreed upon in
the 1979 Peace Treaty
between Israel and Egypt

THE RABIN MEMOIRS

*

BY YITZHAK RABIN

*Expanded Edition
with New Photographs, Speeches,
and an Afterword by
Yoram Peri*

UNIVERSITY OF CALIFORNIA PRESS

Berkeley   Los Angeles

The peace speeches of Yitzhak Rabin are reproduced from the collection of his speeches, 1992–1995, preserved in the Prime Minister's Office, Jerusalem. "On the Road to Peace," written by Rabin for the second edition of his memoirs, is reprinted from Yitzhak Rabin, *The Rabin Memoirs,* 2d ed. (Bnei Brak, Israel: Steimatzky, 1994).

The Rabin Memoirs was translated by Dov Goldstein. The Afterword by Yoram Peri was translated by Maxine Kaufman Nunn.

University of California Press
Berkeley and Los Angeles, California

First paperback edition 1996

Library of Congress Cataloging-in-Publication Data.

Rabin, Yitzhak, 1922–
    [Pinkas sherut. English]
    The Rabin memoirs / by Yitzhak Rabin ; [Translated by Dov Goldstein]. — Expanded ed. with new photographs, speeches, and an afterword by Yoram Peri.
       p. cm.
    The afterword by Yoram Peri was translated by Maxine Kaufman Nunn.
    Includes bibliographical references and index.
    ISBN 0-520-20776-9 (alk. paper). — ISBN 0-520-20766-1 (pbk. alk. paper)
    1. Rabin, Yitzhak, 1922–   . 2. Prime ministers—Israel—Biography. 3. Israel—History, Military. 4. Israel—Foreign relations—United States. 5. United States—Foreign relations—Israel. I. Title.
DS126.6.R32A3613 1996
956.9405'092—dc20
[B]   96-25055
                                                                                       CIP

Printed in the United States of America
9 8 7 6 5 4 3 2 1

The paper used in this publication meets the minimum requirements of American National Standard for Information Sciences — Permanence of Paper for Printed Library Materials, ANSI Z39.48-1984.

CONTENTS

Photographs follow page 376

Author's Note   vii

1   Childhood and Soldiering   3

2   The War of Independence   22

3   Building a Mighty Army   45

4   Rabin Waits for Nasser   67

5   Nasser Waits for Rabin   84

6   The Six Day War   100

7   Introduction to Washington   122

8   New President in the White House   143

9   Anatomy of a Cease-Fire   166

10   The Search for a Solution   190

11   Rounding Out the Picture   219

12   Israel's New Prime Minister   234

13   The Interim Agreement with Egypt   250

14   The Spirit of '76   276

15   Taking Stock   301

16   The Risks of Peace   315

Afterword by Yoram Peri   339

Appendixes

    A. Passage Censored from the First Edition   383
    B. Not a Peace Process, but Peacemaking
      (13 July 1992)   385

C. The Day We Yearned for Will Yet Come
   (20 April 1993)   394
D. What Kind of Israel Do You Want?
   (12 August 1993)   396
E. On Signing the Israeli-Palestinian Declaration
   of Principles (13 September 1993)   400
F. Let the Sun Rise
   (21 September 1993)   403
G. On the Road to Peace
   (December 1993)   410
H. Address to the U.S. Congress with the King of
   Jordan (26 July 1994)   415
 I. On Receiving the Nobel Peace Prize
   (10 December 1994)   420
J. The Last Speech
   (4 November 1995)   427

Index   429

AUTHOR'S NOTE

I MAKE NO pretense to be a historian who evaluates events with a measure of so-called objectivity. This book is a personal memoir, and I have depicted events from my own viewpoint, as dictated by the role I played in them. Nonetheless, I feel obliged to say a few words about documentation, for the sake of the historical record. In writing these chapters, I was assisted by official documents, papers, and cables, including the Israel Defense Forces general staff's war diaries; cables and summaries dating from my period of service as Israel's ambassador to Washington; minutes of meetings held by the Israeli cabinet and other official bodies; and transcripts of political talks held with various parties. In the interests of brevity, I have often been forced to focus on highlights and exercise a degree of selectivity, yet at all times my first interest has been to preserve the accuracy of events and exchanges as reflected in these sources.

Y. Rabin

Ramat Aviv
February 1979

THE RABIN MEMOIRS

Chapter One

CHILDHOOD AND SOLDIERING

SOME MARRIAGES, I am told, are made in heaven. I cannot testify that some otherworldly force guided my parents toward their first meeting. But the crossing of their paths was in itself such an unlikely event that it's almost a wonder I am here to relate the subsequent story of my life. My parents first met in 1920 in Jerusalem, a city in which neither of them resided. They were just barely residents of Palestine, for that matter. My mother was in Jerusalem visiting her uncle when a mob of local Arabs attacked the Jewish Quarter of the Old City. Unable to remain idle, she made her way to the quarter and offered her aid as a nurse, which was far from her vocation. My father, whose last permanent address was Chicago and listed occupation was "tailor," had recently been demobilized in Palestine as a member of the Jewish Legion. Like many of his former comrades-in-arms, he rushed to Jerusalem to participate in the Jewish Quarter's defense. It was there that the erstwhile soldier and the ersatz nurse met.

Both my parents had followed tortuous paths before meeting in Jerusalem, where they became active participants in the Jewish people's struggle for national rebirth. Mother had been in Palestine for a year by then, though she had come to the country purely by chance. She had been born in Russia and raised in a wealthy, traditional home abounding with children (ten, in fact). Her mother had died when she was a child, and in quest of a broad education she defied her father and insisted upon attending a Christian girls' secondary school in Homel. After graduating she moved with my grandfather to Petrograd (now Leningrad), where she worked in his flourishing lumber business.

Very early on, Mother had been attracted to political activism, and the Russian Revolution found her directing a munitions factory. When subsequent attempts were made to dismiss her, the workers went out on strike, and the Communist regime was forced to bow to their will. It was undoubtedly the pressure of this atmosphere that made her decide to leave the Soviet Union, but she certainly did not plan to go to Palestine. On the contrary, even though her uncle, the writer Mordechai Ben Hillel Hacohen, lived in Jerusalem and was one of the leaders of the Jewish community in Palestine (Yishuv), my mother had been strongly influenced by the Bund (a left-wing anti-Zionist Jewish party) and had decided to head for one of the Scandinavian countries or the United States.

In Odessa she encountered a group of young Zionists who were about to board the *Rosslen*, the first ship to sail from Russia to Palestine after the war. For reasons that have never been made clear to me, she decided — somewhat impetuously, I imagine — to join them. This was how she landed up at the collective settlement Kvutzat Kinneret, on the shores of the Sea of Galilee, in 1919. After months of arduous physical labor (to which she was unaccustomed), putting up with language difficulties, and a bout of illness, she had earned a short vacation and naturally turned to her uncle Mordechai in Jerusalem, who was very devoted to her. During her stay, the disturbances broke out, and that was when she met my father.

The path that led him to that meeting had been quite different. Born to a poor family in a small Ukrainian town, he had lost his father at an early age and at fourteen went out to work in a bakery to try and support the family. Like my mother, he was attracted to novel and revolutionary ideas from an early age and took part in a strike led by the Social Democrats, who formed underground cells that included fifteen- and sixteen-year-old boys. In 1905 he fled a wave of pogroms, and after wandering from town to town he finally made his way to the United States, arriving in Chicago lonely and destitute.

Father's first job was selling newspapers, but once he learned English he moved into tailoring. Eager to study, he also registered at the University of Chicago and took classes at night. Soon he became active in the Jewish Tailors' Union and joined the

Poalei Zion party, which brought him to Socialist Zionism. Living in the United States gave him an opportunity to acquire an education and a grounding in the concepts of democracy. His stories about America used to fascinate me, and he might well have settled there. But the publication of the Balfour Declaration toward the end of World War I and Britain's call to enlist in the Jewish Legion and help liberate Palestine from the Turks fired his imagination. The first recruiting office rejected him because of some defect in his feet. He decided to try his luck at another, and to conceal his identity he dropped the name Rubitzov and introduced himself as Rabin. In a way, I suppose you could say that a British recruiting office is responsible for the name I bear. Years later David Ben-Gurion was to tell me: "I recruited your father for the Jewish Legion, and that's why you were born in Palestine." Father would neither confirm nor deny it.

Be that as it may, after twelve years in the United States, my father was posted to Canada, and from there he sailed to Britain to join the Thirty-eighth Battalion (referred to as the "American Battalion" since it was made up largely of volunteers from the United States). They were joined by the exiled Palestinians, including David Ben-Gurion and Yitzhak Ben-Zvi, who later became prominent leaders of the Yishuv and the state. The battalion embarked for Egypt, where one of my father's officers, Vladimir Ze'ev Jabotinsky (later to become head of the Zionist Revisionists), was his first Hebrew teacher. Father held him in great respect and affection, though he disagreed with Jabotinsky's political views.

Ironically enough, the battalion reached Palestine at the end of the war and barely saw action. But when the attack on the Jewish Quarter broke out, my father and some of his comrades rushed to its aid. One thing led to another, and he married my mother in 1921. After being discharged, he took a job with the British mandatory government's postal and telegraph services in Haifa, and my mother worked as an accountant for a timber dealer there. Yet shortly before my birth she returned to Jerusalem to be near her relatives, and so it happened that I was born in Jerusalem on March 1, 1922.

A year later we moved to Tel Aviv, where my father worked for the recently founded Electric Corporation and my mother was an accountant for the Solel Boneh building contractors. (Many years later, when Golda Meir told me that she had been a cashier at Solel Boneh, I said, "So was my mother." "No," she corrected me, "I was the cashier; your mother was the accountant.") Ours was a workers' home, and aside from their jobs, my parents were both deeply involved in public activities, for which they made it a firm rule not to accept payment. Mother was a member of Tel Aviv's Municipal Council, while Father was active in the Metal Workers' Union (whose meetings were held at our home) and a member of the Electric Corporation's workers' committee. I, on the other hand, was a withdrawn, bashful child — traits that some people claim I retain to this day. With both my parents so involved outside the home, our sense of "togetherness" suffered somewhat. Only Friday evenings were reserved exclusively for the family.

Ours was not a religious home, but it was imbued with a pride in being Jewish. Rachel (born three years after me) and I were trained from an early age to assume responsibilities at home: making beds, washing dishes, and sweeping floors. We lived under a Spartan regime, in the best sense of the term. The family fostered respect for property, and no form of waste was ever tolerated. My parents lived with a sense of mission that permeated the atmosphere at home. One did not work merely to satisfy material needs; work was valuable in itself. Public activity was not a way of furthering personal interests; it was a duty owed to the community. Under the circumstances, it was only natural that after kindergarten I was sent to the School for Workers' Children.

The school was a bare wooden structure built in the center of a deserted area. Mother had no time to ease me through those first days of school, or perhaps she believed it was better for me to find my own way. At any rate, I found myself standing there confused and on the brink of tears. My character (which I seem to have inherited from her) always showed a tendency toward withdrawal, but soon I was deeply involved in school — though then, as now, I did not show my feelings or share them with others.

The workers' school was unique in placing education before instruction, inculcating values before imparting book learning. Responsibility, involvement, concern for the welfare of the school and its pupils were of cardinal importance. We cooked our own meals, washed our dishes, cultivated a vegetable garden, and worked in the carpentry shop. From eight to four every school day, the building was a hive of activity, and I was kept fully employed.

At the same time, there was another, somewhat grim aspect of my childhood. My mother suffered from a heart ailmont, and I was dogged by the fear that it would bring her to her grave. Whenever she had a heart attack, I would run as fast as I could to call the doctor, terrified that I would return to find her dead. Rachel and I lived in the shadow of this dread throughout our childhood, and we were very careful not to upset her. Later, she was found to be suffering from cancer as well. She herself was soberly aware of her condition, but my father could not come to terms with it. He spared no effort or cost, contracting large debts in an attempt to have her cured, or at least to alleviate her suffering.

After eight years at the workers' school and two years at a regional intermediary school, I began to dream of going on to the Kadouri Agricultural School, which was then a center for youngsters who planned to establish new agricultural settlements. I should explain that as a city boy I had never really developed a private passion for agriculture. But the return to the soil — and especially the establishment of collectives — was something of a national passion in those days, especially for youngsters who had been raised on the principles of the Labor movement. It was our way of laying claim to the land in the most literal fashion possible. So I took the school entrance examinations and passed, but only conditionally: I would have to take a further set of examinations. My pride wounded, I threw myself into preparing for the exams scheduled in the summer of 1937. Our neighbor, an engineer, agreed to tutor me in mathematics, and I was captivated by the logic of mathematical structures. The second time around I scored high grades, and soon thereafter packed my belongings for the trip to Kadouri.

It was quite a challenge adjusting to life at the Kadouri board-
ing school. Twenty of us lived in a large hall that looked like a
military barracks but made up in atmosphere for what it lacked in
privacy. We lived by the honor code (the teachers would leave
the classroom during an examination) and followed a strict schedule packed with responsibilities. At the same time, no one felt
coerced. In fact, we enjoyed a sense of freedom, because administration of internal matters was entrusted to the students' committee.

One day I was urgently summoned home, where Father
awaited me with tears in his eyes. I rushed to Tel Aviv's Hadassah
Hospital praying that I would find my mother conscious and able
to recognize me so that I could bid her farewell. I think she did
recognize me, though she did not speak. I wanted to believe that
she knew I was on my way and had called up her last ounce of
strength to hold on. Her eyes were open, but she remained silent.
I did not want to cry in front of her but I just couldn't help
myself, and all my grief flooded out.

After the seven days of mourning, I returned to the Kadouri
School with the feeling that I had crossed over the threshold of
manhood. Part of my home no longer existed, and I had to strike
out on my own path. I became withdrawn again and dedicated
myself almost exclusively to work and lessons, finishing my first
year as the top student in the class.

A new dimension was added to life at Kadouri when we were
initiated into military matters. In 1936 Palestine was rocked by
an Arab general strike and bloody riots, and the explosive atmosphere continued until the outbreak of the world war. There were
even several Arab attacks on the school. Being the youngest pupils, at first we served as messengers between the defense positions. Then we were trained in the use of arms. Our instructor
was Yigal Allon, one of Kadouri's first graduates and by then the
highly respected "King of Galilee." (In time, he and I would go a
long way together as soldiers and as politicians.)

At the end of my first year, when Kadouri was closed by order
of the British authorities, I moved to Kibbutz Ginossar on the Sea
of Galilee, where I worked in agriculture and took an active part

in guard duty and in setting ambushes. Eventually I was sworn in as an auxiliary policeman. After some six months, I moved on to Kvutzat Hasharon in the heart of the Jezreel Valley, where we were notified that studies at Kadouri would be resumed in October. A month before I returned to school, World War II broke out.

It was not very easy to concentrate on studies with the world in the grip of a mighty conflict. For the most part the war was remote, yet it was constantly in my thoughts. Nonetheless, I forced myself to stick to my lessons, and at my graduation ceremony the British High Commissioner handed me my diploma as prize pupil of the class. He also solemnly notified me that the mandatory government had awarded me a prize: seven and a half Palestinian pounds, on condition that the money go toward the purchase of agricultural equipment. (Since I failed to fulfill the condition, I have yet to collect that debt from the British government.) More to the point, the school's principal had gone to great trouble to arrange a mandatory government scholarship for me to study hydraulic engineering at Berkeley. I was in a quandary, as such an opportunity could not be turned down lightly. But I was simply incapable of leaving the country, and my friends, during wartime. I managed to resolve the dilemma by promising myself that I would go off to study immediately after the war. That choice turned out to be a precedent that would repeat itself many times over the years for the same or similar reasons. Studying is one of the few dreams I have never brought to fruition.

After graduation, I joined a communal training group at Kibbutz Ramat Yohanan, north of Haifa. Composed of graduates of the Labor youth movement, it was destined, after an appropriate training period, to establish a new kibbutz of its own. I was fond of my companions and the kibbutz way of life, but under the circumstances I chafed within the confines of a life of work, nocturnal discussions, and kibbutz entertainment. Then, at supper one evening in the kibbutz dining hall, the pastoral routine came to an abrupt end for me when I was approached by the local Haganah commander.

The Haganah was the underground military arm of the Jewish

Agency in Palestine. Relations between the British mandatory authorities and our "state within a state," as the Yishuv leadership was more than once described, tended to be schizophrenic at best. Over the twenty-odd years of the Mandate, and especially in the 1939 White Paper — which severely limited Jewish immigration and settlement in Palestine — the British had definitely reversed their policy of fostering a homeland for the Jews. And needless to say, it was illegal for us to possess arms. Yet with most of Europe in Nazi hands, Rommel's forces advancing through North Africa, and the Arab world flaunting its sympathies toward Germany, the mandatory authorities began to mellow toward the idea of having a trained Jewish cadre at their disposal. In 1941, as the Axis forces grew closer to our borders, the Jewish Agency decided to establish special units of permanently mobilized volunteers within the framework of the Haganah. The new units were known as the Palmach (an acronym from the Hebrew words for "assault companies"), and it was to this organization that our local Haganah commander was inviting me to volunteer.

I did so without hesitation and only afterward began to ask questions. But his answers were evasive, and I was sworn to secrecy until I could be interviewed further and have my suitability for membership confirmed. I will never know what prompted him to approach me that evening in the kibbutz dining hall, but the fact of the matter remains that the invitation to join the Palmach changed the course of my life.

Not immediately, though. For weeks I waited in silence before being invited back to the local commander's room, where I first met Moshe Dayan. He asked about the types of weapons I could use, and I told him that I was acquainted with the revolver, rifle, and hand grenade but nothing heavier or more sophisticated. Another couple of questions and then he muttered crisply, "You're suitable." Again weeks passed and nothing happened.

Then, at the end of May 1941, there were rumors that German units had reached Lebanon, with the knowledge and consent of the Vichy government, and the long-awaited order arrived. By dusk the next day, I was in Kibbutz Hanita, on the Lebanese border, together with about twenty equally puzzled but eager young men. In the kibbutz reading room we were met by a group of top-echelon Haganah leaders, including Moshe Dayan, Yitzhak Sadeh, and Ya'akov Dori.

Dori was the first to address us and told of the forthcoming British invasion of Greater Syria, including Lebanon, to prevent Axis forces from using the area as a springboard for invading Palestine from the north and south simultaneously. In response to a British request, the Haganah had decided to cooperate in the campaign, and that is why we had been brought to the border area. I was elated. At last I was about to take part in a battle on a global scale.

In truth, that fantasy was a gross exaggeration. We were divided up into two- and three-man sections and began foot patrols along the border until early June. Then my unit was informed that our task was to cross the border in advance of the Australian forces and cut the telephone lines to prevent the Vichy French from rushing reinforcements to the area. Not exactly battlefield high drama. Furthermore, we drew scant encouragement from a string of warnings: "You men are not soldiers, and if you're taken prisoner you won't fall under the protection of the Geneva Convention. But you don't have to worry about that, because the forces in this sector are Senegalese, and they don't take prisoners." There was another morsel of cheer: "You will have no contact with the Australians. Upon completing your tasks you must return to Palestine as quickly as possible, keeping away from the Australians' line of advance, because they're in the habit of shooting first and asking questions later."

At nightfall we crossed into Lebanon. The route to our objective and back was about thirty miles — to be covered on foot, of course. As the youngest, I was given the job of climbing up the telephone poles. We had received our climbing irons only that day and hadn't had time to practice. Unable to use the irons, I took off my boots (which was the way I was used to climbing), shinnied up the pole, and cut the first wire, only to find that the pole was held upright by the tension of the wires. The pole swayed, and I found myself on the ground. But for lack of choice, up again I climbed, cut the wire, made my way down, and repeated the operation on the second pole. Mission completed, we buried the pieces of wire and made our way back to Hanita by a shortcut, covering the distance quickly. The story of the Haganah's participation in the invasion of Syria might never have been remembered, even as a footnote to history, had it not been for the fact that on that same night, in a clash with a Vichy French force, Moshe Dayan lost his eye.

The Palmach became my full-time occupation from that night until its units were disbanded to become an integral part of the Israel Defense Forces. Throughout the world war, however, membership in the Palmach — indeed, the very justice of its existence — proved to be a source of controversy. Under the shadow of Rommel's advancing forces, the Yishuv leadership called for men to volunteer for the British army, and tens of thousands responded. We in the Palmach held that enlistment in the British army must not come at the expense of an independent Jewish force. Though the likely course of future events was not yet clear, we sensed that the world war would be followed by a set of decisive confrontations in Palestine — both with the British and with the Arabs — and that only the existence of an independent Jewish force could tilt the scales in our favor. The decision of which framework to join was a personal one, of course, and I would be lying if I tried to deny that the appeal of a British uniform — with its shiny boots and smart beret — was not tempting. In contrast, the Palmachnik in his careless, shabby outfit — one part farmer, one part soldier, and one part underground agent sworn to maintain secrecy even before his friends — required strength of character to stick it out.

Even the meager glory derived through association with the British was short-lived. By the beginning of 1943, with Rommel's defeat by the Eighth Army, the British lost interest in cooperating with us; and before long our men were again being arrested for possessing arms. The termination of cooperation with the British sparked a debate about the future of the Palmach and altered our way of life. A good number of people in the Yishuv leadership believed that the Palmach had completed its mission and should now be disbanded, or at least no longer maintained as a mobilized

force. On the other hand, the Palmach's supporters from the settlement movement insisted that it was imperative to preserve a
standing Jewish force. Thus with the assistance of the kibbutz
movement, the Haganah command launched a daring experiment
by forming youth-movement graduates into Palmach units stationed in the kibbutzim. This system created a working army whose
soldiers earned their own keep. Every month, two weeks of hard
work paid for ten to twelve days of training. The atmosphere was
free, on the surface, but at bottom we were bound to the kind of
discipline necessary for any military unit to function. Our legen-
dary life-style — singing and telling yarns around the campfire —
helped to forge the personal and social bonds that unified the
platoon.

As 1943 wore on and more and more reports arrived about the
Holocaust that had overtaken European Jewry, the controversy
flared again. By then, the number of Palestinian Jewish volunteers in the British army exceeded thirty thousand, while the
mobilized units of the Palmach numbered less than one thousand.
I too believed that the Yishuv was obliged to take part in the war
against the Nazis. But I was convinced that once the war had
ended, we would have to fight for our lives in Palestine, and only
an independent Jewish force could undertake such a battle. The
argument raged within the Palmach as well. Here and there,
officers and men left our ranks — whether for personal or ideological reasons — and joined the Jewish units of the British army.
It was not easy to keep up morale or to induce the boys to continue their monotonous service, with its hard work in the fields
and none of the glamour of army service in uniform. Only deep
faith and inner conviction kept the Palmach together.

During and despite the arguments, the Palmach began to develop its own doctrine of combat and to train its members. I
participated in a section leaders' and platoon leaders' course in addition to the agricultural work on the various kibbutzim to which
I was posted. After I had been promoted to platoon leader,
an incident occurred that almost ended my military career. My
platoon, as one of the best in the Palmach in supplying covering
fire, was to present a fire display before a Haganah senior officers'

course. We arrived at the appointed place, conducted the preliminary exercises, and then laid on the display, during which one of the mortar shells failed to fire. It was laid aside, and after the display I decided to filch it. My platoon had mortars but not a single shell for them, and this was a serious defect I felt obliged to correct. From the kibbutz the platoon walked back to Haifa on foot, with the mortar shell wrapped up among my personal effects in my shoulder bag. In Haifa I sent the platoon back to our base by train and I took the bus. If the British should catch me, it was my intention to take the blame on my own shoulders and not involve the platoon in the "crime."

The shell and I arrived safely, and I was thoroughly satisfied with myself. A week later, however, my company commander approached me. "There's a shell missing," he said. "Did you take it?" Like the apocryphal George Washington faced with the evidence of his cherry-tree crime, I could not tell a lie. After being reprimanded on the spot, I was notified a few days later that I was to be court-martialed. The judges were Palmach commander Yitzhak Sadeh and a senior Haganah officer, Yosef Avidar.

For days I walked around in a trance and couldn't sleep at night. Finally I was summoned to a clandestine Haganah office in Haifa, where Avidar's stern expression made my heart stop, though Yitzhak Sadeh was less fearsome. I again confessed the deed and was allowed to explain my motives and mode of operation, after which I was asked to wait outside. The minutes ticked past like an eternity. When Avidar finally pronounced sentence — no promotion for at least one year — I left with a sense of relief, having prepared myself for far worse. As for the shell, it was almost forgotten. But in 1947, when I was serving as the Palmach's chief of operations and we made up an inventory, it turned out that "my" shell was the only one the Palmach possessed!

Early in 1945, the Palmach was reorganized in battalion formations. My punishment was overlooked, and I was posted to the First Battalion as battalion chief instructor — in other words, second-in-command. Then the Palmach inaugurated a national section-leaders' course and I was placed in command.

In June 1945, when World War II came to an end, "illegal" immigration from Europe became a top priority. The Yishuv was torn by a fierce disagreement over how to confront the British. Unlike the Irgun Zevai Leumi (Etzel) and Lohamei Herut Yisrael (Lehi), which had broken away from the institutionalized Yishuv leadership, we believed that our struggle against the British must be linked to two issues — immigration and settlement rights — in defiance of the 1939 White Paper. In October 1945, I was called to First Battalion headquarters and informed that the Yishuv leadership had approved the first operation in the "linked campaign" against the British. Two hundred "illegal" immigrants were detained in a camp at Athlit, on the Mediterranean shore south of Haifa, and we had received information that the British intended to deport them to a destination far from Palestine. The Palmach's First Battalion was instructed to force its way into the camp and liberate the immigrants. The plan was to take them to a nearby kibbutz, whence they would be dispersed throughout the country. We accepted the plan with considerable apprehension. These people were survivors of the Holocaust, the few snatched from the conflagration. We would never be able to forgive ourselves if any harm were to befall them.

I was deputy commander of the operation, and our force consisted of two hundred of the Palmach's finest troops. We took advantage of the fact that the British had permitted welfare workers and teachers to enter the camp by infiltrating a group of Palmach physical-training instructors. Their mission was to organize the immigrants and overpower the Arab auxiliaries guarding the perimeter so that the raiding force could break in.

I commanded the assault force that set out on a moonless night and halted about a hundred yards from the fence of the brightly lit camp. We cut the wire, and before reaching the second, inner fence we ran into our "teachers," who reported that they had managed to break the firing pins in the Arab auxiliaries' rifles. The Arabs cocked their guns, pressed the triggers, and nothing happened. Quickly we forced our way in and hurried past the immigrants' quarters to the British billets. There was no sign of an alert. The plan had succeeded beyond expectations: the British were fast asleep.

Once the immigrants assembled, the pullout commenced in the incomprehensible and menacing silence. Our battalion commander ordered me to remain in the camp for about half an hour until the immigrants could reach the trucks. It was a bizarre sensation. The camp was brightly lit and silent, and a Jewish auxiliary policeman walked right past us, determined to see nothing.

At a quarter to two we withdrew, running as fast as we could to catch the trucks. (In fact we reached them before the immigrants did.) But our detailed planning had overlooked two difficulties, one psychological, the other physical. The immigrants refused to be parted from their bundles, the only possessions they had left; and the infants and toddlers, who had to be carried, hampered their parents' movements. The battalion commander decided to take off with those immigrants who had reached the assembly point and ordered me to wait for the rest and bring them to Kibbutz Bet Oren, on the Carmel ridge. Then a passing British truck opened fire and was silenced, resulting in the death of a British sergeant (the only casualty in the whole operation). To mislead the British, the commander sent the trucks in one direction and led his batch of immigrants off in another. I began to muster the hundred or so survivors whose fate was now in my hands and moved off with about sixty soldiers from various platoons. We made slow progress scaling the Carmel, and I ordered the troops to carry the children on their shoulders. I picked a child up myself. It was an odd feeling to carry a terrified Jewish child — a child of the Holocaust — who was now paralyzed with fear. As my shoulders bore the hopes of the Jewish people, I suddenly felt a warm, damp sensation down my back. Under the circumstances, I could hardly halt.

Dawn broke as we crawled along, and it would be full light before we could reach Bet Oren. We prepared to hide in the woods throughout the day, and I sent two of my people to reconnoiter the vicinity of the kibbutz. They reported having found a gap in the British encirclement of the settlement and thought we could manage to get through. I decided to try. We filtered through as quickly as possible, then dispersed the immigrants and hid our weapons in previously prepared caches. The British brought up reinforcements and tried to break through the kibbutz gate, but in the meantime thousands of civilians from Haifa streamed out to Bet Oren and the kibbutz to which the battalion commander had led his group. The British put up roadblocks, but they were reluctant to open fire on such a multitude. By afternoon the whole area was teeming with people, and the immigrants were swallowed up in a human sea. The British conceded defeat.

My next assignment was to take part in an assault against one of the British police stations headquartering the Police Mobile Force — the unit responsible for the worst attacks on the Yishuv. But in the course of preparing for the operation, I acquired a motorcycle, and it proved to be my undoing. I was cheerfully roaring along on my cycle when I noticed a truck from the Nesher cement factory coming toward me. Opposite the factory, the truck made a sharp left turn, and I knew that I would not have time to brake. The next thing I remember was the wisecracks of an acquaintance who just happened to pass by the scene of the accident and was beside me when I came to at Haifa's Rothschild Hospital. "We found your left ankle," he comforted me. "It was just by your knee." After three weeks in the hospital, I was sent home hobbling on crutches. All I could do was follow the Palmach's operations from an armchair, cursing my fate.

On Saturday, June 29, 1946, I was awakened at dawn by the roar of vehicles in the street. Soon there was a sharp knock at the door and a British paratroop captain (we called them "anemones") asked, "Rabin?" My father nodded in the affirmative, whereupon three squads of paratroopers burst into the flat, armed with Brens and submachine guns. Another platoon had surrounded the house with barbed-wire barricades. This was an imposing military operation! Together with my father and a visitor who was staying with us, I was dragged out to a British army truck and barely managed to clamber aboard. We were taken to a nearby school, where I saw Moshe Sharett, the head of the Jewish Agency's Political Department. He, too, had been arrested. In fact, as only later became clear to us, so had most of the members of the Jewish Agency Executive (fortunately Ben-Gurion was abroad at the time) and thousands of people suspected of belonging to the Palmach. The operation became known in the annals of our modern history as "Black Saturday."

At first we were taken to a tent camp at Latrun, halfway between Tel Aviv and Jerusalem, and two days later we were driven to large warehouses in the Rafah area, at the southern end of what is now the Gaza Strip. During the next few days some sixteen hundred to two thousand Jewish detainees were brought to the camp from all over the country. I was particularly troubled by my father's detention, for which I was to blame. He was in a state of distress because he had been hauled off before he could get to his false teeth, and consequently he could scarcely eat a thing. Fortunately, two weeks later he was released, and after a month our visitor was also freed.

In the camp, we began to get ourselves organized. Dr. Chaim Sheba, who had been sent by the Jewish Agency to take care of us, examined me and had me sent to the camp hospital. Later he tried to procure my release, but the head of British intelligence retorted, "He'll remain in detention even if he breaks both legs!" Still, at Dr. Sheba's request I was taken to the Gaza military hospital for treatment. As I was wheeled to the X-ray chamber, each window was guarded by two British soldiers with submachine guns. "Not bad," I was told by the examining physician. "Come back in another month."

At the end of that month, I was taken back to Gaza to have my cast removed. I found my leg misshapen and lifeless. A British doctor taught me exercises to restore my muscles, and I spent every spare moment at them. But I remained depressed, seeing my life ahead as that of a semicripple and convinced that my leg would never again function properly. I decided to change course. If I was useless in a military capacity, I would set out to study as soon as I was released. So I asked to have textbooks sent to me and spent my days brushing up and learning new material.

Meanwhile we caught wind of rumors that the Palmach was planning to attack the camp from the sea and liberate the detainees. Obviously, with one leg out of order, I would be an impediment and a burden to my companions, and the thought disturbed me greatly. In November, however, the British decided to release us.

With the world war at an end and my sights set on Berkeley, I broached the subject of studying with Yigal Allon. "Out of the question!" he pronounced. "The world war has ended, but our war is only just beginning." I knew he was right, and a week later I took command of the Palmach's Second Battalion. Its three companies were stationed in kibbutzim and divided their time between work and training. I bore a forged identity card in the name of Yitzhak Rosenberg; in case of emergency, I had another one on which I appeared as Rosenbaum. Tension with the British never abated for a moment.

Early in 1947 events began to move toward statehood for the Jews of Palestine at an ever-faster pace. Ben-Gurion took over the defense portfolio in the Jewish Agency Executive, bringing a new spirit with him. He summoned all the Haganah officers from battalion commanders upward and for the first time urged us to prepare for war on a scale never before envisioned. Yigal Allon came back from one briefing elated. Ben-Gurion had asked him whether we were capable of standing up to an invasion by the Arab armies. "We have the basis," Yigal replied. "If the present nucleus grows by substantial numbers and if we get suitable equipment, we could indeed face the Arab armies." But those two ifs were cardinal problems. In April 1947, Ben-Gurion totaled up the arms in the Haganah's possession: "10,073 rifles . . . 1,900 submachine guns . . . 186 machine guns . . . and 444 light machine guns. . . . Heavy equipment consisted of 672 two-inch mortars and 96 three-inch mortars. It goes without saying that there was not one single cannon, heavy machine gun or antitank or antiaircraft weapon, not to mention armor, air or naval force. Nor were there any means of land transportation." In view of this stock of arms, talk of facing up to the regular Arab armies sounded like lunacy.

At that time, my feelings about Ben-Gurion could only be described as ambivalent. Though I respected his breadth of vision, I could not help objecting to his attitude toward the Palmach. Between 1942 and 1947 he showed little regard for the idea of fostering an independent Jewish force and placed an exaggerated stress on enlistment in the British army. Then, upon assuming the defense portfolio, he gave preference to British army veterans over "homegrown" commanders. At the beginning of 1947, when Ben-Gurion foresaw the grave developments ahead, he devoted all his time and energy to surmounting our military shortcomings. The Palmach numbered just over two thousand fully mobilized troops, with another thousand in reserve. Supreme efforts had been made to acquire arms, but the few that reached us were of poor quality. If the Yishuv leadership had given priority to the creation of an independent force, the outbreak of the War of Independence would have found the Palmach with five thousand or even ten thousand troops equipped with better arms. History does not set much store by assessments of "What would have happened if," but it is permissible to assume that had the Palmach gone into battle with a force of that size, the course and outcome of the War of Independence would have been appreciably different.

In October 1947, with tension rising as we awaited the United Nations vote on the partition of Palestine into a Jewish and an Arab state, I was appointed deputy commander of the Palmach. A month before the vote, on November 1, 1947, our units comprised twenty-one hundred people, including women and men unfit for combat. The reserves, consisting of former Palmach members, totaled another thousand. Our complement of arms that day was: 700 rifles, 40 Bren machine guns, 10 Château machine guns, 2 Schwartzlose machine guns, 450 Sten submachine guns, 80 pistols, 5 small-caliber rifles, 10 three-inch mortars, 30 two-inch mortars, 200,000 rifle cartridges, and 10,000 hand grenades (in that account, no mention was made of my shell). There was no way of evading the grim conclusion: in view of the momentous political decision in the offing and the danger of an Arab invasion, we were sorely unprepared. Too much time had been wasted before the Palmach commanders' "private craze" for creating an independent Jewish army had spread to the Yishuv leadership as a whole. There was no way of making up for the time lost.

But events gave us no chance to calculate the balance of forces. On November 29, 1947, a wave of joy swept the country: the UN General Assembly had decided for partition and the establishment of a Jewish state. I joined the jubilant throng in Tel Aviv, but I harbored few illusions. The irony of it all was that the success of our political struggle left us more vulnerable than ever to destruction. We would now have to protect our political gains by force of arms.

Chapter Two

THE WAR OF INDEPENDENCE

MANY BOOKS CUSTOMARILY date the War of Independence from May 15, 1948, the first day of Israel's statehood, when the regular armies of the surrounding Arab states invaded our borders. Yet the war actually began six months earlier on the day after the UN voted for the partition of Palestine, since the Arabs were set on preventing us from bringing that resolution to fruition. There was no formal declaration of war on that day or anything as dramatic as a full-scale invasion. And, of course, the British Mandate was still in force. But as the end of the Mandate loomed in sight, the British passion for maintaining order steadily waned — though this did not prevent their troops from disarming Jews at any opportunity — while Jewish settlements and transport throughout Palestine came under attack by bands of Arab irregulars. Had we waited for our formal declaration of independence before starting to fight back, we probably would not have had much territory left in which to constitute our state.

Since the Jewish underground was so ill equipped and could not allocate its meager resources equally to all parts of the country, throughout the war the most vital decisions concerned the establishment of priorities. Probably the sorest point of all — and we had many during that period — was Jerusalem, where both geographic and political factors came into play. According to the terms of the UN partition resolution, Jerusalem was not meant to be included in either the future Jewish or the future Arab state but would be constituted as an international enclave. Theoretically, therefore, it should not have been a point of contention at all. But beyond the hallowed chambers of the UN, there was nothing theoretical about the state of affairs: the Arabs had categorically rejected the General Assembly decision and were unwilling to share Palestine with the Jews. Their policy was clearly one of all or nothing — meaning all for them and nothing for us. With those lines of battle clearly drawn, it was obvious that Jerusalem would not be spared the agonies of battle merely because on paper it "belonged" to the world at large.

When the War of Independence broke out, there were more than ninety thousand Jews in Jerusalem, making them not only the overwhelming majority of the city's population but a substantial portion of the Jewish population of the country as a whole (which stood at about six hundred thousand people). Yet this relatively large number of Jews concentrated in a single city was all but isolated from other centers of Jewish settlement in Palestine. With the exception of the settlers in the Etzion bloc of kibbutzim halfway between Jerusalem and Hebron (who were in even worse straits from the viewpoint of isolation) and a few scattered Jewish settlements in the Judean Hills to the north and west of the city, Jerusalem had no Jewish hinterland and was wholly dependent on its lifeline to the coastal plain. Strategically, the situation was ideal for the Arab forces, since whoever controlled the road up from the sea to the crest of the Judean Hills held Jerusalem in thrall. Needless to say, the Arab plan was to hold that road and choke Jerusalem's ninety thousand Jews into submission — on the assumption that if Jerusalem fell, the psychological blow to the nascent Jewish state would be more damaging than any inflicted by a score of armed brigades.

When the fighting began the Arabs held the advantage not only of initiative but of geography as well. The main road to Jerusalem ran through Arab-populated areas almost all the way from Tel Aviv to the crest of the Jerusalem ridge, but two sections were particularly troublesome. The first was at Latrun in the middle of the Ayalon Valley, a break in the foothills that precede the sharp ascent to Jerusalem. The valley is a broad expanse, famous as the site where Joshua commanded the sun to stand still in his battle with the Amorites over three thousand years ago. At its heart, however, is some high ground where the Crusaders, in their day, erected the castle of Le Toron des Chevaliers (whence the slightly garbled contemporary name Latrun) and which offers strategic control of the road. During the Mandate the British built one of their Teggart police fortresses nearby to serve much the same purpose. Latrun was the key to that entire section of the road; and to our great misfortune, the Arabs held it.

A few miles farther on, the Ayalon Valley comes to an abrupt end at the narrow entrance to the Judean Hills proper. Today a broad highway runs gracefully through this entire area. But back then Bab el-Wad ("The Gate to the Valley"), as the entrance to the hills was called, was a steep, narrow gorge, and it remained narrow as the road twisted its way up to the crest of the mountains, making any vehicle an easy target from the enclosing slopes. During the first half of the war, these two strategic targets were the primary objects of the Palmach's attention in attempting to safeguard the supply route to Jerusalem. The Palmach was also charged with defending areas like the Etzion bloc south of Jerusalem, the settlement of Bet Ha'arava on the northern tip of the Dead Sea, the potash plant farther south, and, in a more general sense, the settlements in the Negev. But I was given the responsibility of maintaining the route to Jerusalem, and an awesome task it was.

Right from the start, we came to the conclusion that transport to Jerusalem must be organized and protected in the form of convoys escorted by troops. Since our soldiers were obliged to conceal their weapons from inquisitive British eyes, the girls who were assigned to the escort companies played an important role by hiding arms near the more intimate portions of their anatomy. In those days, good manners still prevailed as a restraint on the British when they conducted searches. But the handicap of pulling out guns only in emergencies, together with the increase of attacks on the convoys to Jerusalem, called for different tactics. We began to improvise armor plating for the vehicles to provide some degree of protection for their drivers. We also looked for ways to bypass Arab population centers.

Still, the escort troops faced a savage fate. Sacks of provisions were their only cover from Arab fire, and many were killed. "The drivers and passengers are protected by armor plating," they

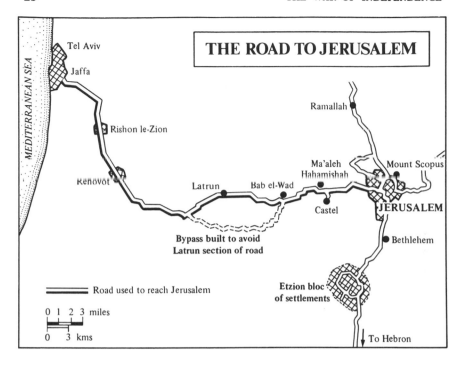

complained bitterly. "Doesn't the Yishuv have enough money to provide us with protection too?" Often they immersed themselves in gruesome mathematical calculations on how long each one had left to live. I tried to keep up their morale, joining them in convoy duty and promising them that homemade armored cars were in production. When they were put into service, the Arabs began to employ their own homemade armor-piercing bullets, and by March 1948 the convoy system had broken down altogether. There could be no further doubt that we had to gain control of Arab areas to prevent attacks on the convoys, rather than trying to fight them off under intolerable conditions.

Out of this need to change our strategy came Operation Nachshon, which was designed to employ the largest concentration of Haganah forces ever fielded under a single command. As a result of the action, we took both a key Arab village blocking our passage in the foothills before Latrun and the vitally located Kastel Hill, the last hilltop bastion before the western approaches to Jerusalem. At the same time, our forces seized strongpoints

along the road so that the convoys could go through while for the
first time their armored escorts could move about freely along the
route. Three convoys succeeded in getting through to Jerusalem
in the context of this operation.

On April 15, 1948, I was placed in command of the newly established Harel Brigade of the Palmach, which was assigned to
complete Operation Nachshon by eliminating the Arab bases
along the Tel Aviv–Jerusalem road. In planning and executing
these operations, I came under constant pressure from our political leaders, who wanted to exploit the breakthrough to rush further supplies to Jerusalem. Preparations were therefore made to
dispatch four more convoys. The first numbered some three
hundred trucks and stretched out over a length of fifteen miles as
it made its way toward Jerusalem. The second was sent on April
19, though by now I sensed that the Arabs seemed to have recovered and were massing to attack again. I therefore suggested postponing the convoy planned for April 20 so that we could undertake offensive operations to prevent the Arabs from deploying.

In the meantime, however, information was received that the
British were going to evacuate the key strategic positions they
held in Jerusalem before the Mandate was scheduled to end on
May 15. In light of this intelligence, a decision was made at the
highest political level to move my brigade to Jerusalem in order
to take the city. With a string of convoys recently sent through
and the Arabs preparing to block the road again, I was ordered to
take the Harel Brigade to Jerusalem and prepare a plan for securing the city. Since our local forces there were tied down in defensive positions, most of the offensive operations would fall to
Harel. Since I did not believe that the British would actually
leave Jerusalem before the end of the Mandate, I objected to the
new plan. But not only was my objection overruled, I was informed that Ben-Gurion and Yitzhak Sadeh would be joining the
April 20 convoy in order to take command of the operations in
Jerusalem. On the evening of April 19, I received firm instructions to move my brigade headquarters and the attached battalion
to Jerusalem with the convoy on the following day.

The convoy set out at dawn headed by the escorting force and, directly behind it, an armored bus carrying Ben-Gurion. The lead vehicles got through without any opposition, but then the Arabs began their attack — perhaps the heaviest onslaught ever launched on a convoy to Jerusalem. Hundreds of Arab irregulars had deployed along the road from Latrun to Bab el-Wad and managed to bring many vehicles to a halt. I received word of the attack as I brought up the rear of the convoy, and I ordered our reserve armored company forward to take up positions and prevent the attackers from reaching the road. The fire was particularly heavy in the Latrun section. Due to the gravity of the situation, I even ordered two stolen British armored cars to be brought out of concealment and sent into action to rescue the convoy. After a prolonged battle, we managed to extricate most of the vehicles. The toll was more than twenty dead, many wounded, and the loss of twenty vehicles. Our troops had fought valiantly, but that was cold comfort in the face of the heavy loss of life. And, of course, the road was again closed behind us. Now the entire brigade was concentrated in Jerusalem.

As I had warned, the British did not evacuate Jerusalem. Nonetheless, Ben-Gurion ordered me to prepare and carry out a plan to capture the northern and southern sectors of the city. For two weeks we fought a series of battles to achieve that objective. The activities in the south centered on the Saint Simon monastery, where a garrison of our troops was besieged by Arab irregulars backed by Iraqi reinforcements. The sheer stubbornness of our men despite a harrowing toll of casualties largely settled the city's fate. Up until the British evacuation of Jerusalem on May 15, there was a significant letup in Arab moves against the city. Nonetheless, the Old City was totally cut off from us.

Two weeks of total siege had left their mark on Jerusalem. It is difficult to describe how it feels to be in a beleaguered city. Jerusalem was almost a ghost town, its ninety thousand Jewish inhabitants totally isolated. At night they would lock themselves in their homes, and during the day they dodged about the streets terrified of snipers. Their expressions remained impassive as they attempted to conceal their anxiety, for to panic would mean to play right into the enemy's hands. But a deep sense of uncertainty hung over the city like a pall. Could the handful of troops in Jerusalem safeguard the lifeline that linked the city to the incipient state? That ominous question tempered any spark of hope in their hearts. When a Palmach unit managed to reach Jerusalem, there were touching scenes in the besieged city. Doors and windows were flung open as the citizens waved and cheered, lavishing their last remaining cakes, candies, and wine on the soldiers.

Early in May, I was summoned to Tel Aviv for consultations at the general staff and flew in a light plane from a small, improvised airstrip in the Valley of the Cross. All through the takeoff, the pilot prayed aloud that we would be airborne before he ran out of runway. Fortunately his prayers were answered and we reached Tel Aviv to find it unchanged. How bizarre it was that a few dozen miles from Jerusalem life went on as usual.

At the time, the chief of operations, Yigael Yadin, was carrying the principal burden of conducting the war, because Chief of Staff Ya'akov Dori was in poor health and under treatment most of the time. My assignment again was to open up the road to Jerusalem, and again my plan rested on seizing the principal strongpoints dominating the route.

In a week of prolonged fighting, Harel secured the route from Jerusalem to Bab el-Wad, but we failed to open the main road because Latrun remained in Arab hands. I was deeply troubled by our predicament. Shockingly short of men and weapons, our units were steadily being depleted. Since moving to Jerusalem, for example, my brigade had suffered over one hundred dead and over four hundred wounded. One of my battalions had lost so many men that I was obliged to reinforce it with a platoon of Gadna troops (youth detachments). I very much wanted to spare these fifteen- and sixteen-year-olds the horrors of battle, but I was left with no choice. We were now paying the bloody price of years of neglect. Now I knew for certain that my assessment prior to the War of Independence had been correct: the Yishuv leadership had not prepared enough weapons of the quality required, and combat forces had not been sufficiently trained. No other people has charged so few, so poorly armed, with gaining and safeguarding its independence.

Considering our mood, there was a mixed flavor to the tidings of May 14, 1948. An ancient radio in Kibbutz Ma'aleh Hahamishah, a few miles outside Jerusalem, conveyed Ben-Gurion's voice to us as he proclaimed the establishment of the State of Israel. Our weary troops strained to catch the portent of his words. One soldier who was curled up in a corner in a state of complete exhaustion opened a bleary eye and pleaded, "Hey guys, turn it off. I'm dying for some sleep. We can hear the fine words tomorrow." Someone got up and turned the knob, leaving a leaden silence in the room. I was mute, stifling my own mixture of emotions. None of us had ever dreamed that this was how we would greet the birth of our state, but we were filled with an even stronger sense of determination now that the state existed.

That same day, the British had evacuated their positions in Jerusalem and the center of the city fell into our hands without a shot. But the next day, May 15, when the armies of five Arab states invaded Israel, our forces stationed to defend northern Jerusalem fled; and by May 17 the whole front on the north of the city was wide open. Arab Legion forces penetrated Jerusalem and reached as far as the Old City, threatening to destroy our gains in the city.

The situation in Jerusalem could only be described as critical when my brigade received an order to resume its efforts to bring convoys into the beleaguered city. I presented a plan calling for the conquest of Latrun and the nearby village of Yalu, giving us control of the entire Latrun ridge. On May 14 and 15 the Arab irregulars withdrew from the Latrun area — except for the monastery and the police fortress — and by the following night we held control of the region. At last we had opened up the road — but the convoy failed to arrive. We were told that there was some organizational hitch, but perhaps it was simply that after so many failures, the convoy's commanders didn't believe we would succeed in our mission and we caught them unprepared. At any rate, we kept the Jerusalem road open all that night, though only a single armored car broke the silence as the brigade's intelligence unit returned to Jerusalem. We called it "the orphan's convoy" — one solitary vehicle.

In the morning I was notified that a convoy was being prepared for the following night. Meanwhile, however, David Shaltiel, the commander of Jerusalem, informed me that he had decided to attack the Old City and asked me to lend him a company or two. I consented but told him I was sending the Harel Brigade's operations officer, Itiel Amitai, and one of its battalion commanders to be briefed on details of the plan. I had little respect for the military abilities of the Jerusalem Brigade's command, and I did not want any part of an operation that was doomed to failure.

While I was busy preparing the units for the arrival of the convoy, Itiel got through to me by phone. "Yitzhak, it's a disaster," he wailed. "You must come to Jerusalem immediately!" At the headquarters of the Jerusalem Brigade, Shaltiel and his staff presented their plan, which called for breaking into the Old City through the Jaffa Gate. They had even prepared a flag to hoist on top of David's Tower. Shaltiel wanted the Harel units to undertake a diversionary attack in the direction of Mount Zion, after which his units would break into the Old City and link up with the Jewish Quarter, which was in desperate straits. To tell the truth, I was appalled, for it was obvious that his plan hadn't the faintest chance of succeeding. "Don't go charging headfirst right into a wall," I warned Shaltiel. "I'll place the whole of the Harel Brigade under your command, but there must be a different plan."

The strategy I proposed was broader in conception. It called for closing in on the Old City from areas under our control in order to isolate it from the Arab forces before attempting to break in. But Shaltiel rejected my proposal and was adamant about implementing his own. I was furious with him and told him outright that his plan was idiotic and bound to fail. But Jerusalem was much too dear to me to refuse even an attempt; we would carry out the diversionary attack as he requested. Since time was pressing, I took my leave of Shaltiel and rushed back down to Bab el-Wad. We managed to get thirty supply trucks through to Jerusalem that night by fighting off Arab attacks.

Itiel radioed me that of Shaltiel's whole plan, only the diversionary attack had succeeded: Mount Zion was in our hands. But it was only later that I learned the full extent of the debacle. The assault force had never even reached the Jaffa Gate, since its com-

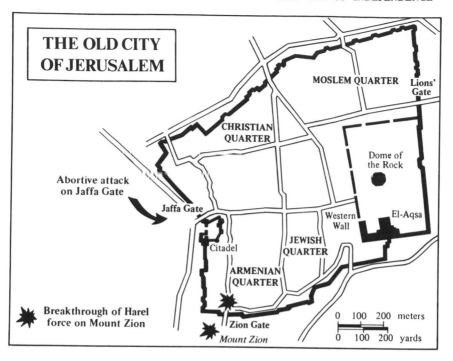

mander was wounded before the attack actually got under way. Now our two companies on Mount Zion, consisting of some forty or forty-five men, were holding out against fierce Arab Legion pressure.

That afternoon I was back in Jerusalem for a further meeting at Shaltiel's headquarters. He proposed that the two Palmach companies occupying Mount Zion break into the Jewish Quarter by way of the Zion Gate. My rage was beyond restraint. "Where are all the troops?" I railed at Shaltiel. "Are the eighty exhausted Palmachniks I lent you the only force that the Jewish people can muster for the liberation of its capital?" I was promised that reinforcements would be sent in *after* the breakthrough. In the meantime, however, the defenders of the Jewish Quarter were sending out desperate appeals for assistance. This was no time for settling accounts or arguing about prestige or authority.

The men who had taken Mount Zion the previous night and spent the whole day in bitter fighting now called up their last ounces of strength to break through the Zion Gate and link up with the defenders of the Jewish Quarter. Some thirty men fought their way in, while fifteen remained behind to defend Mount Zion. Now they waited for the promised reinforcements, who were commanded by an exceptional man, Mordechai Gazit (later to become Israel's ambassador to France). Gazit had managed to pull together some seventy to ninety men, including middle-aged "reservists" with little training and some dispirited youngsters. They were more or less dragged along by soldiers from Harel and brought meager quantities of food and weapons into the Jewish Quarter. Such were the reinforcements that Jerusalem's substantial Jewish population could drum up to maintain our hold on the Old City.

As the Arab Legion intensified its attacks on the Old City and on Mount Zion, it was clear that we could not hold our breakthrough route open. The Palmach detachment was ordered to withdraw, while the reinforcements remained in the Old City as the siege of the Jewish Quarter continued. On the night of May 27, we mounted another attack on the Old City by way of the Zion Gate. It was unsuccessful, as were two other attempts to break through from the north. The legion kept up its shelling without respite. On May 28 I went up to Mount Zion, where I witnessed a shattering scene. A delegation was emerging from the Jewish Quarter bearing white flags. I was horrified to learn that it consisted of rabbis and other residents on their way to hear the legion's terms for their capitulation. That same night the Jewish Quarter surrendered to the Arab Legion.

Throughout this period of dramatic events in Jerusalem, our forces mounted repeated attacks on the Latrun ridge, each one ending in failure. At one point a company of Palmach troops actually fought its way into the police fortress, but when reinforcements failed to arrive it was forced to withdraw again. After yet another abortive attack on June 8, Ben-Gurion's frustration was at a peak. He ordered the Latrun ridge to be taken on the following night, whatever the cost. Yigal Allon and his brigade commanders were in unanimous agreement that the assault should be postponed for at least another twenty-four hours. In addition, a new option had emerged that might allow us to forego Latrun altogether, and we needed time to explore it.

The first hint of an alternate route, beyond the range of fire from the Latrun ridge, had come on the night of May 18, when we had opened the road and the convoy failed to show. That night's "orphan convoy" had covered part of its route on a track to the south of the Latrun ridge, and we realized that this bypass might have great potential. Shortly afterward one of my officers requested permission to leave Jerusalem and descend to the coastal plain for personal reasons. He claimed to know of a route that bypassed Latrun and was sure he could get through. I sent him together with three other soldiers as a test of the route. Later a formation of 150 soldiers, mostly new recruits who had arrived directly from the British detention camps in Cyprus, marched from the foothills up to Jerusalem by the same path that my officer had used going in the opposite direction. Four jeeps had succeeded in negotiating the track as well.

Armed with these tidings, I was sent by Yigal Allon and the famed American colonel Mickey Marcus (who had assumed command of the front) to confront Ben-Gurion. Our proposal was that instead of renewing our attacks on Latrun, we should strengthen our hold on the area surrounding the bypass and channel all our efforts into paving a new stretch of road. Ben-Gurion was furious, and it seemed to me that Latrun had become something of an obsession for him.

"Is it or is it not possible to attack Latrun tonight?" he barked.

"It's possible," I said, "but the chances of success are close to zero."

"Why wasn't I notified yesterday that you had no intention of attacking Latrun?" he flared at me.

"I don't know. I have been charged with submitting this proposal on behalf of Allon and Stone [Marcus's *nom de guerre*]. Latrun is not sacred. The purpose of taking it is to safeguard our link with Jerusalem. If that purpose can be gained by other means, why must we shed our blood over Latrun?"

Ben-Gurion's anger did not subside. "Why didn't Allon tell me that he doesn't intend to attack Latrun?" His rage reached its peak as he shouted, "Yigal Allon should be shot!"

I was astounded, barely able to mumble, "Ben-Gurion, what are you saying?" But he did not withdraw his remark. "Yes, you heard me correctly!" This exchange is depicted in Ben-Gurion's book *The State of Israel Restored.* I have carefully read every word of it, and shooting Yigal Allon is not mentioned. In retrospect, Ben-Gurion must have grasped that he had let his tongue run away with itself.

At the time, however, the prime minister ranted at me for two hours. Finally, he conceded, "You have left me with no choice. I approve." I left general staff headquarters tense and exhausted, contacted our headquarters, and informed Allon and Marcus of the success of my mission. After that, I set out on my way back to Jerusalem. The first truce in the war was due to come into effect on the following day, June 11, at 10:00 A.M., but there were doubts that the Arabs would adhere to it.

The respite came at an opportune moment, since our forces were exhausted and it was essential to reorganize them. During the course of the truce, we also paved the new "Burma Road," opening up the route to Jerusalem, and alleviated two other grave problems: the shortage of weapons and of manpower. Historians will have to judge who is to blame for the Yishuv entering the War of Independence so poorly armed. Yet by the beginning of June 1948, our efforts to acquire arms had begun to bear fruit. Rifles, machine guns, Messerschmidts, and Spitfires were purchased from Czechoslovakia. Whatever accounts Israel and the Jewish people have to settle with the Communist bloc, the parallel column must bear an entry in large, clear letters: without the arms from Czechoslovakia — unquestionably provided at the behest of the Soviet Union — it is very doubtful that we would have been able to conduct our war for independence. Recruitment also improved, and the truce gave us a chance to integrate the immigrants from the Cyprus detention camps into battle-tried units, rather than organize them into separate formations as we had been forced to do during the fighting. We were also blessed with a flow of Jewish volunteers from the United States and other Western countries. They were first-class soldiers, but their principal contribution was to serve as a reminder that we were not alone. Many of these volunteers were directed into the air force, but they also figured prominently in our infantry units.

The first and second truces were divided by ten days of fighting during which our forces went over to the offensive on two fronts: Operation Danny, to secure our gains around the road to Jerusalem; and the occupation of Nazareth to improve our position in the central Galilee. Moreover, the Egyptian offensive in the south was blocked, and we had punctured a hole in the Egyptian line that had sealed the Negev off from the north. The second truce, whose termination date was not specified, was also utilized for the purpose of rest, recovery, and reorganization. The Arab states' appetite for war was waning. Their arms supply was uncertain, and there was no significant improvement in their equipment. At the same time, the newly established Israel Defense Forces (IDF) built up its strength, and the balance of forces shifted to Israel's advantage. The reorganization of the army entailed the establishment of regional commands: the south, Jerusalem, the Sharon (coastal plain), and the north. Yigal Allon was appointed commander of the southern front, facing the Egyptians, and the Palmach command and most of its units followed him south. I was among them.

I also underwent personal "reorganization." On August 23, three days after I transferred to southern front headquarters, Leah and I decided that our prolonged relationship should be formalized under the wedding canopy. Influenced by the times, ours had been a wartime romance. It began with a chance encounter in a Tel Aviv street in 1944: a glance, a word, a stirring within, and then a further meeting. But there were obstacles to the deepening relationship. I was in the Palmach, and leaves were rare. We grew closer in 1945, when Leah joined the Palmach and served in the battalion of which I was deputy commander — one of the rare occasions in our life together when *she* was under *my* command. I did my best to pay frequent visits to the kibbutz where she was stationed, and we took regular rides on my motorcycle. Fortunately she was not with me when I had my accident. As we began to weave our dreams, along came the British and arrested me; our only link was by letter. Then came the War of Independence, with its bitter fighting and heavy toll in lives. Personal plans were set aside, and Leah managed to complete her studies at a teachers' seminary.

During the second truce, we decided to seize the opportunity and seal our ties. The marriage ceremony was held in Tel Aviv, and I can still recall the excitement and jitters, aggravated by the fact that the rabbi was late. All the guests had arrived, everything was prepared, and no rabbi. Years later, a friend was to remind me of my acid comment: "This is the last time *I'm* getting married." If I said it, I said it. We took up residence in a small room of my in-laws' Tel Aviv home until we could move to our own house in the suburb of Zahala in 1952.

About three weeks after formally "settling down," still during the second truce, I experienced something of an emotional upheaval. On September 14, dozens of Palmach officers were summoned to a conference with Ben-Gurion. He began by showering praise upon the Palmach for the outstanding role it had played in the country's defense and for its unique values, which deserved to be adopted throughout the IDF. But — and what a painful "but" that was for us — the existence of a separate Palmach command had lost its relevance. Since the state had formally established a unified army, the Palmach had to become an integral part of that force. Its three brigades would be incorporated into the general IDF structure and come under the direct control of the area commanders and the general staff.

The discussion went on for hours, but I remained silent. In truth, I felt somewhat ambivalent about this latest decision. According to Ben-Gurion's scheme of things, with the Palmach brigades dispersed among various fronts, there was indeed no place for a separate command. Yet if Ben-Gurion really did intend to preserve the values fostered by the Palmach, it seemed to me that the command could be maintained and charged with some special task. Above all, however, it was clear that we had been summoned not to air our views but to be confronted with a *fait accompli*. The Palmach command was disbanded. Yet more compelling than the logic of the move was the feeling that the state's leadership, and the IDF command, were now dominated by men who had a vested interest in diminishing the stature and contribution of the Palmach — our only mobilized force at the outbreak of the war. I sometimes lapsed into wondering how far the move was designed to cover up tracks — or, in this case, the lack of them.

To counter my gloom, I threw myself into planning our strategy for breaking the Egyptian line and liberating the Negev. By late August 1948, the Arab armies showed little inclination to renew the war. The Egyptians appeared to be satisfied with their gains, since the Negev was all but cut off from the rest of the country and their forces were dispersed along the Mediterranean coast to a point just twenty miles south of Tel Aviv. Our plan (code-named Operation Yoav) was designed to slice the Egyptian army into three sections and then attack each one separately In the final phase of the operation, we intended to capture Beersheba and, if possible, Gaza as well. Having taken full advantage of the respite, we were ready and eager for action. But there was one catch. To avoid the political handicap of taking the blame for breaking the truce, we had to find some pretext for renewing the fighting.

The agreement regulating the second truce specified that our convoys would be allowed through to the Negev, but in practice the Egyptians did not honor that clause. Consequently, we decided to send a supply convoy through as a deliberate act of provocation. When the Egyptians opened fire on it, they would provide us with an adequate pretext to renew the fighting. Our only fear was that the Egyptians would change their tactics and actually allow the convoy through! The plan commenced on the evening of October 15, and that is precisely what happened. As the convoy covered every additional mile unmolested, our nerves were stretched to the breaking point. The excuse for our attack was slipping out of our grasp. In the end, with the aid of a random shot here, another there, we had our pretext. The air force launched its bombing raids, and the operation went forward. Two of our forces managed to thrust a wedge into the Egyptian lines; but a third (the only armored brigade in the IDF), which was charged with taking advantage of the fragmentation of the Egyptian army, failed in a daylight attack on a strategic stronghold and was put out of action on the first day of the fighting. Clearly it would take a long time to recover, and we were forced to revise our "divide and conquer" plan in favor of forcing the strongholds at critical crossroads and thrusting forward toward the Negev.

In seven days of heavy and determined fighting — sometimes

hand to hand — Operation Yoav opened up the north-south road to the Negev. On the last day of the campaign, fighting against both the Egyptians and the clock of a UN-proposed truce, we captured the town of Beersheba. When the truce went into effect, the Egyptian army found itself in a most uncomfortable predicament. A force of more than brigade strength spread out along the coast in the Ashkelon-Ashdod area was cut off from the rest of the Egyptian army. Another reinforced Egyptian brigade was trapped in the famous "Faluja pocket" at the heart of the northern Negev. The Egyptian command was forced to take some painful decisions. They decided to abandon the whole of the Ashkelon-Ashdod coastal area without a fight, pulling all their forces south to the Gaza region under the protection of a UN-supervised cease-fire. The Faluja pocket remained intact until we signed the armistice agreement with Egypt in February 1949.

With the termination of Operation Yoav, the War of Independence effectively became an Israeli-Egyptian war, since Arab unity had been smashed and the other fronts remained subdued. Our final major campaign of the war, Operation Horev, began on December 22 and was designed to drive the last of the Egyptian army out of the territory of mandatory Palestine. Most of the fighting in this campaign took place along a front running southwest from Beersheba to the international boundary, which we reached five days after the commencement of fighting. Spurred by the momentum of our victory, once we had obtained the official objectives of the campaign we had little desire to halt and decided to push on into Egypt proper. Our plan was to capture Abu Ageila and try to reach El Arish on the Mediterranean coast. Since this was a major departure from our original orders, I drove to Tel Aviv to obtain Yigael Yadin's approval. Yadin heard me out and gave his consent; but I had neglected to specify our entire plan and confined myself to the capture of Abu Ageila. I had reason to believe that if I were to reveal the whole plan, including the capture of El Arish, the general staff might suspect we had gone mad.

Our forces moved off on December 27, just before darkness fell. With a year of bitter fighting behind them, the troops flashed

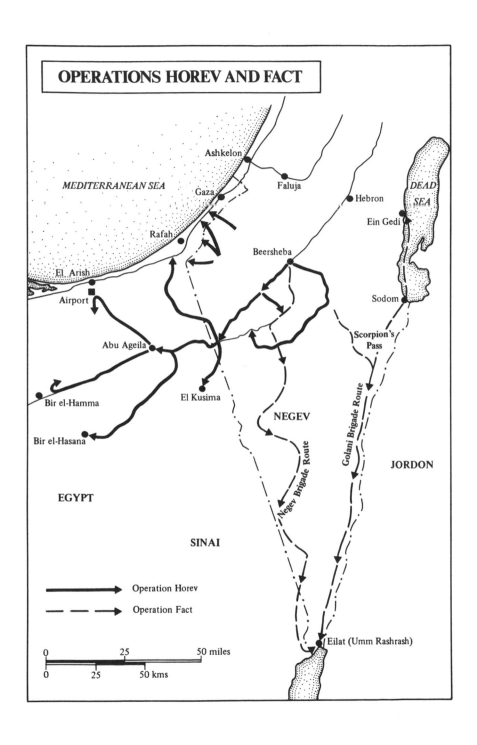

OPERATIONS HOREV AND FACT

MEDITERRANEAN SEA

Ashkelon

Gaza

Faluja

Hebron

DEAD SEA

Ein Gedi

Rafah

Beersheba

El Arish

Sodom

Airport

Scorpion's Pass

Abu Ageila

Bir el-Hamma

El Kusima

NEGEV

Bir el-Hasana

Negev Brigade Route

Golani Brigade Route

JORDON

EGYPT

SINAI

Eilat (Umm Rashrash)

Operation Horev

Operation Fact

0   25   50 miles

0   25   50 kms

smiles of satisfaction at the English signpost reading "Egypt-Palestine Border." There was a sense of profound triumph: at last we were carrying the war into enemy territory. The head of the column encountered an Egyptian position about seven miles before Abu Ageila, where our lead armored car was hit and burst into flames. All that night the burning vehicle served to mark the location of the enemy positions, and the strongpoint was taken in a night attack by an infantry unit. Resuming our advance at dawn, we found that the Egyptians had abandoned Abu Ageila, and we took it almost without encountering resistance.

That morning, without consulting the general staff, we decided to push on to El Arish. It was probably because of this lack of coordination that we found ourselves under attack by Israeli planes, losing several soldiers and jeeps in the raids. When we reached the eastern airfield at El Arish, we were strafed again — this time by Egyptian planes. Just as we were getting over that attack, our own planes appeared once more. The troops opened up at them with every available weapon. I halted one of our jeeps whose occupants were blazing away at a furious rate. "You never fired like that at the Egyptian planes," I commented to one of the soldiers. "Can't you see that they're ours?"

"Sure I can see," he replied. "Our planes are a hundred times more dangerous!"

As the force proceeded westward, we received a message from the general staff: "Our planes report you are advancing on El Arish. What's going on? Halt your advance!" We asked for one more night, and moved on to the second airfield, two miles from the town. But the general staff was adamant. Allon flew to Tel Aviv to get the orders rescinded, but at midnight a radioed message from him shattered our last hope: "No go. Withdraw from El Arish." We carried out our withdrawal in stages as Allon traced Ben-Gurion to his vacation spot in Tiberias, dredging up every possible argument for completing the mission. But Ben-Gurion wouldn't budge.

If El Arish had fallen into our hands, the Egyptian army in the Gaza Strip would have been cut off; the major part of the Sinai would have been ours; and the subsequent military history of

Israel would have taken a different course. But "if only" has little bearing on history. As it was, we attempted to cut off the Egyptian contingents in the Gaza Strip by taking the crossroads south of Rafah. But another — and final — cease-fire came into effect before we could complete what proved to be a difficult operation, and the Gaza Strip remained in Egyptian hands.

Two days prior to the cease-fire, I had an extraordinary experience. At the height of a sandstorm on January 6, I heard the roar of aircraft engines. Then, to my astonishment, I saw parachutes opening as a number of unidentified airmen drifted down to earth. Jumping into my jeep, I drove toward what turned into a bizarre encounter with a British air-force officer whose expression betrayed a mixture of fury and astonishment at the behavior of the Jewish "natives." It transpired that a dogfight between British and Israeli aircraft had resulted in the downing of five British planes, while all our aircraft returned safely to base. What a humiliation! I picked up the pilots one by one and drove them to the safety of one of our kibbutzim, lending a sympathetic — and somewhat amused — ear to explanations that ranged from apology to complaint. They had only been on a reconnaissance mission. Their planes carried no ammunition, and they had strict instructions to avoid combat. And just see what these "barbarians" had done to them!

Operation Horev was, in effect, our last battle against the Egyptians in the course of the War of Independence. Egypt had declared its willingness to conduct separate armistice negotiations even before the operation. Now, however, we enjoyed undisputed military superiority. The Faluja pocket had not been eliminated, but that only gave Israel a further advantage because its existence irked Egypt's military and political leaders more than anything else. Their eagerness to avoid a further setback and to rescue the trapped force (which constituted about one-quarter of the Egyptian army) spurred the Egyptians toward the negotiating table.

Two days after the beginning of the Israeli-Egyptian armistice talks at Rhodes, Yigael Yadin asked for a representative of the southern front to be sent to the talks, and I was chosen. For the first time in my life, I found myself in need of a ceremonial uniform, which I viewed as a dreadful nuisance. A used American uniform of World War II vintage had been purchased at a Tel Aviv secondhand-clothing store to serve one of our envoys in his meetings with King Abdullah of Transjordan. Since then it had changed hands several times, and being very thin at the time I found no difficulty in slipping into it. After consultations at general staff headquarters, I traveled on a UN plane to Rhodes.

My first challenge was getting used to a complete change of environment: peace, and quiet, and the fantastic comfort of the Hotel de Roses. I was immediately impelled to inquire, "What's the Greek word for 'more'?" "*Encore*," I was told. So, seated in the dining room, I repeatedly uttered, "*Encore*," and the kitchen disgorged a series of thick steaks.

The delegations at Rhodes sat around a single table, with Dr. Ralph Bunche conducting the talks and displaying a wealth of experience and good sense. He was assisted by General William Riley, chief of staff of the UN observers. As we got deeper into the issues, the format became more complex. The delegations held a few meetings around the negotiating table, then Bunche and Riley held separate consultations with each delegation. But once the initial feelings of alienation and hostility wore off, we held direct, informal talks with the Egyptians. In fact, the head of the Egyptian delegation, an elegant and polished fellow officer named Saif a-Din, learned one of my most closely guarded secrets.

Before leaving for Rhodes, I had never worn a tie in my life. As part of my uniform, however, I was provided with a British knitted khaki tie. My driver took great pains to teach me how to tie it, but I proved to be a failure at that craft. Finally, he had to rest content with showing me how to loosen the tie gently — without undoing it — so that I could slip it over my head and replace it around my neck by simply tightening the knot. I was terrified of the prospect that the knot might come undone. One day, I walked into the hotel barbershop and who should I find sprawled in one of the chairs if not my friend Saif a-Din. Unfortunately, the barber asked me to remove my tie, so pulling at the knot,

I yanked it up over my head. As I did so, I could see the Egyptian officer staring at me in amazement, and I'm sure he must have been thinking, "What kind of savages am I dealing with here?"

There were smiles and moments of relaxation during the Rhodes talks, but the bargaining was tough. The Egyptians attached supreme importance to extricating their brigade, with its arms, from the Faluja pocket. Contending that the talks were held on the basis of the UN resolution of November 14 (which called upon the sides to return to the positions they held prior to Operation Yoav), they insisted that the IDF give up its subsequent gains. We were outspoken in our rejection of that demand, and at one stage we had the impression that the Egyptians had come to terms with reality. But then they changed their minds and renewed their demand. This time, Yigael Yadin expressed himself sharply and declared that he was astonished by their attitude. Offended, the Egyptians stood up and left the room. The talks were deadlocked. To overcome our boredom, we hired bicycles and built up our muscles by touring archaeological sites in the area. Since the Rhodes talks were my first experience of diplomacy, I should mention that then, at least, I was hardly enraptured by the charms of diplomatic "give-and-take."

Finally the Egyptians consented to accept the international boundary (except for the Gaza Strip) as the armistice line between Israel and Egypt. The IDF then began preparations for Operation Fact, whose purpose was to demonstrate our control of the whole of the southern Negev, including Eilat. It was essentially an administrative operation — stationing troops and hoisting the flag — and since my mind was already filled with ideas about how to implement it, I received permission to return home. As a result, I missed the ceremonial signing of the armistice agreement at Rhodes. But I derived some satisfaction from the fact that our delegation's attitude on demarcation lines was largely influenced by my views and recommendations.

Operation Fact was designed as a race between two brigades (Negev and Golani) through the trackless terrain of the Negev Desert. The finish line was a spot on the Red Sea shore called

Umm Rashrash (now part of Eilat), which was associated in our minds with King Solomon's flourishing Red Sea port of Eziongeber. Golani was to descend the treacherous Scorpion's Pass and follow directly south through the flatlands of the Jordan Rift Valley close to the still unmarked border with Transjordan. The Negev Brigade took a route that ran like a broad zigzag between the central and western Negev and at one point brought it close to an Egyptian position. In each case, orders were to continue south only insofar as no enemy resistance was encountered. At one point fairly close to their final target, the Golani troops found themselves under Jordanian fire. Assuming that no order could deprive them of the right to defend themselves, they returned the fire. The enemy troops fled — and flight, our troops told themselves, could not possibly be interpreted as "enemy resistance." The Negev Brigade got around the Egyptian position by employing a "political" ruse. One of its commanders simply persuaded the Egyptian officer in command that he was in danger of encirclement and would therefore do well to let the Israelis pass through quietly. The race, by the way, had a close finish, with the Negev Brigade reaching Umm Rashrash just an hour or two before Golani.

The War of Independence was at an end. I had been under arms for six years and along the way, without making a conscious decision about the matter, had become a commander in the Israel Defense Forces. But since all endings are simultaneously beginnings of something else, I could no longer allow myself to be swept along by events. For the first time since leaving the Kadouri School, I had to make a choice about my future.

Chapter Three

BUILDING A MIGHTY ARMY

STANDING NOW AT a crossroads in my personal life, I felt a profound sense of moral responsibility, a kind of debt of honor toward the men whose courage and whose very bodies had blocked the Arab advance. It was to these soldiers that I swore an oath of loyalty. At the most tragic moments of the war, tormented by the thought that we were sending these men to face death — poorly armed and frighteningly outnumbered — many of my fellow officers and I undertook a personal commitment: by virtue of our moral responsibility as officers and comrades-in-arms, we would dedicate our lives to ensuring that the State of Israel would never again be unprepared to meet aggression. It was therefore premature to realize my dream of studying hydraulic engineering. I stayed in the army and together with my comrades fulfilled my pledge to the heroes of the War of Independence. We built a mighty army.

In the beginning, though, life in the postwar IDF wasn't easy, particularly because of the anti-Palmach bias displayed by Israel's political leaders. Palmach officers began to leave the army, not really of their own free will, but out of a reluctance to contend with the hostility they encountered. In every sphere, at every level, preference was given to veterans of the British army. It was very painful to see my comrades being treated like the faithful Moor who has done his part and can now be dismissed.

The Palmach command was dismantled in September–October 1948. In May and June 1949, the Palmach brigades were disbanded, and as the commander of a brigade that had just vanished from under him, I wrote to Chief of Staff Dori expressing my resentment. His answer came quickly, going on at length about the necessity to reorganize the army and denying that a deliberate campaign was going on to reduce the influence of the Palmach. "In any case," he wrote, "you would not have been able to remain in command of the brigade, since you are the first candidate to study abroad." He did not elaborate.

With Yigal Allon about to leave on a visit to the French army, I was appointed acting commander of the southern front, and I took up my post feeling isolated and uncertain about my future. But my doubts were resolved by Chaim Laskov, a British army veteran who was later to become chief of staff but was then serving as the head of Training Command. Laskov had previously spearheaded the attack on the Palmach, but he had evidently had a change of heart. He invited me to take over the battalion-commanders' course, and when I went to see him for further clarification I could hardly believe my ears. "Bring in all the Palmach officers," he offered. "I'll make sure that any of them who are willing to remain in the army will be posted there, either as an instructor or as a participant." At first I did not believe it. Yet as things turned out, Laskov kept his word in every detail. In any event, it soon became clear that I had to accept a posting somewhere, because my days at Southern Command were numbered.

While Allon was still in France, Ben-Gurion, in his capacity as defense minister, announced a series of new appointments, including Yigael Yadin as chief of staff and Moshe Dayan as the head of Southern Command. There could be no doubt that Ben-Gurion's move was a deliberate slap in the face to the former commander of the Palmach, leaving Allon with no choice but to resign from the army. As acting commander of the front, I was in charge of transferring the command to Dayan. Everyone was silent and expressionless when he arrived, and Dayan may have felt ill at ease in the company of all those Palmach men. I transferred the command without any ceremony, and the feeling that Dayan would prefer to be rid of me as well was strengthened by our first talk. He was cold, reserved, and laconic. Moreover, he was frank. "Thank you," he said, "I don't need you any longer."

Consequently, I was very glad to accept Laskov's offer, despite the heavy burden of "guilt" I bore for taking part in the Palmach's

farewell rally in defiance of a specific order and at the risk of infuriating Ben-Gurion. While I was still at the southern front, the
heads of the Palmach decided to call their troops together for a
large rally. Whatever the IDF command may have believed, the
gathering had no political purpose; it was planned exclusively as a
leave-taking. Yet Chief of Staff Dori issued firm orders that anyone still serving in uniform was forbidden to attend the rally. I
wrestled with my doubts. An officer does not defy an express
order of this kind unless it is on a clear matter of conscience, and
in my view attending a farewell rally with my comrades-in-arms
was precisely that, as well as the fulfillment of a profound personal need. In the end I decided to attend the rally, not with the
premonition that I would get off scot-free, but out of a readiness
to face the personal consequences.

The rally was scheduled for the evening. That morning I came
north to see the chief of staff, and after a lengthy discussion Dori
told me that Ben-Gurion wished to see me at his home. He
wanted to hear about some shooting incidents on my front. I
drove to Ben-Gurion's and was received very warmly. After I
completed my report, he asked about the minutest details, and I
answered in full. Then Ben-Gurion turned to other matters and
continued to chat in a leisurely fashion. Evidently he was in an
expansive mood that day and he talked on and on, asking to hear
my opinion of various senior officers. As usual, he was very frank
in disclosing his own opinions. He spoke of Yadin, for example, as
"a good officer, but undisciplined and lacking in combat experience"; Allon was "an excellent combat commander, but too
deeply mixed up in politics . . . he lacks the overall view in assessing the principal objectives at each stage"; and Dayan was "a
loner — an incomparably brave and courageous soldier, but a
loner." Meanwhile, hours were ticking past, and unable to conceal my impatience any longer, I finally said, "Ben-Gurion, may I
ask you a question, openly and frankly?"

"Of course," he said encouragingly.

"Why did the chief of staff — certainly with your knowledge or
on your instructions — forbid attendance at the Palmach rally?" I
asked. "Why should those of us who remained in the army be

placed in the embarrassing position of having to choose between our duty to maintain discipline and our duty to comrades-in-arms with whom we have come such a long way?" I spoke at length, probably with some agitation, while Ben-Gurion listened keenly. But he did not reply.

Finally the tense silence was broken by a rather unusual request. "Would you join me for dinner?" he asked. It was out of character for Ben-Gurion to extend such an invitation, and I suspected that he was trying to keep me there until after the rally. So I thanked him but said that I was in a hurry, and took my leave.

By the time I got home, changed clothes, and made off with Leah for the rally, we were conspicuously late. The glances flung in my direction indicated what would have happened had Ben-Gurion succeeded in tempting me to join him for dinner. In the course of the evening, considerable resentment was expressed, both at the disbanding of the Palmach and at the ban on attending the rally. But I did not address the meeting, nor did any of the other officers still serving in the army.

Soon after I took up my post at the battalion-commanders' course, I was summoned to a court-martial for my attendance at the Palmach rally. Rumors were making the rounds that I was going to be dismissed from the army. I was the first to be tried by the chief of staff and was sentenced to a reprimand that would be registered in my personal file. Then Dori lectured me on the need to strengthen discipline in the army, which had to undergo a thorough reorganization now that the war was over. He explained that I had committed a grave misdeed, but under the circumstances he would limit himself to a reprimand. I departed with a sense of relief. In view of what I had expected, we all got off lightly.

On one point Dori was quite right. The army had to be rebuilt, and we used the battalion-commanders' course to fuse the experience gained in the Palmach, the Haganah, and the British army into an entirely new doctrine.

A year later, when it was decided to run a brigade-commanders' course, Laskov and I began preparations. But a change in

orders came from the new chief of staff, Yigael Yadin, appointing
me to head the general staff's Operations Division. I appealed
and Laskov backed me up, trying to get the appointment an-
nulled. But it was to no avail. Resentfully, I left the brigade-commanders' course and at the end of 1950 took up the new post, my
first at the general staff.

The Operations Division was in charge of three spheres: operations (including operational planning), current security, and the
organization and mobilization of the reserves. While devoting vigorous efforts to improving the combat units and organizing the reserves, I also directed considerable attention to a task that, while
not of a military nature, was imperative under the existing circumstances. The great wave of immigration in the late 1940s and
early 1950s, particularly from the Islamic countries, had forced us
to house more than a hundred thousand people in transit camps
under extremely difficult conditions. Since many of them lacked a
vocation and the young state was unable to offer them anything
more than poorly paid manual jobs, the transit camps had the potential to become an enormous reservoir of bitterness and frustration. Placing the army in charge of the camps may have been unprecedented in military history, but it was characteristic of
Ben-Gurion, who regarded the army as the "nation's emissary"
for any and every task. As head of Operations Division, this complex problem fell to me.

Military commanders were appointed in dozens of transit
camps, and the army's Medical Corps shouldered the burden of
providing health services. Soldiers served as teachers and filled
the role of social workers. During the bitter winter of 1951–52,
when heavy rains and snowstorms brought the tents down and
heavy flooding threatened to inundate the camps, IDF engineering units were sent into action and other units were called out to
repitch the tents. No other agency or body in the country would
have been capable of responding to this challenge, and alongside the IDF's other operations, this nonmartial "battle of the
transit camps" will be recorded as one of its most splendid victories.

Interestingly enough, this nonmartial theme was to set the tone for the next few years of my military career. After two years at the head of Operations Division, my turn came to study at a foreign military school as Dori had promised back in 1949. I was posted to the British army Royal Staff College at Camberley for a year and made off for England with Leah and our two-and-a-half-year-old daughter, Dalia. The first stage of my studies included a great deal of technical staff work. For example, I was charged with working out a transportation timetable for an entire division. It was boring, and bizarre into the bargain. Since when did the IDF contain any formation as large as a division? The second stage, however, made up for what the first lacked in interest. It centered on how to assess a situation and prepare an operational plan according to British military thinking.

Toward the end of my year at Camberley, the current chief of staff, Mordechai Makleff, wrote to say that upon my return to Israel he intended to appoint me his chief of Operations Branch in place of Moshe Dayan (with whom he did not get on). Yet before his intentions were anywhere near realization, Makleff was forced to resign from the army, and Dayan was appointed to replace him. Under the circumstances, I requested permission to remain in England for another year in order to study at the London School of Economics, but Makleff wrote back that his successor as chief of staff would have to decide. Soon after, when Dayan stopped over in London on his way home from a visit in the United States, I broached the subject with him.

"What are your instructions from the chief of staff?" he asked.

"My standing instructions were to return to Israel at the end of my year of study."

"Well, then, return to Israel at the end of your year of study." Short and sweet.

Dayan gave me no hint of what position would be open to me when I arrived back home, but upon my return he invited me for a talk and offered me the post of head of Training Branch at GHQ. Coming fresh from my studies at Camberley, I accepted gladly. In the course of preparations to establish our own command staff school, I threw myself into the task of formulating combat concepts, staff work, logistics, and instructional methods of the highest standards. When the chief of staff set out for a tour of U.S. army military schools and installations, I accompanied him — my first opportunity to visit North America and make the acquaintance of the mighty American army. That was a truly instructive visit, and much of what we saw and heard was subsequently applied to IDF training techniques — given the restrictions of our far more limited resources. For example, we adopted the custom of having every combat officer undergo a parachute or commando course on completing Officers' Training School (the members of the general staff were the first to take the parachute course).

In April 1956, a few months after the birth of our son, Yuval, I became a field commander again. Dayan appointed me head (GOC) of Northern Command, and I cannot deny that it was an exciting and refreshing change after years of staff duties. I was acquainted with the northern region from my early service in the Palmach, but the passing years had brought many new problems. The most pressing of them was the constant friction with the Syrians over the demilitarized zones along the border. But from the viewpoint of tension, the strain was even worse on the Egyptian and Jordanian borders. During the mid-1950s, friction had risen to a peak in the wake of the incessant terrorist raids launched from Jordan and the Egyptian-controlled Gaza Strip and the consequent Israeli reprisal actions. One day in the autumn of 1956, all senior IDF commanders were summoned to GHQ and forewarned of the possibility that Israel would initiate an attack on Egypt. The reprisal raids had proved ineffective in dealing with the problem of terrorism, and the leading target of attention now became Egypt, since Nasser gave his full backing to the fedayeen provocations. We were also let in on the secret that the IDF's operations would be coordinated with those of British and French forces. Acting on the assumption that Syria and Jordan would not take part in the fighting, Northern and Central commands were ordered to transfer part of their forces to Southern Command and deploy for defense. Consequently, my involvement in the Sinai Campaign was limited.

Ironically enough, after the problem of terrorism in the south had been settled, it was renewed tension over the demilitarized zones in the north that periodically sent the barometer of war soaring. There was no question about our right to hold those zones or cultivate the land within them, yet our activities irritated the Syrians. Eventually they decided to escalate the tension by shelling our settlements. From the top of the Golan ridge, they had a perfect view of our territory, as well as excellent firing positions. Moreover, the UN observation posts stationed along the border did nothing to reduce the number of shooting incidents. Exposed to the Syrian artillery, our citizens were forced to build shelters, adapt buildings to wartime conditions, and disperse their homes, kindergartens, schools, and public buildings to diminish their vulnerability. Matters reached the point where we were forced to use armored tractors — often manned by soldiers — to cultivate the fields. We also had to deal with safeguarding our fishing rights in the Sea of Galilee. The entire lake, plus a ten-yard strip along the eastern shore, fell under full Israeli sovereignty. But Syrian fishermen were nonetheless in the habit of exploiting our waters, while the Syrian army harassed our fishing boats. This double problem often led to shooting incidents, and Israeli naval units occasionally mounted raids on the eastern shore of the lake to destroy Syrian fishing vessels.

I was in the thick of these problems late in 1957 when Moshe Dayan's term as chief of staff was about to expire, and he summoned a few senior officers to a meeting. He used the forum to air certain proposals regarding his successor and reiterated his opinion that it was desirable for senior officers to take study leave. When he raised my name as a candidate for the latter, it seemed evident to me that Dayan was hinting that my usefulness to the army had run its course and I should therefore terminate my service. All the senior officers in the IDF are aware of the simple fact that only one of them can serve as chief of staff at any one time, while the rest must choose between retirement and taking their chances on waiting their turn. So it was obvious to me that I would have to face this decision someday, though I was not particularly eager to grapple with it so soon. When Dayan raised the subject of study leave, I reminded him of my request to study abroad, for at that time I was exploring the possibility of studying public administration at Harvard. Dayan replied that he was against studies abroad at the present, for reasons of economy. He himself planned to study in Jerusalem after leaving the army and thought that I should do the same. But the notion had no appeal for me. I wanted either to study at Harvard or to remain in the army. As matters turned out, the discussion proved to be purely academic, since Ben-Gurion did not approve of Dayan's proposal for his successor. Chaim Laskov became the next chief of staff, and for the moment I remained where I was in Northern Command.

I was on very good terms with Laskov, and his appointment as chief of staff pleased me. I was also encouraged by the fact that he took a favorable view of my renewed request to study at Harvard. With his permission, I initiated the necessary procedures, was accepted by Harvard, and prepared to leave for the United States in the summer of 1959. But as sometimes happens, the wheel of fortune spins in a different direction; and although I had nothing to do with setting it in motion, its turn was fateful for me.

In April 1959, the army was caught in a serious blunder. A public mobilization exercise had been planned, but due to faulty staff work it was not sufficiently clear to the Israeli public — or the world at large — that the call-up was no more than an exercise. Dramatic radio announcements in dozens of languages galvanized the IDF reserves, as though we faced a grave state of emergency. Israel held her breath — and the whole world with her. That evening I attended a festive concert at Tel Aviv's Mann Auditorium, and as the hall filled with music frantic messengers called the chief of staff to step outside. He was followed by a train of senior officers. Were we at war?

A commission of inquiry subsequently studied the incident and submitted its findings. With the reluctant consent of the chief of staff, Ben-Gurion (as prime minister and defense minister) decided to dismiss the two branch heads concerned: the chief of operations and the chief of military intelligence. Laskov appointed me his new chief of operations, and when Ben-Gurion approved my appointment, I cannot deny my sense of relief; it

had occurred to me that he might still hold my participation in
the Palmach rally against me. Nonetheless, I was sorry to reach
that senior position under circumstances so painful to one of my
long-standing comrades. Not for the last time, I saw that we
sometimes move ahead not only by virtue of our own powers but
in the wake of errors committed by others.

I took up my post as chief of Operations Branch — the second-
highest position in the IDF — in May 1959 and regarded the job
as a challenge of the first order. It was my first opportunity to
tackle problems that embraced every facet of the defense forces.
No one deluded himself that the Middle East could look
forward to tranquillity in view of recent developments: Kas-
sem's revolution in Iraq; the creation of the United Arab Republic
(the Egyptian-Syrian union headed by Nasser); the nationalist
wave sweeping the Arab states; and perhaps most alarming, increased Soviet arms supplies to Egypt, Syria, and Iraq, plus assistance in training and a rise in the number of Soviet advisers. Israel, on the other hand, always operated under two severe constraints in building up her military strength: limited financial resources and her relationships with the Western powers, which
provided or withheld arms according to their own vested interests. Like others in the army, I believed that our almost total
dependence on French arms was imprudent. There were two
reasons behind our line of thinking. First, dependence on a single
source for our arms supplies was too risky, since any change in
that country's policy could endanger our security. Second, the
scope of French arms manufacture and the existent terms of
credit were no match for the massive flow of Soviet arms to the
Arab states.

Prior to Ben-Gurion's departure for a meeting with President
Eisenhower, Laskov and I were set on attempting to break "the
American blockade." Acting independently — and without the
complete approval of the deputy minister of defense, Shimon
Peres — GHQ drew up a long list of military equipment that we
wanted Ben-Gurion to request from the United States. It was
headed by an early-warning system composed of the most modern
radar installations. We urged Ben-Gurion to ask for the equip-

ment as our top priority, since the United States had already consented to sell us weapons of a clearly defensive nature and an early-warning system fitted that definition. Peres, however, did not display much enthusiasm for the idea, contending that recent technological advances had made France capable of satisfying our needs. The commander of the air force, Ezer Weizman, supported Peres's view. This difference of approach was an expression of the two conflicting schools of thought prevailing in the defense establishment. One advocated reliance on Europe (France and Germany) for our arms requirements; the other called for efforts to gain a foothold in the American weapons market. Forebodings that President de Gaulle would change his policy and restrict French arms deliveries to Israel added a sense of urgency to the latter approach.

Ben-Gurion fully comprehended the importance of the United States as a source of arms for the IDF and succeeded in persuading the Americans to sell us the early-warning system. Yet this achievement did not end the debate between the two schools, which grew even more heated in the coming years. Nor was it simple to persuade the United States to sell Israel offensive weapons and eventually become the IDF's major arms supplier. The Yom Kippur War was striking proof of the importance of our efforts in this direction. Had they failed, Israel would have been doomed.

But I am getting a few wars ahead of myself. Not that the prospect of a war was remote to us at the beginning of 1960. As has been known to happen in the Middle East, events unfolded at a rate that escaped the Arabs' control. Following a shooting incident on the Syrian border, we heightened our military preparedness on the northern border. Our movements must have alarmed the Syrians because a few days later, between January 14 and 19, 1960, Nasser visited Syria to assess the situation. The Arabs' suspicions were further nourished by allegedly "authoritative information" provided by the Soviet Union. It concerned Israeli troop concentrations in the north and a plot between the "Imperialists and the Zionists" whereby Israel was to initiate extensive military operations against Syria. (The Soviets repeated this ploy prior to the Six Day War, indicating that on this score, at least, they are consistent.) This report from the Soviet embassy in Cairo, which Nasser received on January 15, was treated with the gravity it deserved. Two days later the UAR army was placed on top alert and Nasser notified the UN forces stationed in the Gaza Strip and Sharm el-Sheikh of the possibility of military action. On January 19, Egyptian infantry and armor began secretly to cross the Suez Canal, and within a short time most of Egypt's military forces were massed in the Sinai.

The first report we received about Egyptian troop movements concerned an Egyptian armored division that had deployed to the west of the canal. On January 23, we sent an aerial reconnaissance mission over the canal — a complex mission and the first of its kind in a long time — but it failed to locate the Egyptian units. We therefore assumed that the divisions had crossed the canal and advanced eastward into the Sinai. Indeed, before long we discovered that the main body of the Egyptian army had crossed the whole of the Sinai peninsula and was massed near the Israeli border! We were taken completely by surprise and had no more than twenty or thirty tanks in the area under the jurisdiction of Southern Command.

At a GHQ meeting held on the evening of January 24, the head of military intelligence reported on the reconnaissance flight and its findings. I scribbled a note to Air Force Commander Ezer Weizman: "We've been caught with our pants down. For the next twenty-four hours, everything depends on the air force." Clearly, if the Egyptians intended to go to war, we would need at least twenty-four hours to get our armored forces to the front; till then, only the air force could block an offensive. As soon as we got the first report, I telephoned the commander of the Seventh Brigade, Colonel Yisrael Tal, and ordered him to prepare his force without delay (at the time, it was the IDF's *sole* regular armored brigade). Infantry brigades also began to move south with all possible speed. In all, we sent about 100–130 tanks to the south.

The following day I flew down to visit the units of Southern Command in a helicopter carrying no fewer than four generals. At one point two of our fighter planes came flying toward us, and their pilots had obviously not spotted our aircraft. Ezer Weizman was the first to sight them and shouted at our pilot, "Dive!" Having avoided a midair collision, we could afford to joke about the rapid promotions that would have ensued if all four of us had been eliminated.

On that occasion, war did not break out. The two armies faced one another in a state of alert, but the cannons did not fire and toward the end of March the Egyptian forces returned to their bases to the west of the canal. Nasser nonetheless reaped the fruits of his "victory": the UAR propaganda organs were jubilant over the Egyptian army's bold action, which had allegedly deterred Israel from attacking Syria.

This mini-crisis, remembered as Operation Rotem (our code name for the deployment against the Egyptians), was laden with lessons for us. The relations between the Soviet Union and the rulers of Syria and Egypt were at their closest, and the Syrian and Egyptian arsenals were overflowing with modern arms. No less grave was the fact that we had discovered the enemy's disposition so late. Alarm bells jangled at GHQ, for it was clearly urgent to improve our early-warning system. But perhaps the most important reason that Operation Rotem remains so firmly etched in my memory is that to some degree the process of events was to be replayed again seven years later — with far graver consequences.

As chief of operations, I cannot deny that I regarded myself as a worthy candidate for the post of chief of staff upon Laskov's retirement. No precise period of office has ever been laid down for an Israeli chief of staff, and Laskov might well have served for another year or more had he not fallen out with Deputy Defense Minister Shimon Peres (which happened to more than one chief of staff) and some of the branch heads. At any rate, primarily under the influence of Peres, Ben-Gurion decided to appoint Zvi Zur, Laskov's deputy, as the next chief of staff.

At the first GHQ meeting following the announcement of Laskov's replacement, Ben-Gurion asked me to remain behind.

"Are you offended that Zur has been appointed chief of staff?" he asked me outright.

"It's not a question of being offended," I told him. "I presume you had your reasons for the choice, and there's no need to explain them to me."

"But I want to tell you why I decided on Zur," he insisted. "True, on one occasion you did disobey orders. And you are cautious" (I think he meant to say "overcautious"). "But these considerations did not affect my decision. Zur is simply ahead of you in the military hierarchy. If I had appointed you, he would have resigned, and I could not ask him to remain in the army."

Ben-Gurion's reference to my disobeying orders — obviously a jab about the Palmach rally — angered me, and I decided to put a nagging doubt to rest once and for all. "I didn't ask for explanations, Ben-Gurion. But as long as we're on the subject, let me ask you a question. I am serving in the army out of a sense of duty. But if you think I should leave, I'll do so quietly. I don't want to hang on by my fingernails."

Obviously perturbed, he cut me off. "Wherever did you get that idea? I want you to remain in the army. It's imperative that you stay! What can I do to convince you of that?"

I told him frankly that I wanted to be nominated deputy chief of staff in addition to my post as chief of operations. Obviously he would have to consult the future chief of staff, so I was not asking for a reply on the spot. But without hesitation he said: "There's no problem about that. You'll be deputy chief of staff." I insisted that the appointment have Zur's approval, but he responded with his familiar wave of the hand, signifying impatience and dismissal.

I left that meeting with Ben-Gurion uneasy about the way the matter was handled, and to my great regret my premonitions turned out to be correct. When Zur took up his post as chief of staff, our relations ran into difficulties. At first he said that he favored my appointment as his deputy, and I, for my part, was prepared to fulfill my role under his unquestioned authority. But weeks passed and still there was no nomination. Finally, Zur made the appointment on Ben-Gurion's intervention. But that in itself did not augur well for our future relationship. Twice during the course of his first term, Zur called me in for a talk to express his dissatisfaction about the state of our relations. Each time I told him that I saw no justification for his complaints. I had always fulfilled his instructions and thought we had done a good job together. But the problem boiled down to one of "chemistry" between us, and I was sure that Zur's discontent was being nourished by some external factor.

I believed that the man who pressed for my replacement was none other than Deputy Defense Minister Shimon Peres. I was a thorn in his side, and he wanted me out of the key post I held. In the dispute then going on between GHQ and the Defense Ministry, I held that priorities in the acquisition and manufacture of weapons should be fixed by GHQ, including the Operations Branch. The decisive viewpoint in building up a military force must be that of the men who employ the arms, not of the men who buy or manufacture them. Peres regarded my view as a menace to his position, and the struggle proved to be a bitter one. It never occurred to me to mix considerations of personal prestige in with such fateful matters. But Peres, I felt, fomented personal conflicts to place his adversaries under pressure.

As time went on, Zur may have hoped for my resignation. But since I showed no inclination to comply on my own initiative, he was forced to take the bull by the horns. Early in 1963, some two years after his appointment, he invited me to his home for a talk and was very candid. Informing me that Ben-Gurion had decided to extend his tenure as chief of staff to four years, Zur laid his cards on the table.

"I've decided that I want a different chief of operations," he said, "and I want you to know that I've asked Ben-Gurion to replace you. Let's wind things up in a dignified manner. As chief of staff, it's my prerogative to work with a different chief of operations, and I intend to insist on that."

I was hardly in a position, or disposition, to argue with him. And obviously I would accept whatever Ben-Gurion decided. "Please permit me to talk with Ben-Gurion," I said. "If he accepts your view, I'll go."

Ben-Gurion received me in his Jerusalem office early in March. "Yitzhak," he began, "I promised that you'd be chief of staff, and you are going to be the next chief of staff." I was absolutely astonished, unable to recall any such promise from Ben-Gurion.

"The intention is for Zur to remain at his post for another year. You wanted to study, and this is a good opportunity. But if you decide that you'd prefer to continue your service now and forgo your studies, that's up to you."

Deeply moved, I thanked him and told him that despite my desire to study, present circumstances did not seem to make that choice appropriate. We were approaching the inauguration of our National Water Carrier — which was designed to divert water from the Jordan River in the north and bring it southward — and I could foresee severe security problems. I therefore wanted to remain in the army.

"Inform the chief of staff of your decision," he said. "I'll see to it that his assistant is informed of the conclusion we've arrived at."

Two days later, on a scheduled trip abroad, I stopped over in Paris, where Peres happened to be at the time. We met to discuss several matters and during the conversation he failed to conceal his impatience about something that perturbed him. I decided to leave the initiative to him. Finally, he said, "Well, I understand you had a talk with Ben-Gurion. How did it go?"

"Very well," I replied.

"What happened?" he asked.

"Ben-Gurion told me that I'm going to be the next chief of staff," I said.

Shimon Peres paled. "Did he say it in so many words?"

"In just so many words."

Of course, I assumed we were talking about events that were still more than a year away. But then the unpredictable happened and served to accelerate that schedule. In June 1963, Ben-Gurion decided to resign his posts as prime minister and defense minister. He acted unexpectedly, and the news left everyone dumbfounded. Since Zur was in Paris for an air show, as acting chief of staff I summoned the head of military intelligence and we decided to go see the prime minister. We told him of our sense of dismay over his decision and tried to persuade him to remain at his post for the sake of the army. I spoke at length of the military situation. France was edging away from us and the Arab countries were growing stronger. Was this a time for Ben-Gurion, who was unique and unrivaled in the eyes of the army, to leave the helm and abandon the IDF?

Ben-Gurion did not confide to us the reasons for his resignation, but he spoke with great feeling of his affection for the IDF and the men and women who comprised it. His words were emotional, and I had the impression that he was deeply touched by our appeal. Later, in his memoirs, he confirmed that more than anything else our words weighed upon him as he stood by his decision to resign. But resign he did, and the changeover occurred swiftly with Levi Eshkol replacing Ben-Gurion as both prime minister and defense minister. At the termination of the last GHQ meeting with Ben-Gurion, two or three days before he left office, he again asked me to remain behind. "I remember my promise to you about becoming the next chief of staff and have told Eshkol of it," he reassured me. "I hope and believe that he will respect it. More than that, I cannot do."

Eshkol stepped into Ben-Gurion's place somewhat awed and apprehensive about his ability to fill the shoes left by his predecessor. At GHQ we all committed ourselves to assisting him. My generation regarded Ben-Gurion with reverence. He stood head and shoulders above his contemporaries and was not a man to concern himself with trifles. His spirit soared toward lofty visions and the broad sweep of statesmanship. In addressing Ben-Gurion, one was often embarrassed at having to force him to deal with details. But Eshkol was made of different stuff. Talkative, overflowing with simplicity and humor, he was first and foremost accessible — and he wanted to know *everything*. Eshkol was a brilliant administrator, a pragmatist, and a master at assimilating every minute detail. He certainly remembered Ben-Gurion's promise to me: whether to exercise his own authority over the defense establishment or for other reasons known only to him, he decided not to extend Zur's term for another year and appointed me as the next chief of staff. My term would begin on January 1, 1964.

I began my tenure as chief of staff just as the National Water Carrier was about to go into operation. Our neighbors were in a full-blown uproar over the project, believing that it would enhance Israel's strength and give her an enormous economic advantage. In truth, they overestimated the significance of the three hundred million cubic meters of water we intended to divert. But Nasser decided to use the issue as a tool to fortify his leadership of the Arab world. During my first month as chief of staff, the Arab states held a summit conference in Cairo and decided that although they were not yet ready to go to war with Israel over the Water Carrier, they would take action to foil our diversion scheme while building up their forces for a full-scale confrontation in the future under a newly established unified Arab command.

As far as current security was concerned, this decision translated into a rise in tension along the Syrian border, primarily because that was where our diversionary apparatus was located. In the course of 1964, the Syrians kept the border in turmoil by employing artillery and armor. The Cairo summit decision to establish the Palestine Liberation Organization gave encouragement to Palestinian terrorists, and the Fatah began to carry out its operations as well. On January 16, 1965, the first explosive charge was found near an aqueduct of the Water Carrier system (it failed to explode), and there were seven further terrorist incursions in the course of 1965.

We replied to these terrorist operations with reprisals, which convinced the Jordanian and Lebanese authorities to prevent the saboteurs from operating out of their territory. But our problem on the northern border grew even more complex in November 1964, when the Syrians began to construct a channel to divert the waters of the Hazbani River (one of the Jordan's feeders) before they reached our territory. The second phase of the Arab plan called for the diversion of the Banias River, another tributary of the Jordan, into a canal that would carry its waters into Jordan. The plan had been prepared by engineering consultants and was technically feasible. There were disagreements in Israel about how to respond to this outright challenge. Some, including former chief of staff Dayan, believed that the only way to prevent the Syrians from diverting the Jordan's tributaries was to seize control of the territory through which the Syrian diversion canal was to run. But I hoped to find an answer to the problem that would not entail going to war.

In mid-November the Syrians laid a heavy artillery barrage on two of our border settlements. Prior to this shelling, I had talked with Eshkol about the option of using our air force as one means of silencing the Syrian guns. He agreed to authorize an air attack if the problem worsened, and on November 13, 1964, I came to the conclusion that the situation warranted the use of our planes. Eshkol approved, and a brief order sent our pilots scrambling on their first mission against the Syrian artillery in the Golan Heights. The results were excellent, and thereafter the Syrians were more prudent about using their artillery. But they did not stop work on their two diversion projects. So I decided to try another tack. Summoning the chief of operations, the commander of our armored formations, and the head of Northern Command, I asked them a simple but crucial question: "Can our tank guns hit the Syrians' heavy earth-moving equipment at a range exceeding thirteen hundred yards?" The idea was elementary: our tanks would take up positions along the border and show the Syrians that we could destroy their equipment without entering their territory.

The commander of the Armored Corps, General Tal, flung himself into the task. You have to know him to appreciate the term "flung." He instituted up-to-date ballistic training; undertook a thorough study to find the shells most suitable for targets of this nature; worked out new firing techniques for tank guns; and improved the marksmanship of the gunners to a standard that was to yield splendid results in the course of the Six Day War. After being briefed on every detail of our plan, Eshkol gave us the go-ahead, and on the appointed day I set out to observe the combat zone. The tanks assigned to destroy the Syrian equipment were manned by our finest officers and gunners. Within a short time, the Syrian earthmovers were wiped out by direct hits with incendiary shells. A renewed attempt to send in earth-moving equipment had the same results. When the Syrians got the hint and shifted their operations farther back, we extended our range. The ability of our tanks to score hits at a range of up to two and a half miles finally convinced the Syrians that their diversion scheme was doomed. In 1965 they discontinued the project.

I wish I could say that with that victory in our column the situation on the Syrian border relaxed for a while. Unfortunately, just the opposite was true. For the next two years, the Syrians kept up the level of tension by periodic provocations of growing intensity. In fact, it was a clash in which our planes downed six Syrian aircraft in April 1967 that sparked the process that climaxed in the Six Day War. Yet the very fact that the Syrians did not relent probably proved to be a blessing in disguise, since it forced us to concentrate on building up our military strength. Once again we worked on improvements in training and dedicated ourselves to solving the ever-growing problem of armament.

Levi Eshkol's most historic decision was to intensify our campaign to break into the American arms market. Even if that had been his only accomplishment during his prime ministership (which it certainly was not), it would have sufficed to secure his fame in the chronicles of modern Israel. We did not have a wide range of suppliers. Planes could be bought in France, but the French had no tanks to match the Soviet T-54s and T-55s being supplied to Syria and Egypt. The British Centurion tanks we bought were available in only limited quantities. Thus without American supplies, we would fail to keep pace with the rapid growth in Arab strength.

When President Johnson invited Eshkol to Washington in June 1964, we focused our attention on two principal items: Skyhawks (subsonic combat planes with four times the bomb-carrying capacity of the French Mirages) and Patton M-48 tanks. Eshkol was successful in his mission and on his return informed us that President Johnson had consented in principle to both requests. Yet matters were not quite that simple. A string of "buts" filtered into the picture between the time when Johnson gave his consent "in principle" and the day we could expect to conclude a formal deal. One reason was that in the meantime Nasser was pressuring Jordan's King Hussein to speed up his own arms-acquisition program and even to approach the Soviet Union if the U.S. was not responsive to his requests. President Johnson was nothing if not a consummate politician. Fearing that Jordan might turn away from the West, he decided to link the supply of arms to Israel and Jordan, thereby thwarting the opposition that might arise from Israel's friends in Congress.

It was primarily to defuse this problem that Johnson dispatched Robert Komer of the National Security Council and America's prestigious roving ambassador, Averell Harriman, to Israel early in 1965. The Jordanian arms deal was a very sensitive issue for both Israel and the United States. While Harriman was set on receiving our consent to the "linkage" plan of that day, we were equally determined to block the idea. At one point during his negotiations, Harriman's frustration peaked and he warned us that the United States would "withdraw" from the Middle East altogether. But we could not take his "threat" seriously.

When Harriman saw that we were adamant on the subject, he changed his tactics. Abandoning his stick, he held up a juicy carrot before our noses. The United States would be prepared to change its policy and provide Israel with planes, tanks, and artillery — offensive weapons that had been withheld till then — provided, of course, that we agreed to a few "minor" conditions. Then came a cascade of terms: Israel would refrain from mobilizing her congressional friends against the Jordanian arms deal; Israel would undertake not to initiate any preemptive strike against the Arab states; Israel would adopt peaceful means (including an approach to the UN) before using force to halt the Syrian diversion operations; and finally, Israel would commit herself not to acquire nuclear weapons.

We began to realize that the longer the list of conditions went on, the more serious each additional one became. In comparison to America's other demands, the initial request that we refrain from actively organizing opposition to the Jordanian arms deal did indeed seem "minor." Needless to say, the subsequent negotiations were very tough, since we were being asked to give in on fundamental strategic issues concerning our right to self-defense. More than once Robert Komer lost his diplomatic step and had to be reined in or soothed by Harriman.

In the end, of course, we compromised and agreed to hold back our opposition to the Jordanian deal. The talks concluded with a written protocol in which Harriman, of his own accord, proclaimed that the United States had an understanding with King Hussein that American-supplied tanks would not cross the Jordan River. (I should add that during the Six Day War some two hundred of those tanks came roaring across the Jordan, making King Hussein's "undertaking" worth somewhat less than the paper our protocol was written on.) In return, we were promised Skyhawks, 200–250 A-2c and A-I tanks (some of which would be delivered from Europe), engine replacement kits, and 105-mm. guns to replace existing 90-mm. ones. There was even talk of supplying us with the more advanced Patton M-48 models.

In anticipation of these American arms, I began to alter the structure of the army, in effect dividing it into two sections — defensive and offensive — and drawing a clear distinction in the quality of manpower, equipment, and resources allocated to each. Defensive operations were assigned to territorial brigades. At the same time, we devoted our efforts to creating mobile armored formations and enlarging and improving our paratroop force, since I envisaged the IDF's assault force as composed of the armored and motorized brigades, the paratroop brigades, and our regular infantry brigades. The air force was programmed first to gain air superiority and then to turn its attention to supporting the ground forces. Our pilots engaged in systematic exercises to destroy the enemy's planes on the ground, as well as refine their interception capabilities.

Thus 1967 found us immersed in a mass overhaul of the Israel Defense Forces in anticipation of a presumably inevitable clash with our neighbors. But then, as if out of the blue, the inevitable was upon us. It was as if the shock waves of a dogfight over the slopes of Mount Hermon had sent a political snowball careening across the Middle East, gathering momentum with every passing day as it charged blindly and inexorably toward war.

Chapter Four

RABIN WAITS FOR NASSER

AT FIRST, the events leading up to the Six Day War appeared to be a replay of Operation Rotem — without the element of surprise. Throughout the 1960s, Nasser had maintained a policy of building up Egypt's military strength and nurturing his alliance with Syria while repeatedly stressing that he would not be drawn into a war with Israel over "a tractor in the demilitarized zone or a border incident in the north." But six Syrian MiGs were not a tractor; and Nasser had at any rate been so constantly needled by his counterparts in other Arab states that he had relinquished his deterrent role by hiding behind the UN force stationed on the Egyptian-Israeli border. So after the downing of the Syrian MiGs in April 1967, he hastened to send a military delegation to Damascus.

Badly mauled, the Syrians urged their Egyptian allies to hit back, but their reply was adamant: "We will not permit the enemy to dictate the timing or circumstances of war. Don't depend on us to come to your aid because of some limited incident. As long as Israel does not perpetrate an all-out attack on Syria, we will not be drawn into war prematurely." The Syrians fumed, but they did not give up. Egypt's reluctance only left them more determined to escalate the tension and draw their ally into a military confrontation.

On May 13–14 Egypt's chief of staff visited Syria, and indications of a heightened state of preparedness in the Egyptian army put us on the alert. It transpired that the Syrians' work had been done for them by the Soviet Union. Between May 11 and 13, the Russians fed the Syrians false information that the IDF had massed between eleven and thirteen brigades on Israel's northern border and was about to launch an all-out attack. Anxiously, the Syrian government passed the information on to Egypt and requested an urgent consultation with the Egyptian chief of staff. Eager to prove that he was capable of deterring Israel from carrying out her "aggressive designs," Nasser began to undertake counter measures. On May 14 I received the first report — vague and laconic — that something was afoot in Egypt. The chariots of war were beginning to roll.

The following day, as I stood in the reviewing stand in Jerusalem watching the IDF's Independence Day parade, firm reports of Egyptian troop movements were whispered into my ear. The Egyptian army was moving through the streets of Cairo on its way eastward toward the Suez Canal. I immediately instructed Southern Command to step up its reconnaissance activities and Northern Command to refrain from superfluous troop movements (so as not to foster the impression that we were planning to attack). The next day our government also took a political step by notifying the American and French ambassadors that the reports of Israeli troop concentrations on the northern border were unfounded. What, then, was going on?

GHQ's Intelligence Branch submitted its assessment that we were facing a repetition of Operation Rotem and that the Egyptians would withdraw their forces to the west of the Suez Canal after a time. Nonetheless, over the next few days we continued to take precautions: heightening the alert of our forces, deploying regular armored units in the south, placing reserved armored brigades on mobilization alert, and laying minefields at vulnerable spots along the Egyptian border. At the same time, standing orders were to refrain from overt movements to avoid an escalation of tension. It was a very delicate situation. We had to react to the military moves in Egypt, both to protect our security and to keep up our deterrent posture. Had we failed to react — giving the Egyptians the impression that we were either unaware of their moves or complacent about them — we might be inviting attack on grounds of vulnerability. On the other hand, an over-reaction on our part might nourish the Arabs' fears that we had aggressive intentions and thus provoke a totally unwanted war.

As we constantly monitored Egypt's moves, events progressed

slowly but steadily toward a more alarming situation. As early as
the evening of May 16, I spoke to the prime minister about the
option of beginning to mobilize reserves. The Egyptian Fourth
(Armored) Division — whose movements were considered highly
indicative of Egypt's intentions — had not yet left its camps near
Cairo. But if it were to move into the Sinai, I felt there was no
way of postponing partial mobilization. Eshkol was understanding
of my position and approved the call-up of a reserve armored
brigade.

The next day, May 17, we learned that the Egyptians had
stepped matters up another notch by demanding that the UN
forces stationed along the Sinai border be removed from their
positions and transferred to Gaza and Sharm el-Sheikh. This
move was a radical departure from the pattern of Operation
Rotem and sufficient reason for alarm. Still, it was a calculated
step and did not necessarily call for an immediate, belligerent
response. First of all, as many people throughout the world expected, rather than respond to Nasser's dictates the UN might
categorically refuse to remove its forces. At the very least, it
would take time for the General Assembly or Security Council to
meet and debate the matter, which would slow down the momentum of developments. On the other hand, by focusing world attention on his martial posturing, Nasser might only be using the
UN as a tool to impress his point on Syria and other Arab states:
he was not hiding behind the UN force. On the contrary, he was
trying to remove it and, by doing so, was sufficiently intimidating
Israel to deter any warlike actions on her part. Seen in this light,
Nasser might even have been banking on the assumption that the
UN would turn down his request.

But even if the UN let him have his way, Nasser assumed that
as long as he did not order the UN force to leave the Gaza Strip
and Sharm el-Sheikh (guarding the sea-lane through the Straits of
Tiran), he would not be confronting Israel with a *casus belli*. Instead, he would be maneuvering us into the uncomfortable position of having to deal with a potentially explosive situation that
nonetheless fell short of being a clear-cut pretext for war, while
he would remain free to dictate all the moves. Or so he thought.

The one possibility that Nasser overlooked was that the UN

would not necessarily play the game by his rules. Commentators and historians have spent much ink on speculations about what would have happened if Secretary-General U Thant had agreed to Nasser's demand for a limited withdrawal of UN forces. But on May 17 we learned that U Thant had presented Nasser with only two options: either the UN troops remained in *all* their positions or they withdrew from the Middle East entirely. Given that choice, Nasser was left with the problem of saving face. His reply was quick in coming: the UN force was to withdraw from all its positions. In the chain of events that drew Nasser into war — perhaps contrary to his original intention — U Thant's action proved to be a vital link.

Our response was no less unequivocal. A GHQ order placed all land, sea, and air units on top alert. On the evening of May 17, Aharon Yariv, the head of Intelligence Branch, reported that the Egyptian forces in the Sinai were equipped with ammunition containing poison gas. At that time we were unprepared for chemical warfare, and our anxiety deepened. Moreover, for the first time in the current train of events, Yariv altered his basic assessment: if Nasser were to order all the UN units to withdraw, we should regard the move as a clear indication of Egypt's aggressive intentions.

Early on the afternoon of May 18, our final uncertainties about the UN forces were dispelled. The Egyptian foreign minister officially demanded the total withdrawal of all UN units from Egyptian territory. I asked the prime minister to approve the mobilization of additional reserves, primarily for the defense of our border with the Gaza Strip, where a Palestinian division with forty-four tanks was stationed. I also notified Eshkol that the entire Syrian army was now on an emergency footing, and he consented to the mobilization of one battalion in Upper Galilee. Yet we still felt bound to act cautiously since any mobilization exceeding our vital needs was likely to lead to further escalation, which we were anxious to prevent.

I held a further conference with the prime minister at eleven o'clock that night and submitted my assessment that the Egyptians were liable to close the Straits of Tiran within two or three days, placing Israel in a situation that would oblige her to go to war. I added, however, that even if the Egyptians refrained from blockading the straits, our situation would be no less difficult. We simply could not keep our reserves mobilized for long, as demanded by the presence of large Egyptian forces in the Sinai. Whether or not the Egyptians were bent on leading the situation to war at present, we were inevitably moving in that direction.

By the next evening, May 19, the UN forces had been withdrawn and Egypt's forces in the Sinai were of an imposing order. Yariv's new assessment was that the Egyptians would continue their buildup and choose one of four options: (1) undertaking no further action but reaping the fruits of victory by declaring that Egypt had deterred Israel from carrying out her "aggressive designs"; (2) instigating a provocation in order to bait us into striking back; (3) initiating an attack without prior provocation, to make the most of surprise; or (4) opting for a long period of tension — thereby forcing us to keep our reserves mobilized — and then choosing a comfortable opportunity to attack.

It was clear to me that whichever option Egypt adopted, Israel would stand alone in her forthcoming struggle. I ordered all commanding officers to make it clear to their men that we were heading for war. Without doubt we now faced the gravest situation Israel had known since the War of Independence. Yet any immediate action on our part was bound by a severe political drawback: the Egyptians had still not presented us with a concrete *casus belli* to justify launching a full-scale war. I agreed with our political leadership that we must not attack as long as the Egyptians had not undertaken some blatantly warlike act — such as blockading the Straits of Tiran or attacking targets in Israel. But deep inside I was convinced that this was only a matter of time; and I naturally assumed that, given a *casus belli*, the IDF would be ordered to attack. In the meantime, however, Nasser was still dictating the moves, and the delicate balance had to be maintained.

May 21 was a Sunday and, as on every other Sunday, the cabinet held its weekly meeting — preceded and followed by a consultation of the Ministerial Committee on Defense. I attended these meetings, replying to ministers' questions and surveying the situation. By this point we were not the only ones engaged in trying to anticipate Nasser's moves. The Americans were likewise sensitive to the question of a *casus belli* and also took a blockade of the Straits of Tiran into account. The United States was committed to the principle of freedom of navigation in the straits, irrespective of the UN withdrawal, and had repeatedly stressed that it would honor its commitment to maintain free passage (given in 1957 after the Sinai Campaign). But the Americans urged us not to initiate any military action as long as political contacts were in progress. They were trying to reduce tension by maintaining contacts with the Egyptians, whom they found jumpy and confused. As a result, our sense of urgency was tempered somewhat. The political assessment was that the Egyptians were in no particular hurry to blockade the straits, leaving considerable time for diplomatic efforts that might avert a war. The message was clear: stay alert but, for the present, wait.

On May 22, nine days into the crisis, Foreign Minister Abba Eban again briefed me on diplomatic developments. I was specifically troubled by the time factor. "If Nasser should block the straits, and the government orders the IDF to attack, how much time would we have before our operations were halted by the UN or the powers?" I asked him. Eban described our political position succinctly: we were isolated; none of the powers would come to our assistance. If a cease-fire resolution were introduced in the Security Council, there was good reason to believe that it would be passed without any objections. He estimated that if we went to war, the IDF would have from twenty-four to seventy-two hours before international intervention halted operations.

Consequently, time was the decisive factor. An army does not go to war without the fundamental conviction that it is capable of achieving its objectives. No nation — particularly not a nation as small as ours — can afford to shed its soldiers' blood with the sand running out so rapidly. On the Egyptian front, our basic military strategy called for a deep thrust to cut off the bulk of the enemy's army in the eastern Sinai and then attack it from the flank and rear. Even the optimists among us knew that the time required for implementing such a plan was more than forty-eight or seventy-two hours. But the main problem was not our plan, which could be altered if necessary. The debate then developing in Israel was over policy. Assuming that Nasser would brazenly challenge us to oppose him, would we go to war?

At that time, the answer to this question was still unclear, which was undoubtedly one reason behind my initiative in arranging two unusual meetings that day — with David Ben-Gurion and Moshe Dayan. Our talks cannot be characterized as purely political or military in nature. Troubled by the course of developments and finding the uncertainty beginning to jar on my nerves, I felt that I needed their advice and perhaps their encouragement. I was carrying a heavy burden. Israel was facing one of the most serious situations she had ever experienced, and I sensed that in its perplexity the cabinet expected me not only to present and analyze the military options (which is the task of the chief of staff), but also to dispel any doubts by telling it which option to adopt. Needless to say, that made me feel very lonely, and I hoped that discussing the situation with Ben-Gurion and Dayan would be of help to me.

By custom, the chief of staff shares his burdens with the prime minister and minister of defense. With all due care, I must stress the respect I felt for Levi Eshkol — as a man, as a Jew, and as an economic expert. I also admired him for what he had done as defense minister during the years preceding the Six Day War. But in May 1967 Eshkol was no longer the same man he had been in 1963, when Ben-Gurion resigned and left the mantle of leadership to him. Relations between the two leaders had progressively deteriorated, and those who followed (or believed that they followed) Ben-Gurion's wishes were impatient to replace Eshkol. They possessed none of Ben-Gurion's stature, authority, or inspiration, but they excelled at intrigue and since 1965 had spared no effort to discredit Eshkol, seizing every opportunity to ridicule him and publicize his every weakness. Now, as tension rose, they spread false rumors about Eshkol and let it be known that in a time of crisis the state in effect lacked a defense minister.

Eshkol was under heavy political pressure as the burdens of the emergency and the libelous campaign against him combined to damage his self-confidence. His authority was undermined in the eyes of other ministers, and senior officers were similarly affected. Eshkol had an excellent instinct and understanding of events. He knew that the moment Nasser blockaded the straits, war was unavoidable. But he found it difficult to control his cabinet, and because of the regrettable circumstances, he did not have the authority that Ben-Gurion mustered when he was prime minister.

It goes without saying that I had taken no part in the bitter struggle that Ben-Gurion and his followers in their newly established Rafi party waged against Eshkol. In fact, I was on Eshkol's side, but as chief of staff I was determined to shun any political controversy and keep the IDF clear of any trace of political involvement. I was therefore surprised when prior to the 1965 Knesset elections I received an invitation to a private political meeting to be attended by Ben-Gurion. I responded that I would not attend any political gathering, regardless of who was taking part. But then the invitation was changed and I was told that it would be a kind of social gathering attended by the former prime minister; the Rafi meeting was to be held later at a different address. Reassured by the explanation, I said that I would come. But upon arriving at the home of Ben-Gurion's daughter, Geula — who happened to be my daughter's teacher — I found myself odd man out as the only guest who was not a Rafi supporter.

At first it was a rather amusing function, with Ben-Gurion's outspoken wife, Paula, needling Moshe Dayan (of all people!) and Dayan evening up the score. After a while Ben-Gurion interrupted the exchange and channeled the conversation in a different direction. "Yitzhak," he said for the benefit of all present, "do you remember when you came to me in 1949 and asked me why I was placing you Palmachniks in the position of having to choose between your duty to obey orders and loyalty to your former comrades-in-arms? Remember what I told you then? That if you feel that way, you can go to the Palmach rally!"

I was struck dumb and remained that way for quite a few seconds. He had never said anything of the sort! And in 1960, twelve years after the Palmach rally, when Ben-Gurion explained why he was making Zvi Zur chief of staff in preference to me, he even reminded me, "You defied my orders." Was Ben-Gurion now trying to retailor history in order to harness me to his political chariot? Was it conceivable that at the end of his days Ben-Gurion's antagonism toward Eshkol had led him to forget the great message he himself had so religiously preached — that the army and its commanders must take no part in political controversy?

"You gave me permission to attend the rally?" I challenged "Then why did the chief of staff put me on trial and find me guilty of disobeying orders?"

Ben-Gurion's eyebrows shot up in amazement. "Really?" he exclaimed, as if hearing of this for the first time. "Why didn't you tell the chief of staff that I had given you permission to attend the rally?"

I remained silent. There was no point in continuing the argument.

There is a saying that goes: "Once burned, twice shy." Yet on May 22, 1967, I nonetheless felt in need of a talk with Ben-Gurion. The Old Man received me warmly, but instead of fortifying my spirits he gave me a dressing down. "We have been forced into a very grave situation," he warned. "I very much doubt whether Nasser wanted to go to war, and now we are in serious trouble. Unlike in the past, we are totally isolated." He asked about the military situation and the balance of forces, and I gave him a brief review. It was painful to see him in his present state: totally cut off from any sources of information and, worse, clinging staunchly to outmoded concepts. He erred in his assessment of the IDF's strength. He was convinced that Israel was in an intolerable political situation and doubted that she could extricate herself by starting a war with Egypt.

As Ben-Gurion proceeded to pour scorn on the cabinet and the prime minister, his words struck me like hammer blows: "The army is all right; the officers are all right; you're all right. But there's no one to tell you what to do! The prime minister and the cabinet should take responsibility for deciding whether or not to go to war. That's not a matter for the army to decide. The government is not discharging its proper duties. This is no way to function in an emergency!" Never have I experienced such a profound sense of disappointment and dismay. But Ben-Gurion kept hammering away. "You made a mistake," he said, referring to our mobilization of the reserves.

"I recommended mobilization to make sure we were ready."

"In that case, you, or whoever gave you permission to mobilize so many reservists, made a mistake," he repeated. "You have led the state into a grave situation. We must not go to war. We are isolated. You bear the responsibility."

Having come to Ben-Gurion for encouragement, I left him feeling doubly despondent. I now felt the entire burden was resting on my shoulders. Many days were to pass before his words stopped ringing in my ears: "You have led the state into a grave situation. You bear the responsibility."

Later that night I met with Dayan — again on my initiative — and again I drew little encouragement on the political question. He too was unsparing in his criticism of the cabinet and the army, although he refrained from personal recriminations. He felt we had erred in placing Nasser's leadership of the Arab world in jeopardy. The nature and scale of our reprisal actions against Syria and Jordan had left Nasser with no choice but to defend his image and prestige in his own country and throughout the Arab world, thereby setting off a train of escalation in the entire region. Dayan was convinced that Nasser would now take further drastic measures, such as blockading the Straits of Tiran, leaving Israel with no choice but to respond.

Unlike his political comments, however, Dayan's remarks about the army were complimentary. He told me that he had been profoundly impressed by the IDF's prowess. He had been more or less aware of the progress made by the air force, but the expansion and qualitative advance of our armored units had surprised and impressed him. He spoke of the IDF with admiration, and I was grateful to him for that. If I was to be blamed for recommending mobilization of the reserves, thereby causing the situation to deteriorate and placing the country in danger, at least no one could accuse me of failing to prepare the IDF for the grave test in store for it.

Nasser did not disappoint those who predicted war. At 3:45

A.M. on May 23, we learned that he had blockaded the Straits of Tiran. According to the official communiqué, the straits had been closed to ships hoisting the Israeli flag or carrying strategic cargoes (soon clarified as including oil) to Israel. On receiving the news, I summoned the GHQ branch heads and ordered the GOC of Southern Command not to move any units until we had decided on our mode of operation. During the meeting with branch heads, further unsettling reports came in. The Damascus-Kuneitra road had been closed to the UN observers and all other foreigners. In addition, the Syrians were increasing their forces on the Golan Heights.

Just after 8:00 A.M., Eshkol reached the GHQ underground command post, known as "the Pit." He told us of a message from President Johnson urging Israel not to fire the first shot or initiate any action without first consulting the United States. As far as we were concerned, Nasser had already fired off much more than a first shot, but the Americans appeared to think differently.

"The post-Sinai Campaign period has come to an end," said Aharon Yariv, speaking for all of us. "It's no longer just a matter of freedom of navigation. If Israel takes no action in response to the blockade of the straits, she will lose her credibility and the IDF its deterrent capacity. The Arab states will interpret Israel's weakness as an excellent opportunity to threaten her security and her very existence."

The chief of Operations Branch, Ezer Weizman, warned Eshkol that, politically and militarily, time was against us, and he recommended striking at the Egyptian air force without delay. On two occasions — May 23 and 24 — Weizman proposed that if we could not undertake a full combined attack, at least our planes should attack the Egyptian air force.

Then a phone call from the GOC of Southern Command temporarily brought our attention back to our principal front. The Egyptians had deepened their forward deployment, and there were preliminary indications that the Fourth Division was about to enter the Sinai. Aware that time was running out, the prime minister expressed his view clearly: "There may be no further point in waiting. But first we must send a message to the president of the United States, honoring his request to consult before taking critical steps." Eshkol regarded the American warnings as ominous. If we ignored them and war broke out, we would find ourselves alone in the international arena. And without the United States to keep Soviet involvement in check, Israel would be in a tough predicament.

At noon the Ministerial Committee on Defense was convened. The meeting was also attended by Knesset members Golda Meir (then serving as secretary-general of the Mapai party) and Menachem Begin and Moshe Dayan (representing the opposition). I described the situation that had arisen since the blockade of the straits and asked whether Israel was prepared to come to terms with the move or would go to war against Egypt. I did not suggest that the decision would be an easy one, for we faced enormous difficulties. We would have to fight on at least two fronts (Egypt and Syria) and possibly a third (Jordan). But I stressed the broader strategic problem at stake in the situation: "It's not just freedom of navigation that is hanging in the balance. Israel's credibility, determination, and capacity to exercise her right of self-defense are all being put to the test."

The committee was, of course, entitled to know what the IDF proposed, so I pointed out that in addition to the question of principle, it was not feasible to fight for Sharm el-Sheikh alone or commence the war there. Sharm was our farthest and most difficult objective. Moreover, the most effective blow we could deliver against the Egyptians would be to destroy their air force on the ground. Together with the air strike, our forces would thrust into the Sinai — or at least occupy the Gaza Strip. Once we went into action, the Syrians would surely strike back — at least by means of their air force and artillery — and we would have to take that into consideration as well. I was asked whether a further forty-eight-hour postponement would decisively endanger the prospects of our offensive. Obviously, it was preferable to act as soon as possible, but I told the committee that I did not think forty-eight hours more or less would be decisive.

That assessment was well received, since neither the ministers nor the representatives of the opposition were inclined to go to war immediately. Mindful of the message from Johnson, they still believed that political moves should be given a chance. Under no circumstances — and particularly on the eve of war — can Israel afford to give less than full consideration to an outright appeal from the president of the United States.

Given the breather, the ministers adopted a resolution to the following effect: (1) the ministerial committee regards the blockade of the Straits of Tiran to Israeli shipping as an act of aggression against Israel; (2) a decision on our response to this act is postponed for forty-eight hours, in the course of which the foreign minister will make inquiries as to the United States' position; (3) should the necessity arise, the prime minister and foreign minister are empowered to decide on dispatching the foreign minister to meet with the president of the United States.

The contradiction between the second and third clauses of the resolution clearly indicates that the forty-eight-hour postponement was not a binding timetable. If the foreign minister were to go to the United States, it would take several days — at any rate, certainly more than forty-eight hours — to hear and analyze his report and adopt a decision about the manner and timing of our response. In the end, Abba Eban went on his tour to France, England, and the United States, and it was clear to me that the delay would far exceed the period stipulated in the committee's resolution.

Later that day, at a meeting of the general staff, various military plans were discussed. I reiterated that the main prerequisite for any operation, whatever its dimensions, was attaining air superiority. Our immediate objective was not the occupation of the Sinai. Instead, we would concentrate on dealing a crushing blow to Egypt's air and armored forces and occupying the Gaza Strip and areas farther south, without deciding now on the depth of our penetration. The commander of the air force, Motti Hod, was full of optimism and guaranteed that our military position would be greatly improved within an hour of our air strike. He had one major concern: Egyptian bombers were liable to strike at Israeli population centers. Our planes would therefore have to destroy the bombers before they got off the ground.

"How can you take the risk? Ben-Gurion didn't risk it, how can you? This war will endanger Israel's very existence!" These harsh words echoed in my ears throughout the nerve-racking hours of

May 23, 1967. I tried to banish them from my mind, for I knew that I must not allow such reproaches to weaken my determination. But they returned again and again like an unrelenting echo.

They were uttered just after the meeting of the Ministerial Committee on Defense by Interior Minister Moshe Chaim Shapira, the leader of the National Religious party. During the meeting, Shapira had been adamant about his opposition to the notion of taking offensive action. Afterward the two of us withdrew to another room. I brought his tirade on myself by asking Shapira why he was so staunchly opposed to the idea of breaking the blockade and dislodging the Egyptian army in the Sinai.

"*You're* the one who owes an explanation," he challenged, and as he went on his agitation heightened. "Do you really believe that the Eshkol-Rabin team has to be more daring than the Ben-Gurion–Dayan team? In 1950 and 1951 the straits were closed; did Israel rush into a war? The straits remained closed up to 1956; did that endanger Israel's security? Ben-Gurion didn't go to war even though the Egyptians were backing terrorist raids against Israel. When *did* Ben-Gurion strike? Only when Israel didn't have to go it alone! France and Britain were still world powers, and *they* undertook to destroy the Egyptian navy and air force. Egypt's army was massed west of the Canal Zone then — not in the Sinai, as it is now. French air squadrons were posted to Israel to safeguard us from Egyptian raids. The British and French fleets defended Israel's shores. Our civilian population was protected. Ben-Gurion did not go to war before he was certain that the fighting would be against Egypt alone; before making certain that at least two powers would veto any anti-Israel resolution in the Security Council. Now Egypt will be fighting on a single front, but *we* will have to fight on at least two, perhaps three. Politically, we will be totally isolated, and we won't receive arms supplies if we run short during the fighting. If we're attacked, of course, we'll fight for our lives. But to take the initiative? To bring this curse down on us with our own hands? Do you want to bear the responsibility for endangering Israel? I shall resist it as long as I draw breath!"

Shapira's words reflected a view that was widespread in political circles. Did Eshkol regard himself as more courageous than Ben-Gurion? Could he and Rabin take the fateful responsibility of leading Israel into a war when she was isolated and abandoned? It verged on lunacy!

For me, it was too late for regrets. Having taken the initiative in inviting Shapira for a talk, I could only try to explain my view yet again. His comparison with the circumstances in 1956 was perfectly accurate. But we faced different decisions now. "Nasser has presented us with a grave provocation," I told him. "If we don't face that challenge, the IDF's deterrent capacity will become worthless. Israel will be humiliated. Which power will bother to support a small state that has ceased to be a military factor? Why bother with a state whose neighbors are growing stronger and subjecting it to humiliating pinpricks? We're going to war over freedom of navigation. Nasser has threatened Israel's standing; later on his army will threaten Israel's very existence. I don't want to go to war either, but there's no way out if the American political efforts fail."

"Israel's existence will be endangered if we go to war," Shapira repeated at me, as if I were an errant pupil. "If we dig in" (that term was being flung around in political circles like some magic charm), "we shall be strong. We'll dig in. We'll fortify ourselves. We can withstand any attack. But we won't fire the first shot!"

Late that evening, after a day of tension and meeting after meeting in smoke-filled conference rooms, I returned home in a state of mental and physical exhaustion. Ever since then I have repeatedly asked myself, what happened to me that evening? How did I get into such a state? Now, twelve years later, I still lack a definitive answer. There can be no doubt that I was suffering from a combination of tension, exhaustion, and the enormous amounts of cigarette smoke I had inhaled in recent days. (I had suffered severe nicotine poisoning on two previous occasions.) The past few days had seemed endless. Meals were taken on the run and only when the occasion arose. I had hardly slept, and I was smoking like a steam engine. But it was more than nicotine that brought me down. The heavy sense of guilt that had been dogging me of late became unbearably strong on May 23. I could not forget Ben-Gurion's words — "*You* bear the responsibility" — and I was haunted by Shapira's harsh indictment. My colleagues and I had prepared the IDF, ensuring that it was properly trained, equipped, and structured in the best manner possible. But perhaps I had failed in my duty as the prime minister's chief military adviser. Maybe that was why Israel now found herself in such difficult straits.

Never before had I even come close to feeling so depressed, and rarely had I allowed myself to share my deepest feelings with someone else. It's just not in my character and never has been. But this time I sensed an urgent need, and I called up Ezer Weizman, the chief of operations. We had often disagreed over various issues, but I had complete faith in his personal integrity. I wanted to pour my heart out to him.

Ezer came immediately and I was frank with him. Although I knew I had done everything necessary to prepare the IDF in every sense, I couldn't shake free of the feeling that I shared responsibility for the worst predicament Israel had faced since the War of Independence. I did not tell Ezer about my exchanges with Ben-Gurion and Shapira. They were not to blame for the way I felt, even though I knew that their words had left a strong impact on me. I simply asked Ezer directly, "Am I to blame? Should I relinquish my post?" Later, in his autobiography, Ezer wrote that I offered him the post of chief of staff. Even though I was very upset at the time, I remember matters differently. I made him no such offer, nor was I empowered to "bequeath" the job to him or anyone else. That is not a chief of staff's prerogative. Be that as it may, Ezer talked me out of any thought of resignation. Over and over again, he told me I would get over it. He would not hear of my resigning and assured me that I would lead the Israel Defense Forces to a great victory.

I thanked him for his encouragement, but when Ezer left I felt no better. Finally, Leah called Dr. Gillon, who had long been my physician. After examining me, he pronounced that I was in a severe state of exhaustion and gave me a sedative. I slept till about noon the next day.

In hastening to notify the prime minister of my condition and in summoning a meeting of the general staff without my knowledge, Ezer was undoubtedly motivated by his concern for the army's command structure and hoped to ensure that it would continue to function properly even if the chief of staff were unable to return to his post. All the same, I felt he had acted rashly. But the real blow came seven years later, when the Labor party was about to vote on its candidate for prime minister and Ezer abused my trust in him by making the conversation we had on the evening of May 23 public. But I shall return to this matter in its proper place.

Having regained my strength, I felt much better by the evening of May 24 and returned to full activity on the following day. I felt obliged to request a private meeting with Eshkol and opened the discussion with my own concerns. "I had a personal problem," I told him, "and I regret it. But I do consider myself fit for duty now. Yet if you think I should relinquish my post, I shall accept your decision without protest."

Eshkol brushed aside the issue with a curt "No problem," and turned to routine matters. I stole one last, hard look at him. He too was under great pressure, and I wondered for a moment what he really thought. I shall never know, of course. But I do know that Eshkol was a warm, wise man. Perhaps he had long known — and I had just then been forced to face — the frightening depths of a man's vulnerability. At any rate, he was right not to dwell on the subject. This was not the time. The key piece of the Middle Eastern puzzle — Nasser's provision of a *casus belli* — had just fallen into place. In effect, the ball was now in our court, and in the words of a popular song that made the rounds during those days, Nasser was waiting for Rabin.

Chapter Five

NASSER WAITS FOR RABIN

WHAT THE COMPOSER of that popular song could not have known was that I stood just one step ahead of the Egyptian president on a long waiting list that extended across the world. If Nasser was waiting for Rabin, Rabin was waiting for Eshkol; Eshkol for his cabinet; the cabinet for Eban; Eban for President Johnson; and Johnson for the other Western "maritime Powers." In retrospect, it seems that a modern-day rendition of the traditional Passover song "Chad Gadya" would have been more appropriate to the situation. At any rate, the next two weeks were essentially spent trying to unravel that web of interdependent relationships so that we could finally take action.

It was only when I returned to full activity on May 25, confident of my ability to conduct operations, that I learned of the meeting of the general staff and heads of regional commands held during my absence. In the course of that consultation, changes were made in the limited plan I had dictated earlier, which called for occupying the Gaza Strip and advancing toward El Arish. Now it had been expanded to include preparations for an advance toward the Suez Canal, moving exclusively along the northern route. Yet even before I returned to work, Eshkol had cooled the enthusiasm of his generals by telling them that no action could be considered before Saturday, May 27. If Eban's report on his talks with President Johnson arrived by then, the cabinet would reconsider the situation.

Ezer Weizman and Aharon Yariv were reluctant to accept the postponement of military operations, and on the morning of May 25 I invited them to my home in the Tel Aviv suburb of Zahala. They subjected me to searching stares, seemingly anxious to find out if I had pulled myself together, but not a word was said about my indisposition. Weizman insisted that it was vital for the IDF to act immediately, while Yariv's assessment of our situation was grim and he predicted that it would get worse. On that basis he proposed that we order a total mobilization. Both men asked me to inquire again whether or not it was feasible for the IDF to attack prior to the foreign minister's meeting with President Johnson. I told them I was sure it was out of the question, but I was willing to consult with the prime minister to remove any lingering doubts.

As expected, Eshkol reiterated the formula worked out by the Ministerial Committee on Defense. In the course of the meeting, I asked Weizman, Yariv, and Chaim Barlev (who had recently returned from France and been appointed deputy chief of staff) to join us. Yariv explained to Eshkol that the situation was deteriorating and that judging by the Egyptian deployment, Nasser was harboring thoughts of launching an attack. Time was the decisive factor, since we faced a confrontation, not only with Egypt, but with the rest of the Arab states as well. And as time went by, the Arab military alliance was growing stronger.

As a result of this meeting, Eshkol decided to cable a message to Eban that time was pressing. He notified the foreign minister of the decisive change in the disposition of the Egyptian forces and of inter-Arab military preparations, making the problem of the straits subordinate to the danger of an enemy attack. By then Egyptian forces in the Sinai alone included four infantry divisions and the equivalent of two armored divisions, with additional Egyptian troops already on their way back from Yemen. It seemed apparent that Nasser's aim was a decisive showdown with Israel. Moreover, the Syrian army was also massing on the border, and the Syrians had consented to the integration of Iraqi ground and air units into their force. Eban was therefore expressly ordered not to present the blockade of the straits as the main issue in his talk with President Johnson. Instead, he must stress that the Arab world was preparing for a war of annihilation against us. Clearly, the time for pursuing political measures was coming to an end.

In that climate of feeling, Eshkol and Yigal Allon (who was then minister of labor) made a visit to Southern Command, where our offensive plans were again reviewed. To tell the truth, though, at that point I did not attach much importance to a precise definition of the size and extent of our offensive. My attention was focused on the question of when the cabinet would decide that, political options having been exhausted, the IDF was to launch its attack. I assumed that the dimensions of our offensive would be dictated by the outcome of the air-force strike againt the enemy's airfields. If we gained absolute air superiority and succeeded in the first phases of our plan, we could extend ourselves beyond the confines of northern Sinai and destroy the Egyptian army throughout the peninsula.

During that tour of Southern Command, Allon told me that he was sure the cabinet would ultimately decide to authorize a preemptive strike. But such a decision could not be adopted before Eban met Johnson. There was consequently no point in urging the cabinet to speed up its deliberations. Nonetheless, on the evening of May 25, Yariv expressed his concern that if we did not take action on the following day, the Egyptians might attack us, and our situation would then be very serious. When I asked Motti Hod about the latest intelligence on the Egyptian air force, he replied that if the Egyptian bombers attacked that night, their priorities would be our airfields and other vital targets inside Israel. For lack of an acceptable choice, we concluded that we had to take the risk of an Egyptian attack that night. I ordered the regional commands to deploy for defense on full alert and also issued orders to complete the mobilization of all our reserves.

Then I asked for a further meeting with Eshkol, which was attended by Generals Yariv and Barlev and officials of the Prime Minister's Office and the Foreign Ministry. I felt obliged to speak bluntly. "We are no longer certain who will take the initiative in commencing hostilities. Do you believe we can extract an American declaration that any attack on Israel will be regarded as an attack on the United States? And if not — since such a possibility does not appear to be likely — what is the point of waiting any longer? We've already forfeited the advantage of strategic surprise. If we continue to wait, we run the risk of losing even the advantage of tactical surprise. That would be the worst situation imaginable. What are we waiting for?"

Eshkol's reply was adamant. "The IDF will not attack before the political options have been exhausted." And that put an end to the argument, for it is an ironclad rule in democracies that the nation places its welfare in the hands of its freely elected political leaders and, only through them, of its generals. As long as the government believed that the political process had yet to run its full course, the army would not be sent into action. We therefore had to gain the consent of the prime minister and his cabinet, not by subjecting them to pressure and forcing them to act against their beliefs, but by convincing them that our options had run out. Some of our political leaders continued to believe (or was it wishful thinking?) that the United States would do the job on Israel's behalf.

Since it had been decided to send a further cable to Eban in America, I asked to take part in wording it. The situation had to be made crystal clear. Either the United States explicitly committed itself to removing the blockade — not of the straits but of our borders, which were swarming with Arab troops — or the Americans must tell us frankly, "You're on your own. If the Egyptians, Syrians, and Jordanians attack you, don't expect any help from us." And if we received the latter reply, I assumed that the cabinet would shoulder full responsibility for the risks engendered by further delay and give the go-ahead for military action.

Working with the directors general of the Prime Minister's Office and the Foreign Ministry, I took care to make the cable to Eban unequivocal:

> Israel faces a grave danger of general attack by Egypt and Syria. In this situation, implementation of the American commitment is vital — in declaration and action — immediately, repeat, immediately, meaning a declaration by the U.S. government that any attack on Israel is equivalent to an attack on the United States. The concrete expression of this declaration will be specific orders to U.S. forces in the region that they are to combine operations with the IDF against any possible Arab attack on Israel. Whatever reply

you get from the United States, limit yourself to stating that you will report to your government. In view of the gravity of the situation, this notification is to be delivered without delay to the highest American authority. In the absence of the president, deliver it to Secretary of State Rusk. . . . We stress the top secrecy of all dealings arising from this cable. Under no circumstances are you to phone us on this matter.

There was nothing more to do now but wait — again. If the American answer left us with no choice other than war, I expected the cabinet to authorize military action on Saturday, May 27, or the day after.

The uncertainty surrounding the foreign minister's talks in Washington may never be dispelled unless some neutral scholar subjects the exact transcript to an impartial examination. For the present, however, there can be no doubt about one fact: the Israeli cabinet was in the dark during the waiting period preceding his return from Washington. On the afternoon of May 26, when a group of ministers convened, Eshkol's *chef de cabinet* attached dramatic significance to a cable just received from our embassy in Washington. It read as follows: "The American Sixth Fleet will take part in reopening the straits. The Egyptian ambassador to the United States has been notified that in the event of an Egyptian attack on Israel, the United States will carry out its commitment to Israel's survival. The president of the United States has warned the Egyptian ambassador that an attack on Israel is tantamount to suicide on the part of Egypt."

The import of the cable appeared to be that the government of Israel was indeed being bailed out by a magnanimous American relative called Uncle Sam. But the encouraging impact of this message was soon dispelled by a further cable. Rusk's reply to Eban was confined to four points: (1) the United States had no information about offensive intentions on the part of Egypt; (2) the president could make no commitment to Israel's security without prior congressional approval; (3) if Israel were the first to take military action, the United States would find great difficulty in extending its assistance to Israel, even on the political plane; (4) the president was taking the initiative in forming an international naval force to break the Egyptian blockade of the Straits of Tiran. Somewhere between Washington and Jerusalem, the Messiah had faltered.

The ministers asked me again for my assessment of the time factor. Unlike my statement on May 23, when I felt that a delay of forty-eight to seventy-two hours was not critical, my reply now was that time was pressing. The later we attacked, the better Egypt's forces would be organized, supplied, and fortified. In addition, we would forfeit the factor of tactical surprise, compounded by the absence of strategic surprise. Taking the initiative would be of decisive importance in determining the length of the war, its results, and the number of casualties it exacted. We were facing a difficult war. If, as I expected, the Syrians and Jordanians joined in, I doubted that we would be able to occupy the whole of the Sinai. But I was convinced that we were capable of dealing the Egyptian army a crushing blow.

Moshe Chaim Shapira, still firm in his opposition to war, asked: "What is our staying power in comparison with Egypt's ability to maintain its present deployment over a long period?"

I replied that we would tire first because the Egyptian army consists primarily of regulars, only a small fraction of the country's enormous population, whereas we had called up most of our reserve forces and were subjecting our economy to severe difficulties.

Shapira did not give up! "And what if we are the first to attack, paying a heavy price in casualties while the whole world turns its back on us? What will we gain?"

Considering my previous bout with Shapira, I required a fund of patience at that moment. Firmly, I reiterated my belief that we were capable of gaining tactical surprise and of hitting the Egyptian army hard.

"But how will we hold out if we take the initiative?" he pressed on. "Egypt and Syria will get full support from the Soviet Union, while we will receive nothing." Again I explained that our first strike was meant to be on such a massive scale that the Egyptians would find it hard to keep fighting for long. As I spoke, I knew that Shapira was not the only minister to hold such views, though the others refrained from expressing themselves so bluntly. In the end, the ministers decided that if we were attacked, the defense minister and chief of staff were empowered to order any response they saw fit. But no decision about launching an offensive would be adopted before the return of Foreign Minister Eban.

Intentionally or otherwise, Eban's meeting with President Johnson was postponed until Friday, May 26, and it was not until midday Saturday that we received our first report on their talk. As usual, it was deficient in details, yet the general point was clear. The president could not conceive of Israel acting alone. Should she nonetheless do so, Israel would remain on her own — in the fullest sense of the term — for the United States would be unable to extend any form of assistance.

In a tense mood, the cabinet convened at the prime minister's Tel Aviv office on Saturday night, May 27. The meeting was also attended by Ezer Weizman, Aharon Yariv, and Chaim Barlev. Aryeh Levavi, director general of the Foreign Ministry, reported on Eban's talk with Johnson, along the lines we had already heard. There was also a report on a harshly worded note from Soviet Premier Kosygin and a tough note from President de Gaulle warning Israel not to fire the first shot. I described the IDF's deployment and argued that our political efforts had gained nothing. If we failed to respond to Egyptian aggression, we would only lose more time — which was working against us — and further endanger Israel's security.

While the meeting was in progress, Eban arrived directly from the airport. Since he had just talked with the president of the United States and had formed an impression of the mood at the White House, I knew that his view would carry particular weight. Eban was strongly opposed to war, claiming that Johnson had told him in no uncertain terms: "Israel must not be the first to act! I need two or three weeks to implement our political plans for resolving the problem."

That meeting was a long session, starting at nine in the evening and going on and on into the wee hours of the morning. Our nerves were taut, and the room turned into a collage of cigarette smoke, bleary eyes, and piles of coffee cups. Arguments in favor, arguments against; none of them was new. The IDF generals backed me up, each one adding a personal note in keeping with his temperament. But the longer the debate dragged on, the more evident it became that the IDF would not attack on the morning of Sunday, May 28. In the course of the meeting, Eshkol passed me a note that the ministers from the National Religious party were threatening to resign if the cabinet voted in favor of war. That was all we needed now — a cabinet crisis with nearly a thousand tanks in the Sinai!

Finally the vote was taken. Nine ministers in favor; nine against. It was a weary stalemate, the most that could be squeezed out of an indecisive cabinet. I could not help recalling Ben-Gurion's words. Eshkol was weary and dejected. With profound inner conviction, he had told his ministers that Israel was bound to go to war and that an order had to be given without delay. But he found himself incapable of tipping the balance, and an Israeli prime minister does not have the decisive vote when his cabinet is deadlocked.

After the meeting dispersed, I remained alone with Eshkol. He told me that in addition to the ministers from the National Religious party, Eban too had notified him that if the cabinet decided for war now, he would immediately submit his resignation. He believed President Johnson's promise that the United States would take action to unravel the situation. Eshkol was not put off by the threat. He had expected the cabinet to vote for war, even if it meant resignations. But the cabinet had not decided. The Egyptian army continued to dig in, and men of ill will continued to undermine our prime minister's standing.

The deadlock was broken when the cabinet met again at three o'clock the next afternoon. Between the two meetings, Eshkol had received a strongly worded message from President Johnson warning Israel against going to war and specifically urging us to permit the United States to explore all political avenues. Under the impact of this message, the cabinet decided to wait two or three weeks, in deference to Johnson's request.

Two or three weeks! My reaction bordered on disbelief, and I could already anticipate the hue and cry when I broke the news to the general staff. Not that I feared mutiny. Yet I believed that our generals deserved a chance to air their feelings directly to the prime minister and minister of defense, so I asked Eshkol to come along and personally explain the cabinet's decisions and policies. He accepted the invitation on the spot, and a meeting was called for that evening at the Pit.

Before coming to address the generals, however, Eshkol broadcast a speech to the nation. His upset and weariness, combined with dejection at his failure to impose his will on the cabinet, led him to stumble. In the brief annals of the State of Israel, that broadcast will be remembered as "the stammering speech," because of Eshkol's difficulties in enunciating. A fluent, nimble conversationalist, he left the impression that he could not control his tongue because of his state of terror. The broadcast was another link in the chain of dismal events that plagued the prime minister at the time.

Allon accompanied Eshkol to his meeting at GHQ, and it began with the prime minister taking something of a tongue-lashing from Yariv. But he replied in a subdued, patient manner, explaining the overall political picture to the assembled generals — the Russian warning that the Soviet Union would not abandon the Arabs if Israel attacked; the American message and his own conviction that the U.S. would work with the British, Dutch, and Canadians to organize a flotilla and break the Egyptian blockade of the straits. Detailing why the cabinet had voted to give the United States time to carry out its commitments, he implied that should the promises remain unfulfilled, the ministers would opt for independent action.

Almost all the generals took part in the subsequent discussion, which was heated. Eshkol heard them out and this time answered back vigorously, trying to impress on his army that Israel could not fly in the face of her friends and still expect their support after the war had ended — regardless of how spectacular the results might be. When a young colonel, who was in charge of our History Department, interrupted the prime minister in an outburst of frustration, Allon proposed that the discussion break for a recess, undoubtedly in order to let tempers cool. Before anyone had time to respond to the suggestion, he and Eshkol stood up and left.

The discussion did not resume afterward, and I became very concerned about the problem of morale. If the men in this room found it so difficult to suppress their frustration before the prime minister, what of the men in the field? The waiting period might last for weeks. Under the circumstances, I attached supreme importance to what officers were to tell their men, and I urged every commander to take great pains in explaining the situation. At the same time, the prime minister agreed, on my initiative, to release thirty thousand reservists and send them back to their homes and jobs. As for the rest, our deployment continued without a clue about how long we would have to wait.

On May 30 Egypt and Jordan signed a bilateral defense treaty identical to the 1960 Egyptian-Syrian agreement — and still we waited. I went off on tours of field units, worried by the signs of impatience, bitterness, and contempt for the cabinet's decision-making capacity. The days dragged on with their burden of nerve-racking meetings and consultations. Everything had been chewed over again and again. Time and time again, we assessed the situation, foresaw options, stationed units, formulated plans — while our political leaders remained captive to their illusory hopes that war might be averted.

On May 31 I met with Eshkol again, but this time our agenda had to do with personal issues — the kind that cannot be shelved even at moments of supreme tension and on the eve of fateful decisions. The prime minister was in a quandary. Moshe Dayan had asked for an IDF post, requesting to be placed at the head of Southern Command. I objected, telling Eshkol that with all due respect to Dayan, I saw no reason to offend General Yishayahu ("Shayke") Gavish, in whose ability I had unfailing faith. But I got the impression that Eshkol's criteria were not only the former chief of staff's military talents. Dayan and his supporters posed a threat to Eshkol's own position as defense minister. With the cabinet torn by doubt and indecision, Eshkol was rapidly losing stature in the eyes of many members of the political and military establishment. I still believe that this was a great injustice that history may yet redress. But at that time, the feeling spread that Eshkol was unfit to lead Israel into the critical confrontation awaiting her. There was growing pressure on the prime minister to relinquish his additional post as defense minister and hand the job over to Moshe Dayan. In a final attempt to protect his position, he consented to place Dayan in command of the southern front in order to appease his supporters and draw attention away from the defense portfolio. I asked the prime minister for time to think the matter over and discuss it with Dayan.

When Dayan and I held our talk, however — in Eshkol's presence — I began to suspect that we were engaged in a game of political hot potato, and now it was *my* position that was being threatened. When I asked Dayan, "Are you prepared to submit to my authority as chief of staff?" the tone of his yes may have been unreserved. But I was concerned by the analogy he attached to it as a rider: "General Maxwell Taylor is the commander of the American forces in Vietnam. Being in command of the Vietnam front, he is, of course, subject to the orders of the Joint Chiefs of Staff in Washington. I presume that our relationship will be of that nature." But that analogy did not accurately reflect Israeli conditions and battle zones; nor did it conform to the chain of command customary in the relations between the chief of staff and the regional commanders. So I asked him frankly, "Do you want to replace me as chief of staff?" "No!" he replied. "You are chief of staff, and I shall obey every order from the general staff. I merely want to take part in the war, rather than watch it from the sidelines. I understand that Eshkol supports my request."

Confirming Dayan's statement, Eshkol instructed me to place him in command of our combat forces in the south. But I still had to face the most difficult part. Summoning Shayke Gavish, I told him that as his commander I was sorry I had not been able to protect him, but I had been ordered by the prime minister and defense minister to appoint Dayan in his stead. I knew he would find little consolation in my assurance that everyone had great faith in him personally. Words cannot soften the gravity of deeds. When I asked him if he would consent to serve as Dayan's deputy, he replied without hesitation, "No. I shall leave Southern Command. I will hand the command over to him as required, and after that you can post me where you will." It was a very painful experience for both of us.

Yet Shayke Gavish never handed his command over to Dayan, for starting on June 1 developments began to take a different turn for everyone. Even though I was skeptical about the prospects of the United States' extricating us from a war, I was surprised by what I heard from the prime minister at our afternoon meeting on June 1. He told me of a cable from Ephraim Evron, our minister in Washington, reporting that Walt Rostow, speaking on behalf of President Johnson, had explained that the president had been misunderstood. He could not fulfill the commitment as worded by Foreign Minister Eban. This gave us reason to believe that Eban's report that, given two or three weeks to organize a naval force, the United States intended to break the blockade of the straits — which had persuaded the cabinet to extend our wait — was less an outright promise by the president than our foreign minister had understood it to be. To clarify exactly where we stood, Eshkol had already dispatched Mossad chief Meir Amit on a mission to Washington to sort out the problem. But before Amit could complete his assignment, the telegram from our minister in Washington arrived like a slap in the face. There was no way of misinterpreting the cable: we could not expect any action on the part of the United States for it was not possible to assemble an international flotilla to break the Egyptian blockade.

Eshkol was thunderstruck. If political moves were merely a charade, why had we attached our hopes to promises? What had been the point of postponing military action? When Nasser learned that American involvement did not extend beyond noncommittal statements, how far would his presumption take him? That cable from Washington had the look and feel of the proverbial last straw. Eshkol had not spoken to me about the moves under way to form a National Unity government by bringing the opposition into the cabinet (which was entirely proper on his part, since the chief of staff plays no role in domestic politics). But when his military aide informed me that all the preparations for constituting such a cabinet had been completed, I had the feeling that it held out better prospects for ending the delay and giving us the green light to break out of the Egyptian noose.

It was only on the evening of June 1 that Eshkol told me of the likelihood that Moshe Dayan would be appointed defense minister in the expanded cabinet. When he asked me for my opinion of the appointment, was it merely out of politeness? In any event, I knew that I could not influence domestic political developments, so I held my peace. Once again I saw Eshkol in a state of despair. He sensed the cruelty (so characteristic of politics) of having to pay the price for the erosion of his authority in the eyes of the public and the cabinet. Had the cabinet already decided to go to war, the outcome would have been so different. Eshkol would have reaped the glory, the nation would have adulated him, and there would have been no need for a National Unity government. Now it was too late. I left Eshkol with a heavy heart and the single consolation that I could now phone Shayke Gavish and tell him he would remain GOC of Southern Command.

That night's cabinet meeting was attended by the three new ministers: Moshe Dayan (defense minister) and Menachem Begin and Yosef Sapir (ministers without portfolio). Aharon Yariv gave the intelligence assessment of the situation, and although no decisions were adopted, it was clear that the hour of judgment was drawing near.

At nine o'clock the following morning, the Ministerial Committee on Defense convened in the war room of the Pit for a joint meeting with the general staff. The ministers listened as we presented our plans for destroying Egypt's military power by an offensive operation. When it came time for the newly appointed defense minister to offer his assessments, we gained strong backing from his words. The urgency regarding our attack, he felt, was related to the question of how long we could operate before international intervention halted the fighting. We would probably be limited to a time span of three or four days. As long as the Egyptian army was not fully fortified in the Sinai, we could break through its lines swiftly and complete the opening phase of the war in a relatively short time. This would give us more time to rout the Egyptian troops and solidify our gains. But if we dallied, the breakthrough phase would take longer; and if we failed to complete our operations, a partial victory would be interpreted by Egypt as a setback for us. In a nutshell, Dayan's message was that the longer it took to decide, the less we stood to gain from a war. And war, after all, was really the only option open to us.

Eshkol still seemed wary. He defended the cabinet's decision to explore every possible political avenue, referring to the fact that the growth in the IDF's strength over recent years would not have been feasible had we not displayed sufficient sensitivity and deference to the wishes of our friends. But as he went on to analyze Johnson's reply to Eban, he was interrupted by our quartermaster general, Matti Peled, who called out: "In that case, what else are we waiting for?"

Eshkol looked angry. "If I haven't made that plain by now, I don't know how I can," he whipped back. "We will still need Johnson's help and support. I hope we won't need it during the fighting, but we shall certainly need it if we are victorious, in order to protect our gains. I want to make it clear to the president, beyond a shadow of a doubt, that we have not misled him; that we've given the necessary time for any political action designed to prevent the war. Two days more or less won't sway the outcome of a war!"

In a way, his words were heartening. If we were really down to two days before H hour, there was little cause for complaint. At midday on June 2, a secret decision was adopted not to attack before Monday, June 5, 1967. Dayan, Eban, Allon, Ya'akov Herzog, and I met at the Prime Minister's Office to decide on that date — subject, of course, to the cabinet's decision. And now that Eshkol and Eban saw eye to eye, there was a much better chance that the cabinet would reach a decision to go to war.

It took two more days for the cabinet to do so. Eshkol's heated rebuke about "two days more or less" turned out to be right on the mark. Sunday, June 4, found the IDF wound up like a mighty spring. Our operational plans had been finalized. Over the weeks of waiting, they had undergone repeated revision as the circumstances shifted on the southern front. We had gone through

Operation Fork and Operation Hoe — what seemed like a whole farmyard of plans — on paper, on maps, with sticks in the sand. Now we would make our way through the final plan with tanks, half-tracks, and trucks. Contrary to earlier proposals, Dayan instructed us not to occupy the Gaza Strip during the first phase of fighting in order to avoid having to cope with a densely populated area right from the beginning of the war. Moreover, he insisted that we not reach the Suez Canal — which was to be regarded as an international waterway — and that we take Sharm el-Sheikh earlier than we had originally planned. But before the tanks began to roll, we would place our fate in the hands of the air force, whose preemptive strike was to destroy Egypt's planes on the ground and give us control of the skies.

Air Force Commander Motti Hod estimated that it would take three hours to demolish the Egyptian planes. Having completed its attack on Egypt's airfields, our air force would then be free to shift its main force to Jordan, Syria, and Iraq if they joined Egypt in the war. The air-force operational plan was daring, since the task of defending the skies over Israel while most of our planes were off attacking Egypt's airfields was left to a total of twelve planes out of two hundred! Prior to the launch of our attack, and long after the Six Day War, I often wondered what would have happened if the air battle against Egypt had lasted more than three hours and Syrian and Jordanian planes had attacked Israel while most of our fighters were away over Egypt. The confidence of Motti Hod and his officers largely dispelled such fears at the time, but their optimism was vindicated only when we received the first reports on our air strike.

On my way back from a final check of operational plans at Southern Command on June 4, I met Dayan at Tel Aviv's Sdeh Dov airfield. He arrived by helicopter straight from the latest cabinet meeting. As expected by then, Dayan informed me that the cabinet had given its approval: the Israel Defense Forces would go into action the next morning. At GHQ we fixed the final hour for the air strike at 7:45 A.M., as requested by Motti Hod. "For the past two weeks, we have been keeping a watch on the precise movements of the Egyptian air force," he explained. "At first light they take off on patrol, staying up for about an hour. Then they return to base and go off for breakfast. Between seven and eight, everything is dead, and seven forty-five in the morning is ideal timing for us. We can send our planes off by daylight. There's no risk of morning mist, either in Israel or in Egypt. And it would be better for our pilots to get a good night's sleep before battle, so we won't get them up too early."

On the night of June 4, I felt calm and relaxed, as if the enormous burden of anxiety and doubt that had weighed on me since May 15 had suddenly disintegrated. I knew that the IDF was well prepared — in its training, its deployment, and the operational plans we had drawn up. Tomorrow morning would be the critical test. Like Motti's pilots — and for the first time in weeks — I went home to get a good night's rest.

Chapter Six

THE SIX DAY WAR

ON THE MORNING of June 5, the IDF faced a powerful constellation of enemies. The Egyptians had the equivalent of seven divisions, including more than eight hundred tanks stationed in the Sinai (with another three hundred to the west of the Suez Canal), hundreds of artillery batteries, and tens of thousands of infantrymen. Their army was backed by an imposing naval force of 7 destroyers, 11 submarines, 18 missile boats, 23 torpedo boats, 2 frigates, 25 minelayers, 80 frogmen, and some 700 marine commandos, and an air force of 242 fighters and bombers, half of them MiG 21s (together with its transport planes and helicopters, the Egyptian air force had 419 aircraft).

On the Jordanian front we faced nine infantry brigades, seven of which were deployed in defensive positions on the West Bank. In addition, there were two armored brigades plus two tank battalions. Altogether, then, we faced more than three hundred tanks, backed by the Iraqi Eighth Motorized Brigade and a further battalion of the Palestine Liberation Army. The Saudi Eleventh Infantry Brigade was also drawn up near the Jordanian border and on alert to move into Jordan. Admittedly, the Jordanian air force numbered no more than 24 Hunter fighters, 7 transport planes, and 4 helicopters. But the Iraqi air force — with its 130 fighters, 21 bombers, 23 transport planes, and 50 helicopters — could come to Jordan's assistance.

The Syrian army comprised some five hundred tanks and about six infantry brigades, five of which were deployed near the Israeli frontier. Their armored brigades were stationed to the rear, but each infantry brigade had twenty to thirty tanks in the front line. Moreover, the Syrian air force had 112 aircraft, 95 of them fighters (including more than 60 MiG 21s, the most advanced Soviet plane).

In comparison with these forces, the IDF was, as always, smaller but tightly knit and well equipped. On the Egyptian front, we had over seven hundred tanks, two infantry brigades, the regular paratroop brigade, two reserve paratroop brigades, and, of course, artillery and engineering units. About one hundred tanks and three infantry brigades were drawn up facing the Jordanian army, and some three hundred tanks and three infantry brigades were stationed opposite the Syrians in the north. Our air force had two hundred fighter planes, as well as some forty or fifty Fuga trainers adapted for ground-support roles by the installation of rocket launchers. Since the Fugas were incapable of taking part in aerial combat, they were not marked for participation in the attack on the Egyptian air force but were to provide air support for our armored thrust against the Egyptians.

The IDF had developed a comprehensive strategic outlook that applied to two basic possibilities: either that the Arab states would initiate a full-scale attack or that the initiative in opening hostilities would be taken by Israel. We knew that initiating an attack would provide us with great advantages — especially in terms of the air war, because the side that achieved air superiority would immediately better its odds in all aspects of the land and sea battles as well. In our case, the achievement of air superiority was absolutely indispensable, for we had to prevent the enemy air force from striking us in our most sensitive area: heavily populated zones.

It was for these reasons that our strategy was designed first and foremost to attain control of the skies by means of a sudden and massive attack to destroy the enemy's air power. The aim was first to put airfields, and especially runways, out of commission; then obliterate planes on the ground; and finally train our sights on radar and maintenance installations. The timing of launching the ground and sea forces had to be coordinated with the progress of the air assault, for the quick achievement of complete air superiority would enable our planes to take part in the ground and sea battles and we knew that a combined air-and-ground action would bring about the enemy's swift and decisive defeat.

As to the ground war, because Israel lacked strategic depth the IDF had an ironclad rule that the war must be fought on the enemy's territory and that the enemy's forces must be defeated as quickly as humanly possible. Due to the skewed ratio of forces between Israel and the Arab states, this policy could be realized only by concentrating our major assault on one front. While that main ground attack was being carried out, our forces on the other two fronts would have to deploy for defense and for coping with the effects of any air attack. Yet even this defensive posture would require limited offensive tactics and the capture of some territory in order to keep the enemy's troops outside our borders.

We viewed the Egyptian army as the main objective, not only because of Nasser's warlike acts, but because Egypt's military might (unmatched by any other Arab state) naturally made it into the most menacing threat in time of war. In consolidating the offensive plan for the Egyptian front, and in the various "war games" that we had carried out over the years, we tried to exploit the IDF's clear advantage in mobile warfare. Our strategy called for destroying the Egyptian army and conquering the Sinai through three axes of thrust. The main effort aimed at penetrating into the open area of maneuver between the Egyptian army's two major defensive zones in the Sinai. The first of these defensive zones was close to the Israeli border in the northern and central Sinai; the second was based around the Gidi and Mitla passes and to the north of them.

The point of departure of our main thrust was the central Negev, since there was no Egyptian defensive line in that area. An armored division was to move along unpaved roads and through trackless areas to attack the first Egyptian defensive zone from the rear, while a second thrust would move along a road parallel to the Sinai coast toward El Arish and a third thrust would move through the middle, that is, between the coastal route and the central Negev. The advantage of the plan was that it provided for attacking the first defensive zone from the front and the rear simultaneously, and isolating the individual outposts and destroying them one by one. In addition to this overall strategy, we had a separate plan for capturing Sharm el-Sheikh, but I did not believe that an isolated attack on this outpost was realistic. It seemed to me that starting the war at Sharm was simply not a feasible option for the IDF.

The plan for capturing the West Bank — should the necessity arise — was based on a broad pincer movement from the north and the south, while a special, independent plan existed for the capture of Jerusalem. As for the Golan Heights, our strategy called for a three-pronged movement coming from the north and south of the Sea of Galilee together with a thrust more or less straight across the heights to take the town of Kuneitra and cut the Syrian forces in two.

Ironically enough, though we painstakingly planned to catch the Egyptian air force off its guard, we began the war from a situation in which it was virtually impossible to surprise the enemy, since all the Arab forces were in a high state of preparedness. I am sure Nasser believed that the IDF would succeed in penetrating the Sinai in certain areas and that bitter fighting would go on for a few days, but then the Soviet Union would go into action at the UN Security Council and bring about a cease-fire and withdrawal of Israel's forces to the armistice lines. This was the most common military view in Eastern and Western Europe, as well as in Egypt and the other Arab states. Yet Nasser (and the rest of the world) erred in two assessments, and the combination of his errors was to prove fatal for his army. He underestimated the Israeli air force's ability to destroy Arab air power with such speed, and he failed to grasp that once we gained total supremacy in the air, Egypt's ground forces would be easy prey for our armor backed by close air support.

Three major questions would be put to the test during the first day of fighting. The first was whether the Egyptian air force could be eliminated as a military factor in a short time (a few hours), leaving our air force free to switch its attention to destroying the air power of Syria, Jordan, and Iraq (if and when they attacked). The second was whether our armor could achieve its breakthrough and fulfill its objectives without massive air support. The third was whether we could withstand ground assaults mounted by Syria and Jordan if these states entered the war immediately to aid the Egyptians.

The plan for the air assault was very daring. All our fighter

planes (with the exception of the twelve left behind to protect
Israeli airspace) would be launched against the Egyptian airfields
in three waves. We were aware that the Egyptian radar and antiaircraft systems could severely impede this tremendous effort,
and I confess to doubt that our objectives could be achieved in
the time set out by Motti Hod. But I also assumed that even if
the attainment of air superiority took a full day, it would still be a
magnificent achievement.

On the morning of June 5, we were all concentrated in the air
force's command post. Emotions reached a peak when the results
of the first wave of the air strike became known: the Egyptian air
force was completely destroyed. A third of its planes had been destroyed on the ground, and most of the runways at the main air
bases were damaged beyond use. The second wave prevented the
Egyptians from recovering their wits, and the third put an end to
the Egyptian air force as a combat formation of any significance.
At eleven o'clock Motti announced that at least 180 planes had
been destroyed and all the installations of the Egyptian air force
were out of operation for at least the next few hours. During
those first three hours of the war, I shuttled back and forth between the air-force command post and the Pit so that I could also
follow the armored advance on the northern axis in the Sinai.
When I was at the air-force command, every so often I would
study Motti Hod. After all, this was precisely how he had predicted events. Was he excited? Did his face show any sign of gratification, any hint of "I told you so"? I was so pleased with him,
and for him, that I was quite prepared to accept such a reaction
with perfect humility. But his features were rocklike in their im-
passivity; not a muscle moved. He gulped down incredible
amounts of water and held his tongue.

Now the air force was free to pursue its attacks on the other
fronts, if necessary. During this first stage, the war was limited to
Egypt, and our instructions from the government were to refrain
from action on any other front. Our planes were to be used only
in response to overt provocation. Israel clearly did not want a war
with Jordan. To prove that point beyond any doubt, the cabinet
sent an official note to the Jordanian government by means of

three channels: our representative to the Israel-Jordan Mixed Armistice Commission (who passed it on to his Jordanian counter-
part); General Odd Bull, head of the UN truce observation teams;
and the American embassy in Tel Aviv. The content of the message was that even though Jordan had already opened artillery
fire on Jerusalem and along the entire armistice line, if the Jordanians stopped firing and refrained from any other warlike acts,
Israel would commit herself to honor the armistice agreement
with Jordan in its entirety. But King Hussein chose for war despite the Israeli warning. Either he was convinced by Nasser's
reports of Egyptian victories or he found himself with no other
choice than to enter battle. Either way, his decision proved to be
a fatal error for his country.

The air forces of Syria, Jordan, and Iraq began to attack their
targets in Israel at 11:50 A.M., and within two hours the Syrian
and Jordanian air forces were destroyed, as was the Iraqi H-3 air
base near the Jordanian border. In all, 400 enemy planes were
destroyed on the first day of the fighting; and that in essence
decided the fate of the war. The Arab air forces still had some 280
planes, but they were not a factor to be reckoned with during the
remaining five days of battle. Moreover, the elimination of Arab
air power was of decisive importance for morale. It undermined
the fighting spirit of the Arab military leadership, as well as of
officers and men in the field, while precisely the opposite happened within Israel's political and military leadership and her
combat units. Still, however, we were not overconfident and
were certainly not itching for a fight merely to demonstrate our
prowess.

The entry of Jordan and Syria into the war raised the questions
of our ultimate objectives on these fronts. For the present, they
remained purely defensive, meaning that the purpose of the fighting was to prevent artillery bombardment of our airports and of
Tel Aviv from positions in the West Bank and to stop the tanks
deployed in the Jordan Rift Valley from reaching Jerusalem. Our
armor was assigned to both these tasks. At the same time, since
Jerusalem was already under artillery fire, Motta Gur's paratroop
brigade was thrown in to capture the northern Arab suburbs of

the city, while the local Jerusalem Brigade fought to the south of the city (after taking the UN compound at Government House from Jordanian troops). On this first day of fighting, the government decided that the Old City was not to be captured.

On the first night of the war, all the troops fighting in the West Bank faced bitter battles — and none more so than Gur's paratroopers in their breakthrough to capture areas heavily fortified by the Jordanians. The air effort concentrated on preventing the Jordanian armor from coming up to Jerusalem, and it succeeded in inflicting enough damage to enable our armor to reach the crest of the hills before the Jordanian tanks did. Meanwhile, in the Sinai, General Tal's armored division had broken through on the northern axis and had reached El Arish by evening, while the other two armored divisions advanced on their targets.

While the Egyptians and Jordanians were immersed in battle, the Syrians remained inert. Their allies failed to achieve any gains, but the Syrians — our bitterest foes and the party that had set off the conflagration — now refrained from coming to their aid. Time and time again, the GOC of Northern Command, David Elazar ("Dado"), protested: "What about the Syrians! Are they going to get off scot-free?" And time and time again (until he finally changed his mind), Defense Minister Dayan forbade him to take any action.

The night of June 5–6 must have been a difficult one for Nasser and Hussein. Never in their worst nightmares could they have dreamed they would be in such a harrowing position after the first day of fighting. Our forces had made a swift breakthrough in both the Sinai and the West Bank, not to mention the fact that we had totally conquered the skies. Military commentators and historians are unanimous in concluding that Nasser lied in his infamous telephone conversation with King Hussein during the night of June 5–6. The Egyptian president claimed that American planes from the Sixth Fleet and British aircraft had participated in the fighting by defending Israel's airspace and aiding in the destruction of the Arab air forces. The two leaders agreed to publicize this story, and at six o'clock the next morning the Supreme Command of the Arab armed forces published the fabrication — which no one outside the Arab world took seriously. But neither at that time nor at any later stage of the war did I totally accept the view that Nasser knew perfectly well that no foreign planes had taken part in the war and was just using the lie to cover up for his debacle. It may have been so, but it is equally conceivable that he simply could not believe that the Israeli air force — whose size was more or less known to him — was capable of carrying out such an enormous task within the space of a few hours. And if the Israeli planes were incapable of doing the job alone, who could have helped Israel destroy the Arab air forces if not the Americans and British?

Be that as it may, by Monday night, at the end of the first day of fighting, all of Israel could afford to breathe a sigh of relief. Not only was the harrowing threat of annihilation neutralized, but our troops were making gains at a phenomenal momentum. I think that Dayan, more than anyone else, was sensitive to the power of our ground thrust. From my perspective, at least, he seemed to be acting as a constant balance for restraint, or at least careful calculation. Throughout those six days of fighting, Dayan was the voice of prudence. Not only did he keep a tight rein on Dado's eagerness to enter battle on the Syrian front, but early on Tuesday morning, June 6, he again reiterated his order to refrain from attacking Jerusalem's Old City. His thoughts at that time were on another matter entirely. At 8:30 A.M. on the second day of the war, Dayan called me over and with a considerable measure of impatience in his tone informed me that reports were piling up about frenzied Russian political activitiy aimed at halting the fighting. "What about Sharm el-Sheikh?" he demanded. "We'll find the war coming to an end before we get our hands on its cause!" Then he ordered me to "get to Sharm and establish our presence there, irrespective of the progress of fighting in the Sinai!"

At my suggestion, we agreed that Sharm would be taken during the night of June 7 by a combined operation of airborne and naval forces. But again the momentum of events outstripped our plans in a bizarre way. On the evening of June 6, after thirty-six hours of fighting and with our forces in the Sinai advancing steadily toward the Gidi and Mitla passes, the Egyptian High Command ordered its army to fall back toward the Suez Canal (only the Fourth Division and units from the Canal Zone command were ordered to stabilize defense lines at the eastern approaches to the passes). As a result, during the night of June 6–7, the Egyptians quietly evacuated Sharm el-Sheikh. On the next morning, when the Security Council decided to call for a cease-fire, we saw the sand in the political hourglass beginning to run out, and it was vital to speed up our operations. I therefore issued orders to move up our assault on Sharm el-Sheikh, but when the navy got there (before the other units), the flotilla's commander reported, "There's no one to fight!" Sharm el-Sheikh had fallen without a single shot. My prewar assessment had been squarely on the mark: once the principal Egyptian forces in the Sinai had been defeated, the capture of Sharm would not be a problem.

June 7, the third day of fighting, was undoubtedly the most remarkable day of the war for me since I experienced both sheer terror and the height of elation within a matter of hours. With the sense that time was pressing, at seven o'clock that morning Dayan entered the war room and finally issued the order for Jerusalem's Old City to be occupied as quickly as possible. The fact that our troops were moving in on the most coveted — and difficult — target in the war left us all with a sharp sense of anticipation. But in the midst of that battle, our attention at GHQ was suddenly torn away to another front and to what appeared to be the most alarming development in the entire campaign.

I was seated in my office at the GHQ command post when I received a message that sounded odd: explosions had been reported in the El Arish area. By that time, El Arish was in our hands and our forces had advanced fifty or sixty miles beyond it along the northern route. An initial guess was that the Egyptians might be coming in from the sea to attack our units in the town, so I ordered the navy and air force to look into the matter. A second report, which arrived an hour later, led to a change in our assessment. A ship had been sighted opposite El Arish. Following standing orders to attack any unidentified vessel near the shore (after appropriate attempts had been made to ascertain its identity), our air force and navy zeroed in on the vessel and damaged it. But they still could not tell us whose ship it was. Then a third message removed all doubts, but it sent our anxieties skyrocketing. Our forces had attacked a Soviet spy vessel! I reported to Eshkol and Dayan and called in the senior GHQ commanders for consultation. It was vital to make preparations, but no one wanted to articulate exactly for what. We did not dare put our fears into words, but the question that hung over the room like a giant saber was obvious: Are we facing massive Soviet intervention in the fighting?

Throughout the period of tension that commenced on May 15 and after the outbreak of war, the Soviet navy had reinforced its fleet in the Mediterranean up to a total of seventy vessels (the U.S. navy had done similarly, though to a lesser extent). Now that the Egyptian and Jordanian armies had been routed and the fighting on two fronts had essentially been decided, would the Soviets take advantage of this incident to join the war and tip the balance in the Arabs' favor? While we were discussing the matter, a fourth report came in and finally clarified the situation. The vessel was American — amazing but true. Four of our planes flew over it at a low altitude in an attempt to identify the ship, but they were unable to make out any markings and therefore concluded that it must be Egyptian. They notified the navy of their attack, and one of our ships finished the task by firing off torpedos at the *Liberty*, leaving the vessel heavily damaged.

I must admit I had mixed feelings about the news — profound regret at having attacked our friends and a tremendous sense of relief stemming from the assumption that one can talk with friends and render explanations and apologies. The frightful prospect of a violent Soviet reprisal had disappeared. After consultation with the prime minister and the defense minister, we reported the mishap to the American embassy, offered the Americans a helicopter to fly out to the ship, and promised all the necessary help in evacuating casualties and salvaging the vessel. The Americans immediately accepted our offer, and one of our helicopters took their naval attaché to the ship.

The scene aboard the *Liberty* was dismal. There were many

wounded and some thirty-two dead, including a number of American Jews serving in the crew because of their command of Hebrew. The vessel's task was to monitor the IDF's signals networks for a rapid follow-up of events on the battlefield by tracking messages transmitted between the various headquarters. The Sixth Fleet declined our services, evacuated their own wounded, and towed the vessel to Naples (one of its home ports) for repairs.

It was only later, while serving as Israel's ambassador to the United States, that I learned further details that cast light on the tragic episode from an American viewpoint. With the outbreak of the fighting on June 5, we notified the American naval attaché in Israel that we intended to protect our shores from Egyptian naval attacks by employing a combination of naval and air units. In the event that Egyptian vessels approached our shores, we would not be able to delay our response. We therefore asked that American ships be removed from the vicinity of the Israeli shore or that the Americans notify us of their precise location in the area near our coast. In the storm of battle, there was no time to check whether or not our request had been fulfilled. During my term as ambassador, however, I learned that Washington had indeed instructed the Sixth Fleet to move its vessels away from the Israeli coastline, but due to a bureaucratic blunder the order failed to reach the *Liberty*.

What we at GHQ could not have known during those tension-filled moments was that this local misunderstanding might easily have set off a far more wide-ranging war. Just as our pilots had failed to identify the markings of the ship (and at one point tentatively surmised that it was Russian), the Americans had failed to identify the planes that had attacked them, and their initial impression was that Soviet aircraft were assaulting a unit of the Sixth Fleet! In his autobiography, President Johnson depicted the incident as one of the most critical moments in his life, for he faced the awesome decision of ordering U.S. aircraft to attack the Soviet fleet in the Mediterranean. I encountered a fascinating parallel: just as we were relieved to learn that the ship was American, rather than Soviet, Johnson and the heads of the American armed forces were reassured upon hearing that the attackers were Israelis. This in no way detracts from the pain of the human tragedy involved, but at least we were not plunged into a third world war.

In any event, to express our goodwill and humanitarian concern, the Israeli government paid thirteen million dollars in compensation to the families of the Americans killed or wounded in the attack. Yet despite repeated pressure, we refused to bear the cost of repairing the vessel, since we did not consider ourselves responsible for the train of errors. Regrettably, the Americans remained somewhat resentful about the affair, at least for the duration of the Johnson administration.

With the *Liberty* incident under control, our attention fell back on Jerusalem. After a day of tough fighting in the Arab-held quarters of the city, Motta Gur's paratroop brigade forced its way through the Lions' Gate into the Old City late on the morning of June 7. I was asked to accompany the defense minister into the Old City, and we flew to the Jerusalem headquarters of Uzi Narkiss, GOC Central Command, where the air was charged with excitement. Uzi had been one of the officers of the Harel Brigade (which fought in Jerusalem during the War of Independence), so it was a great moment for both of us. In 1948 we had been forced to leave East Jerusalem in the enemy's hands, and ever since the outbreak of the present war we had been dogged by the feeling that we must not miss the historic opportunity again.

Driving toward the Lions' Gate, on the eastern side of the Old City wall, we were surrounded by signs of the previous day's fierce fighting. A smoldering tank stood by the gate itself, and the narrow alleys of the Old City, with their shuttered windows and locked doors, were totally deserted. But every now and then the eerie silence was broken by sniper fire from Jordanian soldiers who had failed to flee in time and continued to resist.

As we made our way through streets I remembered from childhood, pungent memories played on my emotions. The sheer excitement increased as we came closer to the Western Wall itself. It is still easy for me to conjure up the feelings that assaulted me then, but it's very difficult to put them into words. The Wall was and is our national memento of the glories of Jewish independence in ancient times. Its stones have a power to speak to the hearts of Jews the world over, as if the historical memory of the Jewish people dwelled in the cracks between those ancient ashlars. For years I secretly harbored the dream that I might play a part not only in gaining Israel's independence but in restoring the Western Wall to the Jewish people, making it the focal point of our hard-won independence. Now that dream had come true, and suddenly I wondered why I, of all men, should be so privileged. I knew that never again in my life would I experience quite the same peak of elation.

When we reached the Western Wall, I was breathless. It seemed as though all the tears of centuries were striving to break out of the men crowded into that narrow alley, while all the hopes of generations proclaimed: "This is no time for weeping! It is a moment of redemption, of hope." Following the ancient custom, Dayan scrawled a wish on a slip of paper and pushed it in between two of the stones. I felt truly shaken and stood there murmuring a prayer for peace. Motta Gur's paratroopers were struggling to reach the Wall and touch it. We stood among a tangle of rugged, battle-weary men who were unable to believe their eyes or restrain their emotions. Their eyes were moist with tears, their speech incoherent. The overwhelming desire was to cling to the Wall, to hold on to that great moment as long as possible.

Although those moments at the Western Wall may have been the emotional climax of the war, the fighting itself was far from over. By the time I returned to GHQ, there was no doubt that the battles on the Egyptian and Jordanian fronts had been decided, but we were still uncertain about the situation regarding the Syrians. As if to refute the accusation that they were willing to fight to the last Egyptian, at 6:30 A.M. on the previous day the Syrians had laid an artillery barrage on our settlements all along the front. Dayan authorized Dado to return the fire but forbade him to step foot across the frontier in an assault on the Syrian positions.

Needless to say, Dado was beside himself with anger and frustration. But the defense minister was filled with anxiety about the prospect of Soviet intervention — and he was not alone in his fears. No one in our political or military leadership could promise that an all-out attack on Syria would not result in Soviet involvement, nor could anyone promise that such a dangerous development would induce the Americans to deter the Soviets. On Wednesday Dayan gave Dado permission to cross the Syrian border up to a depth of a mile or two, at most, but I saw no point in such a move. Reaching the tops of a few hills without producing any fundamental change in the situation did not seem worth the bloodshed.

At 10:00 P.M. on June 7, the cease-fire ordered by the Security Council was to come into effect. An hour before that, I was quite surprised — but not at all sorry — to learn that Nasser had decided not to honor the UN resolution because it did not simultaneously order the withdrawal of Israeli forces. Unwittingly, Nasser was beginning to act more like an ally than an enemy, for we had yet to complete all our plans on the Egyptian front and his refusal to accept the cease-fire made it possible for us to go ahead. Less than twenty-four hours later, however, during the evening of June 8, the Egyptian president changed his mind and agreed to an unconditional cease-fire. There was little doubt about the reason for his change of heart: the Soviet Union could not manage to force through a Security Council resolution linking the cease-fire to an Israeli withdrawal from the Sinai (as it had in 1956). The IDF was advancing on the canal, and the Egyptian army was no longer capable of halting it.

Nasser could not have known that he was not the only one to change his mind that night. Ever since the fighting began, Dayan had resolutely stuck to the view that we must not advance as far as the Suez Canal. Our occupation of the canal bank, he believed, would make it impossible for Egypt to consent to a cease-fire and still avoid an intolerable humiliation. We would therefore have to be careful not to push the Egyptians into a corner, which would inevitably prolong the war. I knew Dayan's reasons against thrusting for the canal (though I was not inclined to concur) but I did not know why he changed his mind near midnight on June 8, after Nasser had announced Egypt's consent to an unconditional cease-fire.

With Dayan's objections gone, there was no further obstacle.

The IDF occupied the whole of the Sinai, establishing its forward positions along the Suez Canal and on the shore of the Gulf of Suez. The Egyptian army disintegrated completely, having suffered at least fifteen thousand dead, and the desert was filled with Egyptian soldiers fleeing for their lives. It was a sight that even the victors did not savor: ragged, barefoot, and terrorized, the troops left their shattered illusions behind and fled back to their homes at the mercy of a triumphant enemy. In order to forestall any errors, I issued explicit orders against opening fire on Egyptian soldiers who surrendered themselves. Of those who fell into our hands, only the officers were to be kept in detention; the rest would be allowed to cross the canal and return home. (This order was issued at a time when we already held between five thousand and six thousand Egyptian prisoners.) Our far-flung forces were already facing supply difficulties, and there was no point in burdening them further with thousands of prisoners.

That same evening, June 8, with Egypt and Jordan out of the war, our undivided attention shifted to the Syrian front. Dado personally came down to see me and made no attempt to conceal his frustration and disappointment. No less insistent were the representatives of our settlements in the north, who submitted their complaints to Eshkol. "The IDF has defeated our enemies to the south and east," they fumed. "Are we going to remain at the mercy of the Syrian guns?" I explained to them that the restrictions imposed by the defense minister made it pointless to storm the Golan Heights, and I asked Eshkol to respond to Dado's request for a meeting. It was obvious that the arguments presented by Dado and the settlers convinced Eshkol that we must act, but under the circumstances the decision was up to Dayan.

All the same, Eshkol decided to convene the Ministerial Committee on Defense and invited the settlers to attend the session. I presented the recommended operational plan, but neither the appeals of the local inhabitants nor the plan I submitted could induce Dayan to budge from his position. Repeating his warnings of Soviet intervention, he managed to sow a sense of grave disquiet among the ministers and persuaded them that no action should be taken on the Syrian front at present.

Just before midnight, I phoned Dado and informed him of the committee's decision. His response was one of utter stupefaction. "What has happened to this country?" he groaned. "How will we ever be able to face ourselves, the people, the settlements? After all the trouble they've caused, after the shellings and harassments, are those arrogant bastards going to be left on top of the hills riding on our backs?" I recalled that the settlers had used precisely the same term in addressing the ministerial committee: "The Syrians are riding on our backs! If the State of Israel is in capable of defending us, we're entitled to know it! We should be told outright that we are not part of this state, not entitled to the protection of the IDF. We should be told to leave our homes and flee from this nightmare!"

Dado asked me to permit him to evacuate noncombatants from the front-line settlements, but I forbade him to do so. The defense minister and the Ministerial Committee on Defense had given express instructions to forbid evacuation, and I was not empowered to override them — though I did give him permission to evacuate children from the front line. And that, it appeared, was that. Yet the unpredictable Moshe Dayan surprised us once again with a sudden reversal.

On Thursday, June 8, when the Ministerial Committee on Defense decided against attacking Syria, the war was effectively over. The Egyptians and Jordanians had been routed and had announced their consent to a cease-fire. Syria, too, had expressed a similar willingness. After four days of fighting it seemed that the guns would fall silent, so for the first time since June 4 I allowed myself the luxury of going home, at 2.00 A.M. Utterly exhausted, I exchanged a few words with Leah and the children before crumpling into bed. I think I was asleep before my head touched the pillow.

If anyone was to wake me at 7:00 A.M., he must have had a good reason. Ezer Weizman had an excellent reason. "Fifteen minutes ago, Dayan contacted Dado," he told me, "and ordered him to attack the Syrians immediately." I rushed to the Pit to find out what had happened. It seems that Dayan had arrived at six and asked the intelligence officers for an assessment of the situation. After hearing about the total disintegration of the Egyptian army, he still maintained his opposition to any attack on the Syrian front. But shortly before seven — for reasons I have never grasped — he ordered Dado to attack. This was no time for petty arguments about lines of jurisdiction. It is up to the chief of staff to give operational orders to the GOC of a regional command, but I had no desire to quibble when the Syrians were about to get their just deserts for malicious aggressiveness and arrogance. Together with officers at GHQ, I reexamined our plans for the Syrian front and ordered the GOC of Central Command to send a brigade and other units up north to reinforce our troops there.

When I contacted Dado by phone, he told me that he had practically fallen out of his chair when he heard Dayan's orders. He could not understand what had changed Dayan's mind. But he added that Dayan had told him that the Syrian units were crumbling and their soldiers had begun fleeing even before the IDF assault commenced. That last comment worried me. Experience in previous wars had taught us that it is dangerously misleading to attack on the assumption that the enemy is in a state of disintegration. "The Syrian army is nowhere near collapse," I warned Dado. "You must assume that it will fight obstinately and with all its strength!"

By the time the helicopter carrying Ezer Weizman and me landed at Northern Command headquarters, our forces had already begun their breakthrough on the northern route to the Golan Heights. At this stage, the Syrian army displayed no signs of disintegration. On the contrary, the battle was tough and stubborn, taking a heavy toll of casualties. Our soldiers had to apply all their skill and devotion in negotiating the steep, rocky tracks. The Syrians' reinforced-concrete fortifications, which were impregnable to shelling, were the scenes of bitter hand-to-hand fighting. From the Northern Command headquarters, Ezer and I watched as our planes attacked the Syrian positions. I have never seen Ezer in such a state of inner turmoil. He murmured the pilots' names as though he were directing the air battle from our vantage, and he begged them to protect themselves from harm. When one of our planes was hit and went down in flames, Ezer knew that the pilot was one of his many favorites, and his features twisted into a grimace of agony.

After returning to the GHQ command post, I phoned Dado
and ordered him to exploit the roads to their utmost in order to
dispatch large forces to Kuneitra, the Golan Heights' principal
town. On completing the call, however, I was notified by Dayan
that all military operations were to cease the following morning — at the latest. I told Dayan I had just ordered Dado to send
an airborne brigade into action, but the defense minister repeated
his order. So I contacted Dado again and transmitted Dayan's instructions. "Sorry," he replied, though I knew he didn't feel an
ounce of regret. "Following your previous order, they began to
move off, and I can't stop them." There was something in Dado's
tone that made me suspicious, but I didn't expend much effort in
an attempt to remove my doubts. Only after the war did I learn
that at the time I was talking with Dado, the brigade was still
awaiting orders miles from the Syrian border.

On Friday the Syrians continued to fight vigorously, and our
forces had to pay a heavy price for their victories. But during the
night the Syrian units began to crumble, even though their
soldiers were not given orders to retreat. Concerned about the
fate of Damascus, the Syrian High Command ordered its forces to
deploy to the north of Kuneitra. That night they asked the Egyptians to send in their commando units stationed in Jordan and
turned to the Iraqis for reinforcements. But as far as the Egyptians were concerned, the war was at an end, and not one of their
commandos was sent to the Syrians' aid. Nasser was unstinting
only with his promises: "If Israel does not honor the cease-fire,
Egypt will renew the war!" Yet anyone acquainted with the state
of the Egyptian army at that moment could not help seeing the
humor in the situation.

Though we knew that time was running out on the Syrian front,
during the last hours of the fighting we were not sure when the
battle was to be terminated. At midday? Earlier? Later? Our
forces were exhausted, and their heroic fighting in the course of
the breakthrough had taken its toll. Moreover, a message from
the American secretary of state induced Dayan to order the fighting to halt by 8:00 A.M. Saturday rather than at noon (as we had
previously expected). Air operations had to cease by 2:00 P.M. at
the latest. As a result, I ordered Dado to forgo the occupation of

Kuneitra and stabilize our line on the existing conquests. But then a Syrian error changed the course of events. At 8:30 Saturday morning, the Syrian radio announced that Kuneitra had fallen to the IDF. There is no way of knowing what prompted this false report. The Syrians may have been trying to create the impression that Israel was threatening Damascus and thereby elicit foreign political pressure on us or force the Soviet Union to threaten direct intervention unless we halted our advance. Or perhaps the report stemmed from Syrian panic and confusion, without consideration of its effect. Be that as it may, the announcement had two immediate results: the retreat of the Syrian troops turned into a panic-stricken flight; and, in view of this turn of events, our defense minister extended the deadline for our offensive until 2:00 P.M. It was eleven o'clock before the Syrians grasped their error and reversed their previous announcement, but by then it was too late to save the town.

The cease-fire with Syria finally went into effect at 6:30 on the evening of June 10, 1967. We spent the next day stabilizing our line (which included advances in which no fighting was involved), and on Monday, June 12, a helicopter-borne force took control of the Mount Hermon strongpoint, which had been deserted by the Syrians. These last moves established the Israel-Syria cease-fire line that was to remain intact from the Six Day War until the Yom Kippur War in 1973. We could have extended the areas under our control. There was no Egyptian force capable of halting the IDF had we intended to occupy Cairo. The same held for Amman, and on June 11 it would not have required much effort to take Damascus. But we had not gone to war to acquire territories, and those we already occupied presented enough of a burden.

Israel now faced three major problems, two of which have troubled us continuously from the Six Day War right up to the present day. The first was that overnight we found ourselves in control of an enormous expanse of territory. The area occupied by the IDF was three times the size of the prewar State of Israel, and we had difficulties in stabilizing new defense lines on all three fronts (particularly on the Suez Canal). We had never before thought of distances in terms of hundreds of miles. In addition, we had to overcome the resultant logistic and transport difficulties with the help of limited manpower, since tens of thousands of reservists had returned to their fields and factories, schools and offices.

The second problem was that a million hostile Arabs — in the West Bank and the Gaza Strip — were now living under Israeli rule. They were not citizens of the state, but they were human beings and had to make a living, eat, receive services, and be permitted freedom of movement. All the while, however, we were conscious of the fact that they would be subject to the temptation to harm us.

Finally, from the very start it was clear that Israel would not be left in peace to deal with the consequences of her territorial gains. The political confrontation commenced even before the guns fell silent, and it was to continue without respite for years to come.

A few days after the fighting ended, I was approached by representatives of the Hebrew University, at the instigation of Professor Yigael Yadin, and was told that they wished to award me an honorary doctorate. The motive was evidently to express the university's gratitude to the Israel Defense Forces, through its chief of staff, for restoring its original Mount Scopus campus; and in keeping with the prevailing atmosphere, the ceremony was to be held at the Mount Scopus amphitheater. I confess that I felt somewhat discomfited by the honor being bestowed upon me, since the IDF is not in the habit of awarding decorations to its senior staff officers. On second thought, however, I decided to accept in order to use the ceremony as an opportunity to talk about the unique nature of the IDF. I also consented to address the assembly on behalf of all those receiving honorary doctorates.

Over the next two weeks, I took time out to prepare my address, and it gave me an opportunity to reflect upon the war and the army that had fought and won it so brilliantly. Again and again, my thoughts were drawn to the phenomenal swiftness of it all, which had both positive and negative ramifications. Obviously, there was never any question — or desire — that the war would drag on for weeks, with all the accompanying tension and losses. Yet we had been so busy deciding whether or not to fight that few had taken the time to think out the consequences of victory. We were left in a somewhat unexpected, if not downright vexing, situation; and it took years for even one of our adversaries — Egypt — to agree to start unraveling that tangle of circumstances.

Second, the lightning pace of the war inevitably gave rise to myths — both in Israel and abroad — about the character of the fighting during those six days. The IDF was portrayed as steamrolling its three adversaries in a breathtaking dash across desert sands and up rocky cliffs. But there was a double edge to that kind of mythmaking, for it simultaneously portrayed the Israeli army as "invincible" and the Arab armies as "pushovers." Nothing could have been further from the truth. Before June 5 I repeatedly warned that if we opted for war, we must know that it would be a difficult undertaking. The fact that our successes exceeded all expectations did not in any way disprove that prediction. A number of infantry and armored assaults — in the Sinai as well as on the Golan Heights — were particularly difficult, and our men fought with determination and great valor. Motta Gur's paratroopers carried on a stubborn and bloody battle for East Jerusalem at a terrible toll in lives to both sides. In those heady days of euphoria after the war, while the mass media around the world were active creating legends, I wanted to keep things in their proper perspective. Sure, we were proud; and we had every right to be — not because we were "invincible" and not because our adversaries were tin soldiers, but because the IDF had earned the praise being showered upon it by its professionalism, creativity, and sheer obstinacy. We had earned the right to feel confident in our military prowess without denigrating the virtues of our adversaries or falling into the trap of arrogance.

When I spoke at the awards ceremony, however, I laid stress most of all on the wellsprings that nourished the IDF's spiritual and moral strength. It was the army of a nation that desired peace but was capable of fighting valiantly when enemies forced it into war. It was an army that displayed all the splendor and virtues of that people whenever it faced difficult trials. It was an army that proved its unrivaled prowess in combat yet even in the heat of battle preserved its humanity. I could not have wished for a finer expression of respect and esteem for the IDF than that ceremony on Mount Scopus. I sensed that my words had a profound impact upon my listeners, including the countless Israelis who heard them broadcast over the radio. If there can be any recompense for the long, anxious nights; for the awful awareness of sending young men to face death; for the heavy burden of responsibility that bore down on me, I gained it at that Mount Scopus ceremony.

For me personally, the Six Day War was the high point of a military career. Yet it also signaled that, having reached the summit of the army hierarchy, I needed to look ahead to my future. With the pressure of the fighting behind us, I turned over the task of studying the lessons of the war to Chaim Barlev (who I presumed would be my successor) and directed my own thoughts back to an idea I had been mulling over for a while: where to go from here.

Chapter Seven

INTRODUCTION TO WASHINGTON

WELL BEFORE THE Six Day War, in March 1967, I had already broached the subject of my personal future with Prime Minister Eshkol. I was due to complete my term as chief of staff after four years in the post, and when I told Eshkol that I wanted to be nominated as Israel's ambassador to the United States, it took him several minutes to get over the shock. "Hold on to me, Yitzhak, or I'll fall out of my chair!" he cried. "That's the last thing I would have expected you to want." Once he had composed himself, however, Eshkol asked for time to think the matter over. "I have to talk to Eban, of course, but I can tell you what my initial reaction is: You're no diplomat! Are you going to stand around at tedious cocktail parties, sit through boring banquets, and play all those other diplomatic games? Are you really up to it?"

"Well," I told him, "I am up to what I consider to be the task of Israel's ambassador to Washington. Cocktail parties don't worry me." What did concern me was our future place in the scheme of global politics. I appreciated the role that the United States played in our region and the need to coordinate our policies with the Americans. It seemed to me that strengthening our links with the United States was our greatest political challenge — not to mention a vital condition for maintaining the power of the IDF. "That is the sphere in which I would like to make whatever contribution I can," I told the prime minister, "and I'm confident that my military and political background as chief of staff will make up for any deficiencies in diplomatic experience." Even though Eshkol did not say so outright, I could already sense that he was taken with the idea.

After the war, in July or August, I had a further talk with

Eshkol, but the most he would say was, "Eban has some reservations. We'll see." The truth is that even then Abba Eban was not
one of my greatest admirers, and in all fairness I should add that
the feeling was mutual. But I did receive considerable support
from Golda Meir (who was then serving as the secretary-general
of the Mapai party) and from cabinet ministers Yisrael Galili and
Yigal Allon. Several of my friends were of two minds about my
request to be posted to Washington and began to drop hints
about my taking up an active role in politics, but I rejected the
idea out of hand. "I may go into politics someday, but definitely
not now," I protested. "I need some time to adjust, a kind of
transition period. And in Washington I can put my knowledge
and abilities to good use." In September, or October, even Eban
came around to the idea, and my appointment was set.

In preparation for taking up my new post, I held a series of
conversations with Eban and a number of Foreign Ministry officials. As is well known, dialogues with Eban have a way of turning into soliloquies, and it was very difficult for me to sound him
out on ideas of my own. Fortunately, my talks with Gideon Rafael, the director general of the Foreign Ministry, and Moshe
Bitan, head of the ministry's North American Division, were
more fruitful; but even there we had some awkward moments.
For example, when I innocently asked, "What does the government expect Israel's ambassador to the United States to achieve?
What are his objectives?" eyebrows shot up at my use of military
terminology. Objectives? No one had any idea.

So I proceeded to turn normal practice upside down. After extensive reading and study, I presented the Foreign Ministry with
a memorandum on the objectives of Israel's policy vis-à-vis the
United States: (1) ensuring that Israel was provided with her
defense requirements; (2) coordinating the policies of the two
countries in preparation for eventual peace negotiations or talks
on a political settlement in the Middle East — or at the very
least, preventing the emergence of too wide a disparity in policies; (3) securing American financial support to cover our arms
purchases and buttress our economy; (4) ensuring that the Americans use their deterrent force to prevent direct Soviet military in-

tervention against Israel in the event of another war. I also sketched the outline of a plan for maintaining Israel's leverage with the American administration and Congress. After submitting the document, however, I did not get the impression that it was given much attention. The ministry officials brushed me off with a terse "All right, that's fine," and I seemed to hear them saying, "Let's see you do all that."

I also took advantage of the opportunity to have a talk with Henry Kissinger when he visited Israel in January 1968. He was still a Harvard professor then (I doubt it even occurred to either of us that within a year he would be offered and accept a crucial post in the American administration), but that certainly didn't make our talk any less valuable to me. The conversation lasted for two hours, perhaps even three — it was so fascinating that I lost track of the time — and Kissinger presented his view of the international scene in his characteristic broad sweep. He explained that the United States' involvement in Vietnam was having a profound effect on its conduct in other conflict zones and on its attitude toward traditional allies, in addition to constricting its freedom of maneuver in relation to the Soviet Union. American liberal circles were even reverting to isolationist tendencies, and there was a strong disinclination to take risks in foreign affairs for fear of further entanglements. The trend was clearly swinging toward withdrawal and a reduction of America's commitment to the fate of other Western nations.

This shift in posture had hardly escaped the attention of the Soviet government, he noted. In fact, Kissinger had come away from his recent trip to the Soviet Union with the impression that America's weakness and inclination toward isolationism were fostering Soviet aggressiveness. Sensitive to the fact that the Vietnam War was a drain on the United States, the Russians had no desire to see it end; on the contrary, they wanted it prolonged. Nor did the Russians display any desire to reach accord with the United States on the reduction of strategic arms. The world situation depicted by Kissinger was a dismal one, and no less depressing was his forecast for Israel. The implications of America's mood of retreat and the Soviet Union's concomitant aggressiveness would have been disturbing to any Israeli, but they were all the more so to one who was about to become his country's representative in Washington.

Early in February 1968, with my groundwork completed, I set off with my family for a trip to Europe. At its end, however, our ways parted in London, with Yuval, our twelve-year-old son, accompanying Leah and me to Washington and Dalia returning to Israel for her final year of high school, to be followed by two years of compulsory military service. Even though we knew that Dalia would be in good hands (she was going to be staying with Leah's sister), it was a difficult parting. Leah and Dalia were in tears. I tried to remain stoic but doubt I succeeded in hiding the ache that every father must feel when he sees his "little girl" going off into the world on her own. And as many an Israeli diplomat can testify, being far from home when a son or daughter is serving in the army is a particularly demanding experience — even for a former chief of staff. Yuval, on the other hand, eventually became so homesick for Israel that he envied his sister's "luck" at being left behind, and I think that during our years in Washington he made as many trips back and forth over the ocean as I did. At any rate, right after landing at Dulles International Airport, we were driven directly to the Israeli ambassador's residence. Whatever else we might say about the "quality" of our life in Washington, we had certainly never lived in such a spacious house!

My first impressions of the American mood convinced me that Kissinger's dismal description had understated the case. The Vietcong and North Vietnamese Tet offensive had left its imprint on 1968 (a presidential-election year), and the credibility of Johnson's administration was at its nadir. Far more serious, the American people had lost faith in their own strength, in the moral fiber of their government, and in the justice of its intervention in Vietnam. Year after year, the administration promised to "bring the boys home for Christmas." But the bloodshed went on and on in the cause of saving a military regime in a distant land that was of little interest to the average American. Although I was careful to avoid being taken for an expert on the Vietnam War, I could well understand why Americans were tempted to seek counsel from the man who had commanded the tiny Israeli army in its mighty victory of 1967. I suppose they found it incomprehensible that the omnipotent United States of America could not overcome a guerrilla force supported by the army of a small and impoverished people when a Middle Eastern country approximately the size of Massachusetts had routed the armies of four Arab states.

Indeed, I too was somewhat puzzled about why the United States was so hopelessly bogged down in the Vietnam conflict. But matters became clearer after I had had a talk with the prominent Washington journalist Joseph Alsop, who invited me to lunch at his home (since Alsop frequently hosted key Washington figures, such an invitation was considered a status symbol). Alsop was a strange man — arrogant, highly intelligent, and fiercely proud of his country and its people (which was rather incongruous with the prevailing mood in those days). His attitude toward Israel had taken a complete turnabout from opposition to the creation of the state (he had feared that it would become a tool of the Communists, whom he detested) to gradually heightened support after he had visited Israel in 1956. We moved from one topic to another and toward the end of our luncheon talk I broached the subject of my puzzlement directly.

"I am not intimately familiar with the war in Vietnam," I confessed, "but I do know two things that hold true for every war: you can't win without spelling out exactly what the military is expected to achieve; and you can't win if the military command does not have a comprehensive plan for reaching those goals. Can you tell me what the military and political objectives in Vietnam are? What would you consider to be a victory? And how can your armed forces achieve it?"

The expression on Alsop's face was of the "I thought you'd never ask" variety. Had he been able, he would have destroyed America's enemies right there on the spot. "We must eliminate the fighting power of the Vietcong and North Vietnam!" he thundered. "There's no other way."

I told him that I had heard similar talk in 1960 from French officers fighting the FLN in Algeria. "If that's the way you see the concept of winning, you'll lose the war in Vietnam. There's no way of eliminating the fighting capacity and spirit of tens of millions of people who are dedicated to the sanctity of their cause."

I had angered Alsop. "Listen," he said with a tinge of warning in his voice, "I believe our generals when they say we're on the threshold of victory. It's only the defeatists in the United States who can deprive us of that."

He certainly was not referring to me, but he had aroused my curiosity. And since the link between the United States' quandary in Vietnam and American policies in other areas remained of profound concern to me, I undertook a more thorough study of the Vietnam War. I asked for briefings from the Pentagon, and Alsop introduced me to the director of the CIA, Pentagon generals, and other prominent journalists. Again and again, I got the impression that the United States had neither clearly defined objectives nor an overall plan for winning the war — and to me, that was incredible.

Then again, 1968 was a year filled with events that seemed incredible to an Israeli newly established in the United States. Together with a group of senators, administration officials, and prominent journalists, I was at the home of Elie Abel, a political correspondent for the ABC television network, on the unforgettable night of March 31, when President Johnson went on the air to announce that he had decided neither to seek nor to accept the Democratic nomination for president. The declaration was met with general consternation, and some people even exclaimed, "He's lying again!" — a striking illustration of Johnson's loss of credibility toward the end of his term. As events were to prove, however, the president was in deadly earnest. Moreover, when Johnson decided to step down, he left the Democratic party in disarray, with Hubert Humphrey, Eugene McCarthy, and Robert Kennedy being only the most prominent figures now in the race for the Democratic nomination. But darker days were yet to come.

The murder of the revered civil rights leader Martin Luther King on April 4 provoked a wave of racial unrest throughout the United States. As seen by a new and inexperienced ambassador, the situation looked depressingly grave. With its looted shops

going up in flames as rioters roamed the streets and large units of
soldiers and police posted around the White House, the nation's
capital seemed about to be swamped in a flood of hatred and in-
terracial strife. The upheaval spread across the country, from
New York to Detroit, Los Angeles, and other urban centers. It
was this unbridled surge of violence that made it possible for
Richard Daley, the mayor of Chicago and the last of America's big
political bosses, to order his police to "shoot to kill."

At one point, even Israel was inadvertently drawn into the turmoil in what was undoubtedly the most bizarre tragedy of the entire period. On June 4 I happened to be in New York when I
received a call from Senator Robert Kennedy's campaign staff asking if I would be good enough to receive the senator at my hotel
and have our picture taken together. I had never met Kennedy
and was certainly eager to do so. But I knew he was on a very
tight schedule (he was about to leave for Los Angeles) and preferred to postpone our meeting to a time when we would be able
to exchange more than just pleasantries. "I wouldn't want the
senator to go out of his way merely to have our picture taken," I
replied in my most diplomatic manner, "but when he returns to
Washington, I shall be pleased to come to the Senate for a more
leisurely talk." To my great regret, that meeting never took place
because the next day (the first anniversary of the Six Day War)
Kennedy was shot and killed by a young Palestinian named Sirhan Sirhan. If Sirhan had thought that by punishing the American
people he would generate a wave of indignation against Israel for
allegedly expelling the Palestinians from their homes, his plan
could not have been more ill conceived. The American people
were so dazed by what they perceived as the senseless act of a
madman that they could not begin to fathom its political significance. All Sirhan had accomplished was to deprive America of yet
another brilliant political figure and leave its citizens more confused and dejected than ever.

It was therefore with a sense of growing concern that I continued to meet with senators, congressmen, administration officials, and leading journalists. I had come to this great democracy — the leader of the free world — with the aim of

generating support for Israel's security and guaranteeing our own democratic regime against the dictatorships surrounding us. What I found was a country in the throes of disintegration.

With the United States engrossed in its domestic affairs and conflicts, the time was hardly ripe for dramatic political efforts to achieve peace in the Middle East. Thus circumstances allowed me to spend a good portion of my first year in Washington in getting to know the lay of the land — and especially the subtle intricacies of the American political system. Since 1968 was an election year, I had arrived just in time for a crash course in the subject. For example, even after Johnson had announced that he would not seek the Democratic nomination, some of his supporters would not abandon the cause. A number of American Jews who fell into that category tried to convince me that no other candidate could be better for Israel. Some stalwarts even suggested that if Israel displayed flexibility and consented to far-reaching concessions, Johnson would be credited with a first-rate achievement and might be prompted to seek reelection after all. But I could not take such suggestions seriously.

On August 7, 1968, I set out for Miami to observe the Republican National Convention, and for the next few days I gazed in amazement at this enormous carnival that would choose the party's candidate for president. There is nothing like it in the political culture of any other country in the world — a festival of pretty girls in multicolored costumes, hats, T-shirts, placards, and balloons all crowded into the conference hall while loudspeakers broadcast over the din. And this was the convention of "straight" America — middle-aged, neatly and tastefully dressed, devoted to "law and order," and pledged to uphold the traditional values of American life. When all was said and done, the delegates entrusted the fate of their country to Richard M. Nixon.

Twenty days after that stunning experience, I expected to relive it at the Democratic convention in Chicago. But I couldn't have been more wrong. Though the trimmings were the same, the Democratic convention was engulfed in tension. Faithful to his policy of "a hard hand," Mayor Daley was determined to smash the "liberals and leftists" who had come to Chicago to demonstrate against America's policy in Southeast Asia, and he loosed his police force on the protesters as they chanted back, "The whole world's watching." Inside the convention hall (ironically enough, a converted slaughterhouse), Senator Abraham Ribicoff made an emotional appeal to stop the violent police action and recess the convention until the bloodletting in the streets was halted. With my own ears, I heard Daley shout back: "Filthy Jew!" But since that did not silence the senator and his supporters, the mayor's henchmen employed a more direct tactic: those delegations "besmirching" Daley's good name had their microphones cut off, and their protests were swallowed by the din in the convention hall. I was torn between staying to follow the political drama unfolding in the hall and rushing to the scene of the confrontation near the Hilton Hotel (where I happened to be lodging for the duration of the convention). But when I weighed the possible consequences of getting caught in a police riot (and since even journalists were being beaten on the streets, I doubted that the Chicago police were bothering to check credentials before wielding their clubs), I decided to stay put. In the end, when the Democrats chose Hubert Humphrey as their candidate for president, the tumultuous events surrounding the convention did not give him much of a send-off on his uphill campaign.

In the course of 1968, I had a number of opportunities to talk with Hubert Humphrey, and I must admit that although I was impressed by his genuine warmth, I harbored doubts about his ability to extricate the United States from its domestic and foreign troubles. Of course, Humphrey was renowned for his friendship toward Israel. But he was also in the ticklish position of being vice-president of the United States as well as the Democratic candidate for president, and he could not readily adopt positions that ran counter to those of the incumbent president. In terms of Israel, this meant that he had to restrict his pronouncements on the most pressing issue of the day — our request for Phantom fighter planes. It is true that Israeli issues were not of crucial importance to the 1968 elections, yet they were a factor in the campaign.

I should explain that at the time it was customary to assume that the voting patterns of American Jews were influenced by a candidate's attitude toward Israel. The Democrats believed that the "Jewish vote" was in their pocket, following a tradition that went back at least as far as the New Deal. Far more disconcerting, however, was that the Republicans also believed that the majority of Jews were a permanent fixture in the Democratic camp. With little prospect of winning them over, there was hardly any point in courting them. I doubt that Nixon himself accepted this view, for when he addressed a closed meeting of the B'nai B'rith he left no doubt about his support for Israel and explicitly promised that, if elected, he would order delivery of fifty Phantoms. In an attempt to balance the score, Humphrey attended a conference of the Zionist Organization of America, but his address there was disappointing. He was very cautious in talking about the U.S. commitment to Israel and ignored the subject of the Phantoms altogether.

Nonetheless, Hubert Humphrey was no novice to American politics, and he was well aware that if he failed to induce the outgoing administration to sell us the fifty planes, his popularity with Israel's supporters — Jews and non-Jews alike — would be damaged. I knew for a fact that Humphrey and the heads of the Democratic party were exerting pressure on Johnson. A letter from seventy senators in support of the sale must also have had its effect, because on October 9 — just three weeks before America went to the polls — the president came around and announced his decision to sell us the planes.

My acquaintance with Richard Nixon went back to 1966, when we were introduced at a dinner given in his honor by the American *chargé d'affaires* in Tel Aviv. He had come to Israel after a visit to Vietnam, and I was naturally interested in hearing his assessments of the situation there. Oddly enough, however, I arrived at the dinner party to discover that as chief of staff I was the senior Israeli guest present. My surprise grew when I found out that ministers and senior government officials had also been invited to meet Nixon, but they evidently did not consider the invitation important enough to accept. When I asked Nixon about his plans for the future, he avoided giving a clear-cut answer. But even then I suspected that his political capital was far from exhausted. At any rate, I invited him to be the guest of the IDF on the following day, and I could see from his expression that he was gratified by the invitation. Needless to say, we gave him the "red-carpet treatment." To be fair, I should add that by the time Nixon returned for a second visit, soon after the Six Day War, the local skeptics had evidently come to appreciate his political potential, because this time the prime minister and other members of the cabinet stood in the doorways of their offices to extend him a warm welcome.

Without detracting from President Johnson's image as a friend of Israel, but for the sake of historical accuracy, I should elaborate on the circumstances. After the Six Day War, the United States suspended the delivery of arms to Israel, including spare parts and ammunition. The gravity of this act is illustrated by the fact that in addition to turning down new orders, the Americans delayed the shipment of orders that had already been approved and signed. The reason for violating these signed contracts was the vain hope that the Soviet Union would reciprocate by cutting down its arms shipments to the Arab states. But the Soviet Union understood things differently. Interpreting the suspension of American deliveries as an act of weakness, the Russians speeded up their arms deliveries to Egypt and Syria. Still, the Americans refused to supply us with so much as a screw, while we were in desperate need of spares to patch up our damaged American equipment.

In light of this situation, by the summer of 1968 it was vital to sound out Richard Nixon, who was likely to gain the Republican nomination for president. I asked to meet him in August, and he responded willingly. Nixon had not forgotten the welcome he received from the IDF at a time when his political stock was far from its peak, and he thanked me repeatedly, adding, "I won't forget it in future, either." While we were on the subject of pleasant memories, I couldn't resist the opportunity to "reminisce" about Nixon's famous statement after a tour of the Golan Heights that if he were an Israeli, he would never give the heights back.

Admittedly, I had come mainly to talk about the question of

military supplies to Israel, but Nixon steered the conversation to
wider topics: the general situation in the Middle East and the
policies of the United States and the Soviet Union. When I asked
him about delivery of the Phantoms, which Israel needed so
badly, it was easy for him to sympathize with my indignation over
the earlier suspension of arms deliveries, since it had been ordered by a Democratic president. But he was more forthcoming
than that. "If the people elect me as their president," he said, "I
promise you that I will advocate a strong Israel, and you will get
your planes."

The promises of presidential candidates should be treated with
a measure of reserve, yet I had the impression that Nixon's outlook on the subject of arms generally coincided with the Israeli
position. That impression was reinforced when he sketched his
views on America's position in the global balance of strength.
Nixon's approach to his country's foreign-policy problems was a
sober one, and he made no secret of his view that Israel had an
important role to play in the power balance between the United
States and the Soviet Union. He also readily confessed that there
was little difference between his views and those of Senator
Humphrey concerning national goals. "Both of us seek peace and
prosperity for the American people, and both of us recognize that
these goals cannot be achieved without reaching an understanding with the Soviet Union," he explained. "The difference
lies in our approach to realizing these goals. Humphrey will continue Johnson's policies and court the Russians. I believe it necessary to reach an understanding with the Soviets, and I am convinced that the only language they respect is the language of
force. You can't reach an agreement with them unless you do so
from a position of strength."

The resemblance between Nixon's ideas on rapprochement
with the Soviet Union and Israel's outlook on the future of the
Middle East was almost uncanny, as I was quick to point out. "We
too believe that it is vital to reach agreement with our adversaries
in the Middle East," I told him. "But negotiations can only begin
when Israel speaks from a position of strength and has concrete
backing."

Nixon is gifted with an unusual ability to listen and pose pointed questions. He was very careful not to undertake commitments unless he found himself in circumstances that required binding statements, and there was no need of that in our talk. But he did make it clear that we saw eye to eye on fundamental policy lines: "In principle, I agree that the correct view of American-Soviet relations also holds true for Israeli-Arab relations. One thing I can promise: You will find considerable understanding from me in everything connected with guaranteeing Israel's strength — including your request for the Phantoms."

It goes without saying that I avoided making any public pronouncement that could be interpreted as an expression of support for one candidate or the other. All the same, I cannot deny my conviction that the changes Nixon was likely to inaugurate in American foreign policy, as well as his overall view of global politics, made him the more desirable candidate from Israel's point of view. America's Jews did not share my opinion, however. Between 88 and 92 percent (the analysts differed on the precise figure) placed their faith in Hubert Humphrey, while only some 8 to 12 percent voted for Nixon. Since the president-elect had no reason to credit his victory to the "Jewish vote," I was concerned that his attitude toward Israel might change for the worse. But in the course of the years, I came to understand that his views on Israel were founded on more than political expediency. My fears proved to be groundless.

Admittedly, much of my first year as ambassador was spent in getting to know my way around and acquiring a grasp of local political mores. Yet I was far from idle on my own political front as Israel's representative to the American government. In order to make clear the nature of my work during that final year of the Johnson administration, it is necessary to fill in some background on the development of both American and Israeli policy before I arrived in Washington.

June 19, 1967, just a few days after the Six Day War, witnessed two major political events that complemented one another (though the fact that they occurred simultaneously was pure coincidence). In Washington, President Johnson formulated a cardinal principle of any Middle Eastern peace settlement by stipulating that "the parties to the conflict must be the parties to the peace. Sooner or later, it is they who must make a settlement in the area. It is hard to see how it is possible for nations to live together in peace if they cannot learn to reason together." He then laid down the five principles advocated by the United States as the basis for a peace settlement in the Middle East:

1. Recognition of the "right of every nation in the area . . . to live."

2. "Justice for the refugees."

3. "The right of innocent maritime passage."

4. Limitation of "the waste and the futility of the arms race."

5. "Respect for the political independence and territorial integrity of all states of the area."

From this point onward, Johnson's statement would be the primary guideline of U.S. policy in the Middle East.

That same day, the Israeli National Unity cabinet adopted a dramatic four-point resolution that was to be communicated solely to the government of the United States. It stated that in exchange for a peace treaty and the full range of interstate relations, Israel was prepared to withdraw to the international border with Egypt. In addition, the Sinai peninsula was to be demilitarized, and appropriate measures would be taken to guarantee Israel's security and freedom of navigation in the Straits of Tiran and the Suez Canal. On the same terms, Israel was prepared to withdraw to the international border with Syria, with the Golan Heights to be demilitarized and proper security arrangements made in the area. The future of the West Bank and the Gaza Strip would be considered separately, as would the problem of the Palestinian refugees.

On June 22, 1967, Foreign Minister Eban notified Secretary of State Dean Rusk of this decision. Strange as it may sound, however, the cabinet's policy was such a closely guarded secret that even I wasn't let in on it — neither as chief of staff nor as Israel's ambassador to Washington. It was only after I had taken up my new post in the United States that I learned of the decision from American sources. A few months later, when I made my first visit back to Israel in May 1968, Chief of Staff Chaim Barlev invited me to address his senior officers on the subject of Israeli-American relations. Assuming that the generals had in the meantime been informed of the cabinet's decision, I mentioned it in the course of my review. My audience was thunderstruck, and I immediately realized that they too had been kept in the dark about this fundamental policy decision. As a result, Barlev asked Defense Minister Dayan to explain the cabinet's position to the general staff. But then something even more incredible happened, for Dayan explained that after having conveyed its decision to the U.S. administration, the cabinet had changed its mind in August 1967 and decided to modify its position. To the best of my knowledge, in May 1968 the United States government still knew nothing of this change. This time the secret was being kept from the Americans!

Meanwhile, events were moving forward and the United Nations became involved in the quest for a peace settlement in the Middle East. On November 22, 1967, the Security Council passed its famous Resolution 242. I have no doubt that the United States based its interpretation of the resolution on the cabinet's decision of June 19, 1967. Although the Americans prevented the Security Council from adopting the wording "withdrawal from the territories" or "withdrawal from all the territories" (the final wording was "withdrawal from territories"), the administration understood the resolution to mean that Israel must withdraw to the international borders in the Sinai and the Golan. The only place where border changes would be open for consideration was the West Bank, in line with the policy that Israel had communicated to Rusk.

In all fairness, however, I must add that at this stage of developments, the question of final border was not even raised, because the primary disagreement centered on the interpretation of another key word in the resolution: "agreement." The Arab states, backed by the Soviet Union, claimed that Resolution 242 did not require the parties to the Middle Eastern dispute to enter into negotiations in order to settle their differences. In their reading of it, the resolution was to be applied as it stood, while a representative of the UN secretary-general would "establish and maintain contacts with the states concerned in order to promote agreement between them." Seen in this light, the UN merely had to set a timetable for the Israeli withdrawal and the arrangements arising from the settlement. Backed by the Americans, we insisted that the term "to promote agreement" required negotiations between the parties. Furthermore, the Arabs and the Russians saw no need for any such "agreement" to be expressed by the signing of a joint and binding document. Presumably, a nod of the head would do!

The bald truth of the matter is that all the dozens of meetings, conferences, and messages relayed between the powers on the interpretation of the word "agreement" were little more than a charade. Even before the Security Council adopted Resolution 242, the Arabs had dug in behind a barrier of self-imposed prohibitions that were spelled out early in September in the "three noes" of the Khartoum Conference: "No peace, no recognition of Israel, no negotiations with Israel." The conference also resolved to continue the Arab struggle for the rights of the Palestinian people, meaning the creation of a Palestinian state not merely alongside Israel — in the West Bank and the Gaza Strip — but on all the territory allocated to an Arab state in the 1947 partition resolution! Once the Arabs had come to an understanding among themselves, the only "agreement" necessary was Israel's consent to pack up and withdraw to the June 4, 1967, lines so that her neighbors could pick up their fight from the same positions they had held at the beginning of the last round.

This inter-Arab understanding was the basis on which Egypt and Jordan rejected UN Ambassador Gunnar Jarring's draft letter in March 1968. (The Syrians did not even accept Resolution 242 until after the Yom Kippur War in 1973.) Representing the UN secretary-general, Jarring wished to invite representatives of all sides to his headquarters in Cyprus. Yet if the UN resolution was self-applicatory, as the Arab states insisted, there was no need for talks. Israel merely had to withdraw from all the occupied territories. But Israel, for her part, kept insisting on various "strange" conditions, such as peace, negotiations between the sides, and the signing of a contractual agreement in which each side made commitments to the other. Such being the state of affairs, Jarring ran aground before he could even set sail.

Keeping in mind the delicate weave of relations between the United States and the Soviet Union — especially in view of America's entanglement in the Vietnam War — I had grounds for concern that the Russians would succeed in eroding the United States' position on the Middle East question. My first confrontation with this problem occurred shortly before the 1968 U.S. elections. On September 4, the Soviet ambassador to Washington, Anatoly Dobrynin, delivered a note from his government to Secretary of State Rusk (I learned of its contents a few days later). Its lopsided description of the causes of the Middle East conflict was in the best Soviet tradition. Yet the document also contained a set of proposals that demanded attention and a response. The gist of the Soviet program was that Israel and the Arab states would declare their acceptance of Resolution 242 and their readiness to implement it. Then, with the help of Ambassador Jarring or by other means (such as deliberations of the Security Council), a timetable would be drawn up for the Israeli withdrawal. Israel would announce her intention to begin vacating the occupied Arab territories on a fixed date, and the withdrawal would be supervised by the United Nations. The states that accepted Resolution 242 would deposit a declaration of cessation of hostilities with the United Nations and would undertake to recognize and respect the sovereignty and territorial integrity of every state in the region and its right to live in peace within secure and recognized borders. Once Israel had completed her withdrawal to the pre–Six Day War lines, the sides would sign a multilateral document binding them to respect all the sections of Resolution 242.

A few days after I learned of the contents of the Soviet note, Secretary of State Rusk invited me for a talk. "From this point on," he told me, "the Middle East conflict will take a prominent place in discussions between the United States and other governments. It is important for us to have more specific information. What does Israel think about the form of negotiations with her neighbors? Does she wish to work with all of them simultaneously or with each one separately? Is there any point in reaching a sepa-

rate agreement with one or two Arab states, or should the envisioned settlement be between Israel and all the Arab states
together?"

His questions deserved replies, and I was glad of the opportunity to present our position. After pointing out that the Soviet
proposals had been drawn up in coordination with Nasser (who
had recently visited Moscow), I urged Rusk to reject the Russian
plan. After all, it lacked the elements that both Israel and
America had agreed must be part of any political settlement In
the Middle East. It did not mention peace, and it did not include
any concrete expression of recognition for Israel or acceptance of
her existence. Over and over again, Rusk asked: "Isn't it enough
for Israel and the Arabs to sign a joint, multilateral document?"
Over and over again, with the persistence so vital in exchanges of
this nature, I explained that we wanted a bilateral, contractual
peace agreement with each and every neighboring Arab state.

The secretary of state had asked for a clear definition of Israel's
position, and that's exactly what he got. But realizing the immense gap between the Israeli position and that of the Arabs and
the Soviet Union, Rusk tried to sound me out on possible points
of compromise. For example, he wanted to know whether we
would consent to the stationing of troops by the Four Powers to
guarantee freedom of navigation in the Straits of Tiran. "Each of
the four," I told him, "has interests of its own, which rarely coincide. Therefore, freedom of navigation must also rest on a bilateral agreement between Egypt and Israel."

Rusk concluded our talk in a somewhat harsh tone. "Look," he
practically ordered, "I want Foreign Minister Eban to come here
with clear views on how to deal with the political situation in the
near future." Despite his gruff manner, however, on October 1,
when I learned the substance of the American reply to the Soviet
note, I was gratified by the results of our talk. The United States
rejected the Soviet view of the causes of the Middle East conflict,
as well as the allegation that America was helping Israel to retain
her conquests. The body of the reply also adhered consistently to
the policy spelled out in President Johnson's five principles for a
Middle Eastern settlement and declared that the conclusion of a

multilateral agreement was insufficient, for "peace must be based upon an agreement that is directly binding upon the sides" (a vague formulation referring to mutual undertakings). The United States further declared that "the cease-fire agreement between the sides must be replaced by a peaceful reality. Resolution 242 calls for withdrawal to secure and recognized borders, but it does not specify that these borders must be precisely the lines of June 4, 1967."

I had little time to rest on my laurels, for it soon came to my attention that upon meeting the Egyptian foreign minister at the autumn opening of the UN General Assembly, the secretary of state had given him an American document that came to be known as "Rusk's seven points." I could not overlook the implied slight to Israel. Even though Egypt and the United States did not maintain diplomatic relations, the Americans revealed the details of their plan to the Egyptians before consulting us or even bringing the existence of the plan to our attention. It was only after making inquiries that I was briefed on the seven points: (1) Israeli withdrawal from Egyptian territory; (2) formal termination of hostilities; (3) reopening of the Suez Canal to the ships of all nations; (4) a solution of the refugee problem based on giving each refugee the option to return to the home he had occupied before the establishment of the State of Israel; (5) an international presence at Sharm el-Sheikh that could not be removed without the approval of the Security Council or the UN General Assembly; (6) general agreement on the level of armament in the region; and (7) the signing of some as yet unspecified document by the UAR and Israel.

I protested vigorously against both the substance of the document and the manner in which it had been presented to the Egyptians. The Americans responded to my indignation with evasive tactics, but soon afterward Assistant Secretary of State Joseph Sisco informed me of the Egyptian reply to the seven-point plan. When I read the text, I was astounded. The Egyptians were reverting to the 1947 plan to partition Palestine. Having commenced in this fashion, they could proceed to pose as the champions of peace by "compromising" on this point and demanding that Israel withdraw "only" to the June 4, 1967, lines.

Meanwhile, the Soviets kept up their side of the combined offensive against the United States by bombarding the Americans with their own documents. Under the guise of moderation and goodwill, they were continually announcing further "concessions" on points that were of no value while adhering to their basic principles: complete withdrawal without a peace treaty or any bilateral agreement between Israel and each of her neighbors. I fought back, proving that the Soviets had no intention of bringing peace. Finally, on January 15, 1969, five days before the end of Johnson's term (and perhaps as an expression of the president's desire to be remembered as Israel's benefactor), Rusk handed the Russians a letter of great significance. It stated that "peace can only be achieved by a process of negotiation between the sides in the Middle East. . . . The parties must sign a contractual agreement that binds each side vis-à-vis the other." For the time being, at least, the United States had in essence adopted the Israeli position. Without precisely defining the character or components of the peace settlement, the Americans left no room for doubt that the cease-fire must be replaced by a state of peace.

The other issue that consumed a considerable portion of my time and attention was the well-publicized problem of the Phantoms. As I mentioned earlier, in something of a pre-election gambit, on October 9 President Johnson had announced the administration's decision to sell the fifty planes to Israel. Yet when Foreign Minister Eban arrived in the United States and met with Dean Rusk on October 22, it was clear that the Americans were in no hurry to fulfill that promise. Rusk referred me to the Defense Department, and I held a series of meetings with Assistant Defense Secretary Paul Vornike. Clearly, and contrary to its protestations of innocence, the administration was resorting to delaying tactics, for once again he asked me to specify in writing why Israel needed the Phantoms. So once again I submitted the relevant documents but protested, "The president has already approved the sale. Why are you asking for further reasons?"

At this point the assistant secretary laid his cards on the table while I sat there stupefied, feeling the blood rising to my face. As its condition for selling the Phantoms, the United States wanted Israel to sign an unprecedented document (never during my five-

year term in Washington would I encounter anything else like it).
We were asked to consent to a U.S. presence in and supervision of
every Israeli arms-manufacturing installation and every defense
institution engaged in research, development, or manufacture — including civilian research institutions such as the Weiz-
mann Institute of Science and Israel's universities. To say that I
was appalled would be a gross understatement; and even though I
promised to pass the paper on to Jerusalem for my government's
response, I told Vornike that any state that agreed to sign such a
shameful document would be forfeiting its very sovereignty!

Hardly recovered from my exasperation, I proceeded to drop
broad hints to Israel's Democratic supporters that upon assuming
office the president-elect was likely to have the Phantoms delivered forthwith — and thereby reap all the credit for the deal.
Presumably my "message" got through to the White House because three or four days before the inauguration, President Johnson put an end to the whole matter by ordering that the sale
be concluded without any further ifs or buts.

Sensitive souls may find the notion of setting a Democratic
president against his Republican successor distasteful. If so, they
will only be demonstrating their ignorance of the ways and means
of American politics. It is not enough to say that in pursuing his
country's welfare an ambassador to Washington is entitled to take
advantage of the ongoing rivalry between the two parties. The
fact is that for his efforts to bear fruit, he is obliged to do so; and
any ambassador who is either unwilling or unable to maneuver his
way through America's political landscape to advance his country's interests would do well to return home.

Be that as it may, before my first year in Washington had
ended, the Phantom deal was finally signed, the U.S. reply to the
Soviet note was favorable from Israel's viewpoint, and Egypt had
rejected "Rusk's seven points" — on the grounds that they were
too generous to Israel. In view of the new president's promises
and his belief that American policy vis-à-vis the Soviet Union
should be conducted from a position of strength — not to mention his similar view on Israel's position toward her Arab neighbors — I could look forward to 1969 with no small measure of optimism.

Chapter Eight

NEW PRESIDENT IN THE WHITE HOUSE

ON JANUARY 20, 1969, President Nixon took up residence in the White House and new men were placed in charge of formulating American policy. To say that we were curious about their attitude toward the Middle East situation would be putting it mildly, and it didn't take long before we were enlightened. In one of his earliest public statements, Nixon hastened to define the Middle East as a "powder keg" that was liable to explode and set off a worldwide conflagration. Experience had taught us that whenever there was talk of a "powder keg," everyone seemed to point to Israel as the only party that could defuse it, by appeasing her enemies. Curiously enough, no one ever seemed to consider placing the onus on the other side.

In point of fact, it was again President Nasser who lit the fuse, in April 1968, by proclaiming a three-stage war against Israel: reconstruction of the Egyptian army, active defense, and the liberation of Israel-held territories. On September 8 he tried his hand at a massive artillery barrage along the Suez Canal, and the fuse continued to burn through October. It took an IDF raid deep into Egyptian territory on October 31 to convince Nasser that his army was not yet up to realizing his plans, and the Suez front quieted down for a relatively long interval. But at the end of January 1969, the Egyptian president took advantage of the lull to visit Moscow and coordinate strategy with the Kremlin, particularly in view of the change of administration in Washington. After his return in February 1969, Nasser visited his troops in the Canal Zone and proclaimed a new phase in the war against Israel: constant military activity along the canal. With this declaration, he sowed the seeds of the war of attrition, which were to bring about decisive changes in the Middle East.

Meanwhile, there had been a dramatic political change in Israel as well. On February 22, 1969, Prime Minister Levi Eshkol died of a heart attack, and soon afterward Mrs. Golda Meir was chosen to head the government until the forthcoming elections. As a result of the new cast of characters involved in the American-Israeli dialogue, Foreign Minister Eban was planning a visit to the United States for meetings with President Nixon, Secretary of State William Rogers, Assistant Secretary Joseph Sisco, and Dr. Henry Kissinger, whom Nixon had appointed as an adviser on national security and foreign affairs.

It was in preparation for that visit that I held a talk with Dr. Kissinger on March 4, 1969. On my way to the White House, I couldn't help remembering a story that another political science expert, Zbigniew Brzezinski (who, coincidentally, was to fill Kissinger's position in the Carter administration), had told me the year before. Brzezinski had long been very suspicious of the Soviet Union's global intentions and had urged the adoption of a very strong policy in relation to the Russians. About a month before the Soviet invasion of Czechoslovakia, President Johnson had called in a number of international-relations experts (including Brzezinski) and asked for their views on Soviet intentions and a possible American response. The president seemed impressed with Zbig's comments at that meeting and asked him to submit a paper detailing his assessments and recommendations. "I, of course, did so immediately," Brzezinski related, "and expected him to summon me for a further talk. But a week passed, and another, and a third, and no invitation, no comment — nothing. Finally I approached a friend who was on the staff of the National Security Council and asked him what had become of my 'paper.' He smiled and told me that the president had passed it on to Averell Harriman — a moderate on the subject of U.S. policy toward the Soviet Union — and when Harriman had read it he was steaming. He rushed off to the president and chided him: 'How can you ask a *Pole* for his opinion of Russia? The Poles imbibe their hatred for the Russians with their mother's milk!' " Sparing no sarcasm, Brzezinski then added his own aside: "Imagine what would happen if an American Jew were asked for his views on the Middle East!"

Curiously enough, that (among many other things, of course) was precisely what President Nixon was asking of Dr. Kissinger and exactly what I was about to find out. One of the questions uppermost in my mind when I entered that meeting was the new administration's view on borders. I should add here that when Eban had met with Secretary of State Rusk five months before, he finally broke the news that the Israeli cabinet had modified its original decision on withdrawing to the former international borders with Egypt and Syria. (In other words, the "secret" that I had been so troubled by was finally out.) Of course, the cabinet's original June 19, 1967, decision had been taken in a mood of ebullience, and its generosity reflected the cabinet's certainty (or should I say fantasy) that at any moment the phone would ring and President Nasser would be on the line expressing his readiness to sit down and talk peace. The message to the Americans was therefore: "He's welcome to have it all back!" It seemed like a fair price to pay for the formal, full peace that Israel was expecting in return.

The phone never rang, of course. And by the time the Khartoum Conference had declared its three "noes" — categorically denying any prospect even of negotiating, not to mention achieving peace — Israel's magnanimity had been replaced by a sense of firm resolve. We were finished storming our way across Arab territory merely to pull back to the international border in return for nothing more than the promise of another round to come (which was pretty much what had happened in 1956–57). This time, Eban told Rusk, Israel wanted border changes, and the exact nature of those changes would be worked out in the course of negotiations with the Arabs and would depend on the overall results of that process. Now that Israel again held some cards in her hand — something to make her neighbors sit up and take notice of her demands — she was not about to squander them in return for nebulous arrangements about the future.

When I arrived for my meeting with Dr. Kissinger, his presentation of the U.S. view was straightforward and to the point: "The objective is peace — that's our position. Resolution 242 is one package; the demand for an Israeli withdrawal cannot be separated from the political quid pro quo required of the Arabs.

There is no substitute for a contractual agreement between the sides in the Middle East, and peace negotiations must lead to a specific, binding agreement. The United States' views on borders and the peace settlement differ from that of Israel" (a characteristic Kissingerian way of putting things). "*You* will have to live within those borders, so I don't want to advise you where they should run. But" (that "but" was the key word in Henry Kissinger's art of negotiation), "having considered the matter, I have some personal ideas on the subject, which are certainly not binding on anyone. If you want to hear my opinion" (interestingly enough, we never told him that we didn't), "I think you should take an interest in practical security aspects — concrete arrangements on the ground to safeguard your security. I find it hard to understand Israel's eagerness for verbal formulations and diplomatic documents. What is really important are security arrangements that create a different reality. After all, even if you have a peace treaty signed and sealed, war can still break out. That happens, you know. And to meet such an eventuality, you have to make security arrangements on the ground."

So much for Mr. Harriman's fears about the "ethnic" sentiments of American policymakers (not, of course, that I had expected otherwise). After completing that outline of American policy, Kissinger informed me of a new development in the efforts to get matters moving toward a peace settlement. "Jarring has been going around for a year and a quarter and has achieved nothing," he noted quite accurately. "He's bogged down and won't extricate himself by his own efforts. So the United States has decided to take part in consultations between the Four Powers to get his mission moving again. When Foreign Minister Eban comes here, it is important that he bring clearly formulated ideas on how to achieve a settlement in the Middle East."

Eban arrived soon after, and Secretary of State Rogers assured him that the United States did not desire an imposed settlement in the Middle East. The purpose of the discussions between the powers was solely to provide UN Ambassador Jarring's mission with new impetus and direction. There was no question that the Middle East conflict had to be resolved by the parties involved

and that the final agreement had to be based on both the cessation of hostilities and the creation of a formal state of peace. At
the same time, the secretary of state was careful to point out that
while the June 4, 1967, lines would not necessarily be the final
boundaries spelled out in a peace treaty, any modification would
have to be justified by vital security needs and be acceptable to
both sides. In asking for Israel's cooperation with Jarring, Rogers
also requested that we employ more practical terms in discussing
the nature of the peace agreement and final borders.

These American positions contained nothing of a particularly
disturbing nature, since they were basically similar to the policy
of the previous administration. What did concern us, however,
was the fact that in the ongoing talks between Joseph Sisco and
Soviet Ambassador Anatoly Dobrynin, the Americans were sparing
no effort to reach agreement with the Russians. Admittedly, Sisco
told Eban: "We don't see ourselves as merely your lawyers, and
we don't want the Soviets to be the Arabs' advocates." But the
Americans were alone in keeping their side of the bargain. At no
stage in the talks did the Russians adopt any position that had not
previously been agreed upon with the Egyptians, whereas basic
American positions were not coordinated in advance with us.
They essentially reflected American interests and concepts that
we were more or less expected to adopt.

The period between March and July 1969 was a difficult one for
us, since Sisco and Dobrynin held frequent talks and rather than
consult us on the position he would adopt at a forthcoming meeting, Sisco would at best brief us after the meeting was over. The
erosion in the United States' position reached such proportions
that our minister in Washington, Shlomo Argov, asked to cable
home a proposal that Israel denounce the current American
moves — even at the risk of sparking a confrontation with the
United States. I could well understand his concern, for as I explained in my reports to Jerusalem, the Americans were determined to reach agreement with the Soviet Union. They still toyed
with the slogan "no imposed settlement," but it was misleading.
We knew perfectly well that if an agreement were reached between the two powers, each would be obliged to "induce" its

"client" to accept it. Nonetheless, I did not believe that a public denunciation was the right approach to our problem. We were best off continuing to pressure through the conventional diplomatic channels.

During May and June of 1969, I also kept a close watch on the war of attrition being waged by the Egyptians along the Suez Canal, because it was clear to me that the military confrontation there was having a direct impact on the Soviet-American talks. The obvious aim of the war was to weaken and inflict damage on Israel. Yet the fact that the fighting was based on coordination between Egypt and the Soviet Union left me convinced that its more subtle and far-reaching aim was to undermine America's position and influence in the Arab world. The Russians were exploiting the fighting to wear down American resistance to their demands. After all, the stakes were high: the PLO was gaining ground in Jordan and posing a threat to King Hussein's rule: King Idris's regime in Libya was collapsing, and extremist elements were expected to take control of the country and its rich oil resources; and the atmosphere of threat even extended to the Saudi monarchy, with its firm ties to the United States. As I saw it, the implied Soviet threat was that the Arab world — and its oil resources — would slip out of Western hands and right into the Russians' lap. Thus even the most halfhearted support for some of Israel's demands would cost the United States a high price.

I believed then — and still believe now — that Israel was disappointing America's expectation (albeit never explicitly stated) that she would deliver a blow strong enough to squelch Egypt's desire to pursue its war of attrition. For as long as that war continued, the United States saw its status in the Middle East steadily losing ground; and the greater the erosion, the more the Americans were inclined to cut their losses in the region by means of reaching an understanding with the Soviet Union. My suspicions about this situation were pretty much confirmed during a luncheon talk I held with Sisco before he left for a visit to Moscow (which I read as a further indication of the erosion in the U.S. position). Sisco and I maintained regular contact on two levels: formal meetings, in which he briefed us on principal points; and informal conversations, usually over lunch. I respected our "quasi-personal" contacts, and because we were not in the habit of making a written record of these talks, we both spoke very frankly.

It was during one of these informal conversations that Sisco laid matters on the line. "Our interests in the Middle East do not center on Israel alone," he reminded me. "Our moral and practical commitment to Israel is by no means toward everything Israel wants or does. Let me tell you frankly: If our friendship with Israel is the only thing the United States is left with in the Middle East, that will be a catastrophic setback for American policy. We must work for a political solution because it's the only thing that will safeguard our own array of interests in the region."

I tried to explain that there was really no contradiction between the interests of our two countries. We also wanted peace in the Middle East, but peace did not mean vague declarations that the parties would agree to ignore one another. "The sides must reach a binding agreement in which they undertake mutual commitments. In order for it to last, peace must have substance: open frontiers, the movement of goods and people, diplomatic relations."

"That would be wonderful," Sisco chimed in, "and the United States would like nothing better. But since the Arabs reject such a possibility outright, the question remains: What is the minimum necessary to put an end to the conflict? We can't force the Egyptians to love you. As far as we're concerned, a solution that falls short of the peace you've described would be sufficient, considering the circumstances. We've got to be realistic!"

I presume it must have been realism of this kind that nurtured the United States' fourteen-point program, which stipulated the basic principles for a peace settlement between Israel and Egypt. Without detailing it point by point, the American plan envisaged representatives of Egypt and Israel meeting under the auspices of Ambassador Jarring to work out an agreement on the implementation of a "just and lasting peace" as prescribed in Resolution 242. After said agreement had been deposited with the United Nations, Israel would start withdrawing her troops from Egyptian territory occupied during the 1967 conflict. The pullback would be to the line agreed upon by the parties as the secure and recognized boundary between them (the boundary was to be marked out on a map that would constitute an integral part of the agreement).

So far, so good. But then a rather incongruous point crept in: Israel would agree that the former international border between Egypt and Palestine would not be excluded as the secure and recognized border between the two countries. For us, this section of the proposal was a clear setback because it constituted the first American attempt to determine in advance of negotiations what the "secure and recognized" borders would be.

I don't know what Sisco's expectations were when he carried this formulation to Moscow in July 1969, but the Russians weren't having any of the State Department's "would not be excluded" phraseology. Nor would they agree to the notion of a formal state of peace (rather than just the end to a state of war) as a prerequisite for an Israeli withdrawal. Sisco returned from his talks in Moscow convinced that he had gained two valuable concessions from the Soviets: they now understood the link between an Israeli withdrawal and the other side's political quid pro quo; and they grasped that the sides must accept mutual undertakings. But I think that what they *really* understood from the fourteen points was that the United States was retreating — slowly and in carefully worded language, but surely enough — and that signal only stimulated their appetite for further concessions.

Although they did not reach agreement on the latest American proposal, the two powers decided to continue working toward understanding, and I continued to be dogged by a crucial question. Did the Americans think that the United States was losing ground in the Middle East because its "client," Israel, was incapable of putting an end to the war of attrition? Were they intimating that Israel's failure to alter the situation in the Middle East was costing her America's support because the United States found itself forced to adopt conciliatory positions vis-à-vis the Soviet Union? Did they expect Israel's forces to take vigorous action to silence the Egyptian guns, thereby depriving the Soviets of a major advantage in the two-power talks?

At the time there was serious concern in Israel that vigorous military action against Egypt was liable to harm our prospects of acquiring additional arms from the United States. I knew of these anxieties firsthand, for in August 1969 I had returned to Israel for consultations prior to Mrs. Meir's scheduled visit to Washington. Inevitably, part of our talks were devoted to the armament needs of the IDF. Now that the first of the fifty Phantoms were beginning to arrive (note: eight months after Johnson had given his final okay), the overriding fear was that the United States would turn down further requests for arms if we stepped up our military operations against Egypt. I did my best to dispel these fears and argued that, on the contrary, we should request additional categories of arms — including tanks and artillery — precisely in order to press the Egyptians even harder.

When I returned to Washington, I was determined to pursue my instinct on this particular point, and after further talks with various administration officials I felt even more convinced that I was right. By September 19, 1969, a few days before Mrs. Meir was scheduled to arrive, I could write to Jerusalem in unambiguous terms:

There is a widespread feeling here that the Soviets are not willing to make concessions in order to reach agreement with the United States about the conflict in the Middle East. The National Security Council is considering the impact of Israeli military operations against Egypt, and the Americans are giving careful consideration to their possible effect on the stability of Nasser's regime. The following lines of thought are beginning to emerge: Continuation of Israeli military operations, including air attacks, is likely to lead to far-reaching results. Nasser's standing could be undermined, and that would in turn weaken the Soviet position in the region. Some sources have informed me that our military operations are the most encouraging breath of fresh air the American administration has enjoyed recently.

A man would have to be blind, deaf, and dumb not to sense how much the administration favors our military operations, and there is a growing likelihood that the United States would be interested in an escalation of our military activity with the aim of undermining

Nasser's standing. Some circles were considering the possibility of Israel destroying the Egyptian army in a large-scale offensive action; and certainly no one here is dismayed by such a prospect. Right now, such thoughts have not been expressed formally. But I have the impression that as circumstances evolve, it is a possibility that the U.S. will take into serious account. Thus the willingness to supply us with additional arms depends more on stepping up our military activity against Egypt than on reducing it.

Five days later, Golda Meir's plane landed at Philadelphia to an exuberant welcome from that city's Jewish community. In the course of her seven or so months in office, she had captured the hearts of millions of people around the world, but nowhere, I think, was her standing as high as in America, where the people looked upon Golda as one of their own. It is a marvelous experience for the ambassador of a small country to observe the marks of respect and affection so unstintingly displayed toward his prime minister by a great country like the United States.

I could well appreciate that affection since I had always been on excellent terms with Golda, and the differences in our ages and the dissimilarities between our generations had never created a barrier between us. She had been generous with her support in helping me secure the job of ambassador to Washington, and for this, too, I owed her a debt of gratitude. A month earlier, when I had visited Israel, Golda had even spoken to me about accepting a seat in the cabinet she hoped to constitute after the November elections, and I was honored and gratified by her offer (even though it later fell through because of internal difficulties in apportioning portfolios for the new cabinet). Golda's personality was a blend of earthiness, Jewish pride, common sense, and iron firmness. Frankly, I just couldn't wait to see her in action in Washington.

Naturally, there was a full schedule of ceremonies, lavish banquets, and cocktail parties. But I have never attached more than minor significance to such spectacular functions, which are merely the outward trappings of respect. Then, as now, the significant events of state visits are the closed political talks, and the importance of such discussions is usually in inverse proportion to the number of participants.

In all her talks in Washington, Golda reiterated our positions forthrightly: there could be no settlement without negotiations between the sides, and the final understanding must take the form of a binding peace agreement. Israel was willing to withdraw, but only to defensible borders and only after a peace agreement had been reached. Once, when Rogers asked whether Israel insisted on sovereignty over Sharm el-Sheikh or would be satisfied if the Egyptians consented to lease her the area for, say, ninety-nine years, Golda replied, "If the offer is serious, we'll consider it." No one so much as blinked an eye. What standing the prime minister of Israel had with the American administration!

The rapport that developed between Golda and the president was fascinating to observe. Nixon was known as a withdrawn, reserved man not given to displays of feeling — particularly of warmth. But he made no secret of his genuine affection for Golda. When she pointedly reminded him of his famous statement about the Golan Heights, I thought we might be headed for an awkward moment. American presidents (like Israeli prime ministers) would rather not be reminded of statements they made prior to assuming office. But having said it, he did not deny it. He simply wanted to keep the record straight. "I repeat, Madam Prime Minister, if I were an *Israeli*, I would find it truly difficult to give up the Golan Heights," he said, thereby making his point with the same brand of wit that Golda herself was so famous for.

Nixon made it a regular rule to avoid enunciating specific commitments. He preferred to confine himself to general lines of policy and leave it to his administration to translate his blanket statements into practical details. (This mode of operation would sometimes cause us no end of frustration, as I shall soon describe.) Yet in a paradoxical way, the president always expressed himself with great precision, and one had to listen very carefully so as to avoid overstating his case in the retelling.

Yes, he still held to his basic view in favor of a strong Israel. The United States and Israel could disagree about exactly what that meant, but as long as he was president of the United States and made the decisions, Israel would never be weak militarily. Beyond this general statement of principle, however, he made no explicit commitment about military supplies to Israel.

The prime minister's visit to the United States in 1969 had one outcome that was far from welcome to Foreign Minister Eban and became a prime factor in disrupting his relationship with me. Nixon believed that national leaders should maintain direct and regular contacts without going through their respective foreign ministries. In his talk with Golda, it was proposed that the two of them set up a line for direct communication, and at a further meeting between them the exact channel was marked out: Kissinger, acting on behalf of the president, would approach me, and I would transmit his messages directly to Golda's personal assistant, Simcha Dinitz, in Jerusalem. The prime minister would do the same in reverse. At the president's request, Golda approved the suggestion. If this proposal expressed a distressing lack of confidence in Eban and Rogers, I certainly was not to blame for it (though inevitably I was the one who felt the brunt of my foreign minister's resentment). Be that as it may, this now became the principal mode of contact between the two countries on the most important issues.

It was also during Mrs. Meir's visit that another idea emerged, though this time it was mentioned while Israeli and American officials sat together outside the Oval Office waiting to join their respective leaders. Rather suddenly, Rogers asked me, "You were at the Rhodes armistice talks in 1949, weren't you? How were negotiations conducted there?" I told him that three methods were used: joint meetings between the parties, presided over by Dr. Bunche or his assistant, General Riley; private meetings between the members of delegations; and, since we were all staying at the same hotel, Bunche would sometimes go from one delegation to another, listening to what they had to say and reporting on what the others had said. All these methods were interwoven and applied alternately.

Then Rogers told me that he had met Egyptian Foreign Minister Mahmoud Riad at the UN General Assembly and asked him the same question. Riad had been a member of the Egyptian military delegation at Rhodes, "but his description differed from yours," Rogers added.

"Ask your archives for the UN reports describing the negotiations at Rhodes," I suggested. "You'll see that my description is accurate."

Rogers was obviously seeking a way to bring the sides together under the auspices of Ambassador Jarring. "Riad talked to me about the Rhodes technique," he offered, "and said it could be acceptable." We had no cause to object to the Rhodes model for negotiations. But since Riad's description differed from mine, I wasn't sure exactly what the Egyptians had in mind. At any rate, Rogers was not forthcoming on that subject, so the matter was dropped — for the present.

On October 4, 1969, after an exhausting tour of the United States marked by media appearances and emotional encounters with Jewish communities, Golda was about to return home when an unforeseen development spoiled her mood. She was approached by Moshe Bitan (head of our Foreign Ministry's North American Division) and told that an American friend had mentioned talk in administration circles about a formula she and Nixon were said to have agreed upon. It was phrased in terms of giving the United States "software" in exchange for which Israel would receive "hardware" — in other words, Israel would agree in writing to the United States' political outlook on the Middle East in return for arms and military equipment. Golda was furious. Summoning me, she asked to speak to Kissinger on the phone and ordered me to listen in and take notes of the conversation. There had been too many private talks — with Nixon and with Kissinger — and sometimes the drawbacks of a private talk outweigh its advantages, for without an accurate transcript neither side can call on any objective document to verify its version of the conversation. Many misunderstandings in international relations stem from conflicting interpretations of statements made at such private meetings.

I listened in as Golda addressed Kissinger in no uncertain terms: "I've been hearing all kinds of things about 'software for hardware.' What is all this? Was any such term mentioned in my presence? And what's all this about a paper that Israel is supposed to provide? Who ever talked to me about such a thing?"

Kissinger was embarrassed — an unusual occurrence that few can claim to have witnessed. His voice actually faltered as he confessed to Golda: "It was not agreed with you, Madam Prime Minister, nor was it discussed with you or mentioned in your presence. . . . The fact is" (once again he hesitated, uncertain about whether or not to say what was in his mind), "there was mention of some kind of deal — you know, hard and soft — in a closed forum here, at the highest level, and there's no way I can understand how it leaked out. . . . I just don't understand. . . . But this was not mentioned to you as United States policy, so there obviously cannot be any agreement with you on the matter."

Kissinger was upset about the leak, but we were concerned (to put it mildly) about its substance. Even though it had not been discussed with Golda, was this now going to be United States' policy? Would the Nixon administration make fulfillment of Israeli arms requests conditional upon Israel's acceptance of its policy? Prior to Golda's departure for Israel, our concern grew even stronger when a friend of Israel with links to the White House warned us: "You are in for a very hard time. The administration has decided to give in on a total Israeli withdrawal, at least in the Sinai."

It didn't take long for that forecast, at least, to materialize. In mid-October, Eban relayed back to me Sisco's notification that the United States intended to modify one of the principal points in the "paper" Sisco had submitted to Moscow that summer. It was the same section that had so disturbed me earlier. But instead of suggesting that Israel would not "exclude" the international boundary as a secure and recognized border between Egypt and Israel, the United States was now prepared to concede to the Soviets that the international boundary would be the final line, negotiations notwithstanding.

Since Sisco was in New York, Under Secretary of State Elliot Richardson was good enough to try to dispel my anxieties by telling me that the government had yet to decide on a move of this nature and was only considering a possibility of this sort. "But I'm not in a position to promise that we won't adopt such a decision," he warned. My first reaction was that Sisco was again engaged in a typical American exercise for testing reactions. An Israeli representative was notified of a "firm decision" when in fact it was still just an idea. If the Israeli reaction was moderate, the Americans interpreted it as a go-ahead to adopt the idea and include it in their guidelines for talks between the powers.

Obviously, a strong reaction was called for on this issue. But I knew that it was not enough to turn up at the State Department armed with vigorous protests (though I did that, too). The key to the erosion in American policy still lay in the United States' declining status in the Middle East, which in turn was directly linked to our handling of the war of attrition. In a cable to Jerusalem on October 25, I therefore proposed that we alter the course of the war, and I stressed that our objectives could not be attained by limiting our counterbombardments to the area of the Suez Canal. We had to undertake deep-penetration raids and strike at military targets in the Egyptian heartland. That was the only way to induce the Egyptians to halt the war. Moreover, delivering a sharp blow to Nasser would help to shore up America's status in the region and thus prevent America from having to back down in talks with the Soviet Union.

In Israel I was regarded as being "on the brink" of losing my mind. I had never been a "hawk," and yet here I was calling for attacks on targets deep inside Egypt. But my proposals had nothing at all to do with "hawkishness." I saw where the war of attrition was leading American policy, and I was horrified. Obviously, however, I wasn't getting through to the cabinet, for I received no meaningful reply from Jerusalem.

That being the case, I was hardly surprised to discover that on October 29 the United States had notified the Soviet Union and the Arab states of a proposal that came to be known as the "Rogers Plan." In a nutshell, it unequivocally established that the international frontier between Egypt and Israel was the secure and recognized border between the two countries (no more "would not exclude" language here) and proposed that a "formal state of peace" would be agreed upon between the parties (without specifying the relationships between the two states that would follow therefrom). To solve such questions as the future of the Gaza Strip, security arrangements at Sharm el-Sheikh, and demilitarized zones, Egypt and Israel would hold "Rhodes-type" negotiations (though the document did not indicate whether that meant the Israeli or the Egyptian interpretation of the term or, indeed, what the Egyptian interpretation was). Three options were open for the Gaza Strip: UN administration, a form of self-rule, or a link with Jordan (the latter could be settled in negotiations between Israel and Jordan).

Mrs. Meir was right in describing this plan as "a disaster for Israel" and in saying that "any Israeli government that would adopt and implement such a plan would be betraying its country." On November 17, I transmitted the prime minister's reaction to President Nixon by means of Dr. Kissinger and took the opportunity to explain to Kissinger that if the United States had already determined what the "secure and recognized" border between Egypt and Israel was, there was no point in Israel's taking part in "Rhodes-type" or any other type of negotiations. We did not suppose that the State Department had adopted this position without the president's approval, and I was therefore asking Kissinger to notify the president of Mrs. Meir's vigorous objection to this latest step.

I also asked Kissinger to find out what was happening about arms supplies. Following Mrs. Meir's talks on the subject with the president, we were again put off by senior officials at the State Department and the Pentagon. The United States never openly admitted that there was any connection between supplying our defense requirements and Israel's compliance with American political views. The Americans used words like "study," "consideration," or other synonyms that equaled evasion. But having got wind of the newest euphemism ("hardware for software"), we had grounds for concern and wanted to know where we stood.

I made the rounds of the White House and the State Department trying to open up the field of maneuver between them and hoping against hope that we could effect a change in this latest

trend before it was too late. But on December 9 Rogers delivered
his thunderbolt by disclosing a considerable part of the plan in an
address before the Adult Education Conference. The only option
left to Israel after Rogers's speech was to protest, and she did so
in an official cabinet announcement dated December 10, and
again on December 16, when Foreign Minister Eban took the
matter up with Rogers in person.

The atmosphere of their talk was far from cordial, for the Americans insisted that the United States had not changed its policy; it
was Israel that had done so by backing down from her decision of
June 19, 1967, to restore the whole of the Sinai to Egypt. "Israel
can't expect to decide on changes and have the United States conform to her policy," Sisco chided us — though I must add that
the State Department generally expected Israel to go along
meekly with revisions in its position. Whether or not the United
States had changed its policy was a moot point. And, of course,
we had already explained to the Americans, dozens of times, that
the June 1967 decision had been modified in response to Arab intransigence! Now we dredged up every conceivable argument to
prove that Rogers's proposal was not the way to establish true
peace. It did not define the nature of peaceful relationships, and
it made no mention of open frontiers, diplomatic relations, or the
free movement of people and goods. But Sisco stuck to his guns:
"That peace is not attainable now!"

In that same discussion, Rogers also mentioned that although
the administration had yet to decide whether or not to deal with
the question of Jordan at the present time, it was probable that
"we shall do something about it, along the guidelines laid down
with regard to Egypt."

Eban informed him that we were holding contacts with Jordan
and preferred to continue them without U.S. interference. "We
are talking with the Jordanians about territorial changes, principally in the Jordan Valley," he told Rogers, "and although our
proposals have not yet proved acceptable to Jordan, if the United
States publicizes its view that Israel must withdraw from all the
territories — including those on the Jordanian border — that will
put an end to the contacts."

The following day Eban again girded his loins for a talk with Dr. Kissinger. I took note of the fact that Kissinger adopted cautious terms and was careful to avoid committing himself to any position. He promised to notify the president of Eban's views and stressed that although the U.S. position might differ from that of Israel on various points, the goodwill displayed by the president in his recent talks with Prime Minister Meir still existed. "The United States honestly and earnestly desires to strengthen Israel's security," Kissinger offered, "and the president again promises to give sympathetic consideration to your arms requests." Kissinger also said that the president was profoundly impressed by Eban's letter to Secretary of State Rogers asking that the United States keep the Jordanian issue off the agenda of the Four Power talks so that Israel could continue to explore the possibility of reaching an agreement with Jordan by means of direct contacts.

The president may indeed have been impressed by Eban's letter, but erosion has a momentum of its own that is not easy to halt. One day after Eban's talk with Kissinger, Elliot Richardson invited me to a meeting and presented me with a *fait accompli*. Without consulting us, the United States had that very day submitted a detailed document on the Israeli-Jordanian conflict to the Four Power forum. I was genuinely appalled. This latest document largely resembled the American proposal for solving the conflict between Israel and Egypt. It called for Israel and Jordan to be summoned for talks under the auspices of Ambassador Jarring, and stipulated that the boundary between the two states would more or less coincide with the 1949 armistice line (border changes would be feasible only if agreed upon by both sides). In addition, the sides would discuss the future of Jerusalem on the assumption that the city would remain united under one municipality but that Jordan would hold the eastern half of the city. There was not even a hint of apology in Richardson's tone, and like his colleagues he adopted the line that the United States could not be held responsible if Israel changed her policy.

I was, of course, obliged to point out his error. "Never, in any of its decisions, has the Israeli government consented to withdraw from the West Bank. The cabinet's decision on June 19, 1967, referred only to the Sinai and the Golan Heights — and even there, withdrawal to the international frontiers was made conditional upon security arrangements that would satisfy Israel. But over and above the substance of the matter," I fumed at him, "how am I to explain to my government the fact that two days before you presented this document to the Four Power talks, our foreign minister spoke with the secretary of state and was not even informed of its contents? One day before you submitted this document, Kissinger told Eban that the president was impressed by our objections to making a detailed proposal on the Jordanian issue at this time. In view of the relationship between Israel and the United States, I cannot comprehend it, and I am unable to explain it to my government!"

Somewhat skirting the point, Richardson replied: "Following the talks with Foreign Minister Eban, the document was modified somewhat — that is, compared to what we previously intended to submit." But I spent hours comparing the Americans' "Egyptian document" and "Jordanian document" and couldn't find a single one of Richardson's so-called modifications.

Deeply disturbed, I cabled Jerusalem proposing that we not enter into detailed discussions of the two documents with the United States. Instead, we should restrict ourselves to a brief message from the prime minister to the president expressing her astonishment at recent American moves and stating that she regarded them as a departure from what the president told her during their talks. It should also be made clear that Israel rejected both documents. At the same time, I proposed that an extensive information campaign be launched in the United States. Our reaction must be public, sharp, and unequivocal.

Sooner than I expected, the answer came back from Jerusalem: "Come to Israel immediately." I left on December 20 and within a week was back in Washington with approval to launch a public campaign against the Rogers Plan. I also brought back a personal letter from Mrs. Meir to President Nixon and therefore asked for an urgent meeting with Dr. Kissinger. I told him that Mrs. Meir still continued to believe that President Nixon was Israel's friend. But she did not understand how this friendship could be reconciled with the recent American steps culminating in the two documents on the Egyptian and Jordanian questions.

"What has changed with regard to the definition of peace since the prime minister's visit?" Kissinger asked me with complete equanimity. "In our talks with the prime minister, did we refer to a kind of peace that differs from what is expressed in the two documents?"

Once again I explained, for what seemed like the umpteenth time: "What is the value of our demand for true peace in exchange for territory if you suggest that we give up all the occupied territories without it? Why should the Arabs consent to give us more than you recommend? Even the 1949 armistice agreements contain more binding formulations about each state's obligation to prevent its territory from being used for operations against the citizens of the neighboring state!"

Up to this point, Kissinger's assistant Harold Saunders had attended our meeting, but I now asked to speak to Kissinger alone. I believed the time had come to put matters clearly on the line. "Let me tell you in complete frankness, you are making a bad mistake," I warned. "In taking discussion of a peace settlement out of the hands of the parties and transferring it to the powers, you are fostering an imposed solution that Israel will resist with all her might. I personally shall do everything within the bounds of American law to arouse public opinion against the administration's moves!"

At least I had penetrated through Kissinger's *sangfroid.* "I don't know how matters will develop," he began cautiously. "What's done is done, and the documents are binding upon the administration. But under no circumstances, I beg you, under no circumstances should you attack the president! It would mean a confrontation with the United States, and that's the last thing Israel can afford. The president has not spoken about the documents yet. He has given Rogers a free hand; but as long as he himself is not publicly committed, you have a chance of taking action. How you act is your affair. What you say to Rogers, or against him, is for you to decide. But I advise you again: Don't attack the president!"

As I was about to depart, immersed in sorting out all the possible implications of that message, Kissinger sprang an incredible move on me. Here we were on the brink of a major political battle with the United States when he suddenly announced: "The president would like to shake hands with you. Shall we go in and see him for a few minutes?" It is almost unheard of for an ambassador to see the president without prior notice or without even requesting a meeting! Crossing the street to the Executive Office Building, we reached the room where Nixon was in the habit of closeting himself whenever he wanted the peace and quiet needed to pull his thoughts together. When we entered, Defense Secretary Melvin Laird was with the president, and the two men were on their feet in the midst of a conversation.

The president welcomed me by wishing me a Happy New Year and without any further preamble said, "I understand this is a difficult time for us all. I believe that the Israeli government is perfectly entitled to express its feelings and views, and I regard that with complete understanding." Then, turning to Kissinger, he asked, "Where do matters stand on Israel's requests for arms and equipment?"

"We are in the midst of examining Israel's needs," Kissinger replied in the usual evasive formula.

"I promised that we would not only provide for Israel's defense needs, but her economic needs as well," the president added, clearly for my benefit.

"The examination covers both spheres," Kissinger confirmed.

Nixon now turned to me again. "I can well understand your concern. I know the difficulties you face in your campaign against terrorist operations, and I am particularly aware of your defense needs. In all matters connected with arms supplies, don't hesitate to approach Laird or Kissinger. Actually, it would be better if you approached Kissinger."

This strange encounter lasted no more than seven or eight minutes, and the president was in a genial mood. When we took leave of one another, I could only guess at the purpose of it all. Was Kissinger trying to prove to me — and by way of me, to the Israeli government — that the president's attitude toward Israel

differed from that of the State Department? Was he inviting me
to drive a wedge between these two branches of the administration, or merely trying to ensure that we keep our fire far from the
White House?

That same day, I learned that Israel was not the only country to
reject the Rogers Plan. Paradoxically enough, the Russians had
done so too, but hardly for the same reasons. They remained en-
trenched in the position that there was no need to convene the
parties for negotiations, making "Rhodes-type" talks out of the
question. Furthermore, a "formal state of peace" would be feasible only after Israel had withdrawn from all the occupied territories. Yet the fact that the Russians had torpedoed Rogers's proposals was of little comfort to me. Their reply clearly indicated
that, having gained major concessions from the United States,
they were out to get more of the same.

Alarmed that additional concessions would soon be forthcoming
and still unable to convince Jerusalem to step up our military actions against Egypt, I threw myself into our public campaign
against the Rogers Plan. Even though the Christmas season is not
the best of times for full-scale activity, I buttonholed senators,
congressmen, and representatives of the media and addressed a
meeting of three thousand Jewish leaders from all over the
United States. On January 5 I had even worked up enough momentum to subject Rogers and Sisco to a forty-minute monologue
on the damage they had wrought on Israel's ability to negotiate
with her neighbors.

Rogers may have felt resentful toward his own president, who
had left him to defend a policy unfavorable to Israel while refraining from giving him any public backing. But it was to me that he
complained about being made into a "scapegoat" and depicted as
"anti-Israeli," as though this were a personal confrontation and
he had private motives for working against Israel when he was
merely implementing American policy. I assured him that there
was nothing at all personal about it. We were only fulfilling our
obligation to defend ourselves against a policy that endangered
our security and the chances of achieving peace. In my subsequent report to Jerusalem, however, I noted that "Rogers is

frustrated over the failure of American efforts to reach an understanding with the Soviet Union" and that that was liable to make his reactions toward us even stronger. I recommended that we continue our public campaign within the United States and, yet again, that we simultaneously escalate our military pressure on Egypt.

This time I got through. Two days after my talk with Rogers, on January 7, 1970, Israel turned the tables in the war of attrition by launching the first air strikes deep inside Egyptian territory. That date was a turning point, and from then on the American administration was gradually to shake free of the depressing feeling that it was backing the loser in the Middle East and consequently losing its own standing in the region. When Sisco invited me to lunch on January 13, he was not in a position to concede that Israel's air operations were equally welcome to the United States. There was no need for him to say it; he knew that I knew. The talks with the Russians had broken down; the United States was not proposing that they be renewed; and the American public's sympathy for Israel was growing stronger every day. I now observed a similar trend within the administration itself, especially on the part of Attorney General John Mitchell, a key man in the cabinet and one of President Nixon's confidants. In his State of the Union address, the president did not even mention the Middle East, and the Rogers Plan, if not dead, was in its death throes. Most important of all, against the background of our deep-penetration raids, the American administration was soon to adopt a new tone in its give-and-take with the Soviet Union.

Chapter Nine

ANATOMY OF A CEASE-FIRE

BY THE END of January, some three weeks after we had begun our deep-penetration raids, President Nasser was sufficiently bruised to make a secret visit to Moscow. According to the intelligence we had on the visit, Nasser asked his Soviet allies for help in strengthening Egypt's antiaircraft defenses (he may even have asked for direct Soviet intervention to defend Egypt's airspace). The Russians, who had no problem reading the handwriting on the wall, were no less concerned about the effect of Nasser's deteriorating position on their own stance in the two-power dialogue. So in a double-edged move designed to rescue Egypt from its predicament and reinforce the Soviet Union's own self-confident posture, on January 31 Premier Aleksei Kosygin addressed a strongly worded note to President Nixon demanding that the United States put a stop to the Israeli bombing raids. The Soviet premier placed responsibility for the fighting along the canal and the raids inside Egypt squarely upon the shoulders of Israel *and* the United States. He also indicated that if Israel kept up the deep-penetration raids, the Soviet Union might provide Egypt with more up-to-date weapons.

Joseph Sisco, who informed me of the Soviet note on February 2, also told me that the president had already worded his reply. He described it as "a vigorous and uncompromising answer" that rejected the Soviet version of events and placed responsibility for the military situation on Nasser, who had broken the cease-fire in the first place by proclaiming his war of attrition. The only way to resolve the situation was to reconstitute the cease-fire. As to the Soviet "threat" to supply Egypt with up-to-date missile systems, the administration had tacked on a kind of "cautionary note" to

Foreign Minister Andrei Gromyko. It declared that the United States was prepared to seek an understanding on a mutual cease-fire and hold talks with the Soviet Union on limiting the arms race in the Middle East. But if the Soviet Union sparked an escalation by supplying ultramodern weapons to the Arab countries, the Americans would be forced to reconsider their arms policy toward Israel.

This was a tone quite unlike the one I had been hearing from the Americans, and it was clear to me that the reversal in America's posture vis-à-vis the Soviets was due to our heightened military action. Sisco did not say so outright, but there was no mistaking his tone. As a result, I could cable Jerusalem: "We have achieved a marked improvement in the United States' position. Continuation of that improvement depends first and foremost on keeping up our air raids in the heart of Egypt."

The raids continued, and there was no approach from the Americans to halt them. In fact, the administration was clearly taking advantage of them to press the Russians toward agreeing to a cease-fire as well as softening their attitude toward America's political proposals. At the same time, the president had another weapon to wield: he had not yet approved Israel's request for another twenty-four Phantoms (over and above the fifty already approved) and twenty-four Skyhawk planes. Nixon was to reach his decision on the sale of these planes within thirty days, and he was signaling the Russians that his answer would be influenced by their attitude toward a cease-fire and peace talks.

Considering that those planes were a pawn in the interpower chess match, I cannot claim that the situation was totally to our liking. But then my generally upbeat mood soured altogether when Joe Alsop whispered in my ear that he had "bad tidings," as he put it: the president's decision on the planes at the end of the thirty-day period would be negative. "It's been a long time since I was as concerned over Israel's future as I am today," Alsop warned.

Alarmed and somewhat bewildered, I instructed Shlomo Argov to contact Kissinger's aide, General Alexander Haig, and make it clear that we had got wind of the president's intention not to approve our request. In my contacts with Haig, I had been deeply impressed by his military and political grasp, as well as his fairness. He and Kissinger made an excellent team, with Haig providing the element of stability during moments of severe tension. At their meeting, Haig would not be explicit, but he did counsel Argov: "Don't press. The president will make his decision public at the proper time, and it would be better for you if that decision were postponed."

Admittedly, that message was cryptic, but the hint about "the proper time" led me to understand that the extra delay was bound up with waiting for the Russian reply to the president's note. In the meantime, the administration did not want to make any overt move that could be interpreted as an American escalation of the war on the Suez front. My foreign minister, however, had his own ideas on the subject and cabled them to me via a channel that bypassed the Foreign Ministry (paradoxically enough, Eban himself used this "second channel" on occasion, even though he continued to complain about its existence). He was not prepared to buy any of the "fabrications" about the reason for the United States' failure to respond to our arms request. Instead, he referred to an article by Peter Gross, the *New York Times* correspondent in Israel, explaining the holdup as an expression of U.S. opposition to our deep-penetration raids. I cabled back that since the raids began there had not been a single American statement — or even unofficial hint — that the Americans were displeased with them. And at the risk of belaboring the obvious, I pointed out that Mr. Gross was the *Times* correspondent in Israel, so that his interpretation evidently came from sources in Jerusalem, not Washington!

Since I had yet to be officially informed of the administration's intentions, I decided to move out into the field and at least signal how unhappy we were about what we *had* heard. I spoke with House Minority Leader Gerald Ford, Senators Barry Goldwater and Henry Jackson, and veteran labor leader George Meany, and each pledged his full support for Israel's needs. I even approached the Reverend Billy Graham, who was known to enjoy the president's respect and admiration and whose unreserved support for Israel never failed to move me.

At the very least, these talks had the effect of getting me an urgent summons to the White House on March 12, 1970, for a confidential meeting with Dr. Kissinger. Strict precautions were taken to keep the meeting secret, and I was admitted through one of the White House's lesser-known side entrances. (In the course of scores of meetings with Kissinger, I must have become acquainted with every possible way of getting into the White House with the exception of sliding down the roof! I never failed to be impressed by the variety.)

Since we both knew what was on my mind, Kissinger got straight down to business. The president's decision on our arms requests would include three parts. The first, which would be made public, was that the United States had decided not to decide — in other words, to put its decision about supplying the planes into abeyance. But it would continue to monitor military developments in the Middle East, and should any change in the situation require a decision on arms supplies, appropriate steps would be taken. The second element was practical: the United States wanted to change the ground rules governing the supply of arms. Instead of a public statement by the president (or administration officials) heralding acceptance, rejection, or postponement of Israel's requests, the United States would undertake to maintain the arms balance in the Middle East by replacing Israel's weaponry on the basis of its attrition rate. The third element was that the president would send a personal letter to the prime minister stressing his commitment to Israel's security and assuring the supply of arms required to maintain the balance of forces between Israel and her neighbors.

Before I could even comment on Kissinger's statement, he added that the Russians had approached him, through Ambassador Dobrynin, proposing an undeclared cease-fire between Israel and Egypt. The terms would require Israel to halt all her air activity to the west of the Suez Canal (meaning not only her deep-penetration raids, but any use of her planes against Egyptian artillery on the canal bank itself) as long as the Egyptians refrained from air activity over Israeli-held territory (which was at any rate nonexistent). Moreover, for a limited period of time, Israel would refrain from responding to Egyptian artillery fire.

These terms were clearly preposterous, for the Russians were demanding that we stop fighting while the Egyptians be allowed to pursue their war unopposed! As to Kissinger's explanation on the supply of arms, it wasn't a flat no — as I had been led to fear — but then again it was the most nebulous yes I could have imagined. And most important, it was not a public yes. If those planes — and the raids they would carry out — were meant to spur the Russians and Egyptians to a meaningful cease-fire, to remove the issue from the public view would be to defeat our joint purpose — and I told Kissinger so in no uncertain terms. But that was not the worst problem.

"You are making an even graver mistake," I warned. "The Russians have promised Egypt up-to-date antiaircraft missiles. What they need is time to get those weapons in place and operational. You come along and tell us, 'Give them that time.' They've made no commitment to maintain any cease-fire, and the minute their missiles are operational, they'll be able to resume the war of attrition."

Kissinger tried to defend the president's position on the planes, telling me that he was under heavy pressure from the State and Defense Departments. But he made no effort to persuade me of the merits of the cease-fire proposal. All he asked was that I personally take it to Israel for consideration. As might have been expected, the reaction in Jerusalem was indignant, and I relayed that response to Kissinger upon my return. He responded by handing me the draft of a letter that the president intended to send to Mrs. Meir. It reiterated that the United States would provide Israel with arms on a replacement basis and continuously monitor the arms balance in the Middle East. If that balance changed, action would be taken to restore it. In addition, the American government would maintain its efforts to reach a political settlement. Finally, the president asked Israel to consent to a sixty-day cease-fire, subject to Egypt's restricting its operations and displaying restraint. No explanation was proffered regarding the terms "restrict" and "restraint."

Immediately after our talk, I transmitted the substance of the letter to Jerusalem. But before my next meeting with Kissinger on the following day, March 18, a cable came from Jerusalem informing me that the Russians had sent a considerable number of personnel to Egypt for the purpose of manning the SAM-3 missile batteries defending Cairo. Kissinger did not say so, but I knew that this information was likewise known to American intelligence. I therefore asked him to have the section referring to the cease-fire deleted from the president's letter to Mrs. Meir. He promised to pass on the request to the president and said that in the evening he would accompany me to see the president personally.

Only Kissinger and I attended that evening meeting with the president. Nixon was cordial and very understanding, referring to Israel as "courageous, daring, and struggling valiantly."

"Let there be no doubt about the United States' commitment to Israel or our responsibility to provide her with the arms needed for her defense," he pronounced. "However" (this and similar terms, such as "but," "all the same," "at the same time," and so forth, did not necessarily contradict the more supportive statement preceding them; they merely prefaced the practical application of such support, which was sometimes rather less pleasing to the ear). "However," said the president, "the basic procedure we have adopted until now is no good. Whenever you request arms — particularly planes — all the media sound off about it and everyone waits for the administration's decision. That's a superfluous and harmful dramatization of the matter. Some sections of the administration are strenuously opposed to supplying arms to Israel at this time. I won't identify them, but believe me, they have spared no effort in trying to convince me. You can be sure that I will continue to supply arms to Israel, but I shall do so in other, different, ways. The moment Israel needs arms, approach me, by way of Kissinger, and I'll find a way of overcoming bureaucracy."

In the absence of any other explanation, I suppose it must have been my state of tension that made me launch into an emotion-charged speech about the perils of a small nation fighting for her life — which is not at all like me. Swept along by my own rhetoric, it took me a while to get down to the point: "Whenever the

U.S. is believed to be reducing her support for Israel, the Arabs revive their old hope of overcoming us by force. And the longer the war of attrition goes on, the more the Soviets will flaunt their insolence. They will interpret the United States' decision on arms as a sign of weakness. And if the Russians can station SAM-3s and man them with their own technicians while America continues to deprive Israel of arms, they will take it to mean they can go even further! Once again, Mr. President, I appeal to you as the only man in whose sympathy and understanding we have trust: Give us the arms we need!"

I was a bit startled at myself — and all the more at the total silence that ensued. Evidently my emotion had been infectious. The pause went on for a minute or so — to me it seemed like an eternity — as the president sat mute with his eyes averted. Finally he said, "Thank you for putting it that way, Mr. Ambassador. I understand you, and I understand Israel's situation. You can be sure that you'll get your arms. I only want to go about it in a different way." He paused again, and when he continued speaking I thought I could detect a strange glint in his eye. "Do you have any more information about the SAM-3s? How do you feel about those missiles being manned by the Russians? Have you considered attacking them?"

Totally flabbergasted, I blurted out: "Attack the Russians?" Strange, I thought to myself, how complex are the motives of a great power. Was the president suggesting that for fear that we would attack the Russian missiles, with all the attendant risks, the United States would avoid strengthening Israel? Or was it conceivable that he meant precisely the opposite? Could it be that the president of the United States was intimating his interest in our attacking the missiles and their Russian crews? And if he knew that Israel intended to do so, would he provide us with all the planes we had requested — and perhaps even more?

The president did not reply further to my outburst, and, frankly, I didn't want him to elaborate on the subject. If he had said, "Yes, go ahead and attack," it was doubtful that Israel would have been able or willing to. If he said, "No, do not attack them under any circumstances!" and developments later made it imperative for Israel to destroy the missiles, she would run the risk of defying the president of the United States and disrupting relations with her strongest ally.

We reverted to talking about the system for supplying arms. Once again the president said, "We will replace any of your planes put out of action."

"That is a long and intricate process," I objected. "We'll report how many have been put out of action, and your people will start bargaining with us. I know the technique."

Kissinger now broke in with a proposal that left me wondering whether he was jesting or meant to be taken seriously. "Why don't we reach prior agreement on the numbers going out of action?"

The president, at least, didn't see any humor in it. "No, not fixed numbers," he mused out loud, and then turned to me. "But it's possible that you'll receive more planes by this method than you did before."

I reported to Israel that we had scored a Pyrrhic victory. The conversation did not refer to the cease-fire, and reference to it had been deleted from the president's letter to the prime minister. On the other hand, I did not believe we had any chance of getting additional planes now even if we changed our minds and agreed to a cease-fire. "If we want planes, we'll have to conform to the new rules of the game."

The reply from Jerusalem was unambiguous: "Israel will not agree to a cease-fire on such terms. Notify Kissinger." When I did so, I had various indications that our negative reply did not cause disappointment in the White House; it was even received with a measure of gratification. After all, the idea of an undeclared cease-fire had been of Soviet origin.

Nonetheless, at the end of March we were forced to call off our deep-penetration raids because of the SAM-3 batteries installed around Egypt's major cities. Once that happened, I had the awful feeling that we were sliding backward again. Those raids had not only changed the balance of power along the fighting front, they had tipped the scales in the superpower confrontation, and now we were regressing to a situation in which the Russians alone would be dictating the moves. On April 7 General Yariv, still head of our military intelligence, came to Washington to address administration officials on the balance of military strength in the Middle East. When he asked what to report back concerning Israel's arms requests, Sisco suggested: "Say that differences have narrowed, that your position has been received with sympathy, and that the United States will not permit the balance to tilt to Israel's disadvantage."

I could no longer restrain my anger. We had, for lack of choice, consented to the new method of supplying arms. "But what are the practical results of that method?" I growled at Sisco. "So far, we haven't received as much as a tail-wing over and above previous commitments!"

Meanwhile, Soviet military intervention in Egypt continued to expand, and in April Russian pilots assumed an active role in defending Egyptian airspace. Mrs. Meir sent the president a personal message expressing her profound concern that despite the growing Soviet involvement in the war of attrition, the United States would not accede to our requests for additional arms. On instructions from Israel, I also submitted a list of urgent items: Phantoms, Skyhawks, additional batteries of Hawk ground-to-air missiles, air-to-air missiles, thousands of bombs, a considerable number of tanks, and radar equipment. But the Americans were embroiled in Cambodia and Vietnam, and it was not convenient for them to admit that there was direct Soviet military involvement in the Middle East, since that would require a firm response. It was therefore better for them to befog the issue in order to gain time.

That policy left us in a pretty bleak position. But there was worse to come. If the momentum of Soviet military intervention continued, and the Russians moved their missile system forward into the Canal Zone itself, there was no way to counter this missile "umbrella." An American friend in the administration put it to me in a painful manner: "If the SAM-2 and SAM-3 missile systems are moved forward toward the canal, we don't possess equipment capable of destroying them. It's no longer a matter of political considerations regarding what to give you and what not. In the war between planes and missiles, the missiles will gain the upper hand. Right now, we just don't possess the military means of dealing with them."

In the light of such talk, I was in a somber mood when I attended Foreign Minister Eban's meeting with the president in May. Considering the drastic change in the situation since I had last spoken with Nixon, he wanted to clarify where we stood. "In view of the Soviet involvement, is Israel's position still — as I once heard Ambassador Rabin say — 'Give us the tools and we'll do the job'?"

"Yes!" I hastened to reply. Eban flung me a reproachful glance, and he was right: it would have been more appropriate for the foreign minister to reply to the president's question. But when an ambassador is anxious about what his foreign minister is likely to say, he is well advised to get his answer in first.

"Good!" Nixon said. "That was all I wanted to know." But instead of elaborating on what he had in mind, the president shifted the conversation to our now-abandoned deep-penetration raids. As Nixon spoke, Eban fidgeted uneasily in his seat (had he not been bound by the rules of diplomatic courtesy, he would probably have interrupted). "If it were just a question of you and the Egyptians and the Syrians, I'd say, 'Let 'em have it! Let 'em have it! Hit 'em as hard as you can!' Every time I hear of you penetrating into their territory and hitting them hard, I get a feeling of satisfaction. I agree with you that the Soviets and the Egyptians are putting us both to the test. But it's not just a problem of Egypt and Syria. The other Arab states in the Middle East are watching us also. I don't have the slightest doubt about that. We don't have any choice. We have to play it so that we don't lose everything in the Middle East." The president turned to Sisco. "You think you can do it, Joe?"

"So-so," Sisco said rather enigmatically.

"We want to help you," Nixon insisted, "and you have to help us without harming yourselves or us. Damn the oil! We can get it from other sources. We have to stand beside the decent nations in the Middle East. We will back you militarily, but the military escalation can't be allowed to go on endlessly. We must do something politically."

That was one of the most openly pro-Israeli statements ever uttered by an American president, and Eban and I were both deeply moved. The president did not elaborate on what he meant by doing "something politically," but I took it as a signal that something was brewing. Sisco later told me that on June 2 Rogers had read out to Ambassador Dobrynin extracts from Israeli newspapers quoting Defense Minister Dayan's statement about a thirty-kilometer-wide (twenty-mile-wide) zone to the west of the canal in which Israel would oppose the entry of Soviet missiles. In doing so, he warned the Russian ambassador that if Soviet-manned missiles advanced beyond that thirty-kilometer zone, the administration would regard the move as an offensive step against the United States that would force it to reconsider its entire position. That was strong language indeed. But the administration no longer believed that warnings alone could prevent a further deterioration of the situation in the Middle East. The only hope of halting the Soviet Union's growing intervention was to advance a political proposal that the Russians would accept.

This must have been the thinking that lay behind the "Rogers initiative" of June 19, 1970, whose professed aim was to "stop shooting and start talking." It was a "package deal" of both military and political elements and proposed a formal cease-fire in place for at least ninety days linked to the resumption of Jarring's mission. The heart of the Rogers initiative lay in the proposed text of a one-page letter from Jarring notifying the UN secretary-general that Israel, Jordan, and Egypt had consented to fulfill the commitments included therein. The letter read as follows:

The UAR[, Jordan] and Israel advise me that they agree:
(a) that having accepted and indicated their willingness to carry out Resolution 242 in all its parts, they will designate representatives to discussions to be held under my auspices, according to such procedure and at such places and times as I may recommend, taking into account as appropriate each side's preference as to method of procedure and previous experience between the parties.
(b) that the purpose of the aforementioned discussions is to reach agreement on the establishment of a just and lasting peace between them based on (1) mutual acknowledgement by the UAR[, Jordan] and Israel of each other's sovereignty, territorial integrity and polit-

ical independence, and (2) Israeli withdrawal from territories occupied in the 1967 conflict, both in accordance with Resolution 242. (c) that, to facilitate my task of promoting agreement as set forth in Resolution 242, the parties will strictly observe, effective July 1 at least until October 1, the ceasefire resolutions of the Security Council.

The U.S. ambassador to Israel, Walworth Barbour, informed Mrs. Meir of the new move and asked her not to reject it before a response came from Egypt and Jordan. A few hours later, I was called to Rogers's office and presented with an identical request. I was also gently notified that U.S. arms supplies depended on our positive response to the new initiative. Of course, I objected to the linkage between arms supplies and our agreeing to American political proposals — as I had done so many times before — but my words made little impression.

Since the Americans were so emphatic about their request that we hold back our reply (Rogers assumed that Egypt would torpedo the initiative), I recommended to Jerusalem that we comply and — despite the shortcomings of the text — restrict ourselves to asking for clarifications from the United States. When Barbour delivered the text of the initiative to Mrs. Meir, her reaction was unequivocal: "I shall bring the proposal to the cabinet for consideration, but my view is entirely negative, and I'm sure the cabinet will agree with me." In response, on June 21 the president sent a personal message to Mrs. Meir again stressing how important it was that Israel not be the first to turn down the initiative. The message called for a response, and I proposed that the prime minister express her disappointment about the linkage between Israel's reply and American arms sales but avoid any statement that would signify rejection of the initiative.

Three days later, when I received the draft of Mrs. Meir's reply to the president, I froze in horror. The prime minister intended to reject the initiative finally and unambiguously! I sent back an urgent cable pleading against such a response and asking to be summoned home immediately to explain my viewpoint. Upon arrival, I held a long talk with Golda and a number of cabinet ministers and advised that we rest content with what the prime minister had told Barbour orally. Golda insisted that she must answer the president's note in writing but finally took my advice about the substance of the reply, toning it down and deleting her rejection of the Rogers initiative — though no one could have construed her message to mean that Israel had accepted it.

Upon my return to Washington on the evening of June 30, I found that all our concerns had been shunted aside by a dramatic development on the military front. During the previous night, the Soviet-Egyptian missile system had been moved toward a new line about thirty kilometers west of the canal and a number of Egyptian-manned missile batteries had been stationed even closer to the canal (though no Russian-manned batteries crossed that line). Furthermore, our attack on the missile system had been unsuccessful and several Phantoms had been shot down in the process. This was a new and far more perilous situation. The next day the president responded sharply by defining the latest Soviet move as an offensive action and sending the Russians a strongly worded warning that the Middle East was a "very dangerous region, like the Balkans before World War I. The two Great Powers would have to be very careful in their action to prevent a confrontation which neither wants."

Israel was now in a terrible double bind. On the one hand, the political text of the Rogers initiative was not acceptable to her (though she had yet to state so publicly). At the same time, however, if the Egyptians rejected the cease-fire proposal, our planes were helpless against the missile system that had crept forward toward the canal. Three weeks went by while both sides remained mute on the subject of the Rogers initiative. Then, on July 22, Sisco notified me that Egypt had defied all expectations and had accepted it. I later learned that they had worded their answer very cleverly, accepting the initiative but simultaneously reiterating their well-known interpretation of Resolution 242.

Anxious about Israel's likely reaction to the Egyptian reply, the president planned to send Mrs. Meir a personal letter asking her to consent to the initiative in order to prevent further bloodshed. Sisco conferred with me on the wording, and when the final draft was sent on July 24, some Israelis considered it a latter-day Balfour Declaration. The president wrote, among other things: "Our position on withdrawal is that the final borders must be agreed upon by the parties by means of negotiations under the auspices of Ambassador Jarring. Moreover, we will not press Israel to accept a solution to the refugee problem that will alter fundamentally the Jewish character of the State of Israel or jeopardize your security. We shall adhere strictly and firmly to the fundamental principle that there must be a peace agreement in which each of the parties undertakes reciprocal obligations to the other." Then he added a sentence of the most far-reaching significance that was long to serve as the foundation for the Israeli position: "No Israeli soldier should be withdrawn from the present lines until a binding contractual peace agreement satisfactory to you has been achieved."

In view of the highly favorable contents of the president's letter, I cabled Jerusalem advising that Israel must under no circumstances reject the American initiative. On July 31, the cabinet indeed adopted a positive decision (which, incidentally, led to the dissolution of the National Unity government, since Mr. Begin and the rest of the ministers from his Gahal party walked out), though the exact wording of its acceptance had yet to be communicated to Washington. And that is when — and why — everything began to go topsy-turvy. The distance between Jerusalem and Washington is less than six thousand miles, and with the refinements of modern communications, messages can be flashed from one capital to another within minutes. But during the period between July 31 and August 10, 1970, those two capitals might as well have been light-years apart for all the "communication" that was going on. Everything was in confusion. Violent accusations were flung about on both sides of the ocean. The relationship between Israel and the United States was in total disarray. And although I, who was right in the middle, can describe it, I'm not at all sure that I can explain it.

In New York, Ambassador Jarring — an inflexible, unimaginative, and imperturbable man — was waiting for official notification from Jerusalem that Israel had accepted the initiative, so that he could resume his mission. When the Americans urged him to deliver his letter to the secretary-general and get things going, he insisted that he had yet to receive Israel's reply (and in retrospect, I must concede that he may have been the only one who had a proper grasp of the situation). At any rate, the Americans were quick to reassure him that Israel had indeed agreed to the initiative (which they understood to be synonymous with the text of the Jarring letter) and that he should go ahead immediately.

Meanwhile, in Israel, Prime Minister Meir was holding talks with Ambassador Barbour over the exact wording of that same letter, trying to rephrase it to coincide with Israel's approach to the resumption of negotiations. As far as Israel was concerned, the "initiative" ("stop shooting and start talking") was in no way synonymous with the Jarring letter itself, and now I can see that here is where the heart of the misunderstanding lay. At the time, however, everyone was at sixes and sevens; no one knew exactly what Israel had accepted and what she had not, which moves she favored and which she resisted, and on what terms the cease-fire would come into effect.

Matters might have been slightly easier if tempers were not already at the flash point and diplomatic conventions did not get in the way. Mrs. Meir asked to talk to Sisco on the phone, but when I transmitted her request to him, he made it clear that he was not empowered to initiate the call. If Golda would do the dialing, everything would be fine! When I explained the problem to Golda, she decided to take the initiative. But that wasn't the end of the problem, for Sisco asked me to come over to his office and listen in on his extension. That was no simple matter for a man in my position, since I could not very well eavesdrop on a conversation of this kind without the prime minister's knowledge. So at one point in their exchange I broke in and told Golda that Sisco had asked me to listen in. There was a pause on the other end of the line, and I knew it could not possibly bode well. At any rate, right after that Golda said that the United States had practically forged Israel's signature. No more and no less. Sisco was astounded: "What do you mean 'forged'?"

"You notified Jarring that we had accepted the initiative before we accepted it!" the prime minister barked. "That's what I mean by 'forged.' I reached an agreement with Barbour, and the United

States now denies that agreement. You can't formulate answers on our behalf. We have our reservations about the text of Jarring's letter."

It was a dialogue of the deaf, which I can only describe as a tragic conversation. Sisco was astonished by Golda's complaint: "You received the text of our initiative weeks ago. One page, one paper — that's the whole initiative. Did you accept it or didn't you?"

Golda could not understand his exasperation. "What do you mean did we accept the initiative? Do we have to accept your formulation? We have a formulation of our own!"

Sisco did not understand what the Israeli formulation was. Golda did not understand why Sisco was getting tough. When I phoned Golda after that abortive conversation, she said: "Talk with Kissinger and get him to talk to the president. I can't go back to the cabinet with a formulation unlike the one it adopted."

"Didn't the cabinet accept it according to the text of the Rogers initiative?" I asked her. Clearly, Golda and I were also talking at cross-purposes.

"We have our position on the political issue and it has to be made clear," she said almost syllable by syllable. "We accept the initiative, but we want to put it in our own words!"

Not really more enlightened on the subject, I nonetheless contacted Kissinger and arranged to see him at the White House late that evening. When we met, he gave free rein to his biting tongue, and I swallowed it all as befits an ambassador whose government is in disarray.

"What do you want?" he asked. "When did you get that sheet of paper called the Rogers initiative?"

"Six weeks ago," I mumbled.

"And six weeks aren't enough for the government of Israel to study and digest the contents of a single sheet of paper? How long does the government of Israel need? I don't understand you people. The paper's been with you for six weeks! If you have any comments, complaints, demands — go ahead, talk! Speak! The Egyptians have accepted our initiative. Have you or haven't you? Let us know clearly!"

"On the basis of the president's letter to the prime minister," I attempted, "we agreed to the initiative but not to the wording you submitted to Jarring."

By this point, Kissinger too was exasperated, and I was equally in the dark as to which portion of the text Israel agreed to and which she opposed. We were at one of the low points in Israeli-U.S. relations. I phoned Golda back and unfortunately I no longer understood what she was so angry about. "Dictate precisely what you want me to tell Kissinger," I begged her. "Word for word. I'll tell him exactly what you say." But she dictated nothing and said nothing.

A phone call from Golda. One from Allon. Another from Eban. Yet another from Yosef Tekoa at the United Nations. And one from Chief of Staff Barlev. Thousands of words, many of them enraged. Golda scolded me furiously, but the entanglement remained unresolved.

Meanwhile, despite the uproar over the political aspect of the initiative, the cease-fire went into effect at midnight on August 7. The people of Israel heaved a collective sigh of relief, and were it not for the terrible tangle I would have shared their joy on August 8, when I arrived in Israel for consultations. But the cabinet's treatment of the cease-fire issue was likewise not what it could or should have been (to put it mildly).

In order to monitor the compliance with the cease-fire, the Americans stressed that they would have to take aerial photographs from U-2 planes before the cessation of hostilities went into effect — otherwise there would be no basis for comparison if either side later complained of violations. But inexplicably, the IDF military attaché in Washington received an order from a senior personage in Israel's defense establishment to notify the Americans that Israel *objected* to aerial photographs being taken just before the cease-fire went into effect! This bizarre cable contained an even more incomprehensible hint: if American planes attempted to take photographs of the battle zone, Israel would intercept them (although everyone knew our air force had no way of intercepting the high-altitude U-2s). Before long, the absence of such photographs was to prove a great obstacle to us in convincing the Americans of the Egyptian cease-fire violations.

In any event, we hadn't reached that bridge yet on August 9, when the Israeli cabinet was still up in arms about the Americans misrepresenting our government's position. Since my own telephone conversations with the prime minister had shown that she was dissatisfied with my opinions on this matter, I was very cautious in expressing myself at this meeting. I tried to make it clear that Israel's answers to the Americans were vague, causing them to wonder whether Israel had accepted the Rogers initiative or not. As far as they were concerned, the initiative was the text of Jarring's letter. And if Israel had accepted the initiative, why was she opposed to the resumption of the Jarring mission on the basis of that letter?

There was much talk and little clarity at that cabinet meeting. I sensed that under present circumstances — after the resignation of the Gahal ministers — Moshe Dayan undoubtedly had a veto right on political issues, and there was no chance of clarifying matters without reaching an understanding with him. So I asked to see Dayan and we met at his office on the evening of August 9. With his customary pragmatism, Dayan analyzed the situation as follows: "Golda can't retreat from the text of her statement in the Knesset on August 4. The Americans can't retreat from the text of the Rogers initiative. Meanwhile, the cease-fire is in force. So the only way out is for the Americans to advise Jarring to shelve the text that Egypt and Jordan agreed to and renew his mission on the basis of Resolution 242. To avoid placing obstacles in his path, Israel will not criticize the Jarring letter publicly." Dayan asked me if there was a chance that the Americans would go along with this. I was 99 percent sure that the matter could be settled with Sisco within ten minutes or less, but I would have to go to Washington to do it. We cleared Dayan's formula with Golda — and to be on the safe side held a joint meeting with her the next morning — and I was out on the first plane to New York on August 10.

Before I could even get to Sisco, however, a phone call from Dayan caught up with me in Washington. "The Egyptians are moving their missiles forward into the standstill zone," he informed me. In other words, the cease-fire had barely begun and it had already been violated! "First things first," I cautioned myself, determined to straighten out the political mess with the

Americans before jumping into the next fray. Sisco readily accepted Dayan's proposal for getting over the "forgery incident," and within a short time he notified me that Jarring was not being fussy about formulations; our proposal was fine with him too. But the military complication wasn't solved anywhere near as easily.

Even though the administration initially refused to admit it officially, the Egyptians had clearly violated the cease-fire by moving surface-to-air missiles into the thirty-kilometer standstill zone. Still, the Americans went about their investigation in a leisurely fashion — taking photographs, developing them, and delaying their conclusions. Even though they insisted that the United States had no sure way of attacking the missiles successfully, I persisted in asking for delivery of their "antimissile package," consisting of airborne electronic systems for disrupting the detection-and-guidance radars of the missile system; Shrike air-to-ground missiles that home in on the radars of the SAM missiles; and cluster bombs for destroying the missile sites. In essence, we wanted two things of the Americans: a public declaration that the Egyptians had violated the cease-fire, and delivery of equipment and weaponry that would enable us to counter those missiles.

I also asked Kissinger to arrange for a meeting between Mrs. Meir and the president for an overall discussion of the post-cease-fire situation, but he put me off by claiming that the time was "not ripe" for such a meeting. A few days later, when I pressed him again, he proposed that I meet with the president. I felt uneasy about the idea, for I could not be regarded as a proxy for the prime minister and I had grounds to assume that such a substitution would thoroughly irritate Golda. But my attempts at persuasion had failed, and we were forced to make do with the less desirable alternative.

On August 17, the president and General Haig received me in the "Map Room" of the White House, which was a particularly suitable setting since I had brought along a pile of maps to illustrate the Egyptian violations of the standstill. It was a businesslike meeting. I began by reviewing the steps leading up to Mrs. Meir's acceptance of the Rogers initiative — in deference to the president's request, against her own better judgment, and at the cost of a cabinet crisis in Israel. And the outcome? In the very first hours of the cease-fire, the Egyptians had moved their missiles forward under cover of the American-initiated agreement. "Now we are expected to enter into negotiations under the auspices of Ambassador Jarring," I said. "But how can we think of negotiations when the Egyptians brazenly violate the present agreement and the United States will not stand by us? Who will guarantee that the Egyptians will stick to their part of any future bargain?"

The president expressed his characteristic understanding and reminded me that, like the prime minister, he too faced domestic political pressures. The American public was in a "peace mood," as he put it, and above all he felt obliged to encourage the start of negotiations to reach a political settlement. I tried to explain again that as long as there was an imbalance between the Soviet Union's unquestioning and uncompromising political support for Egypt — now reinforced by direct and growing military involvement — and the lack of parallel U.S. support for Israel, the prospects for peace were dim. But while I talked about one matter, Nixon pressed on with another. "Israel must not permit herself to be blamed for refusing to negotiate. I will be pleased to meet Mrs. Meir, but not now. Let's see what develops during the next thirty to sixty days."

I left for Israel the next day and once again found the cabinet in turmoil. Everyone agreed that the Egyptian violations were intolerable, but opinions differed as to how to respond to them. A few ministers were in favor of attacking some of the missile sites within the thirty-kilometer zone, even though such a move would be a violation of the cease-fire. I was vigorously against the idea because, when all was said and done, I did not believe we had the effective means to destroy the missiles. We would therefore violate the cease-fire — and be denounced by the whole world for doing so — for no practical gain. I also explained that the president would not consider the cease-fire violations as justification for Israel's refusal to take part in the negotiating process. We could postpone appointing our representatives to the talks while urging the United States to take diplomatic action to remove the missiles; but we could not refuse to take part in the Jarring talks.

After I returned to Washington, the president consented to

meet with Golda on September 18, and it was in preparation for that consultation that Kissinger and I sat down for a talk. He wanted to know what the prime minister hoped to gain from the meeting, and I explained that she wanted Israel to be compensated for the Egyptian cease-fire violations by means of extensive arms deliveries.

"What about the political question?" Kissinger asked.

"As far as we're concerned, the Rogers Plan is nonexistent," I pronounced. "Jarring can convene the parties under his auspices, but we must be given a free hand to negotiate, without preconditions."

"If you come with that kind of talk," Kissinger warned, "you'll hear fine words from the president but nothing concrete. You have to bring the president something more *specific*."

It cannot be said that Kissinger was always right, but he was this time. Golda came and the president pronounced his fine words about the United States' commitment to Israel's security, promising that he would not allow the arms balance to tilt against Israel (though, of course, it already had). It seems that the Egyptian violation was a dead issue, as far as the United States was concerned, and the president's interest had switched to events in Jordan.

Ever since the guns fell silent along the Suez Canal, a grave crisis had been brewing in Jordan. The Palestinian terrorist organizations based there were at the peak of their strength and conducted themselves like a state within a state. As control progressively slipped out of his hands, King Hussein realized that the hour of decision was drawing near, and in September he launched a life-or-death battle against the terrorists. It was a cruel conflict, with the army using tanks and artillery against Palestinian refugee camps. Official casualty figures have never been published, but they are estimated to run into the thousands. With the terrorists on the defensive during what they called their "Black September," Syria saw an opportunity to send armored units across the border — ostensibly to aid the terrorists, but actually to gain effective control of Jordan. The Jordanian army deployed for defense, but it was pathetically inferior to the Syrians in armor and air power.

By that time, Golda Meir had completed her visit to Washington and on her last evening in the United States was scheduled to address a large United Jewish Appeal dinner at the New York Hilton. It was there, at eight in the evening, that I was asked to call Henry Kissinger immediately at his Washington office. When the call was put through, he spoke with a ring of urgency in his voice: "King Hussein has approached us, describing the situation of his forces, and asked us to transmit his request that your air force attack the Syrians in northern Jordan. I need an immediate reply."

"I'm surprised to hear the United States passing on messages of this kind like some sort of mailman," I told Kissinger. "I will not even submit the request to Mrs. Meir before I know what your government thinks. Are you recommending that we respond to the Jordanian request?"

"You place me in a difficult position," Kissinger begged off. "I can't answer you on the spot. Perhaps in another half hour."

After we rang off, I stole Golda away from the cocktail party in progress, moved off into another room, and told her of my conversation with Kissinger. We decided to notify Acting Prime Minister Yigal Allon of this latest development and ask for his opinion. In the meantime, minutes were ticking by and Kissinger had not called back. Golda spoke with both Allon and Dayan and found that opinions back home were split down the middle: the former inclined toward fulfilling the request, while the latter was far more reserved. I suggested that reconnaissance flights be made over the combat zone in northern Jordan and asked our people to explore the feasibility of establishing direct contact between the IDF and the Jordanian command. Battles unfold swiftly, and it would be absurd to have to communicate via Washington.

Over an hour later, Kissinger finally called back. "The request is approved and supported by the United States government," he said.

"Do *you* advise Israel to do it?" I pressed.

"Yes," he said, "subject to your own considerations."

That the Americans were eager to ensure our intervention in the Syrian-Jordanian conflict was underscored by the fact that

Kissinger arranged to have a special White House plane fly me back to Washington that same night. I accompanied Mrs. Meir to Kennedy Airport for her own flight back to Israel, and at 2:00 A.M. a plane was waiting at La Guardia to take me to Andrews Air Force Base near Washington, where I was picked up by a White House limousine and taken home. I called Kissinger again, even though it was already 3:30 in the morning, and while talking to him I had the impression that someone was listening in on our conversation. I later learned that it was the president.

When I met Kissinger at nine the next morning, the American reports on the military situation were still sketchy. But the reports from Israel were encouraging, and I now became the major source of intelligence on the conflict. Although the Syrians had penetrated northern Jordan, Hussein's armored units were holding on to the two routes leading south and had inflicted losses on the invasion force. In response, the Syrians were massing further armored units near the border, but they had refrained from using their air power.

Although Golda had not yet arrived in Israel, the government had worked out its general lines of approach to the United States. I was notified that Israel was prepared to take action, but (one of the few times that I could address this word to the Americans) should our intervention in Jordan lead to a renewal of fighting along the Suez Canal, we wanted the United States to back our response. I also told Kissinger and Sisco that we wanted a written undertaking to provide us with an American "umbrella" vis-à-vis the Russians if the Soviet Union threatened Israel directly, and that we wanted additional arms. Their response was affirmative on the arms, but when it came to the "umbrella" they were in a predicament.

As we were bargaining, events in the Jordanian-Syrian conflict continued to unfold. As the IDF reinforced its forces in the Golan Heights, the Jordanians succeeded in halting the three hundred Syrian tanks and the American moves bore fruit. Israeli-U.S. cooperation in planning the IDF intervention, together with the Israeli troop concentrations near the Syrian border, convinced the Soviets and the Syrians that they were best off halting the advance into Jordan. In weighing their options, the Russians could not have been oblivious to the fact that the Sixth Fleet's aircraft carriers were moving eastward in the Mediterranean and that a group of American officers took off from one of the carriers and came to Israel to discuss operational coordination. "Hints" of that nature may or may not have been subtle, but they were certainly effective, for soon afterward the Syrians withdrew from Jordan and the risk of a broader war was averted. At the same time, these events had a far-reaching impact on U.S.-Israeli relations. Israel's willingness to cooperate closely with the United States in protecting American interests in the region altered her image in the eyes of many officials in Washington. We were considered a partner — not equal to the United States, but nevertheless a valuable ally in a vital region during times of crisis.

On September 25, Kissinger phoned me and asked me, on behalf of the president, to convey a message to our prime minister: "The president will never forget Israel's role in preventing the deterioration in Jordan and in blocking the attempt to overturn the regime there. He said that the United States is fortunate in having an ally like Israel in the Middle East. These events will be taken into account in all future developments." This was probably the most far-reaching statement ever made by a president of the United States on the mutuality of the alliance between the two countries. I had never heard anything like it and still look back on that pronouncement with nostalgia. Now we waited to see how the sentiment would be translated into concrete policy.

Chapter Ten

THE SEARCH FOR A SOLUTION

IN SEPTEMBER 1970, the fighting in Jordan tore attention away from the Egyptian front, what with the cease-fire in effect there anyway. Yet the Jordanian crisis had barely entered its denouement when events in Egypt again stole the spotlight. On September 28, 1970, the news flashed around the world that President Nasser had collapsed and died of a heart attack. He was succeeded by his vice-president, Anwar el-Sadat, a little-known political figure who instantly became the focus of much speculation in the world's major capitals.

Now, nine years after Sadat assumed power, there are many politicians and intelligence men in the United States and Israel — and perhaps other countries as well — who would rather not be reminded of their "professional" assessments of Egypt's new leader. Sadat was viewed as no more than a provisional ruler who would last only as long as it took for a new power bloc to emerge in Egypt and choose a man to succeed the towering figure of Abdel Nasser. In his colorful style, Foreign Minister Eban publicly mocked Sadat as a model of anticharisma, and the new Egyptian president's media appearances provoked mirth.

The ninety-day cease-fire instituted by the Rogers initiative was due to run out early in December, and considering the new political circumstances in Egypt, Israel remained undecided about whether to agree to negotiations under Jarring's auspices or to make her participation conditional upon the restoration of the previous military status quo. The White House displayed no impatience with Israel for delaying the resumption of the Jarring talks. On the contrary, the atmosphere there remained cordial and sympathetic, in view of Israel's cooperative role in the Jordanian affair. I even had the impression that influential people in the White House were not displeased by the sight of Israel taking her time in responding to the State Department's request that she appoint her representative to the Jarring talks.

Early in December, the cease-fire was formally extended for another three months, and the political lull lasted late into January 1971. Then, with the Jarring talks still not off the ground, Sisco confided in me that the American *chargé d'affaires* in Cairo had been approached by an Egyptian general close to President Sadat with a proposal to explore the feasibility of reaching a settlement to reopen the Suez Canal. The suggestion was presented in general terms of an Israeli withdrawal to a line about twenty-five miles from the canal, a limited thinning out of forces on the Egyptian side, and the reopening of the waterway. Whatever else anyone might say about this idea (which, by the way, was originally raised for consideration by none other than Moshe Dayan), it was certainly a refreshing change from the high-stakes, all-or-nothing atmosphere that surrounded all the "final settlement" proposals related to Resolution 242. For that reason alone it merited serious thought.

At first, our own considerations aside, there remained a large measure of confusion about whether or not the United States was interested in having the canal reopened. The Pentagon made no secret of its objection to the idea on strategic grounds related to the Vietnam War, while the State Department tended to favor the Egyptian plan. We would hardly want to respond favorably to a plan that was not to President Nixon's liking, so I asked Kissinger to apprise me of the president's views. The following day he brought me Nixon's answer. "From the viewpoint of our own interests, the United States prefers the canal closed," he told me. "But the Jarring talks are stalled, and the situation in the Middle East could deteriorate and lead to a renewal of the fighting. Since our greatest interest is to prevent such a development, the United States favors discussions with Egypt about reopening the canal." Sisco subsequently described the option in even more appealing terms: reopening the waterway would remove the pressure of deadlines in the negotiations; and if the two armies disengaged, it would improve the prospects of subsequent political talks. These advantages would compensate for the strategic drawback it would present for the United States.

Sisco's hint that exploring this new channel of approach would provide a respite from the pressures to renew the Jarring talks was a welcome one. But evidently no one had bothered to let Mr. Jarring in on the latest turn of events. On February 8, just as the preliminary talk on the Egyptian initiative got under way, the UN ambassador dropped his bombshell in the form of the famous "Jarring questionnaire" addressed to Israel and Egypt. It was one of those black-and-white, no-nonsense moves that was not typical of Jarring's approach (but that eventually thwarted his mission for good). The document asked Egypt to reply to the question of whether or not it was willing to make peace with Israel in return for an Israeli withdrawal to the international border. Conversely, it asked Israel whether she was willing to withdraw to the international border in return for peace with Egypt. Straightforward and simple; no ifs, ands, or buts. Jarring was impatient and demanded immediate, binding answers.

The Israeli government now had to give two replies: to the Sadat initiative and to the Jarring document. In Washington, I complained that Jarring had exceeded his powers. His mandate was to promote agreement through talks, not to impose his views on the parties. But the Americans remained mute on that subject. Their sole comment — which was so familiar from the early days of the Rogers initiative — was: "Don't you be the first to respond in the negative."

On February 17, 1971, Jarring passed the text of the Egyptian reply to Yosef Tekoa (our ambassador to the United Nations), and when I read it I again had the uncanny feeling that we had been through this before. Like the Egyptian reply to the Rogers initiative, it had the flavor of one of those "good news, bad news" jokes that were making the rounds in America at the time. First the "good news": in return for an Israeli withdrawal from the Sinai and the Gaza Strip, Egypt was prepared to enter into a peace agreement with Israel. Strictly speaking, the Egyptians had not answered Jarring's question as posed, since the Gaza Strip did not

fall under the definition of the international border. But I must
concede, their answer was nonetheless a milestone. For the first
time in the chronicles of the Middle Eastern conflict, an Arab
country — indeed, the largest Arab country and leader of the
Arab world — had issued an official document expressing its
readiness to enter into a peace agreement with Israel!

But now for the "bad news" — which was all too familiar by
then: a "just and lasting peace" would not be achieved before
Israel had withdrawn to the June 4, 1967, lines on all the other
fronts as well and agreed to solve the refugee problem in accordance with all the relevant UN resolutions on that subject.

The entire document bore Sadat's evasive imprint. Was there a
definitive conditional link between the two sections of the answer
or not? (This same "linkage problem" would arise again over similar issues following the Camp David accords.) The State Department, for one, was not at all concerned about the "fine print," as
became clear when Sisco shared his "impressions" of the Egyptian reply with me. He characterized the proposal as "serious and
concrete," pointing out that "for the first time it's free of polemi-
cal elements." Moreover, the United States felt that the Egyptian
document satisfied Israel's main concern: a categorical undertaking to make peace. "The Israeli government's desire to make
peace will be put to a test by its attitude toward this document,"
Sisco pronounced. "You will have to reach some hard decisions."

In the wake of the Egyptian reply, I paid a short visit to Israel
for consultations. During my stay the cabinet adopted a resolution
expressing a favorable view of Egypt's readiness to enter into
meaningful negotiations on all matters connected with peace between the two countries. Yet it noted that the Egyptian document
clearly indicated differences between the countries' positions,
particularly on the issues of borders and the refugee problem.
Soon after I returned to Washington and informed the State Department of how Israel intended to reply to Mr. Jarring, Rogers
invited me for a talk to tell me that "the United States government is concerned that the Israeli answer will be interpreted as
being evasive."

Although I worked at keeping my expression calm, that kind of talk infuriated me. No one in the State Department, it seems, had read the Egyptian reply closely enough to see how evasive *it* was! We, on the other hand, hadn't even formulated our reply in writing yet, but accusations about what it "would be" were already afoot. "Our reply to Jarring will be earnest and responsible," I told Rogers. "It has been decided to state clearly that Israel will not withdraw to the June 4, 1967, lines." I also found it pertinent to remind the secretary of state of not-so-distant American commitments. "Last July President Nixon wrote to the prime minister assuring her that the United States would not exert pressure on Israel to accept Egypt's demands regarding a withdrawal from all the territories and a solution to the refugee problem based upon UN resolutions. Now that we actually face the issue, you are doing exactly what the president promised would not be done!"

Rogers retreated a little. "I want to avoid any misunderstanding," he said. "I did not say what Israel's answer should be." But then the exchange grew heated, with Rogers and Sisco alleging that "Egypt's attitude is positive, but Israel's is negative." Throughout my years in Washington, this was the most painful talk I ever had with Rogers. The secretary of state was a genial and gentle man, but on occasion his demeanor would undergo a radical metamorphosis: his eyes flashed, his face reddened, and he spoke very forcefully. "It's just a matter of time before you are forced to face the necessity of making concessions for peace!" he bellowed at me.

I could not have known it then, but Rogers would soon have ample reason to invite me to eat crow at his table. On February 26, when the Israeli reply did materialize and was submitted to Jarring, I was no less disappointed than my American colleagues. To tell the truth, I had recommended a different and clearer reply, similar in form to the Egyptian answer: an expression of our readiness to sign a peace agreement with Egypt followed by a detailed exposition of Isreal's views on the issues of borders and refugees. My proposal was not adopted, however; and the Israeli reply — which quoted at length from previous cabinet decisions and various other declarations — turned out to be a rambling document whose long-windedness was exceeded only by its vagueness. Worst of all, it failed in its main task: presenting Israel's demands in return for peace.

When I brought this statement over to Sisco, I took great pains to conceal my own dissatisfaction with it. His formal reply was only that he would convey it to the secretary of state and the president. But then he asked to comment informally, merely as a friend, and his assessment was grim. Sisco believed that our reply would again undermine the United States' standing in the Middle East and weaken the influence of circles in Cairo and Amman that were truly striving for a peaceful settlement. "For twenty years, you have known no peace," he said with genuine sadness, "and if you continue in this fashion, Israel will never experience peace."

Dr. Kissinger approached the problem from a completely different angle. "What would happen if the United States were to exert pressure upon you by cutting off military aid?" he asked me. "Would Israel still stick by her position?" It was a bizarre situation. Presumably those who planned to exert pressure were asking their intended victims, "How far can we twist your arm without breaking it?" Even the president himself was dropping broad hints when our own president, Zalman Shazar, visited the White House on March 8. "I understand the difficulties Israel faces in exchanging something concrete — territories — for promises and guarantees," he told Shazar. "But you should remember that your pipeline of military supplies is liable to dry up. Under no circumstances will that happen as long as I am president of the United States. But I won't serve forever. . . ."

A few days before Shazar met with Nixon, Egypt had publicly declared that the cease-fire agreement — which had lapsed on March 6 — would not be extended (though Sadat had let the Americans know that it would be maintained *de facto*). Thus the Americans had every reason for concern that the situation in the Middle East was deteriorating again. Jarring was stuck somewhere in the void between Egypt's and Israel's positions (his mission, though never officially terminated, just faded away into history), and no progress was being made on the idea of a partial agreement. Thus when Foreign Minister Eban arrived in Washington a short time later, Kissinger did away with hints and laid matters on the line for him.

"It makes sense for Israel to insist on maintaining a presence at Sharm el-Sheikh," he conceded, "even if she is prepared to withdraw to the international border in return for peace. But we want to know clearly: Is that the Israeli position?" Eban replied that a presence at Sharm el-Sheikh was, indeed, a vital Israeli request, but he could not say that that alone would satisfy Israel. Yet Kissinger was far from satisfied. He tried to sound restrained, but was not wholly successful.

"Gentlemen, would you, at long last, tell us, your friends, what you really want. Are you prepared to withdraw to the international border in return for peace? Yes or no? What are your terms? Sharm? What else? If not to the international border, how far *are* you prepared to pull back? And when? In return for what? And perhaps you would be good enough to tell Jarring, at long last, not only what you are not prepared to accept, but also what you *are* willing to accept. What are your positive proposals? You don't have to accept our position on every subject. But by the same token, you can't totally reject all proposals without advancing some of your own! No one understands you. No one knows what you want. There is serious fear that all you *really* want is to evade any settlement that requires concessions on your part so that you can remain along the lines you hold at present!"

Eban's evasions gave me the impression that he was not empowered to answer Kissinger's pointed questions. But Kissinger would not let up: "To the best of my recollections, reopening the canal as part of a partial settlement was an Israeli idea. All right, along comes President Sadat with concrete proposals. He is prepared to accept such an arrangement. We also submitted some preliminary ideas. Do you agree? Do you object? Don't you have *any* opinion on the subject?"

Eban replied that according to Mrs. Meir's latest notification the Israeli position would be finalized within seven to ten days, but Kissinger found it hard to restrain his anger. "I don't understand. Egypt has given Jarring a detailed answer, and Israel has no such answer. The Egyptians are willing to make an arrangement for reopening the canal, and Israel has no reply. The Egyptians ask us over and over again: 'What do you expect us to do under such circumstances?' And we don't have an answer. What kind of relations do you want with the United States? You ask for close, frank, intimate relations, but you don't tell us what you think or want. Intimacy is feasible only on a reciprocal basis. So go ahead, formulate your positions on an overall settlement and a partial settlement and clarify them to us, at least!"

When the White House and the State Department talk to Israel in a similar tone, there is little reason for comfort; and on March 20 Secretary of State Rogers addressed Abba Eban in a manner reminiscent of Kissinger's outburst. Considering the vehemence of the administration's tone, following these two talks Eban summarized them for the benefit of the cabinet, and this was one of the rare occasions when I could state without reservation that I agreed with Abba Eban. He tried to convey the American feeling that either the Israeli government was unwilling to state where it wanted Israel's border with Egypt to run or it was simply incapable of formulating political policy. The Americans did not demand that we adopt their proposals, or Jarring's, or Egypt's. But they definitely demanded that Israel be frank with all these parties — and first and foremost with her ally, the United States. "At present," Eban wrote, "even our friends are in confusion because they do not know whether we want to hold on to 70 percent of Sinai or 7 percent; whether we want security arrangements or aspire to annex sections of Sinai." Even Jarring had shifted from the demand that we underwrite his proposals to the request that we define our own position, and this had undermined our contention that Egypt's conditions for making peace were the obstacle to political progress.

The cabinet, however, was in no hurry to respond to any of these signs of impatience, and the administration continued to sow its seeds on fertile ground. In addressing the Senate, Rogers succeeded in depicting Israel as inflexible, and to my dismay many of the senators were inclined to accept the justice of this description. Even some Jewish leaders tended to fall in with his severe view, though they were discreet about expressing their feelings in public.

An ambassador can face no more serious quandary than having

to put up an uncompromising defense of his government's policy when he himself disagrees with it. In April 1971 I found myself in such a position. I certainly supported the government's opposition to withdrawal from the whole of the Sinai and found no difficulty in arguing that a "peace" of this nature was a sure recipe for another war. But I could not comprehend why, in the course of two and a half months, the Israeli cabinet had failed to submit counterproposals — at least to the Egyptian outline for a partial settlement (which was, in fact, originally an Israeli idea).

Finally, various ideas on furthering negotiations with Egypt were sent to me from Jerusalem. I found them unacceptable, however, for I did not believe they would elicit a positive response from either the Egyptians or the Americans. For a time, I actually found myself in the rather unorthodox position of negotiating with my own government over a set of proposals for a partial agreement! The main point of contention, as I saw it, was our cabinet's demand that Egypt renounce the state of belligerency in return for an Israeli pullback of just a few kilometers, so that the canal could be cleared and opened for operations. On that point, however, the cabinet remained adamant, and I was instructed to notify the Americans that ending the state of belligerency was a *sine qua non* of a partial agreement. If asked how far Israel was prepared to withdraw, I was to say that I did not know. The Americans were heartily sick of this game of hide-and-seek, and I found that I too needed great stores of self-discipline to refrain from hurling some harsh words at my government and perhaps even requesting that I be recalled from my post.

The most important points of Jerusalem's proposal for a partial settlement, which I proceeded to take to Dr. Kissinger, were as follows:

1. The canal would be open to the shipping of all nations, including Israel.

2. The cease-fire would be unlimited, and Egypt would commit itself not to renew fighting.

3. IDF forces would be stationed a certain distance from the canal, as stipulated in an agreement between Israel and Egypt.

4. Egyptian civilians required to prepare the canal for navi-

gation, open it, and operate it would be permitted into the area vacated by Israel, but no Egyptian forces — regular or irregular — would be allowed into that area.

5. Egypt would thin out its forces on the western side of the canal to an extent to be agreed upon by the two countries.

6. Fifteen days after the agreement came into effect, the prisoners of war held by both sides would be released.

7. The Israeli withdrawal would commence after the canal had been cleared and opened for international shipping.

8. This special agreement would not in any way influence the negotiations under Jarring's auspices to attain a just and lasting peace.

Kissinger reads at an astounding pace, and his reaction to this document was equally swift. "What is this? Where is the new line?" he demanded.

Faithful to my orders from Jerusalem, I replied: "I have been instructed not to discuss the depth of our pullback in precise terms. But if Sadat is thinking in terms of a withdrawal of dozens of kilometers, his expectations do not coincide in any way with the thinking in Jerusalem."

"And you expect me to submit this proposal to the president?" Kissinger roared at me. "If that's your proposal, I don't want to have anything to do with it. Take it to Sisco . . . I won't touch it! It indicates a fundamental misconception of both the basic problem and your standing in the United States. It will lead to stagnation and confrontation. So do whatever you want, but leave me alone!"

In hundreds of meetings, conversations, and contacts, I had rarely seen Kissinger so furious. "Can I leave you a copy of the document?" I asked, in an attempt to reduce the tension.

"You can leave me as many copies as you like," he replied gruffly, "but I won't have anything more to do with it!"

I reported to Jerusalem and asked how to proceed. "Submit the document to Sisco!" was the reply. So once again I spelled out the Israeli plan. Sisco listened attentively to these conditions — and to our requests for arms and aid from the United States — and he said that he would have to bring the matter to Rogers's attention.

Following my instructions, I asked him not to transmit the contents of our proposal to Egypt before the United States had formulated and informed us of its stand.

On April 22 we received the United States' reply to our document and it was notably cautious. The Americans stated that our proposal contained positive parts, and although they were unable to support it as a whole, it offered a positive basis for further attempts to reach an understanding with the Egyptians. Consequently, they would present the document to Egypt and request a positive response.

Early in May, Rogers, Sisco, and Alfred Atherton set out for a visit to the Middle East. After meeting with Egyptian officials, they moved on to Israel and held talks with Mrs. Meir and other cabinet members on political, military, and economic questions. Sisco was very encouraged by his conversation with Moshe Dayan, for he got the impression that Dayan's presentation of Israel's position differed from what had been stated in the document I had submitted to Kissinger and the State Department. When Rogers sent Sisco on a further visit to Cairo (not scheduled in the original itinerary), there were grounds to believe that this additional meeting with the Egyptians was linked to Sisco's talks with Dayan.

Back in Washington on May 12, Sisco told me of his private meetings with Sadat, Prime Minister Mahmoud Fawzi, and Foreign Minister Riad. Though he tried to report factually and unemotionally, it was evident that he had been profoundly impressed by the Egyptian president's desire for peace. He also found Sadat full of understanding for Israel's problems, and Sisco had never heard an Arab leader express himself in such a manner. Placing himself in Israel's shoes, Sadat gave rational consideration — more so than could have been expected from any Arab leader — to Israel's need for security. Sisco also thought that Sadat hoped to reduce Egypt's dependence upon the Soviet Union and was prepared to "do business" with the United States and Israel. "I found a great measure of flexibility in Sadat," he added. "He wants an agreement with Israel, but one that he can defend and justify vis-à-vis the other Arab countries."

Soon after, Sisco left for another visit to the Middle East. Again he claimed to have gained the impression from Dayan that Israel would be willing to withdraw further than the seven to twelve kilometers being discussed. But the cabinet showed no inclination to alter its formal proposal. Nor was there any give on other fundamental issues bound up with the partial agreement.

Then, at the end of September, Sisco "confessed" that the Americans had overreached themselves and told Sadat of Israel's readiness to carry out an extensive withdrawal. That was the impression they had gained from Moshe Dayan, and they based their moves on what he had said to them in private talks. Dayan stated his readiness to pull back beyond the line officially postulated by the Israeli government, and the Americans assumed that in the final analysis his opinion would be adopted by the cabinet. Fearing another "forgery" incident, and concerned that the Americans might commit themselves to Egypt's view on the depth of the pullback, the continued state of belligerency, and a limited military presence on the east bank of the canal, I believed it vital to hold a thorough discussion with Kissinger — who had been keeping an extremely low profile since I first brought him the government's proposal for a partial solution.

On October 2, 1971, we met for a long private talk, and I told Kissinger that I wanted to reach an understanding with him. First off, I had never heard him express any attitude toward the general notion of a partial agreement with Egypt (though I knew his views on the specific Israeli proposal). Kissinger revealed that he did not believe such a settlement could be concluded without an understanding between the White House and the Soviet Union. He also reiterated that our proposal did not seem reasonable to him, and he was not prepared to mislead us or others by handling a matter that he viewed as hopeless. Henry Kissinger was particularly sensitive about failure, and he confided in me one of the cardinal rules of his own personal "success syndrome." "In every sphere of my activity regarding U.S. foreign policy, including relations with China and the Soviet Union, I have developed a reputation for achieving my goals," he said. "I won't handle any matter that looks hopeless to me." Later, as prime minister, I had cause to recollect that Kissingerian "manifesto" when talks broke down over an interim agreement.

Since Kissinger and I had agreed to be candid, I decided to risk some thinking out loud in his presence, though I stressed again that this was a personal talk. "It is possible that after reporting back to the prime minister — which I must do — I will be rebuked for going beyond my powers," I cautioned him. But having delivered that preamble, I proceeded to analyze the benefits of a partial solution for Israel. Reopening the canal was obviously to Egypt's benefit, and Egypt's benefit alone. As far as Israel was concerned, there were two possible motivations for agreeing to such a course: the receipt of an Egyptian declaration of nonbelligerency in return (which I did not see as very likely, and which the United States could not "deliver" anyway); or trading off a partial settlement for America's formal abandonment of the Rogers Plan. "The time may not be right for the United States to make a public declaration that it has abandoned the Rogers Plan," I told Kissinger, "but if President Nixon tells Mrs. Meir that the administration will not place any pressure — political, military, or economic — on Israel to accede to the plan, that would be the minimum that could satisfy her."

Kissinger asked me how far Israel would be prepared to withdraw. "Something on the order of thirty kilometers, with the western part of the Gidi and Mitla passes remaining in our hands. The area we vacate must be demilitarized. Israel might consider the possibility of a *token* Egyptian force being allowed to cross the canal, but then the depth of our withdrawal would decrease." Once again, I stressed that American arms supplies and guarantees of economic assistance must be integral components of the partial agreement. After two or two and a half years, the agreement would be reconsidered and either party could demand changes.

When I reported on this conversation to the prime minister, I tried to forestall her anger: "I may have gone beyond my powers in airing proposals for a partial settlement. But in view of my relationship with Kissinger and my confidence in him — and considering present political circumstances — I thought that Israel ought to make a salient contribution to furthering the political process. We have a vital interest in inducing the president to disown the Rogers Plan, and there is no chance of his doing so unless we inject momentum into the political process in the context of the partial settlement."

Mrs. Meir reacted as I had feared. First, a short cable arrived in which she thanked me for my report. A week later, a further cable came notifying me that the proposals I discussed with Kissinger were unacceptable to her. She regretted that I had aired them, even privately, without first requesting permission. She also expressed her concern that Kissinger might have conveyed the main points of my proposal to the president, thereby weakening Israel's stand in our debate with the State Department over the terms for a partial settlement. Finally, the prime minister told me to notify Kissinger of her sharp reaction, ask him to overlook our private conversation, and tell him to regard my proposals as null and void. If Kissinger had already notified the president of my proposals, I was to ask him to inform the president of the same.

I knew that Kissinger was due to leave for China the following day, so I contacted him by phone and I told him that I had been overruled. Now that I had bitten the bullet, I felt better. Kissinger reassured me with soothing words, telling me he had not yet spoken with the president. Furthermore, he personally was far from eager to handle the partial settlement and proposed that we continue to deal with the matter by way of the State Department. On his return from China, in ten days' time, we would meet again.

On November 5, after his return, Kissinger invited me to the White House under "cloak-and-dagger" conditions. He asked me to come alone, said that he too would be alone, and had me admitted through a side entrance in the West Wing, so that by the time we were face to face my curiosity (not to mention my tension) was at a peak.

"What I am about to say is on behalf of the president, and you must promise that you will report it to no one other than Prime Minister Meir," he began in a conspiratorial manner, "and even to her privately and personally." An alarm bell went off in my mind because when Kissinger asked me to go to Israel and deliver a message to the prime minister personally, there was usually reason to believe that a crisis was in the offing.

What he now told me was of a secret proposal from Leonid Brezhnev relayed to President Nixon by Soviet Ambassaor Dobrynin. Brezhnev was suggesting a deal between the two powers for an overall solution in the Middle East. The settlement was to be effected in two stages: first a limited agreement for reopening the canal; then, after the 1972 American presidential elections (Brezhnev was not insensitive to Nixon's domestic vulnerabilities in an election year), an overall agreement based on the Jarring document. Brezhnev also offered that if the two powers could reach agreement on the character of the overall solution, he would be willing to make concessions in everything having to do with the partial agreement. Moreover, once the overall agreement was reached, the Soviet Union would be prepared to eliminate its operational military presence in Egypt, leaving no more than a small number of advisers, and join the United States both in an embargo on weapons shipments to the region and in measures to safeguard the agreement in whatever form the United States found necessary.

Kissinger paused and looked at me to gauge my initial reaction. I remained silent, judging it better to hear him out before commenting, though I knew he had already made the essence of his point. Ever since the Soviet Union had rejected the Rogers Plan in December 1969, the intensive talks between the two powers had ceased. In the meantime, the Americans had succeeded in bringing about the cease-fire on the Suez front and were now tinkering with the idea of a partial solution. But the implicit threat had always been that if Israel did not make sufficient progress on the political front through either a partial solution or the Jarring talks, the United States would have no choice but to return to the method of interpower negotiations and again evoke the specter of an imposed solution. Over the past few months, the State Department had clearly expressed its impatience with Israel, and now Kissinger was signaling me that our time had run out. Of course, he depicted the initiative as coming from Brezhnev, and I in no way doubted his sincerity on this point. But I could not shake free of the vision of Kissinger and Dobrynin closeted away cooking up deals, with Kissinger subsequently announcing the results to us as a *fait accompli* — much as Sisco had during his earlier talks with the Soviet ambassador. As if reading my mind, Kissinger tried to reassure me.

"I do not intend to negotiate with the Soviet Union, not even at the top level, without close coordination with Israel. I don't think that the United States should negotiate on a matter of fateful importance to Israel without taking her into our confidence at all stages of the negotiations. That is why I want an answer from Prime Minister Meir: Does Israel agree to the United States' entering into such negotiations — on the assumption that the future borders will not basically be different from the June 4, 1967, lines and that the boundary between Egypt and Israel must be the international border?" It must have been my expression, undoubtedly black, that prompted him to add: "I understand your difficulties, and if Israel replies to the Soviet proposal in the negative, I wouldn't blame her. I would seek ways of preventing American–Soviet negotiations on Brezhnev's proposals."

To make a long story short, I departed for Israel, where I submitted a detailed report to the prime minister, and after deliberations everyone agreed that it was vital to reject the Soviet initiative. Golda instructed me to notify Kissinger accordingly. She also asked me to submit to him and to the president information Israel had acquired on the Soviet Union's intention to encourage Egypt to go to war. On November 16, I presented the prime minister's views to Kissinger and suggested that the administration invite Mrs. Meir to come for talks, adding: "Tell the Soviets that you intend to discuss their proposals with the prime minister during the course of her visit and that you consequently cannot give them any reply before she comes to Washington."

Kissinger's hearing was selective sometimes. I was clearly indicating that Golda wanted to settle this matter with the president personally, and that there was little point in our continuing to discuss it now. But he did not seem prepared to let up. He explained once more as he had done on many previous occasions and was to repeat again in the future: "At the highest level, the United States cannot reject Soviet proposals without stating which terms are acceptable. You must understand that interpower relations differ somewhat from relationships in the Middle East. We can't say no to everything! You say no to Rogers! You say no, in effect, to a partial agreement."

I broke in: "We say a decisive *yes* to a partial agreement."

"But your terms are unreasonable, and consequently your yes is actually no," he corrected me. "Look what you say. The prime minister did not accept your views about a thirty-kilometer withdrawal. You talk of a withdrawal of seven to twelve kilometers, and in return you expect Egypt to agree to nonbelligerency and rely on your goodwill in the hope that someday, many years from now, you might give up a few more kilometers of the Sinai! Is that a serious expectation? Then you go on to say that there's no link between the partial settlement and the overall settlement. Forgive me for asking, but within what context do we conclude the partial settlement? What is to guarantee Egypt the right — which it regards as basic and inalienable — to demand your withdrawal from the whole of the Sinai if you insist that it waive its military option while you reject any link between the partial settlement and the overall settlement?"

The discussion went on, but the only matter we did manage to agree on was that the prime minister would come for talks with the president in December. At the same time, Kissinger would try to delay negotiations with the Soviet Union until after her visit.

Golda's meeting with Nixon was held on December 2, 1971, with both Kissinger and me in attendance. On the day before, the prime minister had held a long talk with Kissinger, and of course he had briefed the president on her position before Mrs. Meir arrived in the Oval Office. The essence of Golda's presentation to Kissinger was a reiteration of why Israel could not accept the Rogers Plan and a plea, yet again, to distinguish between consideration of the political problem and the need to keep Israel strong and fully equipped. There was also talk of the partial settlement, and even though I had explicitly told Kissinger that my views on the subject had been firmly rejected by the prime minister, he could not restrain himself from asking, "What about the ideas Rabin put forward about a partial agreement?"

Golda took the path of understatement. "That isn't quite the Israeli position. And there are two points I must insist upon: Egyptian forces will not cross the canal into the territory vacated by Israel; and we will withdraw to the western extremity of the passes — no further." Clearly her position was softening: the depth of the withdrawal was no longer being limited to merely a few kilometers. Yet there was even more to come. "We might be able to do something about the duration of the cease-fire," she added. "That is, we are prepared to consider the possibility of a cease-fire of limited duration, but only on condition that we receive a clear and specific undertaking from the president that the Rogers Plan is not the basis for an overall settlement in the Middle East and does not constitute American policy in any attempt to reach agreement with the Soviet Union."

Evidently my musings out loud with Kissinger had not really been so far off the mark. Israel might indeed trade off her demand for an end to the state of belligerency in return for America's commitment to drop the Rogers Plan. I sensed that if Kissinger played his cards right, we might indeed be able to reach a workable understanding for a partial solution. But he had to be wary.

"Can the ideas presented by Ambassador Rabin constitute a basis for clarifying Israel's position on the partial settlement?" he asked.

What obstinacy! The prime minister had already said that my views did not coincide with those of the cabinet. He was embarrassing me in her presence by placing emphasis on the differences of opinion between us. But far worse, even though Golda was slowly coming closer to the ideas I had talked over with him, he seemed to be handling the discussion in a way that would force her to eat her words! Yet Henry Kissinger, the virtuoso of negotiations, knew exactly what he was doing, and the prime minister's reply took me by surprise. "Egyptian civilian technicians and police will be able to cross over to the east bank," she said. This was the first time that Mrs. Meir had ever given her consent to the notion of Egyptian policemen entering the area to be vacated by Israel — albeit, only after the canal was reopened and in operation.

The next day we all met in the Oval Office. As usual, the president was cordial, courteous, and vague. He began by reassuring Golda that the latest request for Phantom fighter planes would be honored, but he sidestepped the question of how many and when, leaving it to Kissinger to work out the details by the end of the month. Then he turned to political issues and made it clear that concern about the lack of progress toward a political settlement had spread to the White House. The president and Kissinger explained that with a summit meeting between the leaders of the two superpowers looming in May, America had no choice but to hold talks with the Soviet Union on the Middle East question, since the Russians were insisting upon it very strongly. This much was crystal clear. What followed, however, was one of the most amazing examples of the subtleties of diplomacy I was ever to witness. This time it was Kissinger who undertook to summarize the meeting and, consciously avoiding a single concrete reference to any American political position, he proposed the following.

"On December 10, when the prime minister and I meet in New York, I shall bring her a proposal on behalf of the president elucidating the principles of both a partial settlement and an overall settlement. By January, we shall formulate a detailed proposal regarding the Phantoms as well as a draft of the principles for the two settlements. Then we shall examine with Dobrynin the feasibility of reaching an agreement with the Soviet Union on the basis agreed upon between Israel and the United States."

"Madam Prime Minister," the president interjected, "is that acceptable to you?"

Clearly misreading the situation, I was alarmed. Had Golda come six thousand miles to talk these questions out with the president only to be told to settle the matter with Kissinger later in New York? But Golda, who had after all served as Israel's foreign minister for years, was hardly a novice at the wiles of diplomacy, and her rapport with Nixon was often truly extraordinary. She was aware that an understanding was being struck in this room, but formal responsibility for expressing the terms was a delicate matter. So taking the bit between her teeth, she graced the Oval Office with a strong dose of plain speaking.

"I'll tell you how I understand the situation," she began. "There will be no American-Soviet deal contrary to Israel's wishes, and the United States will not exert pressure on Israel to concede to positions reached in any such discussions. The United States understands that, from Israel's point of view, the Rogers Plan is a dead letter as an operative U.S. position. Israel will convey to the United States her views regarding both a partial agreement and an overall settlement; and delivery of arms — including planes — will continue unimpeded."

By now, of course, I had caught on to the rules of this exchange and was not surprised when the president confirmed Mrs. Meir's reading of the situation. And indeed, during their talk on December 10, Kissinger and Golda reached the following conclusions regarding the partial settlement. The Israeli withdrawal would stop short of the western approaches to the Sinai passes while the cease-fire would be for eighteen months to two years, at the very least. Furthermore, Egyptian technicians and a certain "uniformed force" would be permitted to cross the canal within the context of the partial agreement. "I want you to know that I will tell the Egyptians 'a uniformed force,'" Kissinger stressed, "and I don't mean the uniform of a New York hotel porter, so there must be no misunderstanding between us." As to the other side of the coin, linkage between the partial and overall agreements would not bind Israel to the Rogers Plan in any way whatsoever. They also agreed that Sisco and I should explore the feasibility of what were termed "proximity talks" between Israel and Egypt, while the United States would simultaneously try to reach an understanding with the Soviets in anticipation of the Moscow summit — though Mrs. Meir was assured that there would be no deal with the Soviet Union to exert pressure on Israel. Finally, on the matter of arms supplies, it was agreed that the United States would provide Israel with additional Phantoms and Skyhawks in the course of 1972 and 1973.

When Mrs. Meir returned home, everyone seemed to enter a

state of hibernation. "The Soviets are busy with the India-Pakistan war," Kissinger told me. "For reasons of overall global politics, there is no point in us urging them to try and reach an understanding regarding the Middle East. I don't believe that they will encourage the Egyptians to renew fighting in the course of 1972, and it's very doubtful whether the Egyptians would decide on such a course without Soviet encouragement." All of a sudden there was no haste. Everyone had plenty of time. Talks about plane deliveries also went forward at a leisurely pace. Kissinger told me that the president had given precise instructions to the State Department, as agreed with Golda. But Sisco notified me that the United States could not deliver more than two Phantoms every two months — not two planes a month as we had requested.

Then, at the end of January, Kissinger told me that he had recently had a long conversation with Dobrynin that covered a wide range of topics. Since the Middle East occupied only a minor place in that talk, Kissinger's feeling was that no Soviet-American understanding would be reached before the May summit, but periodic talks with Dobrynin would go on. He also mentioned that he had told Dobrynin of Israel's insistence on a presence beyond the former international border with Egypt and that its exact extent would be agreed upon in the peace negotiations.

When I reported back to Jerusalem on our talk, Golda cabled: "Explain what Kissinger meant by a presence in Sinai beyond the former border." Explain what *Kissinger* meant? The problem was to explain what *Israel* meant! "Our position is unclear," I cabled back. "No one outside Israel understands it. Authorized spokesmen state publicly that Israel does not plan to annex any parts of Sinai or place them under her sovereignty; she only wishes to 'control' these areas. I, too, request clarification of that position." The prime minister replied: "Israel's policy aims toward a considerable change in her border with Egypt. That means a change of sovereignty, not just an Israeli presence. We do not employ the term 'annexation' because of its negative connotation."

Annexation or not? Sovereignty changed or unchanged? And what was the meaning of "a considerable change"? Again I pleaded with the prime minister: "The Americans ask me simple questions and I am bound to give them straightforward answers. What does Israel want in regard to her borders with Egypt? How am I to reply?" Mrs. Meir referred me to the cabinet's decision of March 31, 1971: "A secure border for Israel requires changes in the former international frontier, including retention of the Gaza Strip, continued Israeli control at Sharm el-Sheikh, and a territorial link to the State of Israel. Continued control does not signify a presence but rather concrete military control, though the Israeli position regarding the legal form of such control has yet to be formulated."

Not really much more enlightened, on January 27, 1972, I informed Kissinger that "Israel demands border changes, and Dobrynin should be told that." "There's no chance of the Soviet Union agreeing," he was quick to reply, "and that should be made clear to the prime minister."

Golda was worried, and on February 28 she shared her concern with me: "Kissinger constantly reaffirms that he cannot make any promises concerning the commitments Nixon will take upon himself at the Moscow summit. Nixon understood perfectly well that we demand shelving the Rogers Plan and that we demand border changes in Sinai. He told me that he agrees with me." (I must state that I never heard the president express any such agreement in any of the meetings I attended.) "I am afraid that Kissinger is giving the Soviets an erroneous impression concerning Israel's territorial position. As a result, a fundamental political fact is in the process of being established in the Two-Power talks and it is misleading the Russians. I also find a conflict in Kissinger's statements. At times, he declares that there will be no deal behind Israel's back; at others, he says that the United States will not exert pressure upon Israel to accept a deal, which means that one is being put together. All doubt should be removed from Kissinger's mind: if they try to conclude an unacceptable deal for an overall settlement, we won't go for a partial settlement either."

In fact, Golda's concerns were not just products of her imagination. Kissinger was probing for weak spots in Israel's position, and during his talks with Defense Minister Dayan on February 7, he warned: "I cannot say with certainty what conclusion Nixon will reach with Brezhnev at their summit meeting." Dayan reported back to Golda, and this sentence justly aroused her concern. Nor were Kissinger's utterances to me particularly reassuring. On March 7, he informed me that Dobrynin had offered him a package deal: the Soviet Union would withdraw all of its personnel from Egypt if the U.S. would agree that Israel must withdraw to the pre–Six Day War lines. A week later he added that so far he had tried, with some success, to gain time in his talks with Dobrynin. But he was unable to keep it up. "I want to tell you in all frankness," he said, "that when the president meets Brezhnev in Moscow, I'm not at all sure — considering the Israeli position — that the United States will not be forced to revert to the Rogers Plan." Finally, on March 16, Kissinger adopted another one of his customary ploys. He told me that his talks with Dobrynin were deadlocked, and that since it was not his habit to pursue lost causes, he was dropping the whole matter.

Kissinger did, indeed, break off his talks with Dobrynin, but the reason had nothing to do with the Middle East. It was related to a severe reversal in Vietnam — so grave that there was talk of canceling the Moscow summit altogether. The Americans settled that crisis, however, and then Kissinger was sent to Moscow to pursue his preparations for the summit. Brezhnev subjected him to some very tough talk on the Middle East during those preparatory meetings. When Kissinger returned, he repeatedly intimated that if Nixon himself were to be confronted with similar hints about the renewal of fighting in the Middle East, no one could foresee how the president would react. There were also hints that in return for Soviet concessions over Vietnam, it was not inconceivable that the United States would reward the Russians at the expense of Israeli interests.

The words "tell Kissinger" were a regular feature of Golda's cables to me during those days leading up to the summit, and every time I approached Kissinger he seemed to have changed his tune — alternately soothing me and subtly threatening that heaven alone knew what would happen in Moscow. In the end, however, thanks to President Nixon's firm stand, our interests

emerged from the Moscow summit unscathed. As Kissinger subsequently described events to me, during the very first meeting
(with Brezhnev and Kosygin facing Nixon and Kissinger), the Russians adopted extremely forceful language and repeatedly demanded an Israeli withdrawal from all the occupied territories
without any concessions from the Arabs. Three hours of intense,
uninterrupted discussion convinced both sides that the gap between their conflicting positions could not be bridged without additional preparatory work, so Kissinger and Kosygin were charged
with continuing discussions on the Middle East.

Then, under conditions of maximum secrecy, Kissinger showed
me an American-Soviet working paper that included the following
points. The political solution for the Middle East had to be comprehensive and deal with all fronts simultaneously (though it
could be implemented in stages according to the timetable established for each sector). The solution would call on Israel to
withdraw from territories occupied in the Six Day War (rather
than *the* territories, which was the standard Soviet interpretation
of Resolution 242), and changes in border lines would have to be
agreed upon by the parties concerned. (Kissinger attached great
significance to the fact that he had managed to get the Soviets to
consent to agreed border changes without qualifying them as
"minor.") Security arrangements between the parties were essential, and the working paper mentioned demilitarization of the territories and the stationing of UN forces there. But the principal
stress was on firm guarantees by the powers to safeguard the
agreements. Freedom of navigation in the Straits of Tiran and the
Suez Canal would be guaranteed for the ships of all nations, with
Israel to be mentioned specifically.

In contrast to these agreed principles, the United States and
the Soviet Union remained divided on two issues: the Soviets did
not agree with the American view that at some stage of the negotiations face-to-face meetings would be held between the representatives of Israel and of the Arab countries; and the Americans
did not accept the Soviet view that the Palestinian problem
should be solved on the basis of the relevant UN resolutions.

In response to my question, Kissinger told me that this paper would henceforth serve as the basis for talks between the United States and the Soviet Union. Perhaps it wasn't an absolutely ideal outline (from our point of view); but considering what we had prepared ourselves to expect of the Moscow summit, it was a downright achievement, and we had cause to be grateful to the president and his national security adviser.

The summit was like a kind of emotional climax for us all, and afterward things pretty much reverted to the usual pace. Kissinger kept up his contacts with Dobrynin, and I maintained mine with Kissinger and Sisco through the beginning of July. Then, on July 11, 1972, President Sadat returned to the scene — indeed, he took center stage — with a move that stunned the whole world: he summarily expelled the Soviet military experts from Egypt. Everyone was astounded, especially when it turned out that what at first appeared to be a move coordinated with the United States was actually a completely independent step. The American administration was no less surprised than the Kremlin. In moments of distress and confusion, even a masterful ambassador can show faulty judgment, and Dobrynin was no exception. He rushed to Kissinger and informed him that, as a gesture of goodwill, the Soviet Union had already started to fulfill its side of the bargain with the United States by withdrawing its personnel from Egypt. Kissinger retained his cool and merely smiled. He knew no more about Sadat's motives than Dobrynin did, but unlike the Russian (whom Kissinger described as being in a state of panic), he had every reason to be calm and satisfied with this latest turn of events.

Not that that was the end of the Egyptian-Soviet axis. For the present, however, the Soviet Union was left rather off balance. And with the American presidential election coming up in the autumn, the Middle East question was put on the back burner for the next few months. Even after the election, though Dayan met with Rogers (and was told that "status quo is no policy"), Kissinger met with Sadat's adviser Hafez Ismail (and was very impressed by his views), and I saw the president in January for a kind of farewell meeting (the end of my tenure was already established for March 10, 1973), things were pretty stagnant. The

president characterized the situation in the Middle East as "satisfactory" but noted that the diplomatic lull could not go on much
longer. He confessed that he had no new ideas of his own and
hoped that Mrs. Meir would be bringing some when she arrived
for talks at the end of February.

I knew that "new ideas" was a kind of code word meaning that
Israel was expected to contribute further concessions, so I was
put on the alert. It was also clear that the Americans were peeved
by Israel's downing of a Libyan commercial airliner over the Sinai
just a short while before Golda's arrival, and none of our explanations about what had prompted such drastic action could appease
their mood. But I certainly never expected what transpired next.

February 28, the first day of Golda's visit, can only be described as a fiasco. She met with Kissinger and again expressed
Israel's willingness to advance toward both an overall settlement
and a partial agreement for the reopening of the canal. But Kissinger's only response was that "in the absence of any new ideas
or proposals, there will be no progress." Her talk with Acting
Secretary of State Kenneth Rush, at midday, was no more encouraging and only served to underscore the gap between Israel
and the United States on the question of final borders. That afternoon, the prime minister met with Secretary of Defense Elliot
Richardson and Pentagon officials, but the discussion on arms
supplies pretty much ended in an impasse.

By the time she returned to Blair House, Golda was so
dispirited that I felt genuinely alarmed. Sitting silently in the library, in the wing reserved for kings and other heads of state, she
looked absolutely forlorn. "If what the president has in store for
me resembles what I got from the people of his administration,
I'm better off packing my things and returning home before my
meeting with him," she confessed to me. I proposed that we sit
down to work out a number of approaches that I could try out on
Kissinger that very night. Golda agreed, though without much
enthusiasm, and we sat down to work. Still, there was little new
in what we came up with: Israel certainly did not object to further
contacts between the United States and the Soviet Union or
Egypt, but again she insisted that the United States not make

commitments on Israel's behalf. And, of course, Golda had come to raise the question of arms supplies — especially components such as engines that would enable Israel to manufacture the Kfir fighter plane.

New or not, at least I had an outline to show Kissinger, who received me at the White House at 7:30 that evening with an omniscient expression on his face. "I imagine that the prime minister has had a tough and depressing day," he said in what sounded to me like a self-satisfied tone. It goes without saying that he knew about the distressing talks at the State and Defense Departments, but I was not in the mood for diplomatic pleasantries. "I just don't understand any of you," I fumed, "and I can't believe that you were capable of inviting the prime minister here only to send her home empty-handed." However, I hadn't come to argue with Kissinger about manners and with the clock ticking away I showed him the ideas Golda and I had worked out in Blair House.

His response struck me as being novel, even though Kissinger had expressed a similar approach during our very first conversation five years before. Back in March 1968, he had spoken of placing stress on concrete security arrangements on the ground, rather than the precise formulations of treaties — which have been known to be broken. Now he noted that his approach in his talks with Hafez Ismail of Egypt had concentrated on the principle of "security versus sovereignty." Translated into pragmatic terms, it meant that Israel would have to accept Egyptian sovereignty over all of the Sinai but that Egypt, in turn, would have to accept an Israeli military presence in certain strategic positions, such as Sharm el-Sheikh (though he hastened to add that such an Israeli military presence might have to be disguised as a civilian one). He also suggested (perhaps as a way of dispelling the grim mood and ensuring that his proposal would get a fair hearing back at Blair House) that during the next day's talks Mrs. Meir would get a generally positive response on the question of plane deliveries and a positive and specific response on the components needed for the manufacture of the Kfir (though the quantities promised might be less than those Israel had requested).

We ended our talk by agreeing that I would approach the

prime minister with his idea while he would talk to the president prior to the next day's meeting. Then I returned to Blair House, harboring the hope that the prime minister's visit had been saved. Not that it would necessarily be easy to "sell" Kissinger's idea to Golda. It was, in essence, a radical departure from the policy that seemed to insist on official border changes while refraining from stating exactly what those changes would entail. But the fact that the idea was different certainly did not imply that it lacked merit. The question before us was whether or not Israel would agree to have the United States pursue the idea of "security versus sovereignty" with the Egyptians. Golda readily agreed, so long as it was understood that such explorations would be undertaken with Israel's knowledge but not in her behalf. I immediately notified Kissinger, and now we had no choice but to wait and see whether or not the president would be amenable to this solution to our deadlock.

There was no response from the White House that evening, and the next morning, when I tried to get Kissinger on the phone, I was told that he was in the president's office and could not be disturbed. I tried a second time, a third; always the same reply. I watched the clock like a hawk, my nerves growing more and more taut, till finally, just a few minutes before the meeting with Nixon was scheduled to begin, the phone rang at Blair House. It was Kissinger calling from the president's office to announce that Nixon approved of everything we had agreed on the night before. After twenty-four hours of undiluted tension, I saw Golda smile again and felt an enormous sense of relief.

When we arrived at the White House, the president was in extraordinarily good spirits. He sang my praises to Golda (much to my embarrassment) and wanted to know what post I would be offered upon returning to Israel. "That depends on how he behaves," Golda teased. "Well, if you don't need him in Israel, you're welcome to leave him here!" the president offered. "I'll be glad to have him!"

It must have been the tension of the last twenty-four hours that made me forget that it was my birthday. But the president "remembered" and showered me with warm wishes and a score of White House souvenirs bearing his initials. With the mood set so cordially, I knew that it was going to be a successful meeting. Indeed, at its end, both sides appeared satisfied with the outcome. The political process would again be pursued by Dr. Kissinger, and the president had set Golda's mind at rest about military supplies and economic aid.

Since my tenure as ambassador ended nine days later, I should add that although I was fortunate to end my term on an optimistic note, the postscript to this meeting between the president and the prime minister was essentially a sad one. In April, Dr. Kissinger continued his efforts to reach an understanding with Hafez Ismail on the basis of the "security versus sovereignty" formula, but in May President Sadat rejected the proposal — as he had earlier rejected the idea of "proximity talks." By then Sadat was already fully determined to go to war, and he was not interested in exploring any political solution that was not set out purely on his own terms.

As Golda and I stood up to leave that meeting, there was another round of farewells, with the president wishing me the best for the future. The scene remains etched in my memory because none of us could have suspected that the next time we four would find ourselves in the same room would be in Jerusalem and that Henry Kissinger would be secretary of state of the United States; Richard Nixon would be a ravaged man, soon to resign his presidency; and I would be starting out as the new prime minister of Israel.

Chapter Eleven

ROUNDING OUT THE PICTURE

UNTIL NOW I have concentrated on the political aspect of my work as an ambassador because — as I told Eshkol when I first broached the subject with him — that was the job I thought I could do best. Yet I confess to having drawn a rather skewed portrait of ambassadorial life. Those five years in Washington were made up of much more than one meeting after another, drafting cables, and accompanying visiting personages. In fact, I soon found myself involved in a much wider variety of activities — some of which ranged well beyond the conventional duties of a senior diplomat.

Leah and I have never particularly thought of ourselves as "socialites." In Washington, however, being "social" is part and parcel of an ambassador's job, and inevitably we found ourselves going out almost every night, in addition to hosting weekday lunches, Sunday brunches, and our own dinner parties at home. Besides being a welcome form of release from pressure-filled days, the Washington social gathering is another opportunity to "get around," keep in touch with people of influence, and make your country's case heard in a variety of circles, so that even my leisure time was really a mixture of pleasure and business for me.

At first, the social scene in Washington called for a crash course in local tastes and mores, and it was important to pay attention to little things, especially since what might be considered "improper" in one set of company could be most welcome in another. Take cigars, for instance — certainly an innocuous enough subject. Soon after arriving in America, I received a gift of highly coveted Havana cigars from the Israeli minister in Cuba. (The U.S.-Cuban quarrel had no effect on Israel's diplomatic relations with the Castro government.) A short time later, Zvi Zur (then serving as a special assistant to the minister of defense) visited Washington, and I hosted two luncheons in his honor. At the first, for a number of State Department officials, I proudly (and innocently) brought out my Havanas at the close of the meal only to find my offer met by a wall of frozen faces. It seems that the United States had instituted an embargo on all Cuban products, and to the State Department that meant business! Trying to maneuver through my first diplomatic *faux pas* with a maximum of grace, I proceeded to bring out a local brand, and the matter passed without further comment. The next day, however, when the guests were a group of leading Pentagon officials, I was careful to offer Dutch and American products only, while telling my guests of the previous day's embarrassment. "You've got Havanas?" one of the generals asked suggestively, and I could see by the eager grins around the table that the U.S. army would not dream of denying the ambassador's hospitality. So out came the "contraband" to the collective delight of all concerned.

Before long, I had most of the local "social graces" down pat, and any sense of self-consciousness I might have felt in the beginning had dissolved into an easy self-confidence. But soon after President Nixon entered the White House, I was confronted with a perplexing invitation to a reception for the diplomatic corps. At the bottom, it laconically noted "White Tie." Naturally, I had long ago gotten over my tie "trauma," but I simply had no idea what that cryptic expression meant — and I certainly was not about to call the White House and ask. So I paid a visit to my friend Marshal Cohen, the owner of the Madison Hotel, and discreetly inquired what it was all about. Rather than attempt to explain, Marshal merely smiled at me with a gleam of mischief in his eye and sent me off to his tailor, who proceeded to outfit me with all the proper accouterments.

For those of you who have never had the pleasure, "White Tie" consists of a black tailcoat and striped trousers that come equipped with a stiff-fronted shirt that ties in the back, a cummerbund, and, of course, the white bow tie that gives the outfit its name. It may have been the height of formal chic — and the

Nixon White House was famous for its emphasis on formality and ceremony — but it felt like a straitjacket. Although I succeeded in making my way out of the house by moving like a poorly oiled robot, it was almost impossible for me to get seated in the car. Once at the White House, I maneuvered myself back into an upright position and proceeded to make my way around the East Room, trying my best to look as relaxed and poised as my diplomatic colleagues.

Inevitably, however, I drew attention to myself — not because of any hint about how uncomfortable I felt, but because of my lack of war decorations (which were part and parcel of the outfit). Marshal Cohen's tailor had faithfully informed me of this obligatory accessory, but the simple truth is that I don't have any war medals (and seemed to be the only gentleman in the room who did not). Many of my fellow ambassadors from Europe, Asia, and especially Latin America (no few of whom were career diplomats) were laden down with them; and here I was, the former chief of staff of the Israel Defense Forces, without a single medal to his name. Incredible! I had to explain, repeatedly, that the IDF does not award battle decorations to its soldiers. It's simply not our custom and never was. We do award miniature war ribbons and paratrooper wings, but certainly nothing as imposing and cumbersome as a medal! Each time I found someone furtively looking at me as if I were naked, I tried to explain as humbly as possible that the IDF tries to excel at winning wars and hopes that victory alone will compensate its soldiers for their bravery.

My military background sometimes led me into situations that were undoubtedly unorthodox for a diplomat serving in a foreign capital. Even though I tried to avoid becoming involved in matters not directly related to Israel, there were a number of borderline cases in which I responded to the Pentagon's request to clarify how some suggestion currently before Congress might be to Israel's advantage. Once I made Israel's views known to some members of a congressional committee considering the establishment and maintenance of a base for the Sixth Fleet in Greece. On another occasion, when a number of senators opposed the addition of an aircraft carrier to the U.S. navy, I approached several of them with Israel's point of view on the question. In both cases, the Pentagon's proposals were in Israel's interest for obvious geopolitical reasons. After Senator Ribicoff heard me out on the aircraft carrier, he conceded, "You've convinced me. Could you present all that in the form of a written memorandum?" I was pleased to do so, and shortly afterward Senator John Stennis commented to me, "You know, even the navy's memorandum wasn't as convincing as yours!" In the end, Congress approved the construction of additional aircraft carriers, and though that decision was based solely on American interests, my memorandum is on the record.

In the course of my five years in Washington, I was invited to lecture at all of America's major military academies, shared with a special Pentagon committee our experiences and achievements in building the IDF's reserves, and kept the Pentagon up to date on Israel's experience in battle against Soviet military equipment (which was a subject of crucial importance to both countries). My opinion was even solicited on the U.S. defense allocation, weapons development, and the advantages of one weapon over another. In return, I was accorded some exceptional privileges that are not usually the lot of foreign ambassadors. For example, I had the unforgettable experience of a flight in a Phantom jet when the first course for Israeli Phantom pilots reached its conclusion. I even visited the underground command post of the Strategic Air Command and was permitted to become acquainted with the communications systems of nuclear submarines.

One of my appearances as a "consultant" stands out in my mind because even though I had no intention of "showing off," I think I inadvertently put some top American generals to shame. In March 1972 Henry Kissinger invited me to the White House without explaining what the agenda of our meeting would be. This was not the first time that Kissinger had issued an invitation with an air of mystery about it, and I always felt unsettled by that kind of summons. When I arrived at his office, however, it turned out that the subject at hand had nothing whatsoever to do with Israel. He merely wanted some friendly professional advice. The American army was expecting a North Vietnamese offensive, and

Kissinger was interested in my opinion about where the Vietnamese were likely to launch their attack. I was briefed on the situation on the ground and asked for some time to mull the matter over. "Fine," Kissinger said and sat down to gaze at me in silence while I studied the maps laid out before me. After analyzing the situation, I enumerated the possibilities. "They'll probably attack here and here," I told him, pointing out the places on the map. "Your forces are not strong enough on this side, and my guess is that they'll go for a flanking movement and try to encircle you."

"Uhm, interesting," Kissinger mumbled. "You're the only general we've asked who seems to think so."

When the North Vietnamese began their offensive, and a group of generals were bent over maps marking out lines, I'm sure they could not have been pleased to hear Kissinger comment, "You know, the only general who forecast precisely the direction of the enemy's thrust was the Israeli ambassador to Washington!"

Within Washington, my military credentials were certainly an asset and assured me of a rather unusual place in the political and diplomatic fabric of the American capital. Yet my work in America was not limited to Washington. I received countless requests to lecture throughout the country and was eager to comply. On American college campuses, however, the fact that this particular diplomat also happened to be a former chief of staff sometimes made matters less than pleasant — to put it mildly.

The youth of America were angry during the years I served as ambassador. Naturally, I viewed American affairs as an "outsider," but I was not insensitive to their dilemma. They were told to put their lives on the line in a war they perceived as unjust, and the longer that war dragged on, the louder their protest grew. Moreover, as I had seen so dramatically during my first months in America, the country was still grappling with the painful problem of racial tensions; and with the tragic death of such a charismatic leader as Dr. King, radical elements in the black community had rushed in to fill the void. All of which had nothing whatsoever to do with Israel. Yet during my first years in Washington, for reasons that have never really become clear to me, the Students for a Democratic Society (SDS) and the Black

Panthers — each of which had its own ax to grind — entered into an alliance with the Arab students in the United States and they turned their collective fire on Israel. As the chief representative of that country in the United States, I naturally became the personal target of their rage.

Sometimes I would arrive on a campus to be met by hand-painted placards and banners that read THE AMBASSADOR — THE GENERAL — THE MURDERER and similar pleasantries. The Arab students had printed up crude propaganda handbills with a fictionalized biography that "proved" I was personally responsible for civilian casualties. When their efforts to prevent me from attracting an audience failed, their next aim was to make sure I couldn't be heard. Hecklers would infiltrate a lecture hall and sometimes even take up a chant to drown me out. At the University of Colorado, demonstrators burst into the hall carrying immense banners of the variety described above and crowded the aisles to capacity, reducing my host to a state of impotent despair.

I was invited to Stanford University not long after America's invasion of Cambodia (when tempers were running particularly high), and much to my dismay I arrived to discover that my lecture fell on the same day as a recruitment talk by a scout from Union Carbide. Anyone familiar with the mood of America's radicalized youth in those days will understand that the air was already crackling with tension long before I reached the podium. The lecture hall was in a large, glassed-in pavilion, and when the doors closed protesters surrounding the hall began pounding on the glass with their fists. As if that were not distracting enough, before I could open my mouth the fire alarm went off! I had not come to Stanford to brush up on the finer points of California state law, but I did learn a detail that I doubt I'll ever forget. Once a fire alarm is pulled, it is against the law for anyone but a member of the fire brigade to turn it off. So we all sat for ten minutes with that earsplitting bell clanging away until the fire brigade arrived to restore the peace. In comparison to that awful din, the pounding of the protesters seemed downright quiet.

Far more serious than these disruptions, however, were the innumerable bomb scares that seemed to follow me around

America. I particularly remember an incident that occurred at a Catholic college for women in Chicago. As soon as we entered the auditorium, which was filled with students, members of the local clergy, and people from the community at large, the wail of police sirens drew steadily closer. Then a group of police officers burst through the doors at a run and announced that they had received a telephone tip warning that a bomb was planted in the hall. Of course, they wanted the building evacuated immediately and, as one officer suggested, "In view of the tension in the Middle East, the lecture should be canceled." Since this was not the first time that I had been subjected to such a ploy, I proposed that before the program was abandoned, the bomb squad should check out the hall. I also noted that if a bomb had been planted there — which I sincerely doubted — it was meant to injure me personally and would probably be on or near the stage.

When it turned out that the bomb squad could not find anything menacing in the hall, the sister in charge of the program sounded us out on how to proceed. The police still believed that, to be on the safe side, the lecture should be canceled and the hall evacuated. I was very strongly against it and explained to my hostess that ruses of this nature were essentially an extension of the terrorist tactics being used against Israel: airline hijackings, bombs planted in movie theaters and markets — anything that would disrupt normal civilian life. But my countrymen did not abandon flying; they didn't stop going to films or shopping in the markets. I could no more willingly get up and leave than the State of Israel could pack up and vanish because of violence and intimidation. And collapsing in the face of empty threats would only encourage more of this kind of blackmail. Repeating my earlier contention, I suggested, "If there's any bomb here — and you can't seem to find one — it would be directed against me and be somewhere on the stage. So I'll stand on the stage by myself. Let it be my risk and my risk alone."

The officer in charge turned to the sister with a shrug, as if to say "It's his life!" But then she made one of the most moving gestures I was ever to witness in the United States. Responding to my solution, she said, "No, Mr. Ambassador," and then, turning to the police, she added, "We will go on as planned, and I will sit on the stage next to the ambassador." And so she did. Need I add that there wasn't so much as a firecracker planted in that hall? In fact, for all the countless bomb threats that were phoned in to the local police with the aim of preventing my appearances, not a single bomb ever materialized.

I had not come to America to quarrel with its young. Nor did I have any illusion about "saving America from itself," for it was clear to me that the opposition I faced was a function of a purely American problem, some freak (and hopefully passing) revolt against the most cherished values of the American political tradition. I was stung, not by the personal frustration, but by the fact that in this greatest and proudest of democracies, young men and women were pouring so much energy into preventing a man from speaking his mind. Even more painful was the fact that in the very cream of America's institutions of higher learning, I was witnessing a self-righteous crusade based on sheer ignorance.

What did these young people really know of Israel? What did they know of the history of the Jewish people — its struggles and glories, its thousands of years of growth and creativity in the face of rejection? How did they account for hundreds of thousands of people abandoning their homes in Europe, Asia, North Africa, and even America, determined to build their lives in a sovereign Jewish state? Did they ever ask themselves why hundreds of generations of Jews had stubbornly held to the conviction that a Jewish state could be constituted only in the Land of Israel and nowhere else on earth? And how could they explain the obstinacy — perhaps even lunacy — of proclaiming that state despite horrendous odds? Born after the Holocaust, raised in an atmosphere of security and prosperity, these young people were untainted by the memories — be they immediate or vicarious — of that unspeakable human trauma. I could only salute their good fortune at never having experienced even the distant shock waves of that horror, though that did not exempt them from the obligation to know. But they did not want to know. They were determined not to know. And like all those who refuse to learn from history, they were doomed to repeat its mistakes.

The accusation of "murderer" is all too familiar in the annals of Jewish history. It was a favorite anti-Semitic slander that worked like a charm on the ignorant masses of Europe from the Dark Ages right through to modern times. And there was nothing at all new about turning on the Jews in times of domestic strain or crisis. "Read your history" was all I could really say to America's angry young men and women. But they were too involved in their rage, and history was presumably irrelevant — as was the fate of the millions of Jews they recommended be cast into some great unknown beyond the borders of Israel. They merely continued to hurl that age-old indictment at me in the ugly tradition of ignorance, prejudice, and hatred. How profoundly sad and shamed I felt for America then.

In sharp contrast to these fruitless confrontations, my encounters with American Jewry provided some of the most exhilarating moments of those years. I devoted much time and care to cultivating Israel's tie with the American Jewish community, and the concern, warmth, and love that America's Jews displayed for Israel gave me a deep sense of pride and confidence.

One of the intuitive understandings that binds Israel and the United States derives from the fact that both countries have been built through waves of immigration; both are culturally pluralistic societies that have managed to weave a strong national and social fabric without blotting out the ethnic identity of their various population groups. Within America's unique "melting pot," and in a way that is difficult to explain in rational terms, Israel provided the Jews with a "land of origin," a metaphorical "old country" with which they could identify and in which they could take pride. Not that the tie between the Jews and the Land of Israel was an American-Jewish innovation. Indeed, it has been a primary tenet of Jewish life for millennia. Yet in America — perhaps for the first time in history — this feeling found a climate of understanding. Rather than setting the Jews apart, it fostered their sense of belonging and legitimized their status. Along with America's Italian and Irish communities, its Germans and Scandinavians, Chinese and Mexicans, and all its other ethnic groups, the Jews finally had what has been described so successfully as "roots" (and what the blacks of America also began to seek in order to establish their status alongside America's other ethnic communities).

All this was patiently explained to me by none other than an Alabama-born air-force colonel who happened to be seated next to me on a commercial flight from Chicago to New York back in 1957. (I was head of Northern Command then but had been sent to the United States on a mission for the Israel Bonds.) Americans have a way of making friends easily, and he engaged me in conversation. When it came out that I was from Israel and a brigadier general, the natural bond between fellow soldiers (probably helped by the whiskey we had downed) soon had him talking to me without reserve. "I was brought up to — may I speak frankly, general? — to dislike Jews," he told me. But he immediately went on to explain why his attitude had changed; how, with the establishment of the State of Israel, the Jews had become "normal" Americans, freed of the stigma of being "strange." "D'ya understand that, general?" he asked me at the end of his painstaking monologue. That question may have been prompted by the look of astonishment on my face. But it was not the explanation that surprised me, just the extraordinary fact that he had been my mentor on the subject.

Two decades later, I can still find no better explanation for the fact that whatever befalls Israel — her triumphs and setbacks, her achievements and failures — serves as a kind of "index of self-respect" for American Jewry. In turn, the strong identification and unflagging support of a magnificent Jewish community like that of the United States is treasured by the citizens of a small country like Israel.

If I did not always see eye to eye with the American Jewish organizations, it may have been because the situation I discovered upon assuming my post was totally alien to me. Following a deeply ingrained pattern of Diaspora living, some of the leaders of the American Jewish community exercised their influence by means of a *shtadlan*, the traditional intermediary who had sought the favor of the ruling powers in Europe. Every modern president seemed to keep a kind of "court Jew" who served as a channel of communication between American Jewry and the incumbent administration. At first, for lack of choice, I too honored this mode of operation, though I patiently and cautiously tried to change it without offending the sensibilities of the Jewish community's leadership. I believed that the Israeli embassy should assume the principal role of handling Israel's affairs at all political levels and that it was entitled to avail itself of the help of Jews and non-Jews alike, as it saw fit. In fact, it was clear to me that if Israel could rely only on the support of the Jews in the United States, she would be faced with a major setback, so I asked the Jewish leadership to help me foster the support of the entire American people.

It goes without saying that the Jewish leaders in the United States were never under my control. They are not subject to the will of the Israeli government, and there is no foundation for the notion (which occasionally pops up when support for Israel on a sensitive issue is particularly strong) that they have no choice but to obey, even if Israeli policy is not to their liking. Today, with the spread of "single-issue politics" in the United States, I think it is easier to understand the mechanics of Jewish political support for Israel. In a way, the Jewish community pioneered the notion of the "grass-roots lobby" back in the days when lobbies were thought of strictly in terms of salaried professionals hired to influence Congress and the administration. Whatever the mechanics, however, there should be no doubt that the Jews of America have a mind of their own and speak it without hesitation.

A case in point was the sensitive issue of the struggle for Soviet Jewry during Senator Henry Jackson's campaign to prevent the Soviet Union from acquiring Most-Favored-Nation status in its relations with the United States. The heart of this issue was the Kremlin's promulgation of a law that required any Jew wishing to leave the Soviet Union to reimburse the government for the cost of his education. This "ransom" was a precondition for but not a guarantee of receiving an exit visa. The reaction of American Jewry was sharp and vocal, and when Senator Jackson began his campaign in the Senate he had the gratitude and full backing of the entire Jewish community. Yet this was entirely an American issue, a matter between the American people and their government. Israel had not written the Jackson amendment; but once it had been placed on the agenda of the American public, she certainly was not about to oppose it.

The truth is that I was approached by various Americans — from both within the administration and outside it — with the appeal that Israel not support any action that might disrupt Soviet-American relations. I could not agree to such requests. My country had a moral and human commitment to the fate of Soviet Jews and was determined to do everything in her power to guarantee their right to emigrate. Witty as always — though in deadly earnest — Kissinger asked me, "Do you expect us to exert economic pressure on the Soviet Union when you are always insisting that we separate our financial and military aid from political issues?" "The cases are not quite identical," I corrected him. "For us, the supply of arms is a matter of life and death. Are you suggesting that the same is true about granting Most-Favored-Nation status to the Soviet Union?"

Even so, the administration was sorely concerned about the effect the issue might have on the fabric of détente; and when Mrs. Meir saw the president on March 1, 1972, the subject was raised again. Nixon tried to explain why he believed the Senate's strategy was self-defeating. It was a mistake, he felt, to try and back a power like the Soviet Union into a corner, for the Kremlin simply could not accept dictates from the American Congress. "We can get better results if we don't hit them over the head," he told the prime minister. "You can be sure that I shall act to the best of my ability." Mrs. Meir wisely tried to avoid the issue of the Jackson amendment, but the president did not give up easily: "The problem is that the members of Congress say they are guided by the Jewish organizations here. The future of détente with the Soviet Union is liable to be foiled by the Congress. Personally, I can get better results for you."

Then Kissinger intervened in the conversation, and he chose to be brutally direct: "Don't let the Jewish leadership here put pressure on the Congress." The prime minister was left with no choice but to reply equally directly: "You must understand my

situation. I cannot tell the Jews of the United States not to concern themselves with their brethren in the Soviet Union!" But
Kissinger had a different solution in mind. "You don't have to tell
them not to be concerned with their brethren," he offered. "Just
see to it that the senators get the hint regarding the Jackson
amendment. That's sufficient . . ." He did not specify what kind
of "hint" he meant, but he added, "The ambassador has many
good friends in the Senate . . ." Kissinger was asking the impossible of us, and especially of me personally. I could not go about
undermining support for what was obviously a cardinal issue in
the eyes of the Jews of America and Israel alike. Nor could I possibly take any step that would be interpreted as stabbing Senator
Jackson in the back.

I had first met Henry Jackson at the end of 1968 and was immediately captivated by his charm. "It is only we small peoples who
can fully grasp the double struggle against external danger and
great domestic difficulties," he told me then. "It's a battle for survival, for life. It's that feeling which brings Israel so close to my
heart." I was gratified to hear of this "joint front" of small peoples
but was puzzled about why a United States senator felt moved to
speak in such a way. "I am of Norwegian origin," he explained,
"and as an American I can never forget my origin. We always
fought nature, and we were always particular about protecting our
independence against foreign invaders." During the campaign for
the right of Soviet Jews to emigrate, Jackson said to me with the
height of simplicity: "Just imagine. If Norway had instituted a law
similar to the one now in force in the Soviet Union, my father
would not have been able to emigrate to the United States, and I
wouldn't be an American now." The complete sincerity of his
dedication to human liberty always touched me deeply.

Jackson was among my most — and Israel's most — cherished
friends in the U.S. Senate. He combines humanity and liberalism
with political wisdom and a sober strategic grasp of the global
conflict, not to mention an exceptional sympathy and understanding for Israel and her needs. Had it been up to me, I would
have "appointed" him president of the United States. But Jackson
never gained the Democratic nomination for president, and I

therefore never faced the temptation of expressing praise and support for him to an extent unbecoming to the ambassador of a foreign country.

In the end, however, I was accused of doing that anyway — though not in regard to Henry Jackson. For all my caution about staying a safe distance away from U.S. domestic politics, on June 11, 1972 — before the two parties had chosen their candidates for president and the campaign had officially got under way — the *Washington Post* published a report by its Jerusalem correspondent, Yuval Elitzur, claiming that I had affirmed my preference for the reelection of President Nixon. Elitzur's report was based on an interview I had given to the Israeli radio soon after Nixon's return from the Moscow summit. In that interview, I noted that never in America's history had any president gone so far in his pro-Israeli declarations or in expressing America's commitment to Israel's security as President Nixon had in his address to Congress following his return from Moscow. That was a fact — and at most I was bringing it to the attention of the Israeli, not the American, public. I truly cannot understand how my words could have been interpreted as a "campaign speech" when the campaign had yet to begin and I was at any rate addressing myself to an audience that was not going to the polls.

Be that as it may, egged on by its Jerusalem correspondent, the *Washington Post* criticized me for intervening in American domestic affairs and went on to forecast that my statement would anger Israel's friends in the Democratic party and offend many Jewish supporters of both parties. Then, as if to fan the flames of its own fire, on June 15 it published a harsh editorial entitled "Israel's Undiplomatic Diplomat." But the *Post* had severely miscalculated. The chairman of the Democratic party, Lawrence O'Brien, invited me for a talk and affirmed that he knew I did not support either candidate and was not intervening in domestic politics. Some tried to press President Nixon's rival, Senator George McGovern, into publishing a sharply worded letter against me, but he refused to do so. And Senators Jackson and Stuart Symington — both Democrats and among Israel's most outstanding friends — wrote personal letters to the prime minister in praise of my work in Washington. Jackson even wanted to phone Mrs. Meir and dropped the idea only at my insistence.

As to the reaction of America's Jews, the fourteen hundred guests at a dinner sponsored by the Israel Bonds campaign welcomed me with a thunderous standing ovation. Here was my opportunity to set the record straight. "It's been a long time since I received as much prominence in the American media as I've been getting lately," I remarked. "All I did in that interview on Israeli radio was thank the U.S. administration and senators and congressmen of both parties for their aid to Israel. I shall repeat my sin before you here this evening," and I proceeded to express my gratitude once again. A hearty burst of applause indicated that I had not been misunderstood.

The flap continued to occupy the media for weeks, but in November, when the election results were in, it became clear beyond any doubt that my statement in Israel had little to do with Nixon's defeat of McGovern. The president had been reelected by a landslide vote, and only a man suffering from delusions could believe that any ambassador had that kind of influence over the American electorate.

Soon after the elections, I ran into John Mitchell in the lobby of a Washington hotel. Mitchell had left his post as attorney general to serve as chairman of the Committee to Re-elect the President and was obviously terribly pleased with himself and the fruits of his efforts when he said to me, "I hear you've decided to go into politics when you return home in the spring. If you need a good campaign manager, I'm available!" Needless to say, the black humor of that statement would only become evident many months later, as ·the agonies of Watergate gripped the United States. But by then I was home, and Israel was undergoing her own domestic turmoil that would soon accelerate my nascent political career beyond my wildest expectations.

Chapter Twelve

ISRAEL'S NEW PRIME MINISTER

GOLDA MEIR SMILED on March 1, 1973, when Nixon suggested that she leave me in the United States because he could put me to good use. The truth of the matter is that during my tenure in America, I had been approached three times to abandon my ambassadorship and assume a post in the Israeli cabinet. But each time it proved impossible to fulfill that promise — either because of internal problems in allocating cabinet portfolios or because no one could be found to replace me in Washington. The third of these approaches was made in the autumn of 1971, when Golda and I had a long talk at her home and it was decided that I should remain in Washington until the end of 1972, when I would be appointed to the cabinet. But the following summer, when I came to Israel in the role of a man on the (long) way to becoming a minister, the leaders of the Labor party again informed me that there was no chance of my joining the cabinet before the elections in October 1973. By then, I had no more illusions. If I wanted to reach the cabinet, I would have to take the arduous path of politics and not rely on promises. When I returned to Israel on March 11, 1973, no post was lined up for me. The time had yet to come for me to sink into nostalgia about my glorious past, but I still knew nothing of what the future held in store.

The Israel I came home to had a self-confident, almost smug aura to it, as befits a country far removed from the possibility of war. I spent the ensuing months getting settled again, going to South Africa on a mission for the United Jewish Appeal, and finally, being free of any other commitments, becoming heavily involved in the autumn election campaign. I lectured and attended rallies around the country, renewed old acquaintances, made new friendships, and studied the public mood. It was a crash course in local political ways and byways, but I was a diligent student. When the Labor party finally drew up its slate for the Knesset, I found myself in the twentieth spot — meaning that I was assured of at least a seat in the Knesset.

Then, on October 6, the election campaign came to an abrupt halt. At 8:30 A.M. on that Saturday, I received a phone call asking me to join the other former chiefs of staff for a talk with the defense minister at three o'clock the same afternoon. Calling such a meeting on a Saturday — our only day off in Israel — would have been strange enough. But that Saturday also happened to be Yom Kippur — the holiest day of the Hebrew calendar — making such a summons downright bizarre. The day before, my son, Yuval, had arrived home for his first weekend leave from the Navy Training Center where he was serving. No sooner had he arrived home, however, than he received orders to return to his base immediately. My son-in-law, who was a captain in a tank battalion in the Sinai, was supposed to enter the hospital the next day. But when he learned that Yuval had been recalled from leave, he likewise returned to his unit immediately. One didn't have to be a former chief of staff to realize that the IDF was on alert, but even so I never suspected war.

At two o'clock that afternoon, the air-raid sirens began to wail. An hour later, a group of former chiefs of staff gathered to hear Moshe Dayan review the situation. The faces around the room remained expressionless, concealing the stupefaction we all felt. On our way home, we paid a brief visit to the command post, and I felt a strange sensation being there. A tremendous battle was in the offing, and I was totally cut off from it. No one asked me for my advice; no one awaited my decisions.

During the first few days of the war, I accompanied the chief of staff, David Elazar ("Dado"), on his visits to the fronts and served as a sounding board whenever he asked my opinion. On the fourth day, however, I left the military sphere altogether when the finance minister, Pinhas Sapir, asked me to head an emergency-loan campaign. It was an ideal job for an ex-ambassador, and I consented — though without much enthusiasm.

When fighting is in progress, it is difficult for the former chief of staff in me to put his mind to raising money. Nonetheless, I did the best I could and tried to overcome my disappointment about being so far removed from the theater of war.

The elections were postponed until the end of December, and the Israeli public was still stricken when it went to the polls. Considering that they were exhausted, mourning their dead, and having difficulty in digesting recent events or comprehending the significance of them, the voters were merciful toward the Labor party. Not that there was any inclination to forgive the party's leaders or absolve them of their sins of omission. But many people were entranced by the prospect of the Geneva Conference and fervently clung to the hope that it would bring the peace they were yearning for. Labor supported the conference; the right-wing Likud vigorously opposed it, and I don't think that any Israeli political movement ever erred so seriously. The Geneva Conference was convened on December 21 — nine days before the elections — and it failed to bring peace to the Middle East. But it did rob the Likud of its chance to gain power. The Labor Alignment lost a few Knesset seats, but it had clearly won the elections.

At the same time, Labor's relative success failed to salvage the authority of the party's leading figures. Deep personal difference between the party's leaders — hitherto swept under the carpet — now came out into the open as the short-lived grass-roots protest movements raised an angry outcry against Golda Meir, Moshe Dayan, and others. Confusion and depression reigned at the frequently convened sessions of the Labor party's Central Committee. It was against this background that Golda Meir embarked upon the task of setting up a coalition and building a cabinet.

Exactly what induced Moshe Dayan and Shimon Peres — both members of the Labor party's Rafi faction — to refuse to serve in Golda's new cabinet and then reconsider their refusal has puzzled many people. They justified their unwillingness to join the cabinet by citing the party's decision to establish a minority government, but Golda nonetheless kept trying to win them over. When she failed, she offered me the post of defense minister. Naive as I was, it never occurred to me that my appointment was really no more than a ruse to lure Dayan back into the cabinet. I was led further astray when Dayan sent me a warm and friendly note congratulating me on my appointment and adding that he thought it was a good choice. On the morning of March 5, 1974, he even phoned me at home to ask whether he should sign certain documents or leave them for me to sign upon assuming my new post. I replied that I was not yet defense minister, but he countered: "Listen, I know politics. The Central Committee is going to approve the appointment of all the ministers today, and you are going to be defense minister."

As everyone knows, I did not become defense minister. Golda was still determined to step up the pressure on Dayan and Peres, and that same day she announced that she was reconsidering her willingness to present the cabinet to the Knesset. The party Central Committee was in an uproar, and in addressing its meeting I warned that "elections are no game. If we want to halt the process of internal disintegration, we must form a cabinet!" My words were greeted by prolonged loud applause, and cynics later alleged that these cheers were what induced Dayan and Peres to return to the cabinet. But their explanation had a far more noble ring to it.

After that meeting of the Central Committee on March 5, the Knesset Foreign Affairs and Defense Committee convened to study reports indicating that the Syrians intended to renew the fighting. (Similar reports had been received before, though the war they forecast never materialized.) In any event, late that night, at the conclusion of a cabinet meeting, Dayan and Peres notified Golda that in view of the latest military developments, they would agree to join her new cabinet. Golda wept for joy, and my candidacy for defense minister was "terminated." The reentry of Dayan and Peres brought the National Religious party in its wake. When the cabinet was finally presented for the Knesset's approval on March 10, 1974, I was its minister of labor. It was a little less than I had expected — and a little more than some of my colleagues wished me.

With the party's wounds barely patched up, we all sat down to work. But Mrs. Meir's government proved to be extremely short-lived. On April 11 the prime minister decided to resign — and this time her decision was irrevocable. I am in no position to enumerate her reasons for doing so. The most I can say is that the first month of her new cabinet's term was all but totally overshadowed by the findings of the Agranat Commission, which deserve a measure of comment.

The Agranat Commission was established soon after the Yom Kippur War to investigate the conduct of the government and the military on the eve of the war and during the course of the fighting. It was an inquiry commission, not a court of law, and it did not operate according to standard judicial procedure (cross-examining witnesses and the like); yet its findings enjoyed the standing of a court verdict. The most startling conclusion of its interim report was that responsibility for misreading the situation on the eve of the war and for the delayed mobilization lay exclusively with the chief of staff. The civilian leadership was found blameless. When the report's findings were made known to Dado, he was left with no choice but to resign. The public, however, could not accept the justice of placing the blame exclusively on the military, and a great uproar ensued. I viewed the report as establishing a very dangerous precedent. It was clear to me that as soon as the government accepts the recommendations of the military, both share responsibility for the consequences. Any other principle would inevitably undermine the chief of staff's faith in the government's authority and make a shambles of the ironclad rule that the military is subject to the country's civilian leadership.

Mrs. Meir was equally distressed by the results of the interim report and said that even though the commission had praised her conduct, she would find it difficult to continue as prime minister. In the subsequent public outcry, it was Dayan's resignation that the people were calling for. But in the end, it was Golda who tendered her own and — as the rules of parliamentary democracy dictate — brought the entire cabinet down with her. Once again the Labor party was in turmoil as internal conflicts raged within its ranks.

Many people considered Finance Minister Pinhas Sapir a natural choice for prime minister. He had great influence within the party, and if he had wanted the post there is no doubt that he would have gained it. Even when Sapir announced that he would not accept the position, many still believed that he would ultimately come around and "bow to the party's will" — a ritual formula consecrated by an entire generation. Shimon Peres was one of the first to grasp that Sapir was in earnest and would stick by his refusal. The fact is he began canvassing support for his own candidacy while others (myself included) were still clinging to the hope of convincing Sapir.

It was in this context that Peres invited me to lunch and treated me to some smooth talk. "In the final event, the two of us will find ourselves competing for the prime ministership," he told me. "Let us learn from the experience of our older colleagues. Allon and Dayan fought one another, sapped each other's strength, and neither of them became prime minister. Let's conclude a gentleman's agreement to hold a fair contest. Whoever loses will accept the decision in good spirit and be loyal to the winner." I was wary and my inclination was not to believe a word he said. Moreover, I was determined that if he became the next prime minister, I would not set foot in the cabinet. But I certainly had no objection to the terms he suggested, so I replied tersely, "Agreed."

At the time, I was still doubtful that Sapir's refusal was final. But when he personally assured me that it was and that he was prepared to back my candidacy, the contest commenced. Since I was new to the party, support from Sapir and his followers was vital for me, especially since I began my campaign only a week before the date fixed for the Central Committee's vote on the prime ministership. My supporters were cautiously pessimistic, and I too had doubts about the chances of winning. It was only in January that I had entered the Knesset. I had assumed my first cabinet appointment in March. Now, in April, could I honestly expect the party to give me its full backing?

The Central Committee was scheduled to convene on April 22 to choose the party's candidate for prime minister, but just before

that meeting was due to open, "Doctor" Ezer Weizman intervened and dropped his bombshell. In his inimitable narrative
style, he depicted the events of May 23, 1967, on the eve of the
Six Day War, giving a farfetched version of my condition that day.
The timing of the revelation spoke volumes about his motives,
and I could not help recalling Weizman's frequent boast: "I am
not a member of Mapai, but I am a friend of Peres" (Hebrew
employs the same word for "member" and "friend"). Was Weizman now making his own modest contribution to what Peres had
referred to as a "fair contest"?

Gloomy as my prospects may have appeared, the tally of the
Central Committee's secret ballot was 298 votes for me as against
254 for Peres. By this narrow margin, I was elected the party's
candidate for prime minister. Despite the late hour, a stream of
flowers, visitors, well-wishers, and phone calls engulfed my
home. Deeply moved, I thanked them all. Only to my closest
confidants did I confess that this was not how I had imagined I
would ever reach the prime ministership — in the harsh after-
math of the Yom Kippur War, with the disintegration of the
party's veteran leadership.

My next step was to form a government. But while I was busy
picking up the pieces of the previous coalition, Dr. Kissinger was
at work trying to bridge the gap between Israel and Syria in order
to conclude an agreement for the disengagement of forces. Mrs.
Meir co-opted Peres and me onto the Israeli negotiating team,
and while Kissinger shuttled back and forth, we were forced to
conform to his timetable. That left me little time for talks with
possible coalition partners, though the construction of a government was not going to be a simple matter. The National Religious
party (NRP), a traditional partner in Labor-led coalitions, was
coming increasingly under the influence of its younger leaders,
whose views were identical with those of the Likud. They now
took advantage of my "dovish" image to boost their challenge to
the veteran leadership within their own party. Finally, on May
19, 1974, after prolonged and fierce discussion, Labor's Central
Committee decided in favor of forming a cabinet based on sixty-
one Knesset votes (in conjunction with the Independent Liberals

and the Civic Rights Movement). Sixty-one left us with a mere one-vote margin in the Knesset, but the decision left the door open for the NRP to join the government (which it did in the following October).

The time had come to tackle the problem of apportioning cabinet portfolios. I should make it clear that an Israeli prime minister is not free to nominate the ministers of his choice. The question of whether or not he will be capable of working with them — like his opinion of their suitability for specific posts — carries no weight in our form of democracy. The other coalition partners decide who is to represent them in the cabinet, and they are not even bound to consult the prime minister, let alone seek his consent. In fact, a Labor prime minister does not even have a decisive say about the ministers who come from his own party. Yigal Allon was one of our finest commanders during the War of Independence, and I regarded him as the most suitable choice for defense minister. I did not consider Shimon Peres suitable, since he had never fought in the IDF and his expertise in arms purchasing did not make up for that lack of experience. But the choice was not up to me. If Peres had failed to receive the defense portfolio, the Rafi faction of the Labor party would have withheld its support from the new cabinet, thereby ripping the party asunder. So after consultations with Pinhas Sapir and other colleagues, I accepted Peres as defense minister — albeit with a heavy heart. It was an error I would regret and whose price I would pay in full.

I was not guided by "personal accounts" in taking the foreign affairs portfolio from Abba Eban. It was simply my conviction that, after he had served in that post for nine years, Israel deserved a foreign minister with a fresh approach. I offered the job to Yigal Allon, along with the post of deputy prime minister (which he had filled in the cabinets of Levi Eshkol and Golda Meir), and invited Eban to take the information portfolio. Eban was offended, but I think he erred. During his many years as foreign minister, he had essentially explained policies formulated by others, rather than generate his own political thinking. I had a chance to observe this while serving in Washington. Eban's political role was of a most

limited nature — at least in Mrs. Meir's government, where policy was shaped by the prime minister with the active participation
of Moshe Dayan and in consultation with other ministers. I truly
believed that Eban was well matched to the task I had in mind for
him, and at the behest of veteran Mapai colleagues I visited him
at his home in Jerusalem and asked him to join my cabinet. But
his refusal was vigorous, and that was his choice to make.

On June 3, 1974, I was finally able to present my cabinet to the
Knesset and received its approval. Being prime minister is very
different from being a candidate for the post. I was almost physi-
cally aware of the enormous weight of responsibility that I now
bore. The wounds of the Israeli people were still fresh and painful
after the recent war, and deep fissures undermined its faith in its
leaders and government. As I presented my cabinet to our legisla-
ture, I outlined its objectives and guidelines for myself. The
disengagement-of-forces agreement with Egypt — already being
implemented — and a similar agreement with Syria signed three
days before would stabilize the cease-fire on both fronts. Yet no
one had any doubts that these agreements were of limited duration. I wanted to ensure that political negotiations continued and
to influence their direction. I did not want us merely to respond
to outside initiatives — be they American or Arab. At the same
time, it was necessary to make a supreme effort to strengthen the
IDF by acquiring a maximum in arms and military equipment
from the United States in a minimum of time. Only a very powerful IDF could convince the Arab leaders that the only course
open to them was political negotiations. Moreover, the terrorists'
successes in their recent attacks on the towns of Kiriat Shmonah
and Ma'alot made it necessary to take special measures in an antiterrorist campaign.

We also faced a number of pressing problems in the domestic
sphere. Defense expenditure and the long mobilization since the
war had placed great stress on the economy. Immigration was at
an ebb, with a concomitant effect on the progress of housing and
development. Each of these problems would have to be dealt
with in turn, but I had no doubt that top priority had to focus on
moving away from war and toward some state of peace. The situa-

tion was still very precarious. Even Dr. Kissinger, who had masterminded the two disengagement-of-forces agreements, gave the more solid of them (with Egypt) no more than a year. I had not inherited a simple situation.

Less than two weeks after I assumed office, we experienced a political event unprecedented in Israel's history: the visit of an American president. At the time, the Watergate affair had severely eroded Nixon's presidency, but his Middle East policy — conducted by Secretary of State Kissinger — gave the president an exceptional opportunity to alter the global balance of power by restoring the primacy of the United States' influence in the Middle East. Since the United States had played an indispensable role in stabilizing the cease-fire and achieving the disengagement agreements with Egypt and Syria, Nixon came to the Middle East to reap the fruits of his success. If he believed or hoped that he would thereby quell the anger of American public opinion and fend off the attacks directed against him in his own country, his hopes were to be dashed. The fate of one of the most pro-Israeli presidents had already been sealed.

In preparation for President Nixon's visit, we did our homework — hastily, but very thoroughly. The disengagement agreements with Syria and Egypt were structured on three levels: open and direct agreements between Israel and each of the two Arab states; reciprocal undertakings that Israel and the two Arab states had each submitted to the United States (without these undertakings appearing in the documents signed by the parties); and the American undertakings to Israel (and perhaps to Egypt and Syria) in return for entering into the agreements. I was glad of an opportunity to talk to the president about our readiness to continue the negotiating process and the need to ensure that the American commitments to Israel would be fulfilled in every sphere — above all, in strengthening Israel's military power and her economy.

When Nixon arrived on June 16, our citizens stood on the road from the airport to Jerusalem to greet the president who had proved himself such a staunch friend. We could not compete with the cheering multitudes that welcomed Nixon in Cairo, but I assume that he grasped the difference: in Israel, the demonstration was entirely spontaneous. The president failed to conceal his emotion at the sight of a welcoming crowd. "Thank you, thank you," he repeated, visibly moved. "They know what I've done for Israel."

The main subject of my talks with the president was the next stage in political negotiations between Israel and her neighbors. We both agreed that the coming set of talks should be undertaken with Egypt, but I stressed that the outcome of such negotiations could not be limited to a further Israeli withdrawal without some matching political quid pro quo. "Any further agreement that does not contain a meaningful political component will not be a further step toward peace," I told him.

Nixon's impression was that Egypt, in particular, was ready to advance toward a political solution — even though its terms for peace remained unchanged (a total Israeli withdrawal to the June 4, 1967, lines). Yet the president was convinced that Egypt no longer believed in a military solution, but was eager to embark on a program of economic development and improve living standards. "I have come to hear your ideas," he told me, "and we shall go home and formulate our own policy. There will be visits by your people to the United States, and Kissinger may come back to the region to explore more clearly defined ideas."

After all I have written about Richard Nixon in this book, it should not come as a surprise that his resignation — under circumstances unprecedented in American history — caused me deep regret. I was familiar with his virtues and his faults, both of which he possessed in abundance. But above all I had great respect for his broad vision and understanding of global politics. Nixon understood well that the United States could not counter the Soviet Union's aggressive designs unless it spoke from a position of strength, and his doctrine that the United States should help those nations willing to help themselves found very concrete expression in regard to Israel. I cannot deny that we had some tough arguments with Nixon's administration; but neither can I forget that Nixon helped to provide Israel with more arms than any other American president. For this and for his strict avoidance of imposing an unwanted political solution on Israel, he is deserving of this country's profound gratitude.

When Nixon left office, the ideas we had discussed about further negotiations did not fade away. On the contrary, they were pursued and refined over the next eight months until Dr. Kissinger decided to embark on his shuttle mission to secure an interim agreement between Israel and Egypt. My first opportunity to continue the discussion of this issue came on September 10, 1974, when I arrived in Washington for talks with President Ford.

I was acquainted with Gerald Ford from my tenure as ambassador, when he was still House minority leader. Now we were both new in our posts and glad to renew our old friendship. Ford's words of support for Israel in many ways echoed those of his predecessor, and like Nixon he spoke in general terms during our first meeting, leaving details to Kissinger. At our second meeting, however, we talked at greater length about the prospects of a political settlement in the Middle East.

Both Ford and Kissinger felt that an overall agreement was beyond our reach at present. Ford characterized such an agreement as "utopian," while Kissinger felt it was a sure formula for "deadlock." I again explained that we were fully prepared to reach peace by phases, but I did not omit to mention the pitfalls of such an approach. If we were to give up a "piece of land" without getting a "piece of peace" in exchange, the process would end with Israel having relinquished everything she held without achieving her goal. I explained to the president that considerable criticism had been voiced in Israel regarding my policy of a "step by step" approach toward peace. Many of my countrymen felt that if war was inevitable, we would be better off if it broke out while we were deployed along the present lines — not after the IDF had withdrawn further into the Sinai. That is why I felt it imperative for any further agreement to involve a political step toward peace. I also believed it must remain in force long enough for us to observe the Arabs' intentions.

The other subject of our talk that morning was the arms request we had submitted following the conclusion of the disengagement-of-forces agreements with Egypt and Syria. Actually, there were three lists before the president: an emergency list for immediate needs and two long-term lists. It was the emergency list that I was most anxious about, but as soon as the meeting opened I realized that the president was not yet prepared to give me any answer. He apologized for the delay and promised that he would have his reply for me at our third and final meeting the next day, so there was nothing more to be said about that. But I did take great pains to explain why agreement on long-term deliveries was necessary for both our countries. We were eager to reduce tensions with the Pentagon by allaying fears that weapons would be taken out of U.S. army stores (as had happened during the Yom Kippur War). In addition, the IDF needed a clear picture of future arms deliveries in order to plan its own strategy and training programs. Unfortunately, this question of long-term commitments would later develop into one of the major raw spots in our relations with the Ford administration.

That evening the president hosted an official state dinner for me. When the speeches were over and the festive concert had reached its end, the next item was a ball! Beaming and full of self-assurance, the president bore down on Leah, bowed slightly, and swept her off into the brightly lit ballroom. I was in a spot. If only I could dance — even poorly! If only someone would get in ahead of me and invite Mrs. Ford onto the dance floor. But miracles of that nature do not occur at the White House. Deciding to adopt the tactics I follow in every sphere, I strode over to Mrs. Ford, who rose at my approach, obviously convinced that I was about to invite her to dance. But swallowing hard, I explained, "I'm sorry, Mrs. Ford, but I simply don't know how to dance. Not a step. And I wouldn't dream of mauling your toes." Now that the worst was over (or so I deluded myself), I was pleased to see the First Lady rewarding me with a warm smile. But that smile carried a double meaning. "Have no fear, Mr. Prime Minister," she reassured me. "When I was a young woman, I used to teach dance, and I protected my toes from men far less skillful than you. Come along."

My defenses breached, the next thing I can remember I was

being led by Mrs. Ford and doing my humble best to keep the damage to a minimum. After midnight, with the president still as spry as if he had just had a good night's sleep, Dr. Kissinger (himself no great dancer) came to my rescue and managed to get me off the dance floor. If he had never done anything else for Israel, I would still be eternally grateful to Kissinger for that small mercy.

Prior to my third meeting with President Ford, Kissinger came to see me at Blair House, bringing the emergency list of military supplies as approved by President Ford. At first glance, I could see that most of the items had been approved for early delivery — including such weapons as cluster bombs, armament components, tanks, armored personnel carriers, and artillery — and when I arrived at the White House, I thanked the president. In the subsequent discussion, it was agreed that Dr. Kissinger would come to the Middle East in October, when we could discuss our thoughts about an interim agreement with Egypt in greater detail. I left the president with a sense of gratification. When there is understanding on political issues, and the president approves delivery of $750 million worth of arms in the course of seven months, an Israeli prime minister can afford to define his visit as successful.

Upon my return to Israel, we began to prepare for Kissinger's forthcoming visit by formulating a detailed plan for an interim agreement with Egypt. It was clear that we were prepared to withdraw our forces farther back in the Sinai peninsula. The two questions were how far back and what we wanted in return. I had no doubts on the latter score: what we were aiming for was termination of the state of belligerency with Egypt. In return, we would be prepared to pull our forces back another thirty to fifty kilometers. I should explain immediately — since the subject holds the key to all discussions about the interim agreement — that there were two elements of value in the Sinai (bargaining cards, if you will). The first was the oil fields around Abu Rodeis (at the peninsula's western extremity, near the Gulf of Suez), which were mainly of economic value. The second was the Gidi and Mitla passes, of cardinal strategic value, also in the western half of the peninsula. Those passes were the gateway to the Sinai, and the Egyptians would have to provide us with a pretty strong reason for giving them up.

When Dr. Kissinger arrived in Israel on October 12, after making his rounds of the capitals of Egypt, Syria, and Jordan, his report on the mood in the Arab world did not bode well for immediate progress toward an interim agreement. It seemed that we would have to wait for the outcome of the forthcoming Arab summit conference at Rabat, since our three prospective negotiating partners were very much divided on the issues to be discussed there.

Egypt was talking in terms of an Israeli withdrawal to the El Arish–Ras Mohammed line — along the entire length of the peninsula and well to the east of the passes. But Sadat showed very little inclination to offer much in return — and certainly neither peace nor even a termination of the state of belligerency. In a broader context, Egypt was also prepared, in conjunction with Jordan, to negotiate with us about the future of the Palestinians; but Sadat preferred to wait and see what the Rabat Conference would decide on this matter. The Syrians, on the other hand, were concerned that they would find themselves isolated if Egypt reached a separate agreement with Israel, and they were clearly determined to thwart that possibility. Finally, King Hussein was very anxious about what his fate would be at the hands of the Rabat summiteers. Kissinger and his aides suspected that the summit would deprive Jordan of the right to negotiate over the West Bank and "crown" the PLO as the sole representative of the Palestinian people.

It was not a very encouraging picture. And although we would obviously have to await the results of the Rabat summit before pursuing the interim negotiations, Kissinger was meanwhile interested in sounding out the sides. So now it was our turn to brief him.

I told the secretary of state that despite his conviction that Egypt would not be amenable to it, our political objective remained unchanged: termination of the state of belligerency. In return, we were prepared to withdraw to a depth of thirty kilometers in some places, fifty in others. He asked for a map "so that we know precisely what we are talking about." But I objected. It was still too early to draw up precise lines. I was sure, however, that Sadat had his sights on both the oil wells of Abu Rodeis and the Gidi and Mitla passes, so I made it clear to Kissinger that a withdrawal of thirty to fifty kilometers meant that the eastern parts of the passes might still be retained by Israel. Kissinger was not enthusiastic about either part of our proposal and did not believe that Egypt would agree. Above all, he saw no hope for terminating the state of belligerency, but he was prepared to examine the possibility of basing the agreement on certain elements of nonbelligerency. Such a course might, in effect, take Egypt out of the active conflict. That was the best he could offer us now.

When Kissinger left Israel, he made another tour of the Arab capitals and promised to report his impressions through the American ambassador to Israel, Kenneth Keating. Those subsequent impressions contained nothing new. Egypt was willing to advance toward a further agreement with Israel (though the gap between its positions and ours was substantial), but Sadat would reach a final decision on the question only after the Rabat summit. The Syrians, on the other hand, would urge the summit conference to adopt a strong resolution opposing any separate Egyptian–Israeli deal (as well as the very notion of interim agreements) and in favor of convening the Geneva Conference with the participation of PLO representatives. There was nothing to do now but await the results from Rabat.

The summit found King Hussein in less than splendid isolation on the Palestinian issue. Left with no other choice, and in an attempt to extricate himself from his isolation, he added his own voice to the general chorus and voted for a resolution depriving him of the right to negotiate the future of the West Bank. I learned an important lesson from Sadat's conduct at the summit. Shortly before the conference, Hussein had visited Egypt. At the conclusion of his talks with Sadat, the two leaders had issued a joint communiqué specifically recognizing Hussein's right to negotiate on the future of the West Bank. But no trace of this agreement remained in the Egyptian position at Rabat. When Sadat realized which way the wind was blowing, he threw his vigorous support behind the PLO as the sole representative of the Palestinians. His move was a warning signal to me. If Sadat was capable of breaking an agreement with a fellow Arab leader, how was he likely to treat an agreement with Israel if other Arab states placed him under pressure? The results of the Rabat summit reinforced my feeling that the most important part of any agreement with Egypt must not be the commitments it contained but the concrete conditions it established on the ground.

Now, however, it was far from certain that negotiations with Egypt were still possible, since Syria had persuaded the summit to work for an early resumption of the Geneva Conference and to declare that "there can be no separate peace agreement." Would Egypt nonetheless move toward achieving a separate agreement with us? And if, for lack of choice, the Geneva Conference was reconvened and Syria refused to attend unless we negotiated with the PLO (which was out of the question for us), would Egypt agree to go it alone at Geneva?

With these uncertainties hovering in the background, Kissinger returned to the Middle East in November 1974. The principal question then was whether or not the previous guidelines for resuming negotiations with Egypt were still valid in light of the Rabat Conference. Kissinger and his aides depicted Syria's President Hafez Assad in an arrogant mood following his triumph at Rabat. Assad believed that Egypt was now as isolated as Jordan, and Jordan needed Syria more than it needed Egypt. Yet the Americans' impressions of Egypt's position were rather more encouraging. Sadat was willing to continue the negotiations through American mediation, though the Rabat Conference had provided him with a convenient excuse to harden his line. Under the circumstances, it was more difficult for him to enter into a separate agreement with Israel, and he would not be able to make such a "sacrifice" unless his far-reaching demands were met by Israel. At the same time, his political quid pro quo would have to be reduced. Furthermore, Leonid Brezhnev was scheduled to visit Cairo in January 1975, and the Egyptians were using his visit as a warning to the United States that the Soviet option was still open to them. Unless the Americans took steps to appease them, the Egyptians would restore their intimate ties with the Soviet Union.

Kissinger understood Sadat's game precisely and proposed that we initiate negotiations with Egypt but not conclude any agreement prior to Brezhnev's visit. I saw the merits of his proposal from the United States' point of view, but I did not think it would be to our own advantage. We preferred to wait until Brezhnev had completed his visit to Cairo. The situation could be reconsidered in January and February 1975.

It turned out that Brezhnev's visit to Cairo was postponed (which at least indicated that something had gone awry between Egypt and the Soviet Union), and Kissinger was scheduled to visit Israel again on February 10, 1975, after meeting with Sadat in Egypt. In anticipation of that visit, I began to press for the adoption of a more realistic policy. If an agreement on the termination of belligerency was unattainable, we should think in terms of a more modest agreement. It made sense to focus our efforts on a withdrawal of thirty to fifty kilometers (while trying to retain control of the oil fields and the passes) in return for a stabilization of the cease-fire and some positive political features. I also believed that if faced with the choice of relinquishing either the passes or the oil fields, it would be preferable to give up the oil. Not only were the passes of strategic importance, but giving Egypt the oil fields would be a further inducement for it to observe an agreement to the letter. If Egypt were pumping oil with the IDF stationed six or seven kilometers from its installations, any violation of the agreement would have to be weighed against the economic loss it would entail. It was clear that the chances of an agreement being honored were in direct proportion to the interest each side had in keeping it.

When Kissinger came in February, he was convinced that of the various options open to us a partial agreement with Egypt had the best chance of success. Stagnation was no option, and the Geneva Conference would probably lead to stalemate — or worse, an open rift between Israel and the United States on the question of final borders. He therefore concluded that he would return to the Middle East in March and embark on a shuttle mission to secure such a partial agreement. Even if the prospects weren't glowing — as far as I could see — it was certainly worth a try.

Chapter Thirteen

THE INTERIM AGREEMENT
WITH EGYPT

As FEW IN Israel are likely to forget, in March Kissinger came, Kissinger shuttled, and Kissinger left without securing an interim agreement between Israel and Egypt. The problem was not the political element of the agreement, since both sides agreed on a formula that committed them to "the non-use of force" and to solving the conflict by peaceful means. We also continued to press for certain elements of nonbelligerency (reducing the propaganda war, moderation of the economic boycott, and permitting the passage of Israeli merchandise and Israeli-manned vessels under foreign flags through the Suez Canal). But we could not reach agreement on the depth of Israel's withdrawal in return for these political concessions.

When Kissinger first arrived, he brought with him a map drawn up by Egypt's war minister, Abdel Gamasi. It was based on a purely topographical analysis as to where each country's possible defense line could be established in the Sinai. For Israel's defense, Gamasi proposed a line some fifteen to twenty kilometers west of the international border (still inside the Sinai but well to the east of the passes), while the Egyptian army would likewise move forward to the east of the passes and therefore control them. The two armies would be separated by a buffer zone devoid of their troops.

I could see that the Americans were very impressed with Gamasi's analysis, but we could not accept the Egyptian demand for such a deep withdrawal. Instead, our negotiating team (composed of Allon, Peres, and me) offered to pull back to a line west of the passes and stipulated that the Egyptian army must not advance into the area vacated by the IDF. Furthermore, the mandate of the UN peacekeeping force could be extended for one year but the agreement must remain in force for several years. This proposal left us more room to withdraw along the Gulf of Suez (giving up the oil fields), rather than into the heart of the Sinai. However, I again told Kissinger that in return for an agreement to terminate the state of belligerency, we were willing to withdraw to the El Arish–Ras Mohammed line, well to the east of the passes.

During one of Kissinger's sessions in Jerusalem, I suggested that he ask Sadat privately whether he would agree to conclude a separate and full peace agreement with Israel in return for most — or possibly all — of the Sinai. Upon returning from his next trip to Egypt, he told me: "Sadat can't conclude a separate peace agreement, so the question of what Israel is prepared to pay in return is not relevant now." At the same time, in another conversation with Kissinger, Sadat said that in return for an Israeli withdrawal to a distance of about fifteen to twenty kilometers from the international border, "termination of belligerency could be considered."

Kissinger kept up his shuttle trips, forcing us to follow a strenuous regimen. No sooner had my own timetable been arranged than everything was disrupted by Kissinger's schedule. He would leave at abnormal hours, arrive at even more eccentric times, and often meet us for marathon talks that ignored the difference between day and night. No matter when he turned up, though, Kissinger always looked as if he had just had ten hours of sound sleep.

By March 20 Egypt had narrowed the options for solving the territorial question to two alternative proposals. Under the first, both countries would hold the passes — the western parts controlled by Egypt, the eastern parts by Israel — while the two armies would be separated by a ten- to twenty-kilometer buffer zone controlled by UN forces. The second variation was that the armies of Egypt and Israel would take up positions outside and at an equal distance from the passes, Israel to the east and Egypt to the west, while the zone in between would come under UN control. Egypt would not consent to any Israeli presence in the buffer zone, so that we would have to remove our early-warning installation from Um Hashiva. Both these proposals meant that the Egyptian army would advance twenty to thirty kilometers from its existing lines, while the IDF would have to withdraw some fifty to seventy kilometers. The Egyptians also demanded the Abu Rodeis oil fields.

Our counterproposal was that the IDF would withdraw to the center of the passes, with the Egyptian army advancing as far as present IDF positions (this way, we could hold on to our early-warning installations). At a later stage, we agreed to a further concession: the IDF would withdraw as far as the eastern part of the passes and Egypt would receive the oil fields as an enclave. Both sides agreed on "the non-use of force" formula, and we dropped our demand for implementing the aspects of nonbelligerency mentioned earlier. However, the Egyptians refused to be bound by the agreement for more than two years.

Kissinger came and went, but despite his seemingly endless store of energy, the gap did not narrow on three main issues: the depth of Israel's withdrawal and the extent of the Egyptian advance; the Israeli early-warning installation at Um Hashiva; and the duration of the agreement.

During one of our conversations, Kissinger told me that Sadat had posed a question to him: "Does the Israeli government really want to achieve peace? Have the Israelis rid themselves of their security psychoses?" Kissinger replied that he believed in Israel's desire for peace and now advised me to send a letter to Sadat. I wrote the letter and sent it with the secretary of state on his next trip to Egypt. When he returned he told me, "Sadat read it in my presence. He was deeply moved." Be that as it may, I never received an answer.

As time passed, Kissinger grew more and more impatient, and he began to employ strong language to indicate his displeasure. Some of it was familiar to me from my term in Washington: "This will be a setback for me personally, certainly, but that's not the point. The main thing is how the president perceives it. The Soviets will be happy, and there will be an immediate Arab–Soviet demand to reconvene the Geneva Conference. Under the circumstances, I can't promise you anything about American policy."

Finally, downcast and sober, Kissinger prepared to make it

known that his efforts had failed. The announcement would be issued at the last stop of his tour — Israel — possibly with the purpose of hinting that we were to blame for the situation. The extent of the crisis was obvious to me even before it broke. We would have to struggle to win American public opinion by proving that Egypt demanded too much and was prepared to give us little in return. It would be a difficult period — perhaps very difficult.

Before announcing the termination of his mission, Kissinger made a short visit to Riyadh to explain the situation to the Saudis, and while he was there I convened the cabinet. In the midst of that meeting an urgent message arrived from the president:

> Kissinger has notified me of the forthcoming suspension of his mission. I wish to express my profound disappointment over Israel's attitude in the course of the negotiations. From our conversations, you know . . . the great importance I attached to the success of the United States' efforts to achieve an agreement. Kissinger's mission, encouraged by your government, expresses vital United States interests in the region. Failure of the negotiations will have a far-reaching impact on the region and on our relations. I have given instructions for a reassessment of United States policy in the region, including our relations with Israel, with the aim of ensuring that overall American interests . . . are protected. You will be notified of our decision.

If the president hoped that his letter would have a softening effect on the will of the Israeli cabinet, its threatening tone achieved exactly the opposite. Even the most hesitant members of the cabinet now resolved that the negotiating team must remain adamant on its policy.

That evening, I met Dr. Kissinger for what turned out to be the most painful conversation we had ever had. Considering the president's message, I did not altogether trust Kissinger's promise to avoid placing the blame for the breakdown of the shuttle mission upon Israel. He tried to remain composed but could scarcely conceal his profound disappointment, and for the first time he hinted that there had been misunderstandings between the two of us. This was related to a private talk we had had concerning

Israel's willingness to undertake a more significant withdrawal in the Sinai. But I certainly never intended to leave Kissinger with the impression that Israel would be willing to undertake a far-reaching withdrawal in return for anything less than termination of belligerency.

"We have put aside our demand for a termination of belligerency," I told him. "We have agreed to the term 'non-use of force,' which signifies far less than 'termination of belligerency.' Even so, we are prepared to hand the oil fields over to the Egyptians and pull back as far as the eastern part of the passes, with all the risks that entails. We were prepared to allow the Egyptian army to advance from its present positions and occupy the present buffer zone, as well as set up two forward positions at the western entrances to the passes. All of us have displayed considerable flexibility and goodwill to ensure the success of your mission. Under the circumstances, to accuse Israel of fostering expectations and then failing to live up to them, instead of laying the blame on Egypt's intransigence, is a distortion of the facts."

During the evening of Saturday, March 22, when the negotiating team held its final meeting with Dr. Kissinger, even those of us who urged him to return to Egypt and make one last attempt to bridge the gap no longer believed that there was any hope. Kissinger refused. His mission was at an end. The following morning, I accompanied the secretary of state to the airport, where we closeted ourselves in a conference room for a last private talk.

It was important to me that Kissinger understand how deeply I regretted the failure of his mission, for both national and personal reasons. I wanted an Israeli-Egyptian agreement very much — so much, in fact, that we had essentially agreed to a withdrawal in the Sinai without getting a substantive political concession from Egypt. And we were still prepared to accept those terms, despite the sharp criticism being voiced in Israel. I understood that our present position would create tension between Israel and the United States, and nobody knew better than Kissinger how hard I had worked as ambassador to build up a strong relationship between our two countries.

I also felt sad because of the special relationship that Kissinger and I had developed over the years. It was based on mutual trust and cooperation and had proved itself in moments of crisis. "I am fully aware that the situation is fraught with dangers," I told him, including a resumption of hostilities. "And that is not just a political problem for me. I regard every IDF soldier as my responsibility — almost as if he were my son. You know that my own son is in command of a tank platoon on the front line in the Sinai. My daughter's husband commands a tank battalion there. In the event of war, I know what their fate might be. But Israel is unable to accept the agreement on the present terms, and there is nothing I can do but carry that heavy burden of responsibility — the national as well as the personal."

I don't recall ever having seen Kissinger so moved. He may have wished to reply, but his voice cracked with emotion. It was time to go out to the plane, and as we issued a farewell statement he was incapable of suppressing his feelings. In addition to this upset over the failure of his mission, I could see his inner turmoil, as a Jew and as an American. And his emotion was contagious. Some of America's most renowned television and press journalists stood unashamedly wiping tears from their eyes. In the course of time, when I came to meet them again on various occasions, more than one confessed to me: "That day at the airport, I just couldn't control myself. All of a sudden I found myself crying." When Kissinger's plane took off, I stood watching until it had become a tiny speck against the sky. Personal feelings are of little import in crucial negotiations, but I entertained a special regard and affection for that very unusual man.

Even though our talks were often held under pressure and in haste, Kissinger was always a good listener, and his sense of humor (a trait of which few politicians can boast) was an excellent vehicle for releasing tension. On one occasion I told him that I was unable to reply to the proposals he had brought from Egypt until they had been discussed by the negotiating team and the cabinet as a whole. "President Sadat always gives me an immediate reply," he said. "How long do your cabinet meetings last?" I told him that our previous meeting had gone on for ten hours, with Peres adding, "even though several ministers waived their right to speak." Kissinger pretended to be surprised — or he may have genuinely been astonished: "Do you seriously mean to tell me that each of your ministers has the right to address cabinet meetings?" That was indeed our procedure, I told him, whereupon he brought out one of his famous anecdotes.

"Chancellor Adenauer had a minister in his cabinet who was vigorously opposed to his foreign policy. The minister would ask for permission to speak at every cabinet meeting, but Adenauer ignored him completely. Finally the poor man couldn't take any more. At one meeting, he jumped up and stubbornly kept his hand raised to show that he would not give up this time. After repeated attempts of this sort, Adenauer turned to him and said: 'All right, if you want to go to the toilet, permission is granted.' I suppose that wouldn't work in your cabinet, would it?" he added.

Kissinger was more than a virtuoso at negotiations. He was astonishingly well acquainted with the principal figures on both sides and would regale us with descriptions of the Egyptian, Jordanian, and Syrian leaders he had met. (I am also certain that he provided the Arabs with reciprocal — and equally gifted — descriptions of us.) Once he illustrated how familiar the Egyptians were with the Israeli situation and the personalities involved in the negotiations by relating the following story. At Allon's suggestion, we had asked Kissinger to convey to Egypt a certain legal formulation about one of the issues being discussed. On his return, he told us that Egyptian Foreign Minister Ismail Fahmy had only to glance at the document before saying: "There's only one man who could formulate a paper like this — Meir Rosen, the foreign minister's legal adviser." Kissinger said he didn't know who had drawn it up and wasn't acquainted with Rosen. He thought it was worded by Mordechai Gazit, the director general of the Prime Minister's Office. But Fahmy stuck to his guns: "No! No way! The only one who could do such formulation is Meir Rosen!" We did not comment when Kissinger finished his story, but the paper had indeed been drafted by Meir Rosen.

I always listened carefully to Kissinger's characterizations of our Arab counterparts because they were the closest we could get to developing a "feel" for the men with whom we were dealing —

an important aspect in any set of negotiations. Since it was apparent that Sadat alone made the decisions in Egypt, I concentrated on studying his character and intellectual concepts. In addition to going over his speeches, I also tried to glean impressions from anyone who had met him — particularly Americans. One American visitor summed up Sadat's most prominent trait for me by saying, "The fear of war is in his bones." Others defined the Egyptian president as a "treacherous man." I was wary of such generalizations, but Sadat's past actions did give me reason to view him as fickle.

Ever since the time he turned toward Nazi Germany as a young officer in the Egyptian army, Sadat's career had been marked by a succession of sharp and sudden shifts from one orientation to its opposite, from warm friendship to violent hostility. In 1971 he signed a treaty of friendship with the Soviet Union and a year later he expelled the Soviets and switched his affections to the Americans. In 1973 he went to war alongside his "brother" President Assad and then consented to a cease-fire without prior coordination with Syria. Sadat's autobiography (published in 1978) confirmed my impressions by showing that he was flagrantly disloyal to Nasser — first showering him with compliments and then going on to shatter his image with tales of the terrible calamity he brought upon Egypt because of his unsteady nerves.

In a conversation I once held with a group of American businessmen who were visiting the capitals of the Middle East, I asked for their impressions of Sadat and Assad. "It's easier to conclude a deal with Sadat," one of them replied, "but it's doubtful whether he'll keep his side of the bargain. With Assad, it is difficult — sometimes impossible — to reach an agreement, but once he's signed a deal there's a good chance he'll stick to it." For all the differences between commerce and diplomacy, I could not avoid reaching certain conclusions about Egypt's president. I was increasingly convinced that the way to ensure the success of any agreement with him was to establish facts on the ground and structure the deal so that it would pay for him to honor it — or at least hurt him if he did not. But the terms Sadat was offering us did not fulfill either of these conditions.

I had tried to make this clear to the secretary of state and had ample reason to believe that he would understand. The story of Kissinger's contribution to Israel's security has yet to be told, and for the present suffice it to say that it was of prime importance. Yet Kissinger could also be a tough — and occasionally dangerous — rival. His promise not to blame Israel for the failure of his mission was broken while he was still in midair. Before his stopover in London, the secretary of state — in his favorite though thin disguise as "a senior official" — briefed the journalists on the plane, who promptly informed the whole world that Israel's hard line had, once again, led her to miss an opportunity. When Kissinger contacted me from the London office of British Foreign Secretary James Callaghan to "clarify one or two further points," I found it hard to keep from upbraiding him. But I knew that we were only at the start of the quarrel.

A few days later, President Ford officially announced that United States' policy in the Middle East would be "reassessed" — an innocent-sounding term that heralded one of the worst periods in American-Israeli relations. For six months, from March to September 1975, the United States refused to sign new arms deals with Israel (though it continued to honor contracts signed before the crisis broke out). Yet the deeper significance of the "reassessment" lay in how it would be interpreted by Israel's enemies. They had every reason to conclude that the United States was singling out Israel as the principal culprit for the failure of Kissinger's mission and making her pay the penalty while raising a warning finger: if you persist in your refusal to pave the way to peace, don't expect United States support!

As far as I was concerned, any such inducement was unnecessary. My desire to achieve an interim agreement with Egypt rested upon my perception of Israel's needs, rather than on any wish to placate the United States. Evidently President Sadat held similar views, for when he met President Ford in Austria shortly after the suspension of the talks, he expressed Egypt's interest in renewing the attempts to reach an agreement with Israel through American mediation. I therefore welcomed the invitation to go to Washington on June 10 for discussions with President Ford and Dr. Kissinger.

I heard — and voiced — a lot of tough talk during that visit.

Kissinger joined me for breakfast at Blair House on my first day in Washington, and we both agreed that it was best to let bygones be bygones. But first it was necessary to clear the air a little. The administration was less than happy with the results of our public campaign in the United States, which had resulted in a letter from seventy-six senators calling upon the president to support Israel and provide for her defense needs. The manner in which the breakdown in the talks had been handled still rankled me. "I must know where we stand in our relations," I told the secretary of state. "From now on, whenever there is any disagreement between us because we believe that your position endangers Israel's security, do you intend to 'reassess'?"

Kissinger was offended and insisted that the developments arising from the suspension of talks were exceptional. He returned to his theme of a "misunderstanding" between us, and this time I was offended by his recurring claim that I had misled him. When we finally got down to business, he reported on Sadat's attitude toward an interim agreement. Egypt still demanded the oil fields and an Israeli withdrawal from the eastern parts of the passes. On the other hand, Sadat was displaying a measure of flexibility regarding the duration of the agreement and the timing of Israel's withdrawal. We were back to almost precisely the point where the talks had broken down. Sadat had not changed his views, and neither had I. But in the course of that conversation, Kissinger and I did finally concur on one point: he would not renew his mission unless we reached all but total agreement on the terms for an interim settlement with Egypt.

When we went in to see President Ford, I was treated to a mixture of placating words and a subtle threat. With great geniality, which seemed to belie the painful crisis prevailing in Israeli-U.S. relations, Ford told me that he had been looking forward to this meeting ever since the suspension of the Kissinger mission. "I want to tell you frankly what's bothering me," he began, "and then we'll turn over a new leaf." (Contrary to popular belief, politicians and diplomats use up far more paper than journalists; every crisis is followed by a massive turning over of leaves.) The president went on to express his dismay at the fact that his letter to me had been leaked to the press (though he was understanding about leaks being an unpleasant but often unavoidable feature of democratic systems of government). He was also less than pleased by the letter from the seventy-six senators; but considering Israel's treatment at the hands of his administration, I saw little reason to defend our achievement on that score. Finally, we came down to the heart of the matter.

"Our reassessment was not intended to penalize Israel," the president insisted. "Yet after the United States had made a supreme effort to achieve an agreement in the Middle East and failed to do so, we had to reconsider our policies. I have reached my conclusions, but I thought it would not be fair to finalize them before giving you a chance to offer your opinion. I tend toward favoring an overall Middle East settlement to be achieved at the Geneva Conference. It would comprise a peace between Israel and her neighbors, and the final borders would be guaranteed by the powers concerned."

I was pretty sure that Ford was testing to see how firm our position was. Every man in that room knew that the Geneva Conference would lead to hopeless stalemate. Furthermore, I could not believe that the United States was truly interested in a format that would literally invite the Soviet Union to reassume a position of primary influence in Middle Eastern affairs. Yet as long as we were on the topic, I was determined to make my position clear. "No Arab ruler is prepared for true peace and normalization of relations in the Middle East," I told the president. "The Arabs demand a total withdrawal to the June 4, 1967, lines, and those lines were the cause of war. Any significant military movements in the Arab states confront Israel with a harsh choice of launching a preemptive attack or running the risk of an invasion. We must have defensible borders, and those are not the same as the June 4 lines. And we will defend this position at Geneva, if the conference is convened. Let there be no doubt about that."

In a deliberate attempt to lay the matter of Geneva to rest, I began to describe Israel's views on an interim agreement. We unrolled maps of the Sinai, and I explained to the president why it was out of the question for us to give up the passes. In the course of the discussion, it became clear to me that the president preferred an interim agreement to a return to Geneva, but he continued to play "hard to get": "If it's an interim agreement you're after, it must be concluded quickly. There's no time for Kissinger to undertake a mission lasting more than two or three weeks. But if it becomes evident that you can't bridge the gaps between positions, I will revert to my previous plan and formulate an American proposal for an overall settlement."

I had less reason to fear the talk of Geneva than I had to suspect the administration's support for Sadat's two main demands: restoration of the oil fields and a pullback beyond the passes. In fact, during Kissinger's March mission, we had already agreed to restore the oil fields to Egypt as an enclave that would be linked to the city of Suez by a route under UN protection. The Egyptian army would not be permitted into the enclave or anywhere along the route, while the IDF would take up positions nearby. But the passes were another matter entirely.

On the evening of June 12, after a further meeting with the president that day, Kissinger and I met for a talk. He was less friendly and far more demanding outside the Oval Office, and our exchanges sometimes grew loud and heated. "Your insistence on holding on to the eastern parts of the passes prevents any continuation of the diplomatic process," he hurled at me. "As a result, the Geneva Conference will become inevitable, and I don't know what position the United States will adopt there!"

I tried to contain myself, but I felt bound to react at least to his approach. "This is no way to conduct negotiations," I countered. "We will not bow to Egypt's demands! And please don't threaten me with the Geneva Conference. There, too, we will resist any step that endangers our security, and it cannot be assumed that decisions will be reached by a majority vote!" Tempers might have risen further were it not for Joseph Sisco's intervention. "I have the feeling that we're all tired, and that doesn't improve the standard of discussion. Let's go to bed and meet again tomorrow." It was a good suggestion, and Kissinger and I both agreed.

Since there had been so much talk of Geneva during that visit, in one of our less heated, private conversations I asked Kissinger to satisfy my curiosity on one point. "We've known one another for years and have held hundreds of conversations on every subject under the sun. Yet I have never heard you express your view about what Israel's borders ought to be. Now that we're here alone, just the two of us . . ." Smiling back at me, Kissinger said: "You've never heard it, and you won't hear it now. I hope that when the time comes to decide on Israel's borders, I shall no longer be serving as secretary of state."

On the evening of June 13, after a full day of talks with congressmen, senators, and journalists and shortly before my departure for New York, Kissinger, Sisco, Peter Rodman, and Simcha Dinitz (our ambassador to Washington) came to see me again at Blair House. To forestall any continuation of the previous night's argument, I unrolled a map and showed the Americans the line to which we were willing to withdraw. It represented a further measure of flexibility in the northern and southern sectors, while still holding to the eastern ridge of the passes (which constituted a very good defense line). But Kissinger would not accept it as a feasible proposal and "threatened" me with Geneva again. The map did not precisely define the width of the strip linking Abu Rodeis with the city of Suez, and I told Kissinger that I would add this detail after consultations in Israel. In the meantime, the American ambassador to Cairo, Herman Eilts, would be summoned to Washington in order to convey this proposal to Cairo.

I left for New York and at 9:15 that evening received a phone call from President Ford. The president apologized for disturbing me but felt it was imperative that we talk. "After your meeting, Henry came to my office and we went over the subjects you discussed," he told me. "I must tell you, in all frankness, that you have not moved far enough to make me feel that we have indeed made any progress toward an agreement. I am disappointed, and I am concerned about Israel's image in the eyes of the American people."

It seemed that Kissinger had decided to employ the president as his battering ram. I told Ford that everything I had said to Kissinger had been discussed during our two meetings at the White House. I had added nothing. "Israel shows great flexibility, but she can't be the only one to do so." But the president indicated that he had understood differently from our conversations. He had the impression that Israel would show greater flexibility regarding the passes.

From the president's tone, I sensed that he was in a quandary. It seemed to me that at his meeting with Sadat in Austria, he had promised to secure the oil fields and the passes for Egypt. The oil fields had been seen to, but when it came to the passes, he was unable to "deliver the goods."

"I want to make it clear," I told the president, "that at my forthcoming meeting with Kissinger in New York, I will remain unable to change my position. We shall hold on to the eastern ridge of the passes."

When Kissinger and I met the following day, he was still peeved: "What real difference is there between the line you put forward in March and the one you are proposing now? In our opinion, there has been no change." I explained that our latest proposal entailed withdrawing farther eastward.

"Can't you be satisfied with the eastern slope of the ridge?" Kissinger pressed.

"No!" I practically shouted. "I have explained that countless times. It's recorded in every transcript. I must say, I'm surprised at you and your accusations. We have worked together for years, and I can't recall any 'misunderstandings' between us. It's only lately, in March and again now, that I constantly hear complaints of misunderstandings. It sounds very strange to me. I am making myself perfectly clear. In March we proposed that Israel retain the central portion of the passes. Afterward we agreed to move a little bit eastward. Now we are proposing that Israel retain no more than the last ridge on the eastern part of the passes. Do you regard that as inflexibility?"

He took another look at the map. "But the Egyptians will argue that this line leaves the whole of the Gidi Pass in Israeli hands and that Israel is only withdrawing from half of the Mitla Pass!"

"That is open to interpretation. We differ with the Egyptians over the geographic definition of the passes. Do you want to be the arbiter and provide the correct interpretation?"

"I want to repeat what the president told you over the phone," he countered. "We shall convey the Israeli proposal to Cairo without appending our recommendations. And in that case, we shall have to go to Geneva."

"Very well," I said. "Let's go to Geneva!" Israel, Egypt, and the United States all favored an interim agreement, rather than the reconvening of the Geneva Conference, so I had good reason to assume that the agreement would be concluded — even if the obstacles were not easily overcome.

When I returned home, the negotiating team gave its approval to the line I had sketched out in Washington and we delineated the width of the overland link from Abu Rodeis to the city of Suez. My military assistant, Efraim Poran, delivered the map to Washington, but shortly afterward the Egyptians rejected our proposals.

At the end of June, Shimon Peres came up with an idea that he claimed would break the deadlock: the creation of a rectangular zone, including the eastern and western parts of the passes, to be garrisoned by a joint American-Soviet force. The zone would be extraterritorial, meaning that it would not be controlled by either Egypt or Israel. To give greater weight to his proposal, Peres quoted the highest authority: "I have discussed it with Moshe Dayan, and he supports the plan." Peres then offered to fly secretly to the holiday resort where Kissinger was vacationing and present the proposal to him.

I was flabbergasted. This time the defense minister's "political thinking" had soared to unforeseen heights. Had I not, with my own ears, heard a senior Israeli minister propose that Israel take the initiative in inviting Soviet troops into the Sinai, I would have sworn that the defense minister's enemies were slandering him. I told Peres that I did not accept his proposal and doubted that we should suggest even an American military presence in the area, though I would not object to the latter if it removed the obstacles to an interim agreement. I saw no need for the defense minister to set off for a meeting with Kissinger. Ambassador Dinitz could go to the Virgin Islands and talk to the secretary of state about an American presence in the Sinai rectangle.

Meanwhile, the general staff had worked out a withdrawal plan (independent of Peres's latest idea) to meet Egypt's objections to an Israeli presence at the eastern entrances to the passes. The IDF would remain to the north of the Gidi Pass and to the south of the Mitla road while holding on to the eastern ridge running between the two passes. There would be no formal Israeli presence at the eastern entrances to the passes. This would satisfy the Egyptians while allowing us to retain control of the eastern openings of the passes without actually occupying them. Our proposal also called for the Americans to take over all the early-warning installations in the area of the passes and operate them on behalf of both Israel and Egypt. I approved the plan and Dinitz carried it to Dr. Kissinger. The secretary of state was taken aback by the idea of an American military presence and said he would have to discuss it with the president. Yet the Israeli proposal for a new line was acceptable to him, and he thought it might bode well for progress with the Egyptians.

President Ford was not very enthusiastic about the idea of stationing American personnel in the Sinai. In the America of 1975, any suggestion of a U.S. military presence in some distant country evoked instinctive opposition. But Kissinger talked the president around, softening up his objections by suggesting that an American military presence might not be needed at all; it would suffice if American civilian technicians operated the early-warning installations. Then, early in July, the administration informed us that although it was not prepared to send military personnel to the Sinai, it was prepared to man the Um Hashiva installation as well as build and man an additional early-warning station on the Egyptian side. At the same time, the United States again urged Israel to withdraw to the eastern slope of the ridge between the passes.

Soon afterward I set off for West Germany for the first state visit there by an Israeli prime minister. My schedule commenced with a memorial ceremony for the victims of the Holocaust at Bergen-Belsen concentration camp. It was my first sight of a Nazi extermination camp. The terrible anguish of those moments swept away the thirty-five-year time gap separating me — a sabra and a soldier — from the days of the Nazi Holocaust, and I had a glimpse of my martyred people. The camp had been turned into a beautiful spot, green and flourishing with flowers in full bloom. In that eerie stillness, you could almost hear the sound of babies crying.

Upon reaching Berlin, I was welcomed by Mayor Klaus Schutz (now West Germany's ambassador to Israel) and a very special tribute from Axel Springer, who had one of his newspapers greet me with an editorial in Hebrew. On July 9 I held a meeting with Chancellor Helmut Schmidt, and we reached understanding on the extension of trade relations between our two countries. I also talked with the Federal Republic's president, Walter Schell, and with Foreign Minister Hans-Dietrich Genscher and Finance Minister Apel.

On July 13 Kissinger, who was then visiting West Germany, came to see me at the ancient castle of Gimnisch, which served as an official guesthouse of the West German government. Prior to his arrival, American technicians had installed a special system of loudspeakers that emitted incessant bleeps and whistles, which would presumably thwart any attempt to listen in on our conversation or record it. It was, indeed, a very advanced system that precluded anyone's overhearing our conversation, principally because the bleeps and whistles made it nearly impossible to converse. Kissinger's explanation: "You can never know how many Soviet spies are lurking here."

Once again we discussed every ridge and pinpointed every hillock. When we came to the subject of manning the early-warning stations, Kissinger surprised me by stating: "Israel is justified in demanding to man the Um Hashiva station. We have studied the matter, and operating the station requires a large staff. For two stations — yours and Egypt's — we would have to send about one thousand Americans. That is more than we can undertake." On top of the financial and administrative burden, it seemed to me that the United States was reluctant to become overinvolved in the Middle East. America's heavy involvement in Vietnam had likewise begun with the dispatch of a small group of technicians.

Kissinger suggested that the two early-warning stations be considered American, with the U.S. flag flying over them and American sentries guarding their entrances, but that they be manned by Israelis and Egyptians. This was good news. He added the rider that he had yet to receive Sadat's consent to this change, but I assumed that he would not have suggested it unless he had reason to believe that Sadat would agree. Then he added that the United States would be able to construct four additional, smaller warning stations along the roads through the passes, each to be manned by fifteen or twenty Americans.

As to the new line for the Israeli withdrawal, Kissinger asked that we keep it a secret. He intended to instruct Ambassador Eilts to reveal it to President Sadat, while stressing the great efforts the United States was making to persuade Israel to undertake such a far-reaching withdrawal. The virtuoso of negotiations had stumbled once and he did not want to stumble again. During the negotiations for the disengagement-of-forces agreement on the Golan Heights, Kissinger had gained Israel's consent to withdraw to a certain line, but he deliberately tried to lead President Assad into believing that we would only undertake a smaller withdrawal. Assad refused to budge from his demand for a deeper Israeli pullback, while Kissinger, with inexhaustible patience, inched back little by little. Finally Assad decided that the game had run its course. Permitting himself one of his rare smiles, he said, "Haven't you seen today's *Ha'aretz?*" (one of Israel's leading dailies). "Israel has already agreed to withdraw further than the line you claim is the absolute maximum." The secretary of state did not entertain much affection for the Israeli press that day.

After Kissinger and I agreed on a shuttle mission to begin during the second half of August 1975, I left Gimnisch with the feeling that the way was finally open to an interim agreement on terms acceptable to Israel. In March the Egyptians had insisted that there were only two options: either the two armies controlled the respective entrances to the passes or they both took up positions at an equal distance from those entrances. It was now agreed with Kissinger that the Egyptians would not advance beyond the present buffer zone, while the IDF — though giving up the eastern entrances to the passes — would retain full control of the area around them and continue to operate the Um Hashiva early-warning stations. I attached enormous significance to this latter consideration because of the excellence of the early-warning installations.

When Kissinger arrived for his shuttle mission, we gave him a festive reception at the Knesset. But it was marred by the frenzied "welcome" he received from the right-wing Gush Emunim, self-styled "guardians of the faith" who proceeded to put on an appalling display of anti-Semitism right in the heart of the State of Israel. Masquerading as "champions of the Land of Israel," they claimed divine justification for embellishing their religious chauvinism with anti-Semitic slurs. To the horror of Israel's citizenry, the members of Gush Emunim greeted the secretary of state of the United States with the epithet "Jew-boy," while their "spiritual mentor" — the eminent rabbi Zvi Yehuda Kook — referred to him as "the husband of a gentile woman." One so-called intellectual even went so far as to publish an article claiming that Kissinger deserved to meet the same fate as Count Bernadotte, the UN mediator who was assassinated in Israel in 1948 (by an earlier generation of right-wing fanatics). As if all that were not disgusting enough, the members of Gush Emunim stormed through the streets of the capital like common rabble and laid siege to the Knesset in an attempt to disrupt the reception. We barely succeeded in getting Kissinger out through a rear exit and safely back to the King David Hotel.

I felt so thoroughly shocked and ashamed before Kissinger — indeed, before the whole world — that there were no words to express my anguish. I doubt I shall ever witness more deplorable or misguided behavior on the part of my countrymen. If Gush Emunim had an ax to grind, it was with me and my cabinet, not with a guest who had given so much of himself in the pursuit of stability and peace in this region. In fact, there can be no excuse for Jews anywhere to stoop to such obscene behavior. I might not be able to teach Gush Emunim the rudiments of good manners, but I did have a say where rioting in the streets was concerned. The next day I called in the inspector general of the police and ordered him to put a stop to it — by force, if necessary.

Our talks with Kissinger went on from August 21 to August 31. This time the Americans were thoroughly prepared: Kissinger had been preceded by a group of American experts on geography and topography who toured the area with the chief of staff and other IDF officers. They did a fine piece of work in preparing for the talks, producing an enormous trunk containing a precise relief map of the passes and the surrounding area. The map was based upon photographs taken by American satellites and an expert examination on the ground, and the outcome was of an enviable quality. The Americans trundled that relief map back and forth between Israel and Egypt in the course of Kissinger's shuttle mission, since most of the discussions were conducted around it.

During those ten days, we held daylong — and occasionally nightlong — discussions, and there were times when we felt we were flogging a dead horse. Five hours might be spent discussing a stretch of sand one hundred meters long. It was a supreme test of our patience, persistence, and even our physical endurance. Wisely, skillfully, patiently Kissinger inched his way forward between Sadat's difficulties and mine, between proclamations from each side that "this is our final concession!"

Although I never expressed it to Kissinger, my military view was that the width of the buffer zone between the two armies was of far greater importance than a few hundred meters more or less of the IDF's withdrawal. I wanted to rid Israel and our armed forces of the concept of "holding a line," like the Barlev Line prior to the Yom Kippur War. There was neither need nor military rationale to fight for every square meter in the great wastes of the Sinai, as we would do if it were a question of populated areas in the Israeli heartland. A demilitarized Sinai would give us room for maneuver and allow Israel to take advantage of her superiority in mobile warfare beyond the zone of Egypt's ground-to-air missile umbrella. The chief of staff understood this and tried to convince skeptics who were still clinging to outmoded concepts, but it wasn't always easy.

On August 31 the Israeli-Egyptian agreement was completed,

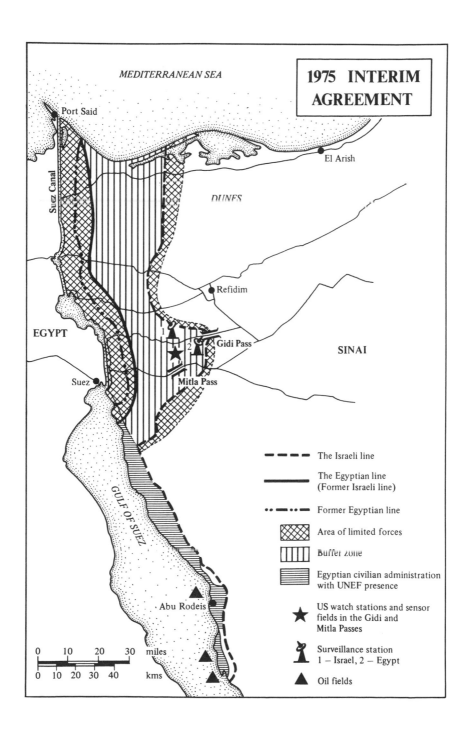

MEDITERRANEAN SEA

1975 INTERIM AGREEMENT

Port Said

El Arish

Suez Canal

DUNES

Refidim

EGYPT

1

2

Gidi Pass

SINAI

Suez

Mitla Pass

GULF OF SUEZ

Abu Rodeis

- - - - The Israeli line

———— The Egyptian line
(Former Israeli line)

-- — --- Former Egyptian line

Area of limited forces

Buffer zone

Egyptian civilian administration
with UNEF presence

US watch stations and sensor
fields in the Gidi and
Mitla Passes

Surveillance station
1 — Israel, 2 — Egypt

Oil fields

| 0 | 10 | 20 | 30 | miles |

| 0 | 10 | 20 | 30 | 40 | kms |

but I explained to Kissinger that the cabinet could not ratify it unless it were accompanied by an American-Israeli agreement (as the two earlier disengagement-of-forces agreements had been). So we went on to discuss the "Memorandum of Understanding" between Israel and the United States, which specified U.S. commitments to Israel following from the interim agreement. The conclusive discussion on the bilateral issues was held on the night of August 31 and lasted until 6:00 A.M. As the hours wore on, participants on both sides dropped out of the discussion, so that by the end it had become a dialogue between Kissinger and me against a chorus of snores all around.

The following day, September 1, the cabinet ratified both agreements, and after many months of tension and uncertainty I had a moment of gratification. I knew that we had taken a first but invaluable step on the long and winding path that would lead Egypt away from war and toward peace. The interim agreement created a new strategic situation in the Sinai that was an improvement for both sides. Egypt could operate the Suez Canal and rebuild the cities on its banks with a greater sense of security. The return of the oil fields moderated Egypt's hostility and gave its leaders good reason to maintain their side of the bargain. Moreover, the agreement gave further impetus to developments already in train, moving Sadat further away from the Soviet Union, depriving the Egyptian army of further supplies of Soviet arms, and widening the rift between Egypt and Syria. In this manner we hoped to leave Sadat with only one choice: a political solution. Egypt might have other options — but not Sadat.

The interim agreement also turned the tide in Israeli-U.S. relations in terms of the scope of financial aid, the supply of arms (including F-16 fighter planes), and a number of fundamental policy matters. In the "Memorandum of Understanding," the United States confirmed that it would not negotiate with or recognize the PLO, initiate any moves in the Middle East without prior consultation with Israel, or diverge from Security Council Resolutions 242 and 338 as the sole basis for peace negotiations (as well as do its utmost to prevent the introduction of any change in these resolutions).

When President Sadat made his historic visit to Jerusalem on November 19, 1977, I was no longer prime minister. Yet that visit — and the subsequent moves toward achieving a peace treaty — could never have come about were it not for the course my government adopted in signing the 1975 interim agreement. That our policy provoked the anger of the Likud opposition (even Moshe Dayan joined in voting against the agreement in the Knesset) has not prevented Mr. Begin's government from reaping the fruits of our labors. Of course, that is how things should be, since the quest for peace is not a contest between political parties. But whenever I hear talk of "peace breaking out" any moment — as if the history of negotiations began in November 1977 — I feel obliged to set the record straight. The 1975 agreement with Egypt was never meant to be an end in itself. As its title implies, it was designed to advance the "momentum" toward peace, and in that sense it has achieved its objective — no minor accomplishment in Middle Eastern politics. I can only hope that the next achievement along the road will prove to be as durable and successful.

Chapter Fourteen

THE SPIRIT OF '76

WHEN I ARRIVED in Washington at the end of January 1976 to continue my dialogue on the future of political negotiations in the Middle East, the plotting of strategy was far more complex than it had been during my last talk with the president six months earlier. Then the choice seemed to be between pursuing an interim agreement with Egypt or reconvening the Geneva Conference. Now that the agreement with Egypt had been signed, the question was where to turn next. Should we continue to concentrate on Egypt and work for a further agreement stipulating the termination of belligerency? Were the prospects of achieving an interim agreement with Syria more promising? (Unlike the situation in the Sinai, there was precious little room for a withdrawal on the Golan Heights, and what the Syrians would be willing to give in return for a few kilometers was highly questionable.) Considering the results of the Rabat Conference and the fact that any territorial compromise on the West Bank would require the calling of new elections in Israel, was there any point in trying to reach an agreement with Jordan?

In my talks with Dr. Kissinger, it was agreed that the aims of further agreements with any of Israel's neighbors would have to be at least a termination of belligerency. Thus before we entered into discussion on possible lines of withdrawal, he intended to find out whether or not the Arab states were prepared to join in negotiations on such terms. I readily consented that the United States should approach Egypt and Syria to see if they were interested. As for Jordan, I had to discuss the question with my cabinet before giving the secretary of state a binding answer. I did agree, however, that if and when talks began with Jordan, we would accept the inclusion of Palestinian representatives from the West Bank and the Gaza Strip as part and parcel of the Jordanian delegation — on the clear and specific understanding that the negotiations were between the two sovereign states.

The other subject taken up during my visit, as might be expected, was the question of arms supplies. At our first meeting, the president handed me the list of weapons he had approved for delivery. (The next morning Kissinger told me that Ford had approved a list costing $500 million more than the sum recommended by the National Security Council and had ordered that Israel be given top priority for weapons deliveries, immediately after the U.S. armed forces.) I had reason to be deeply gratified by the degree to which we had secured the president's understanding for our military needs. Unfortunately, however, the question of future arms deliveries also put something of a damper on what was otherwise a very successful visit to the American capital.

The problem centered on an arms list rather hastily drawn up while we were in the midst of negotiations on the interim agreement with Egypt. It contained some items that were more than superfluous; they bordered on the ludicrous (like a spy-satellite system costing some one billion dollars and so far possessed only by two powers). While the list was being drawn up at the Defense Ministry, my attention was focused on concluding the agreement with Egypt, and I confess that I did not take off time to scrutinize it in detail. In December 1975 Defense Minister Peres delivered the list to the United States as it stood — exaggerated and pretentious. In the course of his talks, he agreed to sift out its superfluous elements and present a modified list, but the members of Congress had yet to receive the revision. I was therefore subjected to some very embarrassing questions by various congressional committees, and it would have been foolish not to admit that we did not need the more outlandish items on the list before them.

As chief of staff, ambassador, and prime minister, I always held that Israel must present her defense requirements in a manner designed to inspire belief in her need for the items she requests.

Any hint of demands based on the assumption that the American taxpayer would foot the bill could undermine the quality of American-Israeli relations. The lists we submitted in December 1975 were frivolous and unworthy of serious consideration, and I said so at a Blair House meeting with a small group of Israeli correspondents. I will not take shelter behind the excuse that the talk was not intended for quotation or attribution. I admit that I erred — not in the substance of what I said, but in the sharp wording I adopted. I referred to our lists as "inflated," but I did not try to evade my share of the responsibility for them.

The journalists literally dashed to their telephones and Teletypes, cabling home reports on things I had said along with things I had not said. Instead of reporting on the generous American response to our defense needs and the understanding reached between Israel and the United States on diplomatic moves, banner headlines highlighted the prime minister's slip of the tongue. The reason for the extravagant response to such a trivial matter was obvious. It was no secret that there was a considerable degree of friction between the defense minister and me. I was determined to prevent our differences from disrupting the smooth running of government, but I was dogged by the feeling that Peres's intentions were precisely the opposite. In that he found an eager ally in the press, which thrives on such subjects as rivalry in high places and pounces on every tidbit that may serve to underscore it. I am sure that copy of that kind sells newspapers; I am not at all sure, however, that it is the most responsible kind of journalism or that it serves the national interest. A case in point: when I returned to Israel, I found that the principal topic of interest was not the concrete results of my Washington talks — the political and supply decisions that would shape Israel's immediate future — but the arms lists!

Be that as it may, following my visit to Washington we did not pick up the thread of political negotiations with the Arab states. Not that our eagerness had waned. But in 1976 the focal point in Middle Eastern affairs shifted radically from Israeli-Arab problems to the conflicts within the Arab world centering on the civil war in Lebanon. In order to understand the significance of that change, it is necessary to review the development of events that led to the fighting.

Lebanon's political and governmental structure was dictated by the "national accord" between the country's two communities — Christian and Moslem — which was designed to create a permanent balance of influence and power. Under the "accord," the hegemony of the Christian community was ensured by a permanent majority in the Lebanese parliament and a Christian president whose powers were greater than those of the Moslem prime minister. But this coalition structure began to crumble with the rise of Moslem nationalism throughout the Middle East and the emergence of left-wing movements in Lebanon. After September 1970 it was turned topsy-turvy when Palestinian terrorists fleeing from King Hussein's army took refuge in Lebanon and transferred their headquarters there. The weakness of the Lebanese government and army and the disintegration of the country's bi-communal regime allowed the terrorist organizations in Lebanon to become a "state within a state" in a natural alliance with Lebanese leftist and Moslem organizations. Seeing the erosion of their position, the Lebanese Christians took a stand to defend their heritage, while Syria lay in wait to extend its hegemony over Lebanon and realize its dream of a "Greater Syria."

The first phase of the Lebanese civil war (from April 1975 to January 1976) was marked by static exchanges of fire between the Palestinian-Lebanese leftist alliance and the Christians, while the Lebanese and Syrian armies stood aside. The second phase, however (from January to May 1976), witnessed a sharp escalation in the fighting, horrifying atrocities, and battles to gain control of various areas. When Lebanon reached a state of collapse, Syria tried its hand at political intervention by summoning the warring sides to Damascus and forcing them to adopt the "Damascus Agreement" — a desperate attempt to preserve Lebanon's basic governmental structure with one major reform: a reduction in the powers of the Christian president in favor of the Moslem prime minister. The latest "concord" proved to be no more than an illusion, however, since the Moslem left and the Palestinians soon broke the agreement. By that point, Syria found that it was unable to extricate itself from the quagmire without losing face before the Arab world. Its first move was to send in the Sa'ika terrorist organization to fight on the side of the Christians (an ironic step that left outside observers finding it difficult to keep track of who was fighting against whom). When that proved insufficient, in June 1976 Syria committed its own regular army to the battlefield.

Of all the moves that exacerbated the civil war in Lebanon, this latest Syrian step had the greatest effect on changing the political and strategic situation in the Middle East. On the one hand, Syria now came under attack from its Arab allies, the relatively moderate Egypt as well as the extremist states of Iraq and Libya (not to mention the PLO). On the other, it found itself in a no less uncomfortable position regarding Israel, because the involvement of the Syrian army in Lebanon inevitably weakened its deployment along the cease-fire line in the Golan Heights. At the same time, it was clear that if the Syrian army occupied southern Lebanon, we would be forced to take pragmatic steps to push it back. Israel could not tolerate having Syrian troops stationed along *two* of her borders! As a result, there was much talk during that period of a metaphorical "red line." Although it was not marked out on any map when the Syrian army first entered Lebanon, we later made it clear that we meant a line running directly east from Sidon to the Lebanese-Syrian border. That line has not been crossed by Syrian troops to this very day.

Within a few months the Syrians killed more Palestinians than the terrorist organizations had lost in all their operations against Israel and clashes with the IDF over the previous thirty years. Even more ironic was the fact that because the Syrians were prevented from moving south of the "red line," southern Lebanon became a haven for the terrorists. We had foreseen such an eventuality and preferred it to Syrian military control of the area bordering on our territory. But that did not reduce the absurdity of the new situation: PLO terrorists, Israel's sworn foes, found asylum under an Israeli "deterrent umbrella" intended against the Syrians.

At the same time, we could not ignore the plight of the civilian population in southern Lebanon, and our response was expressed in the "Good Fence" policy. It was our humanitarian duty to aid the population of the area and prevent it from being wiped out by the hostile terrorists. Israel felt a natural affinity to the Christian community of Lebanon, but under no circumstances could we undertake political or military responsibility for its fate. The aid we extended stopped very far short of involvement in the Lebanese imbroglio.

With the Palestinian terrorists taking such a beating at the hands of their Syrian "brothers," one would have thought they had little time for planning operations against Israel. But we were not oblivious to the possibility that the terrorist organization headed by Wadia Hadad — with headquarters in Iraq, training bases in South Yemen, and ties with such non-Arab terrorist networks as the Bader-Meinhof gang and the Japanese "Red Army" — would attempt an operation against Israeli citizens or institutions on foreign soil. Hadad's operations were marked by a high degree of sophistication, and although we took special precautions in Israel, there was justifiable concern over the "soft underbelly" of our antiterrorist program: the foreign airlines and airports that refused to adopt the strict security arrangements in force in El Al and at Ben-Gurion Airport.

Following the Yom Kippur War, the terrorist organizations developed the tactic of "bargaining raids," whereby terrorists would penetrate into one of our cities or towns, take hostages, and then offer to negotiate for the release of their imprisoned cohorts. In such cases, it was my policy to employ force in order to rescue the hostages as quickly as possible. On our own soil, where we had troops specially trained to deal with such situations, there was no question of capitulation — even though we were painfully aware that we might have to pay a high price for this principle. If Israeli hostages were taken to or in a foreign country friendly to Israel (whether at an airport or an Israeli diplomatic or commercial institution), my policy was to urge that country to emulate our example and attempt to release them by force. We would offer Israeli assistance and extend any help required.

The third and most ominous possibility we had to take into consideration was the hijacking of an airplane to an enemy country or one unfriendly to Israel — in which case military action on the part of the "host" country could hardly be expected. In that event, my policy was to weigh the possibility of taking military action ourselves — even if the operation entailed risks to the assault force and the lives of the hostages — and only if that option proved unfeasible, to negotiate with the hijackers. I should add that there was something of an indirect precedent to this last clause. After the Yom Kippur War, Mrs. Meir's government had agreed to exchange Arab spies and terrorists for the bodies of Israeli soldiers who had fallen in Egyptian-held territory in the Sinai. Since we had released terrorists in exchange for our war dead, it would be inconceivable for us to refuse to do likewise for innocent hostages — provided we were left with no other choice.

The Israeli cabinet's standard Sunday meeting was in session on June 27, 1976, when my military aide entered the cabinet room and handed me a note: an Air France plane, Flight 139 from Tel Aviv to Paris, had been hijacked after taking off from a stopover in Athens. The brief message provided no clue to a series of troublesome questions: How many Israelis were on board the plane? How many hijackers were there? Where was the hijacked plane heading? As further reports came in, we learned that 83 of the 230 passengers on board were Israelis, and the Libyans were reluctantly allowing the plane to land at Benghazi. A special ministerial team composed of Deputy Prime Minister and Foreign Minister Allon, Transport Minister Gad Ya'akobi, Defense Minister Peres, Justice Minister Chaim Zadok, Minister Without Portfolio Yisrael Galili, and I went into action.

The guidelines we followed were self-evident. Israel held the French government responsible for the fate of all the passengers on the plane of the French national airline. Every passenger on Flight 139 was under sovereign French protection, and no distinction could be made between Israelis and others. We urged France to take action without delay and notify us of its moves. The French government confirmed receipt of our message, stating that it shared our view and bore full responsibility for the safety of all passengers on the airliner.

Once the plane took off again from Libya there were various conjectures as to its destination. Was it Somalia? We knew that the Somali authorities welcomed Wadia Hadad and permitted his men to operate from their territory. The hijackers requested permission to land at Khartoum, but the Sudanese refused. At approximately four o'clock on the morning of Monday, June 28, the plane landed in Entebbe, Uganda. I sensed a momentary relief — though it later proved to be erroneous. Compared with my fear that the plane would be brought down in an Arab country, Uganda looked like a lesser evil. Despite my acquaintance with the idiosyncrasies of Doctor Fieldmarshal Idi Amin Dada, I never guessed how far he would go in collaborating with the hijackers.

It wasn't until two o'clock on the afternoon of Tuesday, June 29, that we learned of the hijackers' demands by means of a Ugandan radio announcement. In return for the hostages, the terrorists wanted the release of fifty-three "freedom fighters" imprisoned in five countries (forty in Israel; six German Bader-Meinhof members imprisoned in West Germany; five in Kenya; one in Switzerland; and one in France). The hijackers presented their ultimatum: within forty-eight hours (by two o'clock on the afternoon of July 1), the released terrorists were to be brought to Entebbe. Those freed by Israel were to be carried by Air France; the other countries could decide on their own transportation.

At 5:30 that afternoon I called in the ministerial team and asked my assistant, Eli Mizrachi, to notify the defense minister that I wished the chief of staff to attend the meeting. Motta Gur was contacted on his way to the Sinai and changed course for Jerusalem immediately. When he arrived I opened the meeting by asking him, "Does the IDF have any possible way of rescuing the hostages by a military operation? If you do, that is our first preference. If not, we shall consider negotiating with the hijackers."

The defense minister did not conceal his surprise at the query. "There has been no consideration of the matter in the defense establishment," he said. "I haven't discussed it with the chief of staff yet . . ." Peres was speaking the truth — and a deplorable truth it was. Fifty-three hours after we learned of the hijacking, he had yet to consult the chief of staff on possible military means of releasing the hostages. Gur evaded the defense minister's attempt to prevent discussion of the subject. On being summoned to the meeting, he said, he understood that his military advice would be asked. Consequently he had ordered the chief of operations to start a preliminary examination of whether the IDF had a feasible military option and to estimate its chances of success. One of the major problems was that we lacked information on the attitude Amin and his army were adopting toward the hijackers and their hostages. If the Ugandans would cooperate with an Israeli operation, its chances would be that much better. When it later became evident that Amin and his army were collaborating with the hijackers, we understood that the IDF would have to take the Ugandan army into account as a hostile force. That certainly didn't make Motta Gur's work any easier.

By nine o'clock Wednesday evening, when the ministerial team again convened, the chief of staff reported that the IDF still had no operational plan he could recommend to the government. Since the ultimatum was scheduled to run out at 2:00 P.M. the following day, when the cabinet met on Thursday morning I could only propose that we negotiate with the hijackers on their terms. The reasoning was simple: we had no right to abandon the hostages. If we were unable to rescue them by force, we must exchange them for terrorists held in our country. The negotiations were not meant as a tactical ruse to gain time. We would negotiate in earnest, and Israel would keep her side of any bargain. The defense minister delivered a pathetic address on the implications of capitulation to terrorist blackmail, and I required a considerable measure of patience to keep from interrupting him. Finally, when he had said his piece, I observed: "Our problem at the moment is not rhetoric. If you have a better proposal, go ahead! What do you suggest?" The defense minister maintained a dignified silence.

In view of the sensitivity of the matter, I could not rest content with nods of consent on the part of the ministers, so I demanded a vote. The cabinet unanimously approved the proposal to negotiate the release of the hostages in exchange for terrorists detained in Israel. I told the ministers that the IDF would continue to prepare a military option, but that in no way detracted from the cabinet's present decision to conduct negotiations with the hijackers through the auspices of the French government.

After the cabinet meeting, I went on to a meeting of the Knesset's Foreign Affairs and Defense Committee, where I presented the cabinet's decision and noted that time was pressing. The ultimatum was to run out at 2:00 P.M., and we had yet to relay our decision to the French government. Menachem Begin requested a short interval for consultations, and on his return he said· "This is not a matter for debate between the coalition and the opposition. It is a national issue of the first order. We support the government's position, and we'll make our views known." To tell the truth, I was moved by Begin's support. I myself was less than content about our decision to negotiate with the blackmailers, and this backing from the opposition provided me with a certain measure of relief. When I returned to the ministerial team and reported on Begin's statement, Peres looked surprised. Evidently the opposition's display of national responsibility had descended on him like a cold shower, cooling his demagogy.

After we notified the French of our decision to enter into negotiations, the terrorists announced that they were extending their ultimatum until Sunday, July 4. I informed the army and added that when it had a proposal that the chief of staff could recommend, I wanted it brought to me immediately. Perhaps it was not sufficiently clear, however, that I was talking about a military plan, for at 1:30 that same afternoon a truly bizarre proposal was put before me with the backing of the defense minister and the chief of staff. The idea was for Moshe Dayan to go to Uganda and talk with Idi Amin. My reaction bordered on disbelief. Placing a famous and important individual like Moshe Dayan in the hands of Uganda's unpredictable tyrant? For Amin to mistreat as he had done to another "friend" (a British general who had come to intercede on behalf of an Englishman imprisoned in Uganda)? Further strengthen the blackmailers' hand and leave ourselves absolutely *no* room for maneuver? Obviously I rejected the proposal, and the subject was dropped.

At 10:30 on the morning of Friday, July 2, the chief of staff presented the first operational plan I could consider as reasonably feasible. This was the "Hercules plan" whereby a military force would land at Entebbe by plane (rather than parachute down, which I regarded as risky and not very promising). Two principal features of the plan still remained open to question: How was the assault force to reach its objective by surprise? And how would it take over the area held by the terrorists and the Ugandan troops before they had time to kill the hostages? Various reports convinced me not to trust the hijackers' warning that the old air terminal at Entebbe (where the hostages were being held) was booby-trapped. Ugandan troops were quartered on the second floor of the building, above the hall where the hostages were being held, and I doubted that they would stay in a building that was mined with explosives.

I was not in favor of trying to refuel the Hercules planes at Entebbe airport and preferred them to refuel at Nairobi on their way back from the rescue operation. I took into account the possibility that the released hostages — and their rescuers — might be detained by the Kenyan authorities, but I assumed that they would not be handed back to the terrorists and the Ugandans. Talks in progress with the Kenyan authorities held out a reasonable chance that they would release the passengers, as well as our men. As things turned out, the Kenyans extended all possible forms of humane assistance and provided our planes with large amounts of fuel. The hospitals acted likewise in caring for our wounded. Most gratifying of all, this assistance was a spontaneous display of sympathy on the part of Kenyan citizens.

A rehearsal of the rescue operation was carried out on Friday night at Sharm el-Sheikh, and on Saturday morning, July 3, the chief of staff could say the long-awaited words: "After attending last night's exercise, I can recommend that the cabinet approve the plan." The ministerial team gave its approval, ordering the planes, with the rescue force, to fly to Sharm el-Sheikh and refuel there before setting off on their long flight. Final approval for the mission had to be given by the cabinet.

I summoned the cabinet for two o'clock that afternoon (the religious ministers had made the necessary arrangements so that they could arrive by foot and thus not desecrate the Sabbath) and invited Menachem Begin and Elimelech Rimalt (the leaders of the opposition) and Yitzhak Navon (then chairman of the Knesset Foreign Affairs and Defense Committee) to meet me at three o'clock. When the cabinet convened, I explained that in order to keep to the timetable laid down for the operation, the planes would have to take off from Sharm el-Sheikh before the cabinet reached its decision. But since the flight time to Entebbe was seven hours, if the cabinet withheld its approval, the planes could be ordered back to their base. The ministers were therefore asked to express their opinions irrespective of the fact that the planes might already be in the air.

"We have a military option," I explained. "It has been thoroughly examined and recommended by the chief of staff. As long as we had none, I was in favor of conducting serious negotiations with the hijackers. Now the situation has changed. I believe that the rescue operation will entail casualties — among the hostages as well as among their rescuers. I don't know how many. But even if we have fifteen or twenty dead — and we can all see what a heavy blow that would be — I am in favor of the operation. If we have a military option, we must take it up — even if the price is heavy — rather than give in to the terrorists."

The chief of staff presented the military plan and ministers asked questions. One of them charged that I had placed the cabinet under pressure by permitting the planes to take off, so I again explained that this would not be the first time that forces drawn up for an operation were subsequently called back when the cabinet did not approve its execution. The ultimatum would run out the following day; and since such an operation could not be launched by daylight, this was the last opportunity. In the end, the cabinet vote was unanimously in favor. While the meeting was still in session, I left to talk to Navon and the opposition leaders, and all three gave their full support for the operation.

We decided not to publicize the cabinet meeting. There were reports from the United States that the Americans were talking about a plane being painted some unusual color at Lydda airport, but the U.S. government did not ask any questions.

After the cabinet meeting, I went home feeling calm for the first time in a week. I was convinced of the correctness of our decision. Every detail, every phase of the operation was etched in my brain like an iron casting. The first of our planes would land at Entebbe between two regular commercial flights. That the airport was functioning normally was of enormous importance to us, since the runways would be illuminated to serve regular flights. After landing, the first plane would taxi along the runway and come as close to the old terminal building as possible. Then the assault force would storm the terminal, using Land Rovers and a black Mercedes resembling Idi Amin's limousine. (To this day, I am not certain whether or not the black Mercedes made a significant contribution to the success of the operation.) A second force arriving in another plane would seize control of the new terminal building to open up a possible line of withdrawal, should circumstances require it. The first plane to land would likewise be the first to take off, carrying the liberated hostages and any casualties.

While the planes roared through the night to Entebbe, I grabbed a short (and badly needed) nap at home and then drove to the defense minister's office. A loudspeaker linkup to GHQ was installed there so that we could follow reports from the force at Entebbe. The military transmissions, laconic and dry, heralded the brilliant success of the operation, which was the first ever conducted so far from Israeli territory. It was carried out in an orderly fashion exactly according to plan. The first plane took off from Entebbe within thirty minutes of landing and carried the hostages, the French crew, part of the assault force, and the casualties. The death toll from the operation was four: three hostages and Yonatan Netanyahu, the commander of the force that attacked the old terminal and one of the finest soldiers in the IDF. Mrs. Dora Bloch, who was in the hospital at the time of the raid, was subsequently murdered by the Kampala authorities. There can be no consolation for the bereaved families. Yet considering the circumstances in which the assault was carried out, the number of casualties was smaller than I had dared to hope. The wounded were given emergency treatment on the aircraft and some were transferred to hospitals in Nairobi. One of our men, Sergeant Hershko, suffered a wound in the spine that has left him partially paralyzed.

When the news came through that the last of our planes had left Entebbe, we drank a toast to the success of the venture. A few hours later, people were literally dancing in the streets as a wave of elation swept over Israel. The world joined in with a chorus of admiration for the IDF's triumph. Not since the Six Day War had we witnessed such an outpouring of public sentiment. Later many Americans told me that we even upstaged the Fourth of July Bicentennial celebrations in the United States (though of course we hadn't planned the Entebbe operation as a public-relations spectacular). The Knesset session held later that day gave expression to a united Israel — a rare but invariably encouraging phenomenon.

Yet perhaps I should have expected that someone would try to make political capital out of the affair — and lay the bill at my feet. The truth is that before the hostages had even arrived home, Terrence Smith, the *New York Times* correspondent in Israel, called Amos Eran, director general of the Prime Minister's Office, and asked him to comment on what he had just heard from the defense minister's spokesman, Naftali Lavi. What had he heard? Obvious. The prime minister had consistently opposed any military action, and it was only the persistence of Shimon Peres — who had been in favor of such an operation from the outset — that forced Rabin to consent. Mr. Lavi also took the trouble to relate how Peres had gone about "forcing" me to withdraw my alleged objections. The story was obviously a fabrication — neither the first nor the last to be disseminated by rivals within my own party in order to undermine my standing and advance their own ambitions. But that is a story in itself — with a full complement of ironic twists at the end — and it's best to save it for its proper place in this book.

The war in Lebanon continued to rage into the autumn, and it was clear that we could not make progress toward a solution to the Arab-Israeli conflict until the Arab states had sorted out their own problems. By the time they began to do so (at the instigation of Saudi Arabia), the United States was immersed in its presidential election campaign, which left little room for dramatic foreign policy initiatives. And when Jimmy Carter emerged as the victor in that contest, it was clear that the "lame duck" administration would not renew the momentum of political talks in the closing months of its existence. Thus 1976 will not be remembered as a year of much progress in Middle East diplomacy.

At the same time, we used that year to continue building the strength of the IDF and properly integrating the flow of American arms. The statistics show that from the close of the Yom Kippur War until the end of June 1977 (when Mr. Begin's government succeeded my own), the IDF doubled its overall strength. The number of planes had risen by 30 percent (including fighter bombers of the highest quality in the world — the F-15s); our tank force had grown by more than 50 percent; mobile artillery had increased over 100 percent; and in armored troop carriers the increase was 700 percent! Thus it may sound like an absurd trick of fate, but the fact is that the cabinet I headed — and under whose leadership the IDF's strength grew to unprecedented proportions — was forced to resign in December 1976 as a result of the arrival of the advanced F-15s from the United States.

The whole paradox arose from the fact that the first planes were scheduled to arrive on a Friday afternoon, just before the onset of the Sabbath. The choice of the timing was not ours; it stemmed from the complexities of the Americans' scheduling, including the need to refuel the planes in the air. In any event, this would not have been the first time that American arms were received on a Friday afternoon — or that a ceremony was held to mark their arrival. Since I personally am no ceremony enthusiast, I queried the need for one on this occasion. But I was told that arrangements had already been made, invitations already sent out, and the ceremony would at any rate be a short and modest one saluting the IDF's entry into a new era of technological advancement.

As the chief of staff noted so aptly at that ceremony, with the arrival of the first F-15s, Israel would not be the same as she had been before. He was quite right about that, but for more reasons than he imagined: the next thing we knew the tiny ultra-Orthodox party of Poalei Agudat Yisrael had tabled a motion of no-confidence against the government for desecrating the Sabbath. I did not then and will not now argue the justice of that charge. The cabinet merely issued a statement expressing its regret in the event that the Sabbath had unintentionally been violated. Moreover, the no-confidence motion was defeated in the Knesset — and with that the matter might have ended. But there was a catch involved in the breakdown of the Knesset vote, and I did not view it as a minor one.

At first it seemed that the cabinet ministers representing the National Religious party understood that the no-confidence motion was a trap, and they agreed to rest content with the cabinet's statement of regret. When the vote was taken in the plenum, however, the NRP's Knesset members and two of their three ministers abstained on the question (Minister of Interior Yosef Burg voted against the motion). For those who may be less familiar with the ways and means of a parliamentary system, and especially coalition politics, I should stress that this was an intolerable situation. A no-confidence vote is a clear-cut proposition for the parties that comprise a government coalition. To abstain from expressing confidence in a government of which you are an integral part is essentially equivalent to opposing it. Logically, as well as morally, there can be no middle ground in this case, for a cabinet that does not support itself cannot expect to retain its authority in the eyes of the electorate. It is as simple as that. I was therefore left with only one course: I asked for the resignation of the NRP ministers and then submitted my own resignation to the president, whereupon my cabinet became a caretaker government until new elections could be held. In the event, the elections due to be held in the autumn of 1977 were moved forward to May of that year.

Imaginations ran riot in Israel. My decision was interpreted variously as a "brilliant trick" to deprive the newly formed Democratic Movement for Change of the time it needed to establish itself; a move designed to prevent Peres from picking up support within the Labor party; and an exploitation of the fact that the Likud was unprepared for an early election campaign. Every possible Machiavellian motive was dredged up instead of squarely facing the simple, honest, and just motives that guided me. Basic national order could not tolerate ambiguity of this nature. And I, for one, would not continue to head a government that lacked the express backing and trust of its own members. That was my privilege, and I did not — and do not — see how I could possibly have acted otherwise without making a mockery of our system of government.

As we began preparing for our elections, however, Jimmy Carter entered the White House and decided to speed up the diplomatic process in the Middle East, despite the pending Israeli vote on its national leadership. I was invited to come to Washington early in March 1977, and even though I knew I was not in a position to undertake far-reaching policy decisions so close to election time, I believed it was important to establish top-level contact with the new American administration as soon as possible. After all, the Middle East was still a "volatile" area, and much could happen without warning even between March and May.

In Washington, I found a new president who had visions of curing all the ills of the American people and restoring its faith in the presidency. He was imbued with profound religious conviction and believed that the American electorate had charged him with the mission of carrying through a great metamorphosis in substance as well as in style.

When we met for our first talk, Carter's opening words were music to my ears. He reiterated America's deep commitment to Israel and the previous administrations' promises that no outside solution would be imposed on us. Admittedly, American interests and commitments in the Middle East were not confined to Israel; but the United States' commitment to Israel's security took precedence over any other interest in the area. His questions were equally moderate and courteous. "Do you agree that 1977 is a good year for a concentrated effort to achieve peace? If so, when shall we convene the Geneva Conference? Who should attend it? How can the question of Palestinian representation be resolved?"

I agreed that we should strive to achieve an overall peace settlement during 1977, since every year is appropriate for such an effort. "But let us understand what we mean by the word 'peace,' " I suggested. "We maintain that peace comprises two elements: elimination of the state of war, and the building of concrete relations that establish new realities for everyday life. That is the difference between President Sadat and my government. He is prepared to terminate the state of war in return for a complete Israeli withdrawal; but he is not willing to enter into a peace that means open borders for the movement of people and goods, cultural exchange, and diplomatic relations."

Secretary of State Cyrus Vance, who had visited the Middle East capitals in February, confirmed my exposition of the Arab attitude: "All the Arab leaders told me that the nature of peace is their own sovereign problem. Whether or not they maintain trade relations with Israel, set up diplomatic relations, open up borders for tourists, and so forth, is their affair. As they see it, the first step is terminating the state of war, and that is all they are prepared to discuss."

The president then asked if Israel was prepared to advance toward peace by stages, and I told him that as far back as January 1976 we had accepted the United States' offer to examine the feasibility of conducting negotiations with Egypt, Syria, and Jordan on ending the state of war. Our position had not changed on that score. But when the president asked, "Is Israel prepared to agree first on an overall settlement and implement it by stages?" a warning light flashed in my mind. This was the gist of the "Brookings report," which viewed peace as the final objective in exchange for an Israeli withdrawal to the pre–Six Day War lines. The withdrawal would be conducted in stages, and its completion would coincide with the restoration of peace in the Middle East. My reply was therefore cautious: "Provided that the principles and borders of a real peace are agreed upon, I see no difficulty in implementing the agreement by stages."

That inevitably led to a discussion of borders, and for the first time in the nine years I had been holding discussions with high-ranking American government officials, the conversation took what I could only interpret as an ominous turn. I explained the views of the Labor Alignment (Labor and Mapam parties) and the

Likud opposition on the question of our final border with Jordan. "The first is prepared, in the context of a peace agreement, for a territorial compromise with Jordan. In the context of a more limited agreement, the Labor Alignment would be prepared to share control over the West Bank with Jordan, placing the Jordanians in charge of the Arab civil administration and Israel in charge of security matters. The Likud policy can be summarized in one sentence: no withdrawal from even an inch of the West Bank. But both parties reject any suggestion of a Palestinian state between Israel and Jordan, and both refuse to negotiate with the PLO."

From the president's response, it seemed to me that Carter was set on the Brookings report and intended to "sell" it to me piecemeal. "But there could be a kind of federation between Jordan and the Palestinian state, along the lines of the states in the U.S.A.," he said. "Foreign affairs and defense would be under the supervision of the central government. The West Bank would be demilitarized and enjoy a quasi-autonomous status. I'm not proposing that. I'm just examining the possibility."

"We are vigorously opposed to an independent Palestinian state between Israel and Jordan," I repeated. "For the moment, I won't dwell on the question of how the Palestinians will find their self-expression in a 'Jordanian-Palestinian state.' But no third state should come into being."

"Would you object to a single united Arab delegation to the Geneva Conference, which would include a Palestinian delegation?" the president asked.

"We have no objection to Palestinians being included in the Jordanian delegation, but we want to negotiate with sovereign states," I told him. "It is not our business if the Arab states coordinate their policies at Geneva, as long as we negotiate with every one of our neighbors as a sovereign state."

"And if the Arabs insist on coming to Geneva as a single, united delegation?" Vance pressed.

"We shall oppose such a proposal — for the sake of the conference. A joint Arab delegation to Geneva will go along with the extremist line of the Arab left — with Moscow's backing — and the outcome will be total failure."

"Egypt is in favor of your approach," Vance noted, "but Syria demands a united delegation."

"Obviously," I said. "Syria wants to foil any progress toward a settlement, and it knows that one sure way of doing so is to come to Geneva with a united, extremist Arab delegation."

At lunch that day I discussed the problem of Lebanon with Secretary Vance. Then we reverted to the question of further diplomatic moves, and over and over again it was made clear that the new administration had accepted the Brookings report, which adopted Israel's views with regard to the nature of peace but demanded an Israeli withdrawal to the June 4, 1967, lines with minor modifications on the West Bank only.

That evening some sixty people attended a working dinner at the White House. In the course of the discussion, Speaker of the House Thomas (Tip) O'Neill challenged me with a sharp question that almost sounded like an accusation: "Why don't you negotiate with the PLO? Why can't we ask you to do what we did? We talked with the Vietcong, not just with the North Vietnamese. If that's what we did, as representatives of a great power, why can't you do the same? Why could the French negotiate with the Algerian FLN and conclude an agreement with them? Why were the British able to negotiate with underground movements all over the world — yours included — while you are unable to negotiate with the PLO?"

"Did the Vietcong refuse to recognize the existence of the United States and call for its annihilation?" I asked him in return. "Was their basic program a 'Vietcong Covenant' whereby the United States was to be replaced by a Vietnamese state? How can you compare the two situations? Did the FLN plan to annihilate France? Did the underground organizations in Israel and elsewhere challenge the existence of Great Britain? What basis is there for negotiations with the PLO, whose avowed *raison d'être* is to destroy Israel and replace her with a Palestinian state?"

Other questions arose and the discussion went on until the president bid his guests good night and invited me to accompany him to the presidential quarters of the White House, where we talked alone. In this more intimate setting, he began by asking me what I *really* thought about peace terms. The president was fully justified in asking to speak to me alone. Personal "softening-up" talks are a conventional diplomatic technique. But his question nonetheless irritated me, for it implied that up until then I had been less than frank about our views and that an intimate talk would induce me, at long last, to tell the truth or ease the path to peace by suddenly producing far-reaching Israeli concessions. I could only tell the president that I had already explained what I really thought. I had no other policy. His expectations dashed, Carter's face took on an expression of annoyance, but our conversation maintained its tone of mutual courtesy.

The president spoke at length about his mission to restore the American people's faith in the presidency by eliminating secrecy in diplomacy. He felt that the president was obliged to present clear-cut views, concepts, and intentions regarding his policies and objectives. He must tell his people what he wanted to achieve and how he meant to go about it. As Carter spoke, I grew increasingly concerned about the effect his "new style" would have on our region. If he publicized his views on the Middle East, in keeping with his credo of frank speaking, he would bring comfort to the Arabs and weaken Israel's negotiating position. The Brookings plan had absolutely nothing in common with Israel's views about final borders.

At my third meeting with the president, both sides turned out with a full complement, and the talk only reinforced my feelings of concern. "With regard to the PLO," Carter stated, "Tip O'Neill spoke for many of us last night. We are utterly opposed to terrorism, but there are precedents for negotiations between states and organizations of this nature. I see no evidence of Palestinian leaders other than the PLO leadership. We might be able to find some compromise whereby the PLO leaders join an Arab delegation. I hope that you will be able to accept some such formula after the elections in Israel."

When I reiterated that we would not negotiate with the PLO and that any change in the United States' attitude toward the terrorists would encourage elements equally undesirable to both our countries, the president agreed unreservedly, adding that there was no change in America's attitude toward the PLO. But Vance was dissatisfied. If he understood our position correctly, we would still refuse to meet the PLO or permit its participation in negotiations even if it changed its attitude toward Israel, as the United States hoped might happen. The president joined in saying that if the PLO did change its position and the Geneva Conference was not convened because Israel remained adamant in its refusal to sit down with the PLO, he foresaw a sharp reaction on the part of the American people.

This was tough talk: a "sharp reaction" not only on the part of the administration but from the American people as well indicated that the Carter administration intended to do everything in its power to bring the PLO to the negotiating table. I told the president that I preferred not to enter into a discussion of such hypothetical questions as what would happen if the PLO changed its philosophy and policy (which did not seem very likely — and still doesn't). But he pressed on by asking how we would respond if the Arab states agreed to our definition of peace and the only obstacle remained the presence of the PLO at the Geneva Conference. No one knew what position would be adopted by Egypt, Syria, and Jordan, and there seemed little point in speculating about all kinds of "what if" situations at present. The president had heard our views, and I suggested that he likewise hear those of the Arab leaders. It was agreed that the United States should examine the possibility of reconvening the Geneva Conference, but I again requested that in the course of doing so, the administration not adopt any firm positions. Such a course would only harm the peacemaking process by fostering the Arabs' hopes that they could achieve their ends by means of American pressure on Israel.

Our discussion turned to the subject of arms, the manufacture of F-16 aircraft in Israel (which was a complex problem because of the United States' joint-manufacture agreement with a number of European countries), the sale of Israeli-manufactured arms containing American components, and the subject of American aid to Israel. When we reverted to diplomatic topics, the president assured me that as far as the definition of peace goes, "Israel's views coincide with those of the United States. I have undertaken the difficult task of bringing a permanent peace to your region," he said. "That means that Israel will enjoy peace, open commerce, and freedom of navigation in the Suez Canal. It will be possible for Israel to receive the energy she requires from the oil-producing countries. And Israel will receive massive aid from the United States. Let no one doubt that our countries are friends and allies. Your hopes with regard to the nature of peace are justified, and we shall support them. We'll keep you in the picture all the time. Our job now is to examine whether there is any basis to assume that it is feasible to advance toward an overall agreement."

I have never attempted to mislead the Israeli people as to the gravity of the president's statements on the Palestinian issue. On various occasions, however, our present prime minister, Menachem Begin, described my talk with Carter as the harshest discussion any Israeli prime minister has ever had with an American president. That is clearly an exaggeration. Alongside his disappointing utterances on the Palestinian issue, the president expressed the most favorable views on the nature of peace that we had ever heard, and I don't think that point should be overlooked.

In my meetings in Washington, I was immediately struck by the differences between the administrations of Nixon and Ford and that of Carter. In their mode of operation, the two Republican presidents allocated decisive roles to senior officials like Kissinger, Sisco, and Haig. They did a thorough job of preliminary preparation, while the president's role was to set his seal to an understanding already concluded or apply the weight of his prestige when the groundwork failed to produce results. None of Carter's aides had the stature of a Kissinger, and the president did not delegate power to his subordinates. At that time, he seemed eager to take an active role in the preparatory work through direct contact with leaders visiting Washington. He also announced his own views to the American people in order to gain the support of public opinion through a personal approach.

That evening, at a festive dinner held in the home of Ambassador Dinitz, I was approached separately by Vice-President

Walter Mondale and Secretary of State Vance with reassurances from the president that the contents of our conversations would under no circumstances be allowed to leak out or be publicized in any manner. I was therefore all the more surprised to hear of the president's far-reaching statements at a press conference the next day. The timing of the president's revelations was especially unfortunate. I had accepted an offer from my friend Joe Sisco, who had left the State Department to become president of Washington's American University, to receive an honorary degree. It was after that ceremony, while I was shaking hands with the well-wishers in one of the halls of the Kennedy Center, that reports of the president's comments reached me and succeeded in dashing my spirits.

The president had evidently not intended to comment on Middle Eastern affairs at his press conference, but under pressure from one of the journalists he broke his own promise to me and those delivered in his behalf by Mondale and Vance. In explicating his views on peace, borders, and other issues related to Middle East peace negotiations, Carter practically committed the United States and the presidency to an explicit position — in complete contradiction to all that had been said to me during our meetings. His remark on Israel's withdrawal to the June 4, 1967, lines, with minor modifications, was the worst part of it. No president before him had ever publicly committed the United States to such a position. Even so, it never occurred to me that only ten days later Carter would speak of the need for a "Palestinian homeland," a further dramatic change in traditional U.S. policy.

I confess to feeling totally dismayed about the president's brand of "secrecy." When Secretary of State Vance came to Blair House to escort me on my departure to New York, it turned out that he was no less surprised. I asked him what had brought about the change in the president's decision to keep the contents of our talks secret, but all he could say was, "I cannot explain it. I don't know. I don't even have a text of the president's statement. That statement will place us in an embarrassing position — not only with you, but with the Arabs as well."

After further meetings with the leaders of the Jewish community in New York, I left the United States with the feeling that we were up against a grave problem. In having to cope with an inexperienced administration, Israel would probably have to pay heavily until the new American government acquired expertise and political maturity. Shortly after my visit to the United States, the president took yet another step that was greeted with serious alarm in Israel. Under Presidents Nixon and Ford, Israel had enjoyed top priority in arms deliveries, above and beyond even the United States' NATO allies. But now Carter proceeded to place Israel far down on the priority list for arms deliveries.

I cannot say what the United States gained by the president's statements and moves, but I do know what the Likud got out of them. Just weeks before the elections were due to be held, new disappointments and fears began to grip the Israeli public. If these were the United States' intentions, if Israel was unable to rely upon the United States as a friend and ally, then she would have to entrust her fate to a "tough" and "uncompromising" leadership to protect her vital interests. In the public mind, the word "uncompromising" was linked with the party that had walked out of the National Unity government rather than accept the 1970 cease-fire with Egypt and had voted against the 1975 interim agreement rather than acclaim a move that brought Israel and Egypt closer to peace. Back in New York I had mused that Israel would have to pay part of the tuition for the new administration's education in the finer points of foreign policy. But only after my return home did I begin to understand that the first bill was going to land at the Labor Alignment's front door.

Chapter Fifteen

TAKING STOCK

AFTER THE RESIGNATION of my cabinet in December 1976, and in preparation for the confrontation that would culminate on election day in May 1977, I began to take stock of myself and of my government. Not for one moment did I delude myself into thinking that the two and a half years of my cabinet's tenure had been an unblemished success story. Yet insofar as a man is capable of judging his own actions, I sought objective answers to a variety of questions: Where had we succeeded? Where had we failed? Where had we fulfilled expectations, and where had we been found wanting?

We had ample reason to be proud of our record in the spheres of foreign affairs and defense. At the beginning of 1976, Israel had reached a strategic understanding with the United States on the goal of future diplomatic efforts, and relations between the two countries were at their best. The IDF's arsenals were amply stocked with weapons. Not only had our armed forces been rehabilitated after the Yom Kippur War, but the growth of their strength — qualitatively and quantitatively — was imposing. Furthermore, the hard-won interim agreement with Egypt had created new realities in the region, and for the first time since the creation of the State of Israel there were reasonable prospects of moving away from war and toward peace.

In the course of 1976, I even had hopes that we might establish direct contact with Egyptian statesmen, but unfortunately they were never fulfilled. The first instance was when Peres notified me of an approach from an old friend of his, Karl Kahana of Austria, who had close ties with Chancellor Bruno Kreisky. Kahana proposed that Peres or I come to Austria and meet with Hassan Tohami, a prominent Egyptian figure who had long served as his country's ambassador to Austria. I consented that Peres should undertake the mission, but to our regret nothing ever came of it.

Romania's president, Nicolai Ceauşescu, also tried to lend a hand by sending one of his political advisers on a secret mission to Israel to discuss the feasibility of setting up an Israeli-Egyptian meeting for direct negotiations. When the envoy arrived, we reached an agreement whereby President Ceauşescu would try to arrange such a meeting between Israeli and Egyptian representatives — preferably at a high level but, if that proved out of reach, on whatever level he could achieve. The Romanian envoy promised to notify me as soon as possible as to whether or not his president's efforts had borne fruit. I have not heard from him to this day.

There were also various abortive "feelers" from Sadat regarding visits to Egypt by a delegation of leaders of the World Jewish Congress and later of Rabbi Alexander Schindler (then chairman of the Conference of Presidents of American Jewish Organizations), but they never came to pass. Besides, it was not intermediaries that we lacked, and I was never very enthusiastic about the idea of introducing more "third parties" into the situation. We were eager to meet directly with Egyptians; President Sadat was not yet ready for such a move.

The frustrated efforts on this plane notwithstanding, had my government been judged solely on its political and military record, I am sure that its achievements would have earned it extensive support — and the Labor party would probably have remained in power. Yet these two spheres were not the only test. The crucial nature of political and military issues forces every Israeli prime minister to place them at the head of his priorities, but his government must also cope with the country's economic and social problems. In fact, the latter are often the principal concern of the average citizen because of their direct influence on his daily life. To some degree the division of attention between these two spheres creates a cruel paradox: a government whose efforts succeed in preventing war is forced to pay the price for its failings in the domestic sphere; but if war breaks out and the IDF is victorious, all sins seem to be forgiven.

Israel has no lack of economic problems and the social friction that invariably follows in their wake. There can be no question that, judged by the standards of industrialized Western nations, life in Israel is really very hard. Few contemporary Western peoples have been subject to the combined burdens that Israelis have carried for more than three decades. Everyone must serve in the armed forces and be ready to take up his country's defense on the battlefield at a moment's notice (certainly no exaggeration considering our experience on Yom Kippur in 1973). We also live with the constant threat of terrorist attacks on the streets of our cities and towns and even in our own homes. Added to that, Israel is a developing country blessed with few natural resources, so that our citizens must contribute the best of their talents in every sphere of creativity, while the financial rewards for their efforts are limited by the need to pay heavy taxes to support the objective needs of the state. All this has always been true of life in Israel — even before the state came into being — and every generation made its sacrifices in the hope of creating a better life for its progeny. That is one of the facts of life here.

As I am neither a sociologist nor an economist, it is impossible for me to state exactly when and how the domestic situation in Israel began to falter. But I do know that by the time I entered office in June 1974, Israel was possessed of a booming "black market," which made our objective and already unwieldy economic problems all the more difficult to handle. The gap between the "haves" and the "have nots" was not only growing wider, it was becoming far, far more conspicuous. While the self-employed found it relatively easy to conceal portions of their income from the tax assessor, salaried workers began to express their disgruntlement over carrying more than their fair share of the national economic burden — often by disrupting the economy through strikes. At the same time, a segment of the poorer strata of the population emerged in open revolt over lack of attention to their plight. Under such circumstances, appeals to the public to "tighten its belt," "reduce consumption," and "exercise restraint" were treated with undisguised scorn.

Because of my own preoccupation with defense and foreign affairs, I was forced to delegate the handling of these economic problems to Finance Minister Yehoshua Rabinovich and other

ministers working in related fields while promising them my full
backing. And there is no question that they scored some truly impressive gains in the difficult struggle to set the economy back
on track after the heavy blow of the Yom Kippur War. Through
stubborn and consistent efforts, the government succeeded in increasing exports, cutting down on imports, and in 1976 reduced
the balance of payments deficit by $600 million. At the same time,
it channeled enormous sums of money to the underprivileged
classes of our society through the National Insurance Institute,
guaranteeing them a minimum standard of living. Finally, the Finance Ministry instituted a far-reaching reform in the income-tax
system by reducing the maximum rate to 60 percent (whereas it
had previously reached as high as 87.5 percent, even for a salaried worker) while requiring two hundred thousand self-
employed taxpayers to keep books. The simultaneous introduction of the value-added tax was both a strong inducement to keep
accurate financial records and an aid in assessing the true sum of
income tax due from the self-employed.

I cannot claim that the new tax system was a cure-all for the nation's self-inflicted economic ills. But it was a frontal attack on the
"black market," which was clearly eating away at the social and
moral fabric of our society. What it could not do, however, was
instantly dissolve the resentments that had been brewing for so
long against the background of economic disparities and injus-
tices. All that was lacking, it seemed, was evidence that the cynicism and corruption that seemed to set the tone in commercial
dealings had penetrated into public life as well. And then, as if on
cue, a rash of scandals began to break. They started with the dis-
covery of an enormous amount of money missing from the Britain-
Israeli Bank, followed by an uproar over shady dealings by the
director of the Israel Corporation, Michael Zur (who had for many
years served as a director general of a government ministry and
was on close terms with government and Labor party officials).
Neither of these affairs was related to the government, but when
a scandal broke regarding Asher Yadlin's conduct as the head of
the Histadrut (Labor Federation) Sick Fund, even the cabinet
found itself damaged by the fallout.

The embarrassment to the cabinet derived from the fact that

right after Yadlin had been appointed to the prestigious post of governor of the Bank of Israel, he was arrested on charges of financial misconduct during his term as director of the Histadrut Sick Fund. When the arrest occurred, we were caught in a vise between two cardinal moral principles. There was never any question but that a governor of the Bank of Israel must be a man of impeccable scruples and moral stature, and Yadlin's reputation was already severely damaged by the fact that enough evidence had accumulated against him to justify his arrest. Yet even in the course of a campaign against crime, the fundamental tenet that a man is innocent until proven guilty cannot be disregarded. If the government had canceled Yadlin's appointment on the basis of the fact that charges had been brought against him, it would appear as if we had already tried the case and found him guilty — and that is not the role of the country's cabinet. In the end, Yadlin confessed to some of the charges before his trial, thereby freeing the case of any possible ambiguity, and his appointment was canceled. But the damage had already been done in terms of casting a shadow on the government's judgment for appointing him in the first place. Later it was claimed that Yadlin's misdeeds were committed not in order to line his own pockets but to help finance Labor party expenditures. This charge was never corroborated by any evidence. But in the emotion-charged atmosphere that surrounds a public scandal, allegations have a miraculous power of their own, while the basic need to prove them seems to get lost in the frenzy. Sometimes the mania goes on until some shocking event finally makes people realize that things have gone too far.

In the case of the scandal fever that gripped Israel at the end of 1976, it took the tragic death of a cabinet minister to bring matters back into proper perspective. On November 10, 1976, a correspondent of the weekly *Ha'olam Hazeh* submitted a written complaint to the head of the Investigations Branch of the police enumerating offenses allegedly committed by Housing Minister Avraham Ofer during the period he served as director general of the Histadrut's housing company, Shikun Ovdim. A team of four officers was duly appointed to examine the accusations and decide if there was any basis for a formal inquiry.

To make a long and very agonizing story short, the media pounced on the issue with undisguised glee, and for close to two whole months the public was regaled with reams upon reams of fabrications. I have always detested trials by the press; and in this case, before a shred of evidence was found suggesting Ofer's guilt, the papers had already massacred him. All during that time the police were investigating whether there were grounds for a formal inquiry. Ofer had not been told what charges had been raised against him or what kind of investigation was being conducted, yet details of the police's work were constantly leaked to the press. Since he had not formally been accused of any crime, he could not exercise his right to defend himself. I knew that the police had checked the complaints submitted by the *Ha'olam Hazeh* correspondent and found no foundation for them. But in the frenzy of those days, new "suspicions" arose and the police claimed they needed more time to check them out. It seemed to me that the entire affair was a glaring mockery of justice, yet all I could do was complain to the attorney general about the intolerable manner in which the case was being handled. For reasons known only to himself, however, the attorney general was not at all forthcoming in his help.

When Ofer came to see me on January 2, 1977, the toll that the affair had taken of him was all too visible. He had come to plead his innocence before me, but I could only express my confidence in him and offer my support as a personal friend. I begged him to be patient for another week or two, for I knew the truth would come out. But he was already a broken man and could not withstand the incessant pressure. The next day Avraham Ofer committed suicide. To my mind, the trigger of his gun had been pulled by an intemperate public and a press that permitted itself to condemn a man before he was even accused of a crime. It was a tragic and sobering experience, and I can only hope that its lessons will be long-standing.

The residue of the scandals — genuine and fabricated — was especially bitter for the Labor party, since 1977 was an election year and incumbent administrations are always an easy target of public agitation and discontent. Clearly the time had come for the party to close ranks and dedicate a maximum effort to preparing for the upcoming contest at the polls. But in the weeks before the Labor party's Central Committee was scheduled to meet and officially choose the head of its electoral slate, Shimon Peres was engaged in his own private race for the prime ministership; and instead of engendering unity on the eve of the battle, he tore the party into two opposing camps.

By the time Peres openly threw his hat into the ring, few were surprised by his move. I was dogged by the feeling that he had been "running" for prime minister ever since April 1974, when the Central Committee vote chose me as the Labor candidate to form a government. Before that vote, Peres had approached me with talk of a "fair fight" and "loyalty to the winner," but after he lost I saw little evidence of the loyalty to which he was pledged. The reports disseminated by the Defense Ministry's spokesman immediately after the Entebbe operation were just one example of the broad interpretation applied to that term.

I cannot imagine an Israeli cabinet — or any government forum, for that matter — whose members do not have differences of opinion. Yet in order for a government to maintain its authority and credibility, once a decision is reached by majority vote the entire cabinet is obligated to stand behind it. There can be no greater threat to the public's confidence in its government than having cabinet squabbles splashed across the pages of the daily papers. On a number of occasions, however, the defense minister behaved as if he was out to challenge the cabinet's authority by taking his differences to the public. When we clashed over the defense budget — which had at any rate grown to mighty proportions during my tenure as prime minister — Peres chose to make the issue a subject of public debate. When the cabinet adopted a policy that excluded the establishment of new settlements in the heavily populated area of Samaria on the West Bank (in the belief that Jewish settlement there was not justified by security considerations and would only serve as a provocation to the Arab population), Peres raised the banner of "settlement everywhere." With his characteristic rhetorical flourish, he proclaimed that "the hills of Samaria are no less lofty than the hills of Golan" — as though politics was a mountaineering contest. Public statements of this kind naturally encouraged the Gush Emunim movement to challenge the government to a show of strength, though it is difficult to fathom why a cabinet minister would be interested in encouraging defiance of his own government's policy.

At the same time, our government was plagued by a sinister rash of leaks. Probably the most infamous of all was that of the classified stenograms of talks between Mrs. Meir's government and Dr. Kissinger, which were passed on to *Ha'aretz* correspondent Matti Golan. This wasn't a matter of a "tip" to a journalist friend; Golan actually came into possession of entire transcripts! The aim of the move was clearly to destroy Kissinger's trust in the feasibility of conducting frank and intimate talks with the Israeli government and to undermine the cabinet's public standing by impeding its ability to function in the sphere of foreign affairs.

The leaks did not come mainly from cabinet meetings; they were related to matters handled jointly by the Prime Minister's Office and the ministries of foreign affairs and defense. Obviously, I could not investigate each and every incident, but one was of such exceptional gravity (the secret visit to Israel by two Soviet representatives) that it called for exceptional measures. I consented that the officials of the three ministries who had access to the classified information on that visit (from their respective ministers) should undergo lie-detector tests. The tests failed to single out any one of them, so I called in Yigal Allon and Shimon Peres to consult on how to handle this insidious threat to our conduct of foreign policy. When Allon suggested that the three of us likewise submit to the test, Peres threatened to resign rather than do so. I decided that a lie-detector test would not be necessary. I would never claim that resorting to lie detectors was a pleasant or dignified choice for us, but the leaks were not merely a minor annoyance — they threatened to disrupt the conduct of our policy on issues of the most sensitive nature. Again, we were never able to get to the root of it.

When Peres announced that he was a contender for the Labor

party's nomination for the post of prime minister, at least his fight was finally out in the open. He invoked the principles of democracy to justify his candidacy, though there was no precedent for a cabinet member challenging the prime minister from his own party without first resigning his cabinet post. However, I did not and will not argue the merits of the case regarding democratic theory. The problem was essentially one of logic and credibility. If a party discredited its own prime minister (as Peres was asking the Labor party to do), how could it reasonably expect the electorate to place any confidence in its next candidate for the post? Since June 1974 the Labor party had consistently backed its prime minister in every parliamentary vote. Why withdraw its support from him now in an internal party forum? Because he was unworthy of the position? Then a responsible party should have deposed him long before the elections were due. Because some far better candidate had come along in the meantime? Perhaps, but that could not be said of Mr. Peres; he had already contended for the post (quite legitimately) in 1974 — and had lost.

No one seemed to be able to make Peres see that challenging the incumbent prime minister was a formula for political disaster. If he lost the internal party vote, he would only have succeeded in flaunting the party's disarray before the electorate. If he won the vote, he would turn the Labor party into a laughingstock and completely debase its credibility at the polls. But he would not listen to reason, so the Central Committee held its vote — and Peres lost again.

The greatest irony was that after I withdrew my candidacy and Shimon Peres was chosen to head the Labor party's slate, he and his supporters reaped the bitter fruit of their long campaign to cast aspersions on the cabinet, harm its credibility, and flay it for its sins of omission. The public believed them, but it could not follow the twisted logic that blamed all the country's ills and tribulations on a "hapless prime minister" and claimed that with Peres at its head, the Labor party was worthy of the electorate's confidence once more.

The reason why I forfeited my nomination is well known, but I believe that the story surrounding the incident demands some elaboration in the interests of accuracy. Two days after I returned from the United States in March 1977, an *Ha'aretz* correspondent published the fact that the joint bank account Leah and I had used during my tenure as ambassador in Washington remained open. The existence of the account was beyond dispute, as was the fact that it ran counter to a Treasury regulation forbidding Israeli citizens to keep foreign currency accounts abroad. Presumably that regulation was instituted to prevent people from spiriting money from "black market" transactions out of the country in order to evade taxes. The two thousand dollars in our account on the day its existence was reported represented what remained of our savings from the period when we had lived in Washington. During the intervening years there had been withdrawals, but no deposits, and the amount progressively dwindled until the entire balance was transferred to Israel.

Leah has always been our family "finance minister," and in the case of the Washington account all withdrawals were made on her signature. That may have been the source of the subsequent references to "Leah Rabin's bank account." But to my mind, there could be no question that morally and formally we shared responsibility equally. We were joint signatories to the account, and since the problem was that the account existed — not how it had been managed — I did not see any grounds to draw a distinction between us. As soon as the affair became public, I sought the advice of Minister Without Portfolio Yisrael Galili, in whose good sense I had often placed my trust. I told him that if my candidacy were a liability to the party in the elections — or if certain members thought it might be — I was prepared to withdraw it immediately. After consulting other colleagues, Galili asked me to wait and see the results of the inquiry to be carried out by the Treasury.

The need for an inquiry arose from the fact that there was no clear-cut legal formula for resolving the matter; the law merely empowered the finance minister to decide how to act in the event that an Israeli citizen possessed foreign currency contrary to regulations. As soon as the *Ha'aretz* story was published, my

lawyer contacted the Finance Ministry's foreign currency super-
visor and gave him the relevant details. I also contacted the attorney general, Aharon Barak, and notified him of the procedure my
lawyer had adopted. Barak's tone was gentle and conciliatory as
he played down the gravity of the whole matter. His attitude
went a long way toward reassuring Leah.

Since the law was so vague, Finance Minister Yehoshua Rabinovich decided to appoint a committee to examine the matter. But
while the committee was conducting its examination, the attorney
general reversed his position. After previously disassociating himself from the matter, he announced that he objected to an investigation by an internal Finance Ministry committee. He wanted
the committee to be appointed by the head of the Foreign Currency Division and to include representatives of the ministries of
finance, police, and justice. Soon afterward I heard that the attorney general had decided to take the whole process under his control and that the finance minister would not be able to accept or
reject the new committee's recommendations without his approval.

The new committee was duly formed, and on the afternoon of
April 5, 1977, I was notified that its conclusion was to require Leah
and me to pay a fine. But the following day, the attorney general
decided that if the finance minister adopted this recommen-
dation, he would not be able to defend it should it be challenged
in court. The justice minister concurred with his view. Instead,
Barak came up with a new proposal whereby a distinction would
be drawn between Leah and me. I would be required to pay a
token fine, whereas she would stand trial before a district court.
To this day I cannot understand the legal justification for drawing
that distinction, and at the time I sensed a growing resolve to
reject the offer with a resounding no. I would do everything possible to share full responsibility with my wife.

As a result, I arrived at a further decision: I could no longer
remain the party's candidate for prime minister. As the experience of the past few days had shown, the gravity of the offense
was open to a broad range of interpretation. But I had committed
an offense, and although the attorney general viewed it as a tech-

nical infringement, I felt that I had to render my own personal and private account, which demanded consistency and courage. Friends tried to dissuade me from taking any fateful steps, but a man is always truly alone at such times. And alone, my conscience and I came to three interconnected decisions: I would withdraw my nomination as the candidate for prime minister; I would share full responsibility with Leah; and I would try to resign my post as prime minister, so that the Labor party's nominee could fill the post up to the elections (when he would head the slate).

I intended to notify the nation of my decision in a broadcast that same evening, April 7. Some friends still tried to dissuade me in the hope that after further reflection I would change my mind. "Out of the question this evening," they said. "Tonight is the live telecast of the basketball game between the Israeli and Italian teams for the European championship." No one could *dream* of competing with the European championship game (which Israel won, by the way). So I waited until the game was over and then informed the Israeli people that I was forfeiting my nomination and seeking ways of resigning my post as prime minister, even though the law precludes the resignation of a caretaker cabinet.

I immediately felt the kind of relief that can only be entertained by a man who knows he has been honest with himself and true to his own conscience. Yet the law remained in force. I wanted to resign as prime minister but was told that for the head of a caretaker cabinet that was out of the question. Left with no other choice, I took a leave of absence until after election day, while Shimon Peres was chosen to serve as chairman at cabinet meetings. In such an event, the law does not relieve the prime minister of his overall responsibility, so I made the appropriate arrangements to receive current reports on political and defense matters. Then Leah and I set off for an extended tour of the Sharm el-Sheikh area, far from the heavy atmosphere of Tel Aviv and Jerusalem.

We returned home a few days before Leah was scheduled to be tried at the district court. Once again good and well-intentioned friends begged me to stay away from the court when Leah was tried. "Your presence will only turn the whole thing into a great show," they insisted. "As it is, the matter has been inflated beyond all reasonable proportion." They had a point, and when Leah insisted that I not join her in the courtroom I respected her wishes. On the morning of April 17, 1977, I accompanied her to the court and then left to await the verdict. The judge, who had a reputation for strictness, was consistent with his fame: he fined Leah a quarter of a million Israeli pounds. We decided not to appeal, and with that the case was closed.

For weeks after the trial, every delivery of mail brought letters that touched us both very deeply. People from all over the country and all sectors of society expressed their sympathy and some even offered financial assistance. One citizen advised us not to pay the fine and volunteered to serve the alternative prison sentence in Leah's stead. Leah spent days replying to each of the thousands of letters personally and gratefully refusing the checks that often accompanied them.

I think that the most moving experience of all, however, occurred at a Memorial Day ceremony for our fallen soldiers. Although I was officially on leave, no one in Israel can ever take a leave of absence from the heavy price we have paid for gaining and defending our independence, and I felt impelled to attend the ceremony as a citizen of the state. When the ceremony ended, an elderly man walked up to me. I did not know him, but I could see that he was in a highly emotional state. "I am a bereaved father," he said, "and there's something I want to tell you. Here, on this hallowed ground, *here* you have no account. And that is what is truly important." Then he silently extended me a warm handshake, turned, and walked away. I was stunned, and his words reverberated in my mind: "*Here*, you have no account . . ." I also attended a memorial ceremony in Haifa, and although such events are conducted in an atmosphere of silence and formality, befitting mourning, when I was called upon to address the ceremony thunderous applause broke out. Afterward bereaved parents came up to say a few words of encouragement. Deeply touched and embarrassed, I could only mumble my gratitude.

On the evening of May 17, 1977, when I heard the first election results and forecasts of the final outcome, it was clear to me that the Labor party had been called upon to pay the price for the intrigues, conflicts, and internal dissension that had divided its ranks. For the first time in Israel's history, the people had voted for a change of the ruling party. I therefore decided to resume my post as prime minister in order to ensure the orderly and proper transfer of power to the new government. During the month it took for Menachem Begin to constitute his coalition, our cabinet meetings were devoted mostly to a summary of the government's three years in office. The ministers themselves were often astounded by our achievements, for when such matters are viewed in toto they have a powerful impact. (It is truly a shame that the Labor party failed to convey the impact to the public, but that accounting would have to be made in another forum.)

Finally, at midday on June 21, 1977, Menachem Begin and I met in the Prime Minister's Office to execute the popular will. In a brief and modest ceremony, I formally passed the reins of government into his hands, and we wished each other success. Then Prime Minister Menachem Begin took his seat and Knesset Member Yitzhak Rabin left to assume his duties as a member of the loyal opposition.

Chapter Sixteen

THE RISKS OF PEACE

BUT THAT IS emphatically not the end of the story — neither of my own story nor of the political saga first set into motion by my government. As for me personally, serving in the opposition in no way means languishing in the wilderness or laying down one's political burdens. On the contrary, as a member of the Knesset, and especially in my role as a member of its Foreign Affairs and Defense Committee, I have spent the last two years actively monitoring, analyzing, and responding to the political developments that have taken place in the country and the region, and I have remained alert to every twist and nuance in our present government's policies. Moreover, I have traveled, lectured, written political analyses for the press, and devoted no small part of my time to the internal affairs of the Labor party, which has tried to exploit this period in opposition to regenerate its vigor from within while fulfilling its role as a responsible critic of policies that run counter to the interest of its constituency.

Being on the "outside," as it were, allows a political leader to view events from a different and sometimes broader perspective. This is not only an advantage but the responsibility of a party that finds itself in political opposition. As many dramatic political developments have occurred in the Middle East since I left office, I believe it would be constructive, and perhaps enlightening, to take a look at the forces and processes that have brought Israel to the threshold of a new age and, as a direct result, to a time of renewed introspection about who we are and what we aspire to become.

When I left office in June 1977, the positions of the countries most actively engaged in the peacemaking process — Egypt,

Israel, and the United States — had already begun to diverge on certain key points. As I saw it, Egypt's efforts to solve the Arab-Israeli conflict by peaceful means — a process that began after the Yom Kippur War and concentrated first on resolving the Egyptian-Israeli conflict — was a policy that had passed the point of no return. By the summer of 1977, it was impossible for Egypt, as long as it remained under the leadership of Anwar Sadat, to reverse its course of action, for Sadat had burned all his bridges to the Russians by then and consequently found himself left with only one option: to negotiate a solution to the Middle East conflict (rather than revert to the use of force). The disengagement agreement of 1974 and, even more so, the interim agreement of 1975 had essentially left him with only one way to go: further negotiations until the achievement of peace.

Meanwhile, under the Carter administration, the United States continued to pursue the policy that the president had described to me during our meetings in March 1977. The Americans had set for themselves a single operative political goal: full-fledged and comprehensive peace. Carter was determined to achieve peace between Israel and all her neighbors simultaneously and to solve all the outstanding issues that had maintained the Arab-Israeli conflict for so long. This was an ambitious goal, to say the least. But the Carter administration was convinced that without a solution to the three major and complex issues that nurtured the conflict, true peace would never be achieved. Moreover, the Americans had clearly defined views about each of these three major issues. When it came to the nature of peace, they called for nonbelligerency *and* full normalization of relations. As to the boundaries of peace, they called on Israel to withdraw to the pre–Six Day War lines. And as a solution to the Palestinian problem, they postulated the establishment of a Palestinian "homeland" in the West Bank and the Gaza Strip after the withdrawal of Israeli forces from these areas — meaning the establishment of an independent Palestinian entity whose future would be decided by the Palestinians themselves with the cooperation of the other Arab countries.

When the new Israeli government under Mr. Begin assumed

power, one of its first moves was to institute a radical departure from the policies that had been advocated and pursued by my government. On the one hand, it joined President Carter in proclaiming that the only operative goal should be full-fledged peace; but from there on, it parted ways with the Carter administration regarding the other positions advocated by the United States. On the territorial question, Mr. Begin's government took an extreme position, essentially demanding the extension of Israeli sovereignty over the West Bank and the Gaza Strip. And, of course, it came out strongly against the creation of any Palestinian entity there, because the Begin government stipulated the inclusion of Judea and Samaria (the biblical names for the West Bank) and the Gaza Strip within the sovereign State of Israel as an integral part of any final settlement.

When Prime Minister Begin visited the United States in July 1977 to meet with President Carter, he instituted a departure in another sphere as well: the traditional understanding between the Israeli and American governments regarding the need to coordinate political policy. I had always believed — as had Labor prime ministers before me — that prior to embarking on any political initiative, it was imperative for our two governments to reach an understanding, even though in order to do so we might be called upon to make certain compromises. Naturally, in the course of hammering out a coordinated policy, differences of opinion and tensions may well arise. But these can hardly be characterized as a "breach" or a "confrontation"; and at least, once the discussions were completed, we would have a common strategy with the United States — no minor achievement for a small nation in today's world. However, when Mr. Begin saw that the gap between the position of his government and that of the United States was so wide that it appeared unbridgeable, he revised this traditional policy and proclaimed, with what was undoubtedly meant to be a reassuring smile, that Israel and the United States had "agreed to disagree." In doing so, Begin relieved the Americans of the necessity to coordinate policies with Israel before taking any political initiative vis-à-vis the Arab countries regarding negotiations on a final settlement.

For those who did not understand the full implications of that change in the relationship between the United States and Israel, the "cordial" ring of Mr. Begin's slogan led to the impression that his visit to the United States had been a resounding success. And to reinforce that impression, upon his return to Israel he went on to accuse me of almost bringing Israel into a confrontation with the United States by advocating the coordination of policy between the two governments. His motto now became "No confrontation!" "I saved Israel," he claimed, "from what Rabin almost wrought." There are probably few political leaders today who can compete with Mr. Begin in their enthusiasm for their own slogans. But all his enthusiasm for this latest phrase could not cover up its inherent twisted logic. Indeed, when future historians set to charting the development of the "credibility gap" that has plagued Mr. Begin's government, I believe they will find it was born in this very statement made so early on in his term as prime minister.

In any event, during the course of 1977, the United States continued to pursue its policy and, for the first time, committed the presidency to the demand that Israel withdraw to the June 4, 1967, lines and accept the creation of a Palestinian entity in return for peace in the fullest sense of the word. President Carter made his position clear to a number of Arab leaders, including President Sadat, King Hussein of Jordan, President Assad of Syria, and King Khaled of Saudi Arabia. Yet in following through on the assumption that peace could be achieved between Israel and all the neighboring countries simultaneously, the United States inevitably found itself having to court, with unprecedented vigor, the extremists in the Arab world — namely, Syria, and even, to a certain extent, the PLO. As a result, during the summer of 1977, and particularly when Secretary of State Vance visited the Middle East in August, he convinced Egypt — and later on Israel as well — to agree to a concession demanded only by the Syrians: the Geneva Peace Conference would be conducted not by separate missions sent from each individual country but rather by Israel facing a single, unified delegation from the Arab side. Egypt was in fact totally opposed to such an arrangement.

But Sadat was forced to accept it because it had become American policy, and he was essentially left without any choice but to follow whatever process the United States devised.

As far as the PLO is concerned, Israel witnessed an alarming reversal in American policy during that same Middle Eastern tour by the secretary of state. In the memorandum of agreement between the American and Israeli governments that followed from the interim agreement of September 1975, the United States committed itself not to maintain any diplomatic contacts with the PLO as long as the latter failed to accept United Nations Resolution 242 and recognize Israel's right to exist. While he was in Saudi Arabia, it was suggested to Secretary Vance that the United States, and preferably the president himself, should come out and declare that he would view the PLO's acceptance of Resolution 242 as its tacit recognition of Israel's right to exist (without the PLO having to spell it out in so many words). Furthermore, it should then be made clear that the United States would understand the PLO's acceptance of the resolution as being qualified, since neither the name "Palestine" nor the term "Palestinians" is mentioned in that document. It would therefore be understood that the PLO, while accepting Resolution 242, would retain the right to raise the Palestinian issue in any way it might choose.

While the secretary of state was in Saudi Arabia, President Carter was spending a long weekend at his home in Plains, Georgia; and in his efforts to bring the PLO to the negotiating table, he called upon representatives of the various American television networks and spelled out precisely what the Saudis had suggested to Vance. Even that was to little avail, however, for despite the fact that the president's statement was a clear-cut departure from a signed commitment to the Israeli government, the PLO refused to budge. For us, however, this new trend was ample cause for alarm.

It would not be the last cause. In continuing its pursuit of comprehensive peace, the United States harbored the illusion that the Soviet Union had the power to influence the extremists in the Arab world toward moderation. It was with that in mind that the American government entered negotiations with the Soviets that led to the joint communiqué of October 1977. Obviously, Israel was profoundly upset by this latest turn in American policy. But even more significant, I believe that this return to joint talks with the Russians was the proverbial last straw for President Sadat, for it made him realize that the Americans were practically forcing him into a situation that could be detrimental to his regime. First U.S. policy had given President Assad a veto right over Sadat. Now, with the purpose of achieving a comprehensive peace settlement, the Americans were bringing the Russians back into the picture — in complete contradiction to the efforts of former administrations, following the Yom Kippur War, which had been designed to neutralize the Russian factor and consequently bring about a change in Sadat's posture from a warlike policy to a peaceful one. Unlike the Americans, Sadat had no illusions about the role the Soviets would play. He knew they had one thing in mind: to undermine his regime and thereby play a more active role in finding a "solution" to the Middle East conflict that would best serve their own global interests.

I am convinced that this latest reversal in American policy forced Sadat to reassess his own posture. He quickly grasped that if the United States were allowed to continue moving along its present lines, he would soon find himself in a very awkward situation. Sadat knew that the Geneva Peace Conference — should it indeed convene in 1977 — would only lead to deadlock. If that happened, he would practically be forced to follow the Soviet-Syrian-PLO line at the conference, rather than continue to work on the basis of an earlier understanding between Israel, Egypt, and the United States that these three countries would guide events in the region. Thus in yet another ironic twist of political life in the Middle East, I would venture to say that by default of its policy, the Carter administration can actually claim credit for President Sadat's historic decision to come to Jerusalem.

Sadat exploited lines of communication that had been opened between Israel and Egypt even before 1977, for while I was still prime minister, Morocco had tried to serve as a mediator between the governments of Israel, Egypt, and Syria. The Egyptians were well aware that the possibility of establishing contact with Israel through Morocco — without the United States' being involved or, indeed, even knowing — was readily available to them. When Morocco's initiative was launched in 1976, the idea behind it was to hold direct negotiations between the parties and avoid the influence of either one of the superpowers. Thus, as has become public knowledge, it was through the "Moroccan connection" that a meeting took place between the deputy prime minister of Egypt, General Tohami, and Israeli Foreign Minister Dayan to pave the way for President Sadat's visit to Jerusalem.

As matters turned out, I happened to be visiting the United States at the beginning of November 1977 when President Sadat made his famous statement before the Egyptian parliament that he would go to the ends of the earth — even to Jerusalem — in the pursuit of peace. Soon after I arrived in Washington, I met with Secretary of State Vance at the State Department for a talk on the situation in the Middle East. I asked the secretary and his advisers how Egypt had reacted to the joint American-Soviet communiqué issued a few weeks earlier, and I was amazed to see to what extent they misinterpreted the true state of affairs, for they replied that Egypt's reaction had been quite positive. When I went on to ask how they evaluated the chances that a meeting would actually take place between Begin and Sadat, they replied "about fifty-fifty." After I left that meeting, it took only a few hours for Walter Cronkite of CBS News to replace the State Department and, through a joint interview with Begin and Sadat broadcast on the evening news, bring about that barely probable "meeting" between the two leaders and President Sadat's subsequent visit to Jerusalem.

Naturally, when I learned that Egypt's president would indeed be coming to Jerusalem, I cut short my visit to the United States and rushed back to Israel, arriving a day before he did. There could be no doubt, even then, that Sadat's decision had opened a new chapter in the relations between the Arab countries — particularly Egypt — and Israel. As I saw it then, his move was both a courageous and a desperate one. Courageous, because until then such a step had been absolutely unthinkable — and still was unthinkable in most of the countries in the Arab world. Desperate, because Sadat realized that if the policies of the United States were allowed to develop along the lines favored by the Carter administration, they would bring about the destruction of almost four years of dogged efforts that had been conducted in a very cautious, low-key manner but had produced, for the first time after a generation of hostility and stalemate, both negotiations and the signing of an agreement between Egypt and Israel. Thus I believe that Sadat came to Israel with a twofold purpose in mind: to open up new opportunities by bringing down the walls of suspicion and eliminating the deeply rooted psychological barriers that existed in Israel vis-à-vis his intentions; and to force the United States to revise its policy on the Middle East.

I confess that as I stood on the receiving line waiting for President Sadat's plane to land, I was possessed by a strange feeling. Even though I had participated in negotiations with Egypt in 1949, subsequent events had reinforced an idea that had been with me since my youth — that Egypt was the enemy. And even though, during my term as prime minister, we had done everything possible to move closer to peace, I cannot say that I really expected Egypt's head of state to visit Israel, openly, and with all the pomp and formal ceremonies, at such an early date. As the plane taxied up to the reception area and the door opened, the tension of the crowd waiting at the airport began to soar. But when President Sadat appeared in the doorway and moved out to the top of the steps, our emotion peaked in a way I hadn't thought possible. It was a uniquely electric moment for us all; one of those moments that remain etched in your memory forever; the kind that people call upon to date a generation. Yet for me, that "moment" seemed to stretch on and on. As the national anthems were played by the Israeli military band, and especially when President Sadat followed his military escort to review the honor guard of the Israel Defense Forces, I felt that I was caught up in a dream. Despite the evidence of my own eyes and ears, what was happening around me seemed quite unbelievable.

When I greeted President Sadat on the receiving line, there was no time for anything more than a brief exchange of pleasantries. Yet it was the first time I had ever seen him in the flesh, and I was enormously impressed by the poise with which he handled himself in a unique situation. Here he was meeting all his former archenemies, one after the other, in the space of seconds, and he nonetheless found a way to start off his visit by saying exactly the right thing to each and every one of them. Either he had done an uncommonly thorough job of diplomatic homework or he has an enviable talent for saying just the right thing at the right time.

If that alone were not enough to win us over, Sadat's speech before the Knesset can only be described as a political coup. After all — putting aside the formal and legal aspects of the address — what did he say to us? In practical terms, and in the most impressive way — by coming to the country, addressing the Knesset, and creating a true revolution in our attitude toward him and toward Egypt — he made Israel a brilliantly calculated offer: accept President Carter's positions — full-fledged peace with normalization of relations, a withdrawal to the lines of June 4, 1967, and an independent Palestinian entity — and I will make a concession that goes beyond what even the United States is willing to offer. If you agree to American policy positions, I am prepared to make peace with you without waiting for the other Arab states to agree. It's true he added that if we agreed, he would call a summit meeting and present the same terms to the other Arab countries. But it was clear, without his spelling it out, that if the other Arabs rejected his terms for peace, Sadat would go it alone. In other words, our archenemy came to Israel and offered us terms that were even more forthcoming than what our best friend in the world, the United States, was prepared to extend. President Sadat all but said: Accept the American concept of peace, and I won't wait for Mr. Arafat or President Assad or even King Hussein.

At the same time, he also succeeded in disarming some of our most basic, ingrained attitudes when he proclaimed: "I understand your need for security, but not for land." Of course, there is an inherent contradiction buried in that statement. Yet the mere fact that an Arab leader who had waged war against Israel came forth and stated that he understood our need for security and that a way must be found to meet our legitimate concern was absolutely revolutionary. It was a statement we had never heard before — even from some of Israel's best friends! Furthermore, Sadat did not make a point of demanding that Israel negotiate with the PLO. On the contrary, he spoke of the "Palestinians" and never mentioned the PLO by name, which in a way made him more forthcoming than the United States.

Finally, there can be no doubt that had Sadat made the same proposal to Israel during a secret meeting with Prime Minister Begin or in a televised speech in Cairo, it would not have had anywhere near the same dramatic impact on Israel. The idea of delivering the offer to the Israeli people in person, in Jerusalem, was a stroke of genius, and I don't believe that without it there would have been much readiness on the part of the Israeli public to make so many concessions.

As to the second purpose of Sadat's trip, it took the United States about two weeks of hesitation to adjust to the new reality that had been created by the Egyptian initiative and the Israeli response before and after Sadat's arrival in Jerusalem. By then the American administration found itself forced to shelve its declared policy that peace cannot be achieved on any one front but must be secured on all the fronts of the Arab-Israeli conflict simultaneously.

The psychological impact of Sadat's visit was enormous, but then so was the gap between the positions held by the two sides. Yet his appearance before the Knesset forced Israel's government, as well as its citizens, to reassess what they had formerly considered to be their minimal demands for peace. Then Mr. Begin came out with his famous peace plan, in which the Israeli government agreed openly, for the first time, to the restoration of Egyptian sovereignty over every inch of the Sinai and raised the idea of autonomy to avoid dealing with the question of a change in the pre–Six Day War lines on the eastern front. Furthermore, to be on the safe side — and it's not for me to pass judgment now on whether or not it was a mistake — Prime Minister Begin decided that rather than continue the dialogue directly with Egypt, he would first go to the United States and try to mobilize backing for his peace plan there.

In a subsequent talk with some American diplomats, I learned
that while they were surprised by Israel's readiness to make the
concessions offered by Mr. Begin during his visit to the United
States in December 1977, there was nonetheless some sort of
misunderstanding about the reactions to his peace plan. Begin
presented the plan on the first day of his visit during a meeting
with President Carter. Then the Americans suggested that they
would explore its ideas with Egypt and elicit Sadat's reaction. The
next day, either there was a misunderstanding between Mr.
Begin and the Americans or the terms that were employed were
open to different interpretations, for Begin returned to Israel believing that his peace plan was fully acceptable to the Egyptians.
A few days later, however, at the Ismailia Conference, the differences of opinion between Israel and Egypt became painfully
clear and stalemate was imminent, because Egypt's demand that
Israel commit herself regarding the other countries concerned in
the conflict — especially on the issue of withdrawal — was obviously unacceptable to our government.

The consequent deadlock, which came out into the open with
the failure of the Political Committee's talks in Jerusalem in February 1978, stretched out through the spring and summer. As the
months went by, it was clear to me that unless a total effort was
made at the highest level, all would be lost, for the logistics of the
situation demanded the equivalent of a summit. In Egypt there is
only one man who can make decisions — President Sadat. In the
United States, the decision-maker is of course the president. And
while in Israel this function is less clear-cut, it was beyond question that only Begin had sufficient influence over his own party to
convince it to swallow the concessions that would be inevitable.
Even for Begin, this task became more and more difficult as time
went on. But other than Begin, with his long-standing authority
as the leader of the Herut party and as the head of the Likud bloc
since its inception, no one had the slightest chance of bringing
the right wing in Israel to the point of resigning itself to the necessary compromises.

A few days before the Camp David summit was called, I sensed
that the moment was ripening, and I wrote an article in one of
Israel's evening papers forecasting that the next step must be a

summit meeting — otherwise the game was up. President Carter's timing in calling the summit was very well calculated. Eight months of stalemate had gone by, and both sides realized that the situation could not be allowed to drag on any longer without some move being made. Even more important, once you have convened a summit meeting, it must bear fruit for the simple reason that after a summit there is nowhere else to go. The last option has been exhausted, and you are faced with the responsibility for unmitigated failure. Carter was therefore right to wait until all other means had been exhausted — meetings at lower levels, exchanges of views in direct and indirect ways — for it is necessary to reach a certain stage in the development of a crisis or a stalemate before both sides realize that now — at a given moment, at a given level, in a given set of negotiations — they are in a "make it or break it" situation, once and for all.

As we all know, the summit meeting lasted for thirteen days, with its inevitable ups and downs. During that time, each side came to realize the awesome responsibility that would be placed on its shoulders if the meeting did not produce concrete results. So what emerged from the Camp David talks were two framework agreements, and without going into their legal formulations here, they looked to me like a simple, practical package deal in which both sides had made painful compromises. The package was composed of three parts.

First, an agreement was reached between Israel and Egypt to make peace immediately (that is, within three months). To achieve agreement on this point, Israel forfeited the whole of the Sinai peninsula and agreed, in a departure from her original peace plan, to eliminate every trace of Israeli presence (military or civilian) from the Sinai according to a definitive timetable. Thus every last inch of what had been sovereign Egyptian soil prior to the Six Day War would be returned to Egypt. The Egyptian compromise was that for three years following the ratification of the anticipated peace treaty, Israeli forces would remain along a line running from El Arish down to Ras Mohammed at the southern tip of the Sinai peninsula, meaning that for that period about 40 percent of the Sinai would remain in Israeli hands. Far

more important, however, is the fact that for over two years of
that period, full, normalized relations would be maintained between the two countries — meaning that ambassadors would be
exchanged, borders opened, and cultural and commercial in-
terchanges conducted for more than two full years while Israel
still retained 40 percent of the Sinai under her control. I cannot
overemphasize the importance of testing Egypt's intentions, not
merely by virtue of what the Egyptians say, but by what they do
for more than two years while Israel continues to hold on to such
a large proportion of the Sinai.

The second point of the package deal is that since the Egyptians did not want to sign a document that could be interpreted as
a "separate peace," and because they wanted to ensure that a process would be instituted to solve the complex issues of the Palestinians, the future of the West Bank and the Gaza Strip, and
peace with Jordan, it was inevitable that they would ask Israel to
agree to certain demands regarding these issues. The negotiations
at Camp David revealed that the gaps between the positions of
the two sides on these questions were so wide that they could not
be bridged. Each side presented its views on the questions of
withdrawal, sovereignty, the future of Jerusalem, the solution to
the Palestinian problem, the future of the Israeli settlements in
the West Bank and the Gaza Strip, and the future of the Israeli
military presence there, and it was clear to all that their respective ideas on each one of these issues were diametrically opposed.
The two countries therefore "agreed to disagree" and to postpone
tackling these issues for a few years. In the meantime, however,
their differences would not interfere with the building of the
peace between Egypt and Israel.

The third point is that the period during which we will be
engaged in building peaceful relations with Egypt, on the one
hand, and working toward an agreement on a permanent settlement eastward of Israel, on the other, will serve as a transitional
stage of five years during which the Arab inhabitants of the West
Bank and the Gaza Strip will enjoy "autonomy" (though no
agreement was reached at Camp David about the content or nature of such autonomy). The essence of the package deal was

therefore to allow Israel and Egypt to first build peaceful relations, in the fullest sense of the term, during a transitional period of five years, and then, toward the end of that transitional stage, to work out a permanent settlement through negotiations. The objective was to have peace with Egypt during this first phase while sweeping the more difficult issues under the carpet to be dealt with at a later date. At the same time, the package deal is governed by a timetable. Within a year of the ratification of a peace treaty, Israel and Egypt are obligated to negotiate an agreement on the modalities of the elections for the self-governing authority in the West Bank and the Gaza Strip and on the power of that elected authority. We are not committed to conclude the agreement within a year, but we are committed to make every effort to do so. Then, not later than three years after the establishment of the self-governing authority, the two sides are obligated to begin negotiations on a final settlement and to commit their efforts to concluding such negotiations toward the end of the five-year transitional period. The peace treaty between Egypt and Israel must therefore be seen within the context of this package deal. Any attempt to view it as an entirely independent affair is a gross distortion. It is true that there is no legal or operative linkage between the two agreements signed at Camp David. Israel was very cautious to ensure that point. But when it comes to the question of a political linkage, I can see how there might well be different interpretations of the question.

When Mr. Begin returned from Camp David, the issue of the accords he signed there was raised before the Knesset, and I voted in favor of them. I have always believed — as I made clear when I served as prime minister — that it is an illusion to think we can achieve peace all at once — within a month or six months — with all of our neighbors. As my record in the prime ministership shows, I held to the view that the key to the future relations between the Arab states and Israel lies in Israel's relationship with Egypt. Egypt led the Arab countries into every war with Israel; it was always the first country to halt the fighting by agreeing to a cease-fire; and it has always been the first of the Arab countries to conclude agreements with Israel. From the armistice agreements of 1949 up to and including the peace treaty of 1979, no accord has ever been concluded between Israel and any Arab state without Egypt's signing it first and alone.

Even more to the point, the building of peaceful relations between Israel and an Arab country is no simple matter. So even though we paid a very heavy and painful price by agreeing to uproot our settlements in the Sinai, and even though I do not support the idea of autonomy as a permanent solution to the Palestinian problem and the key to peace eastward of Israel, I do believe that Israel's ability to move toward peace with Egypt and test it over three to five years of day-to-day experience *before* turning our attention to the far more complicated issues is absolutely imperative. Had peace been linked conditionally to solving the more complex issues we face on our eastern frontier, without first giving Egypt and Israel the chance to experience living together and realizing that we *can* live in peace and create an atmosphere of mutual confidence, I don't think we would ever have moved an inch closer to a solution to the broader conflict. But as the Camp David accords stand, I have reason to hope that once our peoples on both sides of the border — and perhaps even other Arab nations — see for themselves that peace is not some impossible fantasy but a feasible reality that benefits both sides, the pockets of opposition in both countries will wither away.

The difficulties that arose after the signing of the Camp David agreements were not related to the central issues of the bilateral relations between Egypt and Israel. They had to do mainly with the question of the linkage between the Egyptian-Israeli peace treaty and what will happen or not happen thereafter regarding the other sectors of the Israeli-Arab conflict. So it took twice as long as the three parties to the Camp David summit expected to reach a final peace treaty, but all along I never doubted for a moment that the treaty would eventually be signed.

Naturally, I was very gratified by the invitation to join the delegation going to Washington to witness the signing of the treaty. Mr. Begin was kind enough to invite me as a former prime minister and, I like to believe, in recognition of my contribution in paving the way for the final peace process. The White House lawn was a rather unusual setting for sitting down to play a game of chance. But in essence the treaty signed there is exactly that — a tremendous political gamble — and the stakes are very high; for we all know that if our efforts fail and our trial with peace does not work, Israel will find herself facing the most difficult period of her existence since the War of Independence.

In gauging the odds of success, much will depend upon the nature of developments in three directions over the coming five to seven years. First is to what extent the peace between Egypt and Israel is truly beneficial and satisfies the expectations of their respective peoples. What worries me most is the degree to which Egypt can meet — even in only a limited way — the exaggerated expectations of the Egyptian people that peace will bring them swift progress and prosperity. I believe that more than anything else, including the Palestinian problem, the factor that will decide the stability and durability of the peace and Egypt's adherence to its commitments is the extent to which the economic situation in Egypt shows definite improvement. I hope that now that the formal treaty is signed, the countries that spoke so promisingly of peace and coaxed and cajoled the sides at every opportunity — the United States, Canada, and the European nations — will pay more than just lip service to peace. Just as there was little chance of Europe's developing as a democratic part of the world after World War II had it not been for the Marshall Plan, without providing concrete economic support to Egypt — and to Israel — those who preach peace will not be able to prove that their vision is truly valid.

As for Israel, I am convinced that during the first phase we must devote all our attention to building the fabric of human relations, and there are many pitfalls awaiting us. It would be lethal for us to try to teach the Egyptians what to do. The worst mistake Israelis can make would be to patronize our neighbors because of advantages in our educational system and technology. And though there has been much talk about the size of the Egyptian market, I believe it would be an unforgivable error to try to "cash in" on it through commercial ties. Instead, during the coming years it is necessary to focus on getting to know each other by meeting with groups of people of various occupations — farmers, industrialists, doctors, educators, laborers — and learning to appreciate each other's problems. Not that I think we should turn down explicit requests for cooperation in defined spheres. But our main objective in the coming years should be to achieve the far more subtle but invaluable goal of starting to build confidence, eliminating suspicion, hatred, and a misunderstanding of each other's problems. After all, what is the core of peace if not the relations between peoples?

The second direction in which we must work is to neutralize the dangers from the east. I have grave doubts that Israel and Egypt can reach agreement about the establishment of autonomy simultaneously in the West Bank and the Gaza Strip. Yet I believe that we must look upon the whole issue of autonomy as an instrument to facilitate the building of peace with Egypt during the transition period without getting bogged down in crises, tensions, and clashes over the Palestinian issue. I would therefore recommend working out some arrangement regarding the Palestinians as early as possible so that we will be able to spend the next three or four years concentrating on experiencing peace with Egypt before we must anyhow start negotiations on a permanent settlement regarding Israel's eastern border.

As long as we have arrived at the subject, I think it important to stop and dwell a bit on the Palestinian question, for with the exception of the highly sensitive issue of Jerusalem's future, it is undoubtedly the thorniest problem we will have to face in the coming years and the greatest pitfall on the way to the full realization of peace. In addition, with all the violence, bitter propaganda, and charged emotion surrounding the Palestinian imbroglio, I would venture to say that it is probably one of the most befogged issues on the international agenda today. Since I have already stated that I do not accept the notion of autonomy as a basis for the ultimate solution to the Palestinian problem, this is probably as good a place as any to dispel some of the fog, take a hard look at the facts, and explore what I believe to be the only feasible answer to this very complex and painful issue.

As I see it, there is really no ideal solution to the Palestinian problem. A terrible human tragedy has taken place, and we believe that it was created by the Arab countries in 1947–48, when they rejected the United Nations' partition plan and continued to struggle (some are still struggling) against the very existence of the State of Israel. But regardless of where the initial responsibility lies, by this point Israel owes it to herself to become an active partner in seeking a solution to the problem, for unless it is resolved the chances are poor that comprehensive peace will ever be realized in the Middle East.

Essentially there are three basic options for solving the Palestinian problem. The first, advocated by the Palestinian extremists (basically the PLO) is to create a sovereign Palestinian state in the West Bank and the Gaza Strip. The second position, which is advocated by Mr. Begin's government — and tends toward the opposite extreme — is to grant the Arabs living in the West Bank and Gaza the right to run their lives under an autonomous self-governing authority. They will have the right either to choose Israeli citizenship (and those who do so will have full rights as Israelis) or to maintain the Jordanian citizenship they hold today. But regardless of the citizenship of its Arab residents, the West Bank and Gaza Strip will become an integral part of the sovereign State of Israel. At Camp David, Mr. Begin agreed to have the autonomy arrangement for the transitional period, during which negotiations on a final settlement will take place. But his government's position is that autonomy should be the permanent solution to the Palestinian question. The third option — which I support and to which the Labor party adheres — is that within the original borders of mandatory Palestine (which includes Israel, the West Bank, Gaza, and what is now called the Hashemite Kingdom of Jordan), there should be two states: Israel, basically a Jewish state (though not all the Jews will live there and not only Jews will comprise its population), and, to the east of it, a Jordanian-Palestinian state that would include considerable portions of the West Bank and the Gaza Strip (mainly the densely populated areas). This Jordanian-Palestinian state will allow for the expression of the unique identity of the Palestinians in whatever form they choose to exercise their right to self-determination.

I can already hear (because I have already heard) the cynics jumping to their conclusions: "Very generous of you, Mr. Rabin, offering shares in King Hussein's domain to a third party!" But here is where I think we must stop and take an honest look at the demographic facts in order to see where the Palestinians actually live. The largest single concentration of Palestinians today — at least 900,000 people — is to be found east of the Jordan River in what is today the Hashemite Kingdom of Jordan. In fact, the Palestinians now residing in Jordan constitute over 40 percent of that country's population! The West Bank contains over 700,000 Palestinians (likewise citizens of Jordan) and the Gaza Strip over 400,000, about half of whom are refugees (meaning not indigenous to the Gaza area). By simple arithmetic, that means that some two million Palestinians presently reside in areas that could become parts of a Jordanian-Palestinian state. If we continue the count, Lebanon contains over 300,000 Palestinian refugees (from parts of mandatory Palestine that became Israel), Syria has about 100,000, and an additional 100,000 Palestinians are scattered throughout the other Arab countries, making a total of about 500,000 Palestinians living outside of Jordan, the West Bank, the Gaza Strip, and Israel (which has about half a million Arab citizens).

Now if we reconsider the concept of a Jordanian-Palestinian state, we can see that four-fifths of the total Palestinian population (excluding the Arab citizens of Israel) in fact already reside within its envisioned borders. Furthermore, there is ample room to resettle all the refugees from Gaza, Lebanon, Syria, and anywhere else to constitute a total population of about two and a half million Palestinians. I am convinced that anyone willing to hold his emotions at bay long enough to look at these facts will be forced to agree that this is an eminently just and reasonable proposal.

Moreover, I believe that Jordan is ready to accept such an approach. After all, until the extremists at the Rabat Summit Conference barred Jordan from pursuing such a policy, King Hussein accepted the principle of representing the Palestinians and assuming responsibility for their affairs. Having once been stung by the extremist camp, it appears that Hussein prefers to "play it safe" for the meantime and side with those who demand to have matters their way or not at all. I can only hope that in the coming months or years, he will have a change of heart and agree to negotiate with us over our common future in the area. At the same time, I hope no less that Mr. Begin and his supporters will come to see that territorial compromise is not anathema and that it may well be the only truly feasible solution precisely because it is the most just.

Although Labor and the Likud differ in their views on the solution to the Palestinian question, we both oppose in the strongest terms the creation of a Palestinian "mini-state" in the West Bank and the Gaza Strip, first and foremost because it cannot solve anything. It certainly will not be able to absorb the almost million and a half Palestinians who currently reside beyond these two areas; and just as surely it will be ruled by the most extreme faction in the Palestinian political spectrum — the PLO. Such "internal" Palestinian politics might not be any of Israel's business were it not for the fact that the leaders of the PLO have declared — and I believe them — that they view such a "mini-state" as but the first phase in the achievement of their so-called secular, democratic Palestine, to be built on the ruins of the State of Israel once all the Jews who arrived after 1917 (or, with slight modification, after 1948) have been expelled. Given that scenario, there is little wonder that the overwhelming majority of Israelis are so strongly opposed to this "option." And though attitudes have changed before and may well change again in the next few years, I doubt that my countrymen are likely to mellow toward the prospect of their own destruction.

Which brings me back to the third direction in which developments are likely to move in the next few years, namely, the need to ensure that Israel will remain strong. By that I mean not just in the military sense, but in terms of our moral and social fabric. The price of peace for us, calculated in hard currency, is not going to decline. On the contrary, it has taken a little time, but by now every Israeli realizes that peace will actually be more costly. In the context of the defense budget alone, in the next three to five years we will have to invest at least two billion dollars to replace what the IDF built in the Sinai over eleven years — without adding anything to our military strength. At the same time, we have not yet begun to calculate the psychological and social impact upon us of peace. I have no doubt that the imminent threat from the outside was the most powerful force uniting the people of Israel. Now we live in a time of both peace and war, and we have never experienced anything like it before. No one can predict how it will affect the motivation of our people, their readiness to bear heavy burdens, and the efforts needed until we can fully realize the benefits of peace with at least Egypt. But if that peace with Egypt is consolidated, as I hope it will be, later on we may begin to move toward some sort of peace agreement eastward of Israel — with Jordan and hopefully with Syria too (though I don't see that materializing in the immediate future). Only then, I think, will my countrymen begin to realize that we are already standing on the threshold of a new era in Israel's life, and perhaps likewise in the history of the Jewish people as a whole.

I recently heard one of our young writers speak on the meaning of peace for Israel, and I was very impressed by his analysis of this current phase in the broader context of our history. Embarking on an age of peace, he said, marked the end of the era of the establishment of the state — not merely the proclamation of its independence (as the word "establishment" usually denotes here), but the actual physical establishment of Israel as a permanent reality on the Middle Eastern landscape. It has essentially taken us more than a generation to accomplish that, a generation in which we invested much of our energy in the struggle to survive — simply to maintain our very existence. In fact, the need to ensure Israel's survival has in itself become something of a leitmotiv, a set phrase in practically every speech by national leaders friendly to Israel and Jewish spokesmen in the Diaspora. Yet given pause to reflect, it seems terribly sad that an entire nation should have been all but preoccupied for so long with much minimalist aspirations. Now we finally have an opportunity to break out of those narrow straits and consider a vision of our future. It may have taken us over a generation, but we have built our house on solid foundations. Now it is time to devote our attention to the appliances and furnishings that make a house a home — in this case the identities and values with which we will surround ourselves in our national home.

One could say that the beginning of the peace marks the end of the heroic period of the Zionist movement. The future will not be an age symbolized by the settler and the soldier working side by side. But although it may be a less romantic time in our national history, we will nonetheless have to deal with very fundamental, if less dramatic, issues. We will have to decide what will make our Jewish state a unique place in which to live and nurture future generations; what forces, other than the threat from beyond our borders, will keep our people united in their vision and purpose; and what kind of relationship we want to foster with the Jewish communities abroad. Whenever Israel has been faced with a mortal threat, the Jews of the Diaspora have stood firmly behind her. But Jewish history shows that the Jews have always stood together in times of trial, while in tranquil days each community turned to tending its own garden. How, then, will we maintain the ties with our people once the drama and romance in our life recede? Peace will demand that we change certain of our basic attitudes and philosophies; that we devise new methods to reach and educate our public; and that we set new goals that capture the imagination of Jews around the world, motivate them to join us in our venture, and help them exploit their talents to the maximum.

It may sound peculiar, but I believe that Israel will face many dangers even — or perhaps especially — in peace. And when I speak of dangers, I mean real threats to her existence, though they will be different from those we have grown accustomed to coping with. In the past we devoted too little time and attention to the challenge of living in the Middle East, as a Jewish state, in peace. Now the specter of Israel losing her way because of the blessing of peace should not be ignored. For all that, however, I must say that as a man who has led his country's struggle both on the battlefield and in political negotiations, who has been privileged to amass a unique combination of experience as a soldier, a diplomat, and a head of government, there is no doubt whatsoever in my mind that the risks of peace are preferable by far to the grim certainties that await every nation in war.

AFTERWORD

Rabin: From Mr. Security to Nobel Peace Prize Winner

BY YORAM PERI

Let the sun rise
and illuminate the morning;
the purest of prayers
cannot bring us back.
Bitter tears will neither awaken
nor restore
those whose candles have gone out,
those buried in the dust.
No one will bring us back
from the deep dark pit.
Neither the joy of victory
nor songs of praise are of any use.

So just sing
a song to peace.
Don't whisper a prayer,
better to sing a song to peace
with a loud shout.

Let the sun penetrate
the flowers;
don't look back,
make way for those moving forward.
Lift your eyes in hope
not just in good intentions,
Sing a song to love
and not to war.
Do not say "the day will come,"
but make it come,

because it is no dream;
all the town squares
are going to ring out with peace.

This "Song of Peace" was written in 1970, while the cannons were roaring over the Suez Canal. The War of Attrition between Israel and Egypt was at its height. This deadlocked conflict — in the wake of the Six Day War of 1967 — had gone on for seventeen long months, and the younger generation of Israelis, who had suffered 721 killed and 2,659 wounded, was tired of war. In the highest echelons of the Israel Defense Forces, there was concern about this new mood, which was interpreted as weakness. General Rehavam Ze'evi — adviser to Prime Minister Yitzhak Rabin in the late 1970s and later head of the extreme right-wing Moledet Party — outlawed the playing of the "Song of Peace" in the army.

Twenty-five years later, Prime Minister Rabin, painfully shy and unable to carry a tune, stood in Tel Aviv's central square and, uncharacteristically, sang this song in public. The song concluded a rally — whose slogan was "No to violence; yes to peace" — in which Rabin had been the keynote speaker. "Violence is eating away at the foundations of Israeli democracy," Rabin had declared. "It must be condemned, denounced, and isolated. It is not the way of the state of Israel. . . . This rally must send a message to the Israeli public, to the Jewish public throughout the world, and to many, many in the Arab world and the world at large, that the people of Israel want peace, that they support peace." When he finished speaking, he received a thunderous ovation such as he had not enjoyed in a long time.

With the conclusion of the song and the rally, he folded the sheet of paper upon which the words of the song were printed and put it into his jacket pocket. As he finished descending the twenty-six stairs from the stage and stepped toward his official car, Yigal Amir approached him from the rear. Twenty-five years old, thin, cool, and collected, the assassin drew his pistol and shot Rabin at point-blank range. Two dumdum bullets penetrated his body, knocking him to the ground. A moment later he was in the back seat of his car speeding to the hospital. His stunned driver asked him how he felt. "My back hurts, but it's not so bad," was the response from the back seat.

Then Rabin's head fell forward as his blood began to stain the sheet of lyrics red.

The shock at Rabin's death was unprecedented. For the first time in the history of the forty-seven-year-old state, a prime minister had been assassinated. When people heard, they sobbed as if a close and dear relative had been killed. National mourning was declared for three days but continued for a full week. Eight heads of state from around the world attended the funeral. They included, first and foremost, President Bill Clinton of the United States, as well as King Hussein of Jordan, President Hosni Mubarak of Egypt, and Chairman Yasir Arafat of the Palestine Liberation Organization — the three Arab leaders visiting Jerusalem for the first time in their life. "Your prime minister was a martyr for peace, but he was a victim of hate," declared Clinton. And Israelis, in their quest for meaning in this shocking murder, filled the country's streets with placards proclaiming, "In his death, he commanded us to seek peace."

How did this man, so identified with Israel's military might, become a "martyr for peace"? What brought the man who ordered the breaking of Palestinians' bones during the Intifada to shake the hand of the man who, more than any other, personified the Palestinian resistance — Arafat? How did Israel's "Mr. Security" become one of the winners of the 1994 Nobel Prize for Peace?

The debate over the relationship between leadership and history will probably continue to the end of time. Was Thomas Carlyle right in claiming that history is the biography of great men? Or was Rosa Luxemburg more accurate when she contended that a leader is like the foam on the sea, which catches our eye but is carried on the backs of the waves, and it is the people who hold the leader up and are more important? Even a person who leans toward Rosa Luxemburg's version — "Rosa," by the way, was the name of Yitzhak Rabin's socialist mother — will run into difficulty when confronted with leaders who have brought their people to a dramatic turning point in their history: Charles de Gaulle, who came to power promising that Algeria would remain French and then brought about its independence; Mikhail Gorbachev, who came from deep within the Communist Party and launched *glasnost* and *perestroika,* which in turn led to the collapse of the Soviet empire; F. W. de Klerk, who emerged from the ranks of the apartheid Nationalist Party in South Africa to bring democracy and black majority rule to his country. How much influence did these leaders have on the history of their peoples? Would Algeria have remained a part of France, the Iron Curtain still divide Europe, and the white minority still be subjugating a black majority deprived of human and civil rights in South Africa, had de Gaulle, Gorbachev, and de Klerk not arisen?

Rabin's rise to power in 1992 was accompanied by the expectation of historic change. In fact, it was this expectation that led to his election after fifteen years of rule by the dyed-in-the-wool Likud guardians of the status quo. But would this native-born Israeli, who had spent much of his life looking at Palestinians through a gun barrel, be capable of making peace with them like a de Gaulle? Was Rabin endowed with the qualities of a leader who could alter the course of history? What actually are the attributes of such a leader?

Rabin resigned as prime minister in 1977, a beaten and disappointed man. Three years earlier, with the fall of Golda Meir's government in 1974 following the debacle of the Yom Kippur War, the reign of the founding fathers and mothers of the Labor movement had come to an end. Hopes were high as Rabin stepped into the shoes of David Ben-Gurion, Levi Eshkol, and Golda Meir. Now, at last, the younger generation was about to open a new chapter in the life of the nation. In Israel, Rabin was compared to President John F. Kennedy, and his wife, Leah, regarded Jacqueline Kennedy as worthy of emulation.

But it was not to be. Labor lost the 1977 elections. The defeat was blamed on the failings of Rabin's government, corruption at the highest levels, and the internal disintegration of the ruling party. But beyond that, there was far deeper disappointment with Rabin and his generation. A political sociologist called them "a barren generation," and he dubbed the Labor party barons who had ruled the country for forty-four years "an elite without successors."

Rabin felt a need to present the public with an accounting of his government's accomplishments, and he devoted two years to writing the autobiographical *Pinkas Sherut* (published in English as *The Rabin Memoirs*). In it Rabin described the difficult circumstances that prevailed following the 1973 war and the efforts he invested in salvaging the situation: the rebuilding of the army, the strengthening of military and economic relations with the United States, and the signing of interim agreements with Syria and Egypt. These were the agreements, he rightly claimed, that laid the groundwork for the peace accord signed by the Begin government in 1979.

But Rabin did not forego his desire to rehabilitate himself politically, to recapture the party leadership and the office of prime minister. His conduct when his wife's foreign bank account was revealed — standing by her and taking personal responsibility — won him unprecedented credibility and the confidence of the public. Thus Rabin discovered an additional basis of public support for him: if the first was the primacy of security in his worldview, the second was his un-politician-like code of conduct. Rabin made a conscious decision to build on this credibility, knowing that while the Israeli people do not expect credibility in their other politicians, they regard it as the most important quality in a prime minister.

The years of political penance spent in the opposition were good for Rabin. Israel, lacking elder statesmen, found in Rabin someone to fill this role. The media pursued him relentlessly for his analyses of statecraft and security. The positions he advocated placed him at the center of the political spectrum and, freed from the need to defend the party line, he took a centrist position, sometimes supporting policies of the Likud government.

Since he was not yet ready to lay claim to the party leadership, his biographer Robert Slater correctly explains, Rabin supported Yigal Allon's candidacy in 1979 and 1980, in an attempt to oust Shimon Peres from the post.[1] And then, on February 29, 1980, Allon suddenly died. The new circumstances created a vacuum that Rabin was glad to fill. The public supported him, but Peres had the stronger grip on the party apparatus and won the internal party contest. Peres, however, was unable to ignore the strength of Rabin's support. The Labor Party thus continued in the opposition, with the two rival leaders unable to rid themselves of each other.

A tie vote in the 1984 elections compelled the two major parties — the Likud led by Yitzhak Shamir and Labor headed by Peres — to set up a National Unity Government. They agreed to rotate the office of prime minister: Peres for the first two years, followed by Shamir. In

1984 Rabin was able to return to his favorite portfolio, the Ministry of Defense. He loved that job, and made the most of his special status as head of Labor's right wing and thus in the center of the political spectrum, between Labor and Likud. In this he was consciously following in the footsteps of Moshe Dayan, the prototypical member of the "1948 generation" — the native-born generation that reached maturity around the time of Israel's War of Independence. Dayan, in many senses, served as their role model. During the National Unity Government, which lasted six years, two events of historic significance took place, influencing the course of Rabin's life and the history of his people: the collapse of the Soviet empire and the start of the Intifada, the Palestinian popular uprising.

The key concept in Rabin's political doctrine was power. "Nations and states operate out of concern for their own interests and not for other reasons or considerations, and the way to achieve one's interest is through power," he wrote in *Pinkas Sherut*.[2] The great weight that he assigned to the component of power in interstate relations is what made Rabin such a thorough embodiment of the Zionist revolution — "the dream-lad of Zionism," in the words of author Yoram Kaniuk. The Zionist movement had been the product of a decision by Jews without a homeland and lacking political authority to take charge of their own fate and reenter the flow of history. The only condition under which this could be done was for them to have power. Moral right, in and of itself, was far less important than right as a means, in that a sense of being in the right contributes to national staying power. On issues of national security, there was no doubt which took precedence, absolute right or *raison d'état*.

This attitude toward power had begun in Rabin's younger days, as evidenced by the description in his memoirs of the unsuccessful battle over Jerusalem during the 1948 War of Independence. If at first this attitude was a direct outcome of the difficult life in the young state, Rabin later expanded it to encompass a much broader worldview. His mentor in this was Henry Kissinger, the man who, more than any other, influenced the development of the young sabra Yitzhak Rabin — first during Kissinger's visit to Israel in 1966 and later during Rabin's term as Israel's ambassador in Washington. The unpolished Israeli, lacking higher education, was captivated by the doctrine advanced by this Harvard professor of international relations. "I spent some of the most wonderful hours of my life with him," testified Rabin.[3]

What particularly entranced Rabin was Kissinger's theory of "balance of power." It seemed to him applicable to the conflict in the Middle East as well as to relations between the superpowers. In fact, during the 1970 debate over the Rogers Plan with President Richard Nixon — a president revered by Rabin — the young diplomat remarked, "Be so good as to recall, Mr. President, what you told me even before you became president about how to negotiate with the Soviets: negotiations must be conducted from a position of strength, otherwise they have no chance of success. . . . I said to you that this also applied to relations between Israel and its neighbors, and that in the Middle East, no negotiations would lead to concrete results unless Israel participated from a position of power."[4]

Since relations between the superpowers were a key factor in the Israeli-Arab conflict, Israel's security, indeed its very existence, according to Rabin, was dependent on maintaining close ties with the United States.[5] Rabin saw it as his supreme national mission, first as ambassador and later as prime minister and minister of defense, to strengthen Israel's ties with the leading superpower. In the view of Martin Indyk, a Middle East expert who became U.S. ambassador to Israel, he succeeded. More than any other Israeli politician, Rabin gave expression to his affinity for things American, and during his second term as prime minister, he became Israel's foremost advocate of the American way of life and tried to instill the "American dream" into Israel's social-democratic culture.

Faith in the language of power — along with other traits, especially pragmatism, that characterized such members of Rabin's generation as Moshe Dayan and Yigal Allon — has in recent years come under fire in a wave of critiques of the first native-born generation. Some critics have even accused them of militarism, but that is a distorted reading, despite the importance attributed to power and military might in this generation's value system.[6] The best way to demonstrate this point is through an analysis of Yitzhak Rabin's perception of war.

Whereas the military mind regards war as a fact of life and even a desirable state, Rabin viewed war as a means to an end. In contrast to Menachem Begin, for example, Rabin did not see Israel as fated to be in a constant state of war. "Our fate is that in the land of Israel there is no way out of having to fight with total dedication. Believe me, the alternative is Treblinka," Begin told his ministers on the eve of the war in Lebanon in the summer of 1982, while comparing Arafat to Hitler.[7] Rabin's approach to war was not propped up by religious motifs, such as the conclusion in the Passover Haggadah that "in every generation they rise up against us to annihilate us." "The whole world is against us" is a legacy passed on to Israel's children, from kindergarten on up, with almost every national holiday, focused on this theme — on the impending danger of the destruction of the people and their salvation from that fate.[8]

This was not Rabin's view of security. He was free of such cultural paranoia. He would never call Arafat a Hitler, nor would he compare Gamal Abdel Nasser to the Hellenistic king Antiochus, or Khomeini to Haman, the villain in the Purim story, who sought to annihilate the Jews. In categorizing the attitudes that foster war, Yehoshafat Harkabi, a professor of international relations, has distinguished between the "expressive" and the "instrumental," and Rabin exemplifies the latter approach. "In the expressive approach, one is 'pushed from behind' by the 'cause,' whereas in the instrumental approach, one is 'pulled ahead' by the reason for the war in order to achieve some specific outcome."[9] Thus, starting a war for the purpose of enabling "an honorable existence" was characteristic of Begin, but very far from Rabin's style. Likewise, a military action launched for revenge would seem legitimate to Rafael Eitan, but alien to Rabin. Rabin regarded war as an instrument for thwarting enemy threats only, to ensure the survival and security of the country.

Rabin's approach to war was one of political realism. He thought it was possible to use force to improve the state's political position. He therefore did not hesitate to initiate penetration bombing of Egypt in 1970 during the War of Attrition, a step that earned him harsh censure from his opponents. Abba Eban, foreign minister at the time, regarded Rabin as a dangerous hawk and described him in the understated language he loved to use: "He had sudden outbursts of strange aggressivity."

Given this approach to war, Rabin did not hesitate to employ an iron fist policy to forcibly suppress the Palestinians in the territories each time they tried to improve their situation by force. He did not believe, however, that it was possible to achieve far-reaching political goals by means of force. This perception was not so much the out-come of moral scruples as of utilitarian considerations. "When it is a matter of war or a preemptive strike, the question is not whether it is right or wrong, but rather what it is for: Is it worthwhile, necessary, desirable from our point of view?" he wrote.[10]

Rabin explained that his perception of war originated "from the recognition that there is neither moral right nor practical benefit in the illusion of the efficacy of force to attain fundamental political objec-tives or conclusive political solutions to the Arab-Israeli conflict in the Middle East."[11] The moral reservations in this statement were rooted in his utilitarian appraisal that the use of military force for the achieve-ment of definitive political goals is not realistic — it is an illusion.

Rabin was one of the principal architects of Israel's concept of the defensive war. His depiction as a militarist by some critics arises from a misunderstanding of his doctrine. His stance was apparent in how he dealt with the territorial dimension of the Israeli-Arab conflict. Rabin's forceful approach caused him to be regarded as a hawk on this subject as well, although he was not. His attitude toward the occupied territories did not really change in any significant way in all the years since 1967. It was never emotional or religious. His approach was solely strategic and geopolitical. Because of this, from 1967 until the day of his death, he was willing to compromise on ter-ritory. He wrote, "We must view the territories that we conquered as bargaining chips for negotiations with our neighbors for the attain-ment of peace or for the advancement of political objectives aimed at amelioration of the Israeli-Arab conflict," adding, "That is what I thought then in 1967, and what I think today."[12] This was his attitude toward the Sinai Peninsula and later toward the Golan Heights and the West Bank.

Rabin's political map of the Israel of the future did not include those areas of the West Bank heavily populated with Palestinians. This he reiterated countless times. At an appearance before students at a Jerusalem high school on March 17, 1988, for example, he stated: "What is important for Israel is a unified Jerusalem as the capital of Israel, preservation of the Jordan River as its security border, as well as other security areas, including the Etzion Bloc and the Jordan Valley." In his final speech to the Knesset, he again presented his projected map of Israel. On October 5, 1995, when submitting the Oslo II Accord for approval, he spoke of retaining blocs of settlements in the territories as part of the final agreement. But this too was the restatement of a principle he had articulated as far back as the 1970s, when he stated, "I don't care if I need a visa to get to Gush Etzion."

As with war, so too on the territorial issue part of commentators' failure to differentiate between Rabin's individual tactics and his fundamental convictions led to a misinterpretation of his stance. In 1976 Shlomo Avineri, a political science professor who was then director general of the Foreign Ministry, perceived Rabin's openness to extensive territorial compromise. But, Rabin told him, 1976 was not the proper time for territorial concessions because of the heavy cloud that had descended on Israel's strategic positions after the Yom Kippur War. Israel's current task was to improve its strategic, diplomatic, and psychological position following the trauma of that war. Rabin did not think that it would be correct for his government to negotiate peace agreements during that period. According to Avineri, Rabin claimed: "My task is to improve the morale and equipment of the army, to strengthen United States support for Israel, and to get it out of the Arabs' heads that a weak Israel is willing to make concessions. Only in another five years, when we have reached a position of strength, will Israel be in a position to make compromises."

This approach, Avineri later explained in an article published in *Yediot Aharonot* after Rabin's assassination, was hawkish and dovish at the same time: generous regarding concessions as part of a peace agreement, but unyielding regarding the manner in which this agreement would be reached. This was Rabin's stance until 1992, and it reinforced his hawkish image, increasing confidence in him on the right, while causing the left to mistrust him. Both sides were misreading him. But, in Avineri's opinion, Rabin could not reveal his strategy without spoiling his chances of carrying it out. Few understood him, not even all his ministers. Only after signing the Oslo Accords in September 1993, could Rabin publicly disclose his overall perspective in clear terms. And indeed, when it became known that he was prepared to make far-reaching concessions in the Golan

Heights, this revelation was a severe shock to some of his longtime friends, who felt that he was betraying his principles. Several joined an initiative by two members of his own party to form a new faction, the "Third Way." Rabin's assassination brought some of these back to the Labor fold.

Soviet support of the Arab bloc put Israel's very existence at risk, but it also made radical change possible in Israel's relations with its neighbors, once the international status of the Soviet Union began to decline. When President Hafez al-Asad of Syria went on a visit to Moscow in 1978 to promote closer cooperation with the USSR in the context of Asad's "strategic balance" policy (a code word for a military solution to the Israeli-Syrian conflict), Gorbachev suggested that he abandon that idea and try to resolve the conflict politically. This was the first sign of the end of the cold war in the Middle East. The collapse of the Soviet Union changed the entire picture, removing this superpower from a potential military confrontation with Israel.

Rabin, a pragmatist who did not assign cosmological significance to the world map, had praised the USSR for aiding Israel during the War of Independence, and he was now able to detect the changes wrought by *perestroika* and *glasnost,* and to state categorically, "a new international era has begun." After Egypt's exit from the circle of hatred for Israel, Syria became Israel's most dangerous enemy, and now it had lost its military support structure. The option of a military operation against Israel was becoming less feasible. If the Arab states surrounding Israel wished to achieve their political objectives, especially that of regaining the territories that Israel had conquered from them in 1967, they would have to do so through negotiations leading to political settlements. A window of opportunity for peace had opened.

Thus Rabin was able to state, in a speech introducing his new cabinet to the Knesset on July 13, 1992, "In the last decade of the twentieth century, the atlases and history and geography books no longer present an up-to-date picture of the situation. . . . We are no longer of necessity 'a people that dwelleth apart' and no longer is it true that 'the whole world is against us' " (see appendix B for this speech). Rabin would return to this theme countless times in his public speeches during the three years until his death.

British historian E. H. Carr, in a brilliant series of lectures published under the title *What Is History?*, differentiates between two types of great leaders in history. The first kind, leaders like Napoleon and Bismarck, rode to greatness on the back of already existing forces. The second type, those like Cromwell or Lenin, helped mold the societal forces that carried them to greatness. Rabin certainly belonged to the first group. In the words of G. W. F. Hegel, "The great man of the age is the one who can put into words the will of his age, tell his age what its will is, and accomplish it. What he does is the heart and essence of his age; he actualizes his age."[13]

It was in relation to the Palestinian people — this Siamese twin of the evolving Israeli nation — that the greatest change in Rabin's views took place. Rabin was a leader who understood the will of the people and was determined to carry it out. It is in this, particularly in his resolute decision to realize the newly created potential for peace, that Rabin's greatness was manifested.

When it became clear that the establishment of a national home for the Jews in the land of Israel was encountering stubborn resistance by the Arabs of the region, two schools of thought on the Israeli-Arab conflict emerged. One, the "Palestinists," held that the core of the conflict was the contradictory interests of the two national movements, Jewish and Palestinian, in this small plot of land. The second, the "Jordanists," reckoned that the core of the conflict was the unwillingness of the Arabs to recognize the state of Israel and their strategic decision to put an end to the "Zionist entity." This school of thought had been dominant among Israel's political and military elite since the founding of the state, and even before that, and led to decades of secret understandings between Israel's leaders and the Hashemite royal house in Jordan at the expense of the Palestinians.

However, the outcome of the Six Day War gave impetus to developments that would lead to the establishment of a Palestinian national entity. Under the steamroller of the Israeli occupation, Palestinian national consciousness became increasingly consolidated and national institutions were established. Golda Meir, the arch-Jordanist (she met secretly with King Abdullah on the eve of the founding of Israel to map out political and military understandings with him), expressed the narrowest version of that school of thought when she declared after the Six Day War, "There is no Palestinian people." But in the 1970s, when she presented the Palestinian issue as solely a refugee matter that could be resolved in the context of a settlement between Israel and the Arab states, this way of thinking was already in decline. The secretary general of Meir's own party, Knesset member Lova Eliav, dared to propose the opposing view, that the conflict was the outcome of a collision between two legitimate national movements, and that the only desirable solution was mutual recognition and division of the land.

In his perception of the conflict, Rabin too was a Jordanist and close to Golda Meir. But as a pragmatist, he was unable to ignore the Palestinian issue. When he replaced Meir as prime minister in 1974, Rabin made a first small step by stating that he acknowledged the existence of "the Palestinian problem,"[14] a comment that marked the beginning of his move away from the mainstream disregard of the Palestinian people's existence, even though he still envisioned a solution in the context of an agreement with the Arab states. A long time would pass before Rabin would agree that even if the Israeli-Palestinian conflict was not the source of the Israeli-Arab conflict, its resolution was a necessary condition for achieving any political settlement with the Arab states.

What detracted from the standing of the Palestinians in Rabin's eyes was his complete contempt for them — his scorn for their culture, their values, their leaders, and their way of life. Unlike Moshe Dayan and Yigal Allon, who sometimes tended to romanticize the Levant, Rabin's attitude toward the Palestinians was a reflection of his veneration of power: If you aren't powerful, you're worth nothing. For this reason, Rabin mocked the efforts that were being made in the late 1970s and early 1980s to cultivate moderate elements with whom negotiations for peace could be conducted. For this reason, also, he supported Operation Peace for the Galilee, the "war of choice" launched by Defense Minister Ariel Sharon in Lebanon in the summer of 1982. Despite his being one of the leaders of the opposition, a significant proportion of whose members opposed the war, and despite earlier statements, Rabin supported the operation and its initial, limited objectives.

Indeed, in November 1981 Rabin had stated that "it is an illusion to assume that, by means of a military operation, it is possible to destroy the terrorist organizations in Lebanon and to undermine their will to act against Israel."[15] During the war, however, he was in favor of "the destruction of PLO bases in southern Lebanon . . . making it difficult for terrorists to attack northern Israeli communities."[16] Even though he opposed Sharon's plan to invade West Beirut, he remained true to his *macht politik* (power politics), reasoning that "war is war" and that the military course of action should be exploited to reap the maximum benefit from it. Thus, he did not refrain from expressing his support for Defense Minister Sharon when the Israel Defense Forces besieged the capital of Lebanon and advised him "to tighten the siege." The famous picture of Rabin standing beside Sharon, both wearing flak jackets and observing the siege, intensified his militant, hawkish image for years to come.

But as early as the second stage of the invasion, when the IDF, deviating from the announced objectives of operating against the PLO in southern Lebanon, began to strive toward the more far-reaching political objectives set out by Sharon, Rabin began to speak out publicly against continuation of the war. Preemptive action to expel the Syrians from Lebanon, to set up a stable government there, or to destroy totally the PLO in Lebanon — all of these appeared excessive to him, and he expressed concern that the IDF would become mired in what he called "the Lebanese swamp." Years later, at a study day in memory of Ben-Gurion where he lectured on "The Limits of Force in the Preparation and Conduct of War," Rabin stated, "I do not see any constraints on the use of military force by the state of Israel to attain two defense objectives: guaranteeing national political survival and ensuring the security of the state. An Israeli military force that is not capable of performing these tasks places the very existence of the state in peril." However, "can the very existence of military force serve as an instrument for the achievement of far-reaching political objectives" such as "bringing the war to an end, imposing peace, or establishing a new political reality more convenient for Israel?" To this he answered in the negative. "If you were to attempt to learn from the two wars [the Sinai campaign in 1956 and the Lebanon war in 1982], they had far-reaching political objectives that were not attained. Was this a coincidence? Was it an accident?" The answer is no. "There is a fundamental error in the approach that uses military might to achieve the total imposition of our political will over an Arab state or a group of Arab states."[17]

The war in Lebanon demonstrated that the PLO's political power was not destroyed, despite the heavy beating it took. But this lesson was not enough to change Rabin's attitude toward the PLO and the Palestinians. What did bring about this revolutionary change was a dialectical process: recognition of the limitations of Israel's military might against them. In other words, Rabin learned to respect the power that was actually a product of Palestinian weakness. True to form, when the Palestinians proved to him that they were strong, Rabin began to see them as worthy partners for dialogue. What brought about this change was the Intifada.

In 1981, upon my return from a three-year stay in London, Rabin and I had a long conversation about the Palestinian issue, a conversation that is engraved in my memory. I thought then, actually long before then, that the conflict in our region would not be resolved without recognition of the PLO and negotiations with it. Since I knew Rabin's view on this, I said, "Okay, not the PLO. But why don't you conduct talks at least with moderate Palestinians in the territories, those who are prepared to talk with us and reach an agreement?" His response reflected Rabin's characteristic way of thinking. He did not answer on the moral plane, as does the ideological right, that the Palestinians have no legitimate moral claim to share the land with us. Nor did he answer, as he would at a later date, that speaking with the PLO was tantamount to conducting negotiations about the establishment of a Palestinian state. His answer reflected the "balance of power" school of thought: "There's no point. When I speak to one of them, he tells me that he has to consult with the king [Hussein of Jordan]. When I speak to another, he says he has to consult with the president [Mubarak of Egypt]. When I speak to the third, he has to consult with the other president [Asad of Syria]. The fourth says he must consult with the chairman [Arafat of the PLO]. So what's the point of speaking with proxies? It's better to speak with those who have the power to decide."

The Intifada altered his attitude toward the Palestinians, but even this did not happen at once. Rabin the conservative was slow to change his positions, slower still in his decision-making processes. He would concentrate on working on a central issue, whatever seemed to him the most pressing, and even with such an issue, he would put off a final decision as long as possible. During the first weeks after the outbreak of the uprising in December 1987, he was a prisoner of his old perceptions of the Palestinians. So convinced was he of their weakness, he could not imagine how a people so lacking in power could have any control over its own fate. Even though he had pointed out that the United States had been defeated in Vietnam and the French army had lost the war against the FLN in Algeria because they both underestimated the strength of freedom fighters — even though he stated, "It is impossible to wear down the power of the fighting will of a people that fiercely believes in the sanctity of its objective" — he fell into the very same trap when faced with a similar situation.[18]

So strongly did Rabin believe that this uprising, like those that had preceded it, would be a passing phase, that he did not even cut short his visit to the United States when the fighting broke out. "The purpose of the visit was to obtain attack helicopters for Israel, and these seemed far more important to the strength of the IDF and the security of the state than dealing quickly with demonstrators and stone-throwers in the towns of the West Bank and the Gaza Strip," General Amos Yarón, then IDF attaché in the United States and organizer of Rabin's visit, recounted in an interview. No wonder that upon returning home a week later, he assumed that the Palestinians were being incited from outside the territories and began various attempts to suppress the Intifada, all of which had one thing in common: the use of force. This was the background to the harsh policy he adopted: the use of live ammunition, then after many deaths and international outcry, the shift to rubber bullets, and after that to billy clubs and the policy of "breaking their bones."

When it became evident that the Palestinians were prepared to sustain casualties, it eventually dawned on him that it would be impossible to quash the Intifada by means of force, even though he reckoned that the level of Palestinian violence could be reduced. As a result, he enraged the opposition by not giving the army a free hand "to wipe out the Intifada." At the time Rabin rejected the theory that

I proposed to him, that in all the "little wars" since World War II, it was not the side that spilled more of its rival's blood that was victorious, but the side prepared to sustain the heaviest losses. However, in March 1988 he began to speak of the need for a policy that stands on two legs, military and political: "Any policy supported by only one leg will never bring about a solution."[19]

Here again is the gap between the positions Rabin showed the outside world and those that Avineri referred to when discussing Rabin's territorial concept. While Rabin was still outwardly expressing hawkish views — scorning and mocking the left's "moralistic atti tude," attacking the judiciary for restricting freedom of military action against participants in the uprising, mocking human rights and civil rights organizations for their "formalistic arguments" against the use of excessive force in the struggle against the uprising, and continuing to support an iron fist policy — he had begun, in conversation with those close to him, to speak of a dimension that he would not dare to expand on publicly: that the war against the Intifada was damaging the IDF's fighting spirit, hurting army morale, and undermining the status of the IDF as a people's army.

After Rabin's death, his bureau chief, Eitan Haber, revealed in an interview how serious an issue this had been for the prime minister: "First there was the recognition that it was not possible to suppress the Intifada by force. After that, he gradually recognized that we would not be able to continue to rule two and a half million Palestinians against their will. The indications of moral deterioration that had appeared as part of our rule over the Arabs in the territories led him to recognize that we must not continue to dominate another people. The scenes of what the occupation was doing to the IDF and the behavior of soldiers at roadblocks or in the pursuit of demonstrators concerned him greatly. After a large number of court martials of soldiers from elite army units and officers, some of high rank, for violent and illegal behavior, Rabin understood that the IDF was in deep trouble."

What is interesting, in any case, is the discrepancy between Rabin's support for the use of tactical force and his public denial that the Intifada was harming the army and Israeli society. Here, too, Rabin's pragmatic nature is apparent. Unlike the left, which used moral arguments to oppose the manner in which the Intifada was being suppressed, Rabin arrived at his conclusions through political realism. The damage to the esprit de corps, the crumbling of internal military discipline, and the deterioration in performance were what worried Rabin, because they were contrary to the principles of how a professional army, especially a people's army, should function.

By now it had become clear to him that it was necessary to talk to the Palestinians and that there was, in fact, someone to talk to. "Was it not possible to talk to them previously?" I asked on the flight to Washington for the signing of the Declaration of Principles in September 1993. And he replied, "No. Because before, they were only proxies. With the Intifada, they proved that for the first time in their history, they had decided to take charge of their fate." Nevertheless, he did not easily liberate himself from his ties with the Jordanist, anti-Palestinian school of thought. With exactly which Palestinians to talk? The "who," he used to say, determines the "what."

Recognition of the PLO would open discussions about their right to an independent state, and this Rabin was not prepared to concede. Therefore, he could not speak with those representing the national body, that is, the PLO leadership in Tunis. Thus, the first step in the evolution of Rabin's perception in the wake of the Intifada was a willingness to talk to representatives of the Palestinians in the occupied territories only. His reasoning was practical: They are the ones who are suffering under the yoke of the occupation and will be ready to compromise more in order to lighten this load. With them it will be possible to reach an agreement to halt the Intifada without making a commitment to establish a Palestinian state.

Thus began the practice of differentiating between the PLO "inside" and "outside" the occupied territories. For the first time since 1967, Rabin was prepared to talk to "moderate Palestinians" from the territories. In this spirit, and with the help of Peres and the agreement of Shamir, then prime minister, Rabin developed his peace plan, which became known as "the Shamir Plan" on May 14, 1989. Its essence: Elections would be held in the territories to choose representatives with whom Israel would conduct negotiations for a settlement granting self-rule to the Palestinians for an interim period. During this period, negotiations for a permanent settlement between Israel and Jordan would be held, in the context of which fundamental problems, such as Israeli settlements, Palestinian refugees, the status of Jerusalem, and permanent borders, would be resolved.

Shamir, however, did not really plan to reach a settlement with the Palestinians, just as two years previously he had sabotaged the clandestine agreement with King Hussein to begin peace negotiations that his foreign minister, Shimon Peres, had signed in London. Shamir's rigid stance meant that a new American initiative intended to capitalize on the situation after the Gulf War would not fare well. In October 1991 an international peace conference opened in Madrid amid great fanfare, but the talks in bilateral working groups, Syria and Lebanon in one and Jordan and the Palestinians in the other, were soon deadlocked.

The next stage would come only after the Israeli general elections. In the Labor Party primaries, Rabin defeated Peres, and in the general elections of July 1992, Labor, under his leadership, beat the Likud, headed by Shamir. Rabin returned to the prime ministership, and the public expected him to fulfill his campaign pledge to — within six to nine months — deliver an autonomy agreement with the Palestinians that would bring an end to the Intifada. The bilateral talks with the Jordanian-Palestinian delegation resumed in August of that year in Washington. But again there was no progress in the negotiations after a full month of talks. Rabin understood that now Arafat was holding them up; the delegation of Palestinians from the territories would not lift a finger without his guidance. The attempt to differentiate between "the PLO inside" and "the Tunis PLO" had failed.

Had Rabin been a leader like Ben-Gurion — or Oliver Cromwell, to use one of Carr's examples — at this stage he would have been striving to consolidate societal forces in order to shape reality to his liking. But Rabin was reactive rather than proactive. Half a year had passed since he had risen to power and had promised to solve the problem of the Intifada, and nothing had happened. Violence only increased during the first six months of Rabin's premiership. The media, which had built up high expectations of his government, began to criticize it. This infuriated Rabin. He accused the Palestinians of stonewalling. When terrorist attacks by Palestinians, by the Hizbullah in southern Lebanon, and especially by Hamas inside Israel increased in frequency, he vented his rage. In December he expelled 415 Islamic fundamentalists, creating a mess that preoccupied the major players in the conflict for many months and held back the peace process. In March he began a "closure" of the territories, sealing them off from Israel to prevent the infiltration of terrorists. He was not yet ready to reshuffle the deck in regard to the PLO.

"Man lives consciously for himself," wrote Tolstoy in *War and Peace*, "but he is unconsciously an instrument in humanity's attainment of historic universal aims." At this point a dramatic event took place, which extricated Israel and the Palestinians from their stalemate and eventually led to an interim agreement between them. Deputy Foreign Minister Yossi Beilin, a young protégé of Foreign Minister Shimon Peres, who later became his political colleague, had been promoting a series of informal talks with PLO representatives. Many such meetings between Israelis and PLO members were held during the 1980s in various parts of the world, mainly in an academic context or under the auspices of research institutes. Beilin, who headed a circle of doves in the Labor Party, had been of the Palestinist school of thought since the late 1970s. He had therefore — on his own, through other members of his circle, and through academic channels — arranged several meetings with Palestinians, including PLO supporters. In late 1992 and early 1993, following Labor's return to power, Beilin became one of the prime agitators for repeal of the law prohibiting meetings between Israelis and PLO members, which had been legislated by the Shamir government during its final term.

As early as January 1993, Beilin used his contacts in Norway to arrange for the first talks there between Israelis and Palestinians. "This was one of many academic meetings, and at that stage, I did not believe that anything would come of it," Beilin later told me. Even when his associates, Professor Yair Hirshfeld and Ron Pundak, had met with Arafat's moderate representative, Ahmad Qurai ("Abu Alaa") in London, Beilin did not anticipate far-reaching results. "Only after the third meeting in Oslo, on January 20 and early February in 1993, did I understand that it would be possible to reach an agreement in principle with the PLO on a political plan. I reported this to Peres, and he agreed and brought the matter to Rabin."

Beilin explained that it was his intention to create a relaxed, informal venue where understandings and agreements could be reached and subsequently brought before the negotiators in Washington. "We did not think that this would be the principal venue, but that it would be a clandestine channel through which Rabin and Arafat would eventually come to secret agreements, in the absence of mutual recognition." And why would Rabin buy the idea? "In the course of the talks in Oslo, we came to understand that only if Israel recognized the PLO would it be able to demand that the latter end terrorism, even that of other Palestinian organizations. The surprise was that Rabin not only sanctioned the clandestine contacts, he was even willing to make the matter public at a certain stage."

As the tedious negotiations between the official Jordanian-Palestinian and Israeli delegations ground on in Washington, contacts on the Oslo track continued in absolute secrecy, remaining compartmentalized within the Israeli administration. In May 1993 Rabin decided to give the talks in Oslo a more "official" status, and he dispatched the director general of the Foreign Ministry, Uri Savir, to Norway. Another trusted Rabin associate joined Savir in June, lawyer Yoel Singer, whom Rabin had met when he was minister of defense and Singer was head of the international law division of the IDF. But even at this stage, Rabin did not believe that these talks would succeed. Hence, he kept them secret from Washington and from his colleagues in Israel, too. If they failed, he felt he could always claim that they had been an aborted attempt by the Foreign Ministry and Shimon Peres. But the talks did succeed, and thus on the ninth and tenth of September, Rabin and Arafat exchanged letters of mutual recognition, and on the thirteenth of that month, they astounded the whole world with their historic handshake on the White House lawn.

The great shift in attitude that Rabin had undergone was in his willingness to recognize the PLO, not in his views about the territories. Even this change had occurred, as was Rabin's wont, not as the fruit of a planned initiative, but in response to one presented to him by Beilin and Peres, virtually ready-made and in reaction to a change that had taken place in Arafat. Rabin recognized the PLO only after Arafat had made a series of concessions of his own: not only recognizing Israel — which the PLO had already done in 1988, even though

Rabin had regarded it then as a publicity stunt — but also agreeing to an interim settlement, agreeing not to raise the demand for a total Israeli withdrawal from the territories during the interim period, agreeing that the Israeli settlements remain in place, and agreeing to halt the Intifada and to work actively for the prevention of terrorism by other Palestinian organizations.

Rabin believed that these developments affirmed the fundamental principles that he had stood for over the years. First, he was able to avoid simultaneous negotiations with several Arab states, preventing a situation where the group could line up behind the state with the most extreme stand. Holding separate negotiations made it possible to play the Arab powers off against each other. Indeed, at a certain stage, the most effective pressure on the Palestinians was the threat that if they did not accept the Israeli position, Rabin would walk out of the negotiations and shift to the Syrian track. A second principle, which he had learned from Kissinger and strictly adhered to, was for a solution in stages — one step at a time. This incremental approach was justified by the argument that events could be observed as they unfolded, to assess the degree to which the other side was serious and how the public was adjusting to the new situation. In truth, this approach was largely the fruit of Rabin's disposition — a man of incremental thought, suspicious and cautious, and a great believer in "muddling through."

This approach typified the 1948 generation and had been perfected to an art by Moshe Dayan. It had originated in reaction to the generation of the founders, whose lives were encumbered with ideological baggage and whose day-to-day existence was governed by lofty and compelling dogma. The members of the second generation were tired of high-sounding words. It was difficult for them to live according to preset plans. Perhaps living with uncertainty, incessant war, and a changing environment caused them to evolve a worldview like that fervently espoused by British historian Lewis Namier, who wrote, "The less man clogs the free play of his mind with political doctrine and dogma, the better for his thinking."[20]

But would not an interim settlement inevitably lead to the establishment of a Palestinian state at the final stage of the process? Rabin remained true to the old school. He preferred a solution of only two

states between the sea and the desert: Israel and Jordan. Any
arrangements that might subsequently be made between the Jordanian regime and the Palestinian population mattered less to him. Nevertheless, he did not recoil as strongly from the idea of an independent Palestinian state now that there was no longer a danger that it
would become a Soviet base. Although Rabin continued publicly to
oppose a Palestinian state, a change had taken place in his statements
after the Oslo Accords. One of his close aides explains: "In his public
statements during the last two years of his life, Rabin used interesting
wording. He was careful to say 'I am against a Palestinian state at this
stage.' The impression was that he opposed a Palestinian state, but
the way I see it, the emphasis was on the note of hesitancy and the
words 'at this stage.' Add this to the fact that ever since becoming
prime minister, Rabin had spoken of 'a Palestinian entity that is less
than a state.' In my estimation, he was prepared to accept a Palestinian state, but without an army." Indeed, familiarity with the incremental character of Rabin's thinking suggests that this interpretation
is correct.

To this end, it is necessary to say something about Rabin's grasp of
history. Despite the fact that he was present at the birth of the nation
and was a participant in the molding of its history, Rabin lacked a
profound historical perspective. This would seem to be a strange situation, since, in the words of historian Sir Frederick M. Powicke,
"unless we have a constructive outlook over the past [and, I would
add, into the future], we are drawn either to mysticism or to cynicism."[21] And Rabin was far from either. He lacked all religious feeling, believing in neither a "higher power" nor a "guiding hand," and
certainly not in institutionalized religion. He even scorned its ritual
expressions. This was one reason for his lack of success in relating to
American Jews, in addition to differences of opinion over their role as
mediators in the dialogue between Jerusalem and Washington. He
was secular in a way that only the children of socialist immigrants to
the land of Israel in the 1920s could be.

This was why he felt such deep alienation from the religious settlers of Gush Emunim (the bloc of the faithful). As a pragmatist,
Rabin had a revulsion for their ideological fanaticism. As one brought
up on social-democratic values, he was particularly disgusted with

fundamentalist religious ideology. So these settlers, who operated from a messianic worldview driven by power politics, aroused his concern. When they demonstrated against Secretary of State Kissinger during his shuttle diplomacy in the 1970s, Rabin wrote in his memoirs, "In Gush Emunim, I see an extremely grave phenomenon — a cancer in the body of Israeli democracy." And he was worried, when an Israeli newspaper at the time published an article by them declaring that "Kissinger deserved to meet the same fate as Count Bernadotte," the UN mediator who was assassinated in Israel in 1948 by a gang from Yitzhak Shamir's organization.[22] What a twist of fate that fifteen years after Rabin wrote these words, a similar "sentence" was passed on him, the prime minister of Israel, providing sufficient justification in the warped mind of a young Israeli to carry out the deed.

However, Rabin was far from being a cynic. Schooled from childhood to a life in search of the common good, he had always been an involved citizen. This is not compatible with cynicism. Lacking both religion and cynicism, he was motivated by a belief in life's possibilities. This belief was always at odds with his pessimism, which made him envision the worst at every crossroads. This pessimism perhaps originated in his mother's persistent illness and absences from home during his early childhood years. He himself recounted that the most terrible fear in his life as a child was that his sickly mother would die. But his hopeful attitude toward life — a psychologist might say that this was a way of overcoming his fears and persuading himself that the pessimism was not justified — allowed him to carry on. And this attitude, which stayed with him from the beginning, was reinforced by his infatuation with the "American way of life."

Rabin was enthralled by the American worldview and, above all, by its faith in progress. If one were to speak of his historical perspective — though he himself would have scoffed at such an analysis — it would be the view of history as an expression of progress. Progress less in the European sense of "enlightenment" than in the sense, found in American popular culture, of getting ahead — of success, individual achievement, social mobility, subduing nature and dominating the environment, improving life. Progress — not as the fulfillment of an all-embracing abstract vision, not according to some great preordained plan, not with highfalutin words — but slowly, with measured steps, sometimes with setbacks, but on the whole, onward and upward. To Rabin, this seemed the correct perspective for both personal life and the life of society as a whole.

Although Rabin acknowledged that he must sign the agreement with the PLO, he was assailed by anxieties about how things would develop. He was concerned that the Israeli public might not be willing to accept the concessions. He was worried that the agreement would be approved by only a slim margin in the Knesset and that the opposition would continue to claim that this majority was won solely because of the votes of the Arab members. He even was anxious lest the extra-parliamentary opposition stir up unrest in the streets. But the process among the Palestinians concerned him even more than Israeli reactions. Rabin found it difficult to believe that Arafat would be able to impose his views on his opponents, and he worried that terrorism would continue. Essentially, he was not so sure that Arafat would want, or be able, to stand by his commitments.

The story of Rabin's relationship with Arafat is itself of interest. Rabin did not hate his greatest enemy, but he was disgusted by him. It was the typical attitude of revulsion and scorn held by members of the 1948 generation toward the "ugly representative of the Palestinians." This attitude turned the necessity of shaking Arafat's hand at the signing ceremony in Washington into a positively intolerable ordeal. But Washington had resolved that this would be a part of the ceremony, and the thought gave Rabin no rest. He usually took advantage of the flight from Israel to New York to get a good sleep, but this time he was unable to do so. "He got ready for bed, put on his sweatsuit, and got into the bunk at the front of the plane. But very soon he got up and began pacing up and down the length of the plane in obvious agitation," recounts Uri Dromi, head of the government press bureau. The following day, the whole world witnessed Rabin's body language. He radiated unease, ambivalence, apprehensiveness, and lack of enthusiasm at the contact with Arafat.

Rabin, this straightforward man unable to be manipulative in interpersonal relations, whose body language was frank and open, was instinctively aware of the importance of this handshake. As Eitan Haber recalls, "We analyzed the situation in advance. On the one hand, Rabin was obliged to shake Arafat's hand in order to persuade the public that a new chapter was beginning in Israel's relationship with the PLO. On the other hand, had he not been so restrained and hesitant, he would not have succeeded in bringing the public along with him." What he chose was the "right dose." He was correct, and for the Israeli public, he radiated credibility.

But Rabin was not at peace with himself even after the Washington encounter. Only after several months had elapsed did his attitude toward Arafat begin to change and trust begin to replace suspicion. When it became apparent that Arafat was actually taking action against the terrorism of Hamas and the Islamic Jihad, Rabin began to respect him. In the meetings that followed, he was more relaxed and open. Their mutual respect and closeness also increased through the awareness that their personal fate depended on the success of the agreement they had signed. When Arafat paid a condolence call to Leah Rabin at her home, providing the occasion for a rare photograph of him with his bald head not covered by his ever-present kaffiyeh, his visit to Israel was taken almost for granted.

Nevertheless, despite this sea change, despite the fact that he praised peace frequently in all of his speeches and expressed confidence in this path, Rabin was feeling weighted down and devoid of enthusiasm. Because, in spite of his two reasons for changing his political stance — the collapse of the USSR and the Intifada — his basic attitude toward the world had not changed. Rabin remained pessimistic. Just as in the past he had not treated Arab hostility as a permanent condition, he did not now think that a Kantian era of eternal peace had arrived. "The Arab states are not making peace with us because they have joined the Zionist federation," he would often say. The name of the game was still "national interests."

Until the day he died, Rabin remained disappointed with the peace with Egypt. Only out of a desire not to harm relations with that country did he not reveal his thoughts regarding Egypt and its leaders. Immediately after being elected prime minister, Rabin had traveled to Cairo to meet with President Mubarak, to signal his desire to carry on a deep and intimate dialogue as a basis for a Jerusalem-Cairo alliance that would carry weight in the Middle East. Mubarak's chilly reception disappointed him. The Egyptian president did not even take the trouble to reciprocate with a return visit. When he finally did come to Israel, it was for Rabin's funeral. Until the very day he died, Rabin carried anger in his heart for Egypt. He blamed its foreign minister, Amro Musa, who was the primary influence on the president's behavior.

If this was how Egypt, the first to sign a peace agreement with Israel, behaved, what did that portend for the other Arab states? Rabin did not hide his scorn for those who believed that a new reality had been created in the Middle East, and that Israel was about to be integrated into the region. Among those close to him, Rabin would mock the notion of "a new Middle East," a term that Foreign Minister Shimon Peres liked to bandy about. The map of the new Middle East as seen by Rabin was entirely different; it showed a situation where two states — Iraq and Iran — were on the verge of nuclear weapon capability without having abandoned the Arab dream of "throwing Israel into the sea." Even while in the opposition, Rabin had expressed his concern that Israel would lose its nuclear monopoly, and he had supported — again in contrast to his partner-rival Shimon Peres — the blowing up of the Iraqi nuclear reactor. While Labor criticized the deed as election propaganda and Peres continued to condemn it for many years, Rabin expressed his support after the operation was completed.

But if the nuclearization of the states on the periphery of Israel was seven to ten years away, Rabin was concerned about a more immediate and much closer threat: the spread of Muslim fundamentalism from the radical states and the takeover by fundamentalist forces of moderate states like Jordan, Egypt, Saudi Arabia, and Algeria. "This subject was really an obsession with him," comments one political adviser. "He never stopped talking about it in the conversations he had with any foreign diplomats and politicians. It got to the point where they were begging me to stop him from preaching about it." For example, during an appearance at a conference held by the International Center for Peace in the Middle East on December 17, 1992, Rabin declared, "Today Iran is the leading disseminator of fundamentalist Islam in the region. Iran has replaced Iraq in its megalomaniacal ambitions in empire-building. Within seven years, this will be the threat in the Middle East. We have this time in which to resolve the problems."

The fact that the danger from the outer circle of Arab states threatened not only Israel, but also its traditional "confrontation states," made Israel, to Rabin's way of thinking, a potential ally of these inner-circle states. Similarly, just as the creation of an extremist element among the Palestinians — the fundamentalist organizations — had turned the PLO into Israel's ally, so had the fundamentalists ruling Iran made partners of the pro-American Arab states. This situation also justified making territorial concessions to them, even withdrawal from the entire Golan, so long as those states, including Syria, would provide a friendly, or at least a neutral, buffer against the more distant enemy. Thus, while good friends of his in the Labor Party continued to oppose a pullout from the Golan Heights for fear of a future Syrian attack, Rabin's answer was that they were fighting yesterday's war. Our problem tomorrow will be Iran and not Syria, and the need to have the Israeli air force fly over Jordan, close to the Iraqi border, is more important than holding on to another hill beside Nablus or Hebron.

What strengthened this belief was the Gulf War of 1991. For the first time it was possible to see how the new Middle East would look. On one side was a threat from a radical state, Iraq, which was not afraid to launch Scud missiles against Israel, had unbridled ambitions of territorial hegemony, and was closer than previously supposed to having a nuclear capability. And opposing this threat was a coalition in which Israel was a partner, though a minor one. From one war it is possible to learn about the character of the next war, and especially about the handling of fighting forces and long-distance weaponry, in an era when the territorial component of war has changed its significance.

However, the Gulf War also provided a third reason for Rabin's pessimistic estimate that time was ultimately not on Israel's side, but that a window of opportunity had opened. This reason was related to the question of Israel's stamina as a nation.

The Middle East of the early 1990s was ostensibly the most congenial ever for Israel. The United States had responded to requests for strategic reinforcements to Israel's air force, giving the Jewish state an unprecedented qualitative military advantage. Its international standing was also firmer than ever: in the course of the Rabin government's term in office, and especially following the peace agreement, the number of countries with diplomatic relations with Israel rose from fewer than 100 to 150 (in 1995).

Under Rabin, the Israeli economy was booming like that of Southeast Asia, with a per capita gross national product exceeding $15,000 in 1995. When Rabin was prime minister in 1975, the per capita GNP had been just $3,400. That year the GNP was $12 billion, equal to half the combined GNPs of Egypt, Jordan, and Syria. In 1995 it reached $85 billion and exceeded the combined GNPs of those three countries by fifty percent. The immigration of nearly 700,000 people from the former Soviet Union, most of them highly educated and skilled, brought the population of Israel to 5.5 million, with a constantly rising level of education and other economic indicators that forecast further gains. Poised on the other side was the Arab world — having lost its political support, the USSR — weak and divided, torn between the radical fundamentalist and pro-American camps, suffering from a variety of political ills, and especially from economic difficulties.

But during this sanguine period, Rabin had a growing sense — which had first taken hold during the Intifada — that Israel's staying power for a continuous state of war was diminishing. The fact that half a million Tel Avivites had fled the biggest city in Israel every night during the Gulf War for fear of falling Scuds seemed to him inconsistent with the ethos of "we won't budge" on which he had been reared. The public's overwrought reaction to the terrorist attacks in the ensuing years seemed to him contrary to formerly accepted norms. He was especially critical of the media. He accused them of irresponsibility, of cynically exploiting the tense situation to produce newspaper-selling drama, thereby sowing panic, instead of exerting a calming, strengthening, and encouraging influence. This matter requires some elaboration.

When Rabin assumed his post as prime minister, relations between him and the media were very good. They had been built up during his years in the opposition, when he had served as a patient commentator, cultivating — since he always dealt with issues of security — the image of the credible politician, that is, the anti-politician. His campaign pledges to effect a change in national priorities and to bring peace closer were compatible with the political leanings of the major newspaper editors and columnists in the country, and the media supported him in the race for prime minister in 1992.

However, relations between Rabin and the media had been tense during his first term as prime minister in the 1970s, and this happened again and for the same reason: he regarded the media as "irresponsible." I remember one enraged criticism made at a cabinet meeting on October 25, 1992, regarding publication of a leak about Israel's willingness to withdraw entirely from the Golan. "*Davar* has been irresponsible," Rabin lashed out at the daily, of which I was editor in chief at the time. Another motif of his criticism was the harm to public morale that the media fostered following terrorist attacks. This was linked to his concerns over a weakening of the public's staying power for a state of war that he knew would persist throughout the peace process.

He aimed the first criticism of this sort at the huge headlines in the newspapers during the 1991 Gulf War. But this was just a harbinger of things to come, given the journalistic style developing in the early 1990s. The crueler the terrorist attacks became — a wave of knifings followed by suicide bombings — the more dramatic the reaction of the media. The two tabloids vied with each other for gigantic headlines: "Back in Hell," "A Nation in Fear," they trumpeted. The television channels competed for close-ups of blood-drenched body parts scattered in the bus explosions. Rabin was furious. Appearing on the prime time news of the public television channel in March 1993, he stated, "I saw today's headlines about the stabbing of several youths [by Palestinian terrorists]. They were three times the size of the headlines in the papers at the outbreak of the Six Day Way. Even the media have a role in calming the people." Although he was a great proponent of the American way and believed in a free press, Rabin had little tolerance for liberal sensibilities when it came to the media. He essentially preferred the media to be responsible and committed to the national interest, and he made sure to criticize them whenever this dimension was missing from their reportage, in his opinion.

Rabin's personal relations with the media were not at all simple. After all, it was a newspaper scoop — the revelation of his wife's U.S. bank account by *Ha'aretz* — that caused his resignation as prime minister in 1977. But beyond that, he was not enamored of the dovish leanings of the media, most of whose members he regarded as belonging to the "bleeding heart" school of liberals. During Rabin's first term as prime minister, the term "left-wing Mafia" was coined to describe Israel television and its personnel. This description was not actually Rabin's, but it did express the prevailing mood in his office in response to the critical style that the Israeli state media had begun to adopt following many years of more established and disciplined reporting.

Veteran radio and television broadcaster Micha Friedman attributes Rabin's attitude to elements of his personality: "He can be described as a figure with a dualistic and ambivalent attitude toward the media. This is because his purely rational thinking is subject to a strong emotional influence, which is not always under his control, and sometimes interferes with his functioning. This built-in conflict in his personality is reflected by gaps between the rationalistic positions that he proposes and his conflicted emotional world. There is an intense dissonance between his conscious thought and his character: between the analyst and the redhead, as journalist Yoel Marcus so aptly put it. Rabin's perception of the specific value of the mass media sometimes receives a distorted expression because of his difficulties with interpersonal communications. Rabin was a great champion of the American way of life, but had difficulty adjusting to the style of behavior and the political culture it entailed. He is exposed but reveals nothing, close but distant, open but disconnected, willing to hear criticism but vulnerable."[23]

It is perhaps more accurate to attribute Rabin's ambivalence toward the media to his republican and anti-intellectual bent. His abstract style of thinking and preoccupation with process were the flip side of his inability to touch people or feelings. Even in *Pinkas Sherut,* the chesslike style of the life he describes is apparent. People are pawns on the board more than flesh and blood possessed of feelings. His difficulty in expressing feelings, in talking about personal matters, in making small talk, drove him to discussions of strategic and international concerns. For this reason, his book *Conversations with Leaders and Heads of State* is dry as dust. It lacks poetry, feeling, or metaphor; makes no reference to matters of the spirit or problems of society, not even to soccer, which is what he most loved to watch on television. His abstract and analytical style gave him an intellectual image, though he actually didn't like intellectuals and mocked "eggheads," preferring the company of successful business-men and being most at ease in the company of military men.

As far as Rabin was concerned, media personnel and intellectuals were part of the Israeli left and represented neither the people nor their beliefs, fears, or desires. Of this he was convinced. The "peace camp" included those involved with rights or law, whether in the state legal system or in academic institutions, who placed restrictions on antiterrorist activity. They demanded strict adherence to the law even in the struggle to quash the uprising, and maintained a cold legal attitude even toward fundamentalist terrorists, "who are seeking through their suicide missions to kill the peace process," in Rabin's words. He believed that activists from the various civil rights organi-zations who applied moral scruples where the more primary consid-erations were those of the good of the state were not strengthening Israel's moral fiber, but were, in their naiveté, weakening the nation. How great was the similarity between Rabin's perspective and that of the pair Nixon and Kissinger. For that reason, Rabin felt that their analysis of post-Vietnam trauma in American society corresponded to what might occur in Israel.

Rabin did not, in any case, regard the "new Middle East" as the dawning of an era of optimism and peace, but as a period to prepare for the troubles to come. It was an opportunity to take advantage of the international situation — the collapse of the Soviet Union and the fear among the confrontation states concerning the rise in power of Muslim fundamentalism — to reach political agreements with these states in anticipation of the possibility that in seven to ten years a new conflict with the outer circle of Arab states would emerge. Or at least to delay the next war. This was far from the rosy picture painted by the Israeli peace movement, and he did not make much mention of it in his speeches to the general public. Rabin's speechwriter must have been aware of the discrepancy between his personal beliefs and the pose he assumed for public consumption. From this point of view, his behavior was reminiscent of Ben-Gurion's on November 19, 1947. While everyone else was joyfully celebrating the UN resolution to establish a Jewish state, Ben-Gurion sat there, sunk in introspection, realistically (or so he believed) worrying about Israel's security.

The only hint Rabin gave in his speeches about his concern had to do with his anxieties regarding a decrease in the nation's staying power and motivation. Immediately following the Six Day War, this motif appeared in positive terms: "I believe that the people of Israel is mobilized and does battle differently when it feels assured that everything possible has been done to avert war, but that ultimately there was no choice but to fight. This feeling, common to all the nation, is a tremendous source of strength." During the 1980s, Rabin reformulated this statement more pessimistically: Should there be a war in the future, those called to arms would know that he or his successor had done their utmost to prevent it, because it would be a war that they had no choice but to fight.

Historians who will some day examine the peace agreements that Rabin signed with the Palestinians and Jordan from a more long-term perspective will surely grapple with the questions of how much influence was exerted by the man standing at the helm at that specific historical juncture or whether what transpired was an inexorable historical process. Sir Isaiah Berlin, the liberal thinker and humanist from Oxford, dealt with this question in his essay on historical inevitability, in which he derided those who assume that "vast impersonal forces" (an expression from T. S. Eliot), rather than flesh-and-blood human beings, are the determining forces in history. E. H. Carr, the astute and sharp-tongued historian from Cambridge, disputed this approach — how could he not? — stating, "The desire to postulate individual genius as the creative force in history is characteristic of the primitive stages of historical consciousness."[24] Individuals do not act in a vacuum, he noted, but exclusively in a social context, and the historian must not play the amateur psychologist in analyzing heroes, but must also examine the unanticipated consequences of their actions. This is certainly true regarding the question of whether the 1993 accord with the PLO was the result of inexorable historical forces or the doing of a hero. Since 1967, relations between Israel and the Palestinians had been evolving in the direction of rapprochement and mutual acceptance, and a 1993 survey of Knesset members from Labor revealed that a majority were willing, ultimately, to recognize the PLO. But the recognition itself, and especially a formal agreement, were believed to be many years away. The 1948 generation would first apparently have to leave the stage, allowing the generation born after the founding of the state — politicians like Yossi Beilin — to launch Israel into a new chapter in its history.

It was a fortuitous combination of a historic moment and three heroes — Beilin, Peres, and Rabin — that turned out to be the formula for success. Beilin made the mental breakthrough and did the groundwork. Rabin, with his reactive style of action, would perhaps not have responded to Beilin's initiative as quickly as he did, had he not had, at that particular moment, an ally with qualities that complemented his own — his foreign minister, Shimon Peres. Rabin needed someone like Peres — dynamic, restless, full of initiative, and a great believer that only motion creates successful politics — to present him with the opportunity, lay the proposal before him, and sweep him up in his enthusiasm. The partnership of these two longtime rivals was what made the process possible.

Domestic peace is generally a precondition for peace with external enemies. But in the Labor Party some used to joke that signing a peace treaty with Hussein and Arafat would be worth it just to reach peace between the two partner-adversaries, Rabin and Peres. When Rabin published *Pinkas Sherut* in 1979, the book was partly intended as a weapon against Peres, to prove Rabin's claim that a large share of his government's ills and failures was the result of sabotage from within. Rabin was astonished at the harsh criticism of the book, even among his supporters in Labor. Party members did not like the bitter attack on Peres, they didn't think it was entirely accurate, and certainly it wasn't useful. After Rabin resigned and Peres was chosen party leader, it was in the party's interest to set aside this internal dispute. Rabin was unable to accept this and was not sorry when Peres lost the election in 1977 and again in 1981.

All that time, even while serving as a minister in the National Unity Government in the late 1980s, Rabin was goaded by his rage toward Peres and his sense of having been treated unjustly, awaiting the moment to unseat his rival. Since, as party leader, Peres dominated the centers of power within Labor, it was necessary to go about this indirectly. Rabin, the America-phile, again found a solution in an import from the United States: primaries. He became an enthusiastic proponent of this method.

When differences of opinion between the two parties composing the government heated up in mid-March 1990 because of Shamir's unwillingness to advance the peace process — the issue was the inclusion of Palestinians from East Jerusalem in the Palestinian delegation to the talks in Cairo — the two-headed coalition split apart. A month earlier, on February 19, Rabin had engineered a change in the Israeli political game. Instead of the 450-member party central committee that had chosen him to head the party for the first time in 1974, or the 1,450-member party convention that had chosen him in 1977, this time the party held its first primary election with 150,000 party members participating. This internal democracy worked to Rabin's advantage. He won 54.80 percent of the votes, while Peres received only 40.59 percent. After fifteen years, Rabin had returned to the leadership of his party.

Rabin was determined not to repeat the errors of his first term. He conducted his campaign on a personal basis, although this angered Peres's supporters. He also prepared to run the government in a quasi-presidential style, an intention that he expressed as early as his victory speech on election night: "I will lead, I will navigate, I will decide," a flushed Rabin declared in his gravelly voice from the television studio. It was a hint as subtle as an elephant. And, indeed, the relationship between him and Peres continued to be tense during the early part of his administration. Decades of antagonism, mistrust, lack of mutual respect, and bad chemistry could not change overnight. But reaching the age of seventy, during what seemed as if it might be the final term in office for both of them, the two veteran leaders of Labor realized that their fates were intertwined. The party was tired of their rivalry. Two other candidates had taken part in the primaries, and even though they had together received less than twenty percent of the vote, the ballots cast for them were an expression of anger toward the "old men." A sense that this time it was a war between the generations, the two of them versus their young successors, brought them closer to cooperation with each other.

What most benefited their relationship was, in fact, the peace process. The recognition that it would be possible in the course of this term to reach a peace agreement with Jordan, an interim agreement with the Palestinians, and perhaps a settlement with Syria became the engine that propelled them with all its force. For Rabin, the belief that his first government in the 1970s had disappointed the nation spurred him on to prove himself; this time he must succeed. "I had learned," he wrote in his memoirs, recalling his failure in a mathematics examination in the summer of 1937, "that failure is sometimes a strong impetus to success."[25] For both men, historical considerations began to take the place of short-range concerns. The Nobel Prize did not enter Rabin's mind, but he spoke of "closing the circle," of the idea that someone who had been part of bringing Israel its independence in 1948 and liberating Jerusalem in 1967 should conclude his life by procuring peace for Israel. Only after his nomination for the Nobel Prize was made public did he take pleasure in it, in no small measure because this implied a kind of leveling out of his relationship with Kissinger, who had won the prize in 1973. The mentor had become a colleague.

If the conflicting qualities of Rabin and Peres had hampered their cooperation in Rabin's first government, this time round they complemented each other in advancing the peace process. And now their roles were reversed. In 1974–77 it was Rabin who was the dove and Peres, the hawk. This time it was the other way around. Having established his status as a dove during the 1980s, Peres continued to fulfill that role in the second Rabin government, whereas Rabin remained security-minded. Peres the dynamic, entrepreneurial visionary, farsighted and optimistic, was willing to move the process quickly. Rabin the cautious, suspicious, conservative pessimist, with his emphasis on security, checked and double-checked every angle. Whereas Peres was able to lift the public on the wings of his vision, Rabin's critical and careful approach ensured the support of the political center. Peres understood that without Rabin, he would not be able to sell peace to the general public. Rabin sensed that Peres's diplomatic skills, authenticity, and political initiative — and the peace movement's support for him — were advantageous for his government. This did not turn them overnight into a pair of lovebirds, but they learned to work with each other.

The power games did not end completely, however. Rabin had prepared to fly alone to Washington for the signing of the agreement with Arafat. Peres heard about this on the radio and was wounded to the quick. He was added to the delegation. When it became apparent that a decision was in the works in Norway to award the Nobel Peace Prize to Rabin and Arafat, European leaders who were friends of Peres and who believed, rightly, that his part in the process had been equal to Rabin's, sprang into action. Rabin conducted the negotiations for peace with Jordan directly with King Hussein and through the deputy head of the Mossad, bypassing the Foreign Ministry and the man who headed it. When criticism of this was heard, those close to Rabin responded, "And who started the Oslo process behind the prime minister's back?"

But these setbacks pale beside the routine cooperation, mutual acceptance, and especially the enthusiastic response of the public to what resembled a belated honeymoon. Every revelation of cooperation between the two set off a wave of rejoicing among party activists and evoked expressions of satisfaction from the general public. Each compliment that one of them paid the other increased the public's warmth and love for both of them manyfold. "The fact that peace brought with it so many honors made it possible for the two of them to divide the spoils without either of them feeling deprived," stated one of their close associates. And so it happened that one of the highpoints of the mass rally at Tel Aviv's Kings of Israel Square on the evening of November 4 was when Yitzhak Rabin clapped Shimon Peres on the back in an uncharacteristic physical show of affection and closeness. The crowd roared with joy.

After Rabin's assassination, Peres understood, with his acute political antennae, that this recent good relationship with Rabin would be an important source of legitimacy for him as successor. He described at length the friendship that had grown up between them, and the media, influenced by the assassination and revelations of hatred among political camps in Israel, bought his description at face value, without passing it under the usual lens of cynicism and mockery. The public needed a familial atmosphere like this, and the story of the new friendship acquired an almost romantic dimension.

The murder of Yitzhak Rabin, the very fact of the assassination of a prime minister, the dramatic fashion in which it was committed, and the personality of the victim, sent unprecedented shock waves through

Israel. Albums, books, audiocassettes, and compact disks commemo-
rating him were turned out in hundreds of thousands of copies. Both
Israeli television channels produced videos of his life; authors and
poets outdid one another in paying homage to his memory. The
mourning ceremonies and political rituals that went on for an entire
week fostered the myth of the man, who at his death had turned into
a legend. But if not for his assassination, Rabin would not have been
considered by Israelis to be the second most important leader after
Ben-Gurion. The one founded the state and the other fought to preserve it and bring it peace.

If Ben-Gurion was part of "the generation of the desert," those
who had immigrated to Israel in order to turn it into a haven for the
Jewish people, Rabin belonged to the first generation born in the
country, and he was the first among them to reach the highest level of
the nation's leadership. Rabin embodied many of the stereotypical
attributes of the sabra, be they real or not: prickly on the outside but
sensitive inside; direct, genuine, plainspoken and unaffected, not one
to beat around the bush, honest, fair, courageous, and a fighter. But
especially, a man who eschewed fine words, preferring deeds.

After Rabin was elected prime minister in 1992, Anthony Lewis of
the *New York Times* described him accurately as not a visionary or
someone with an extraordinary message, but an ex-general whose philosophy, "if one can call it that," was pragmatism. He had no ideological learnings, said Lewis, and what a difference that made, for
throughout most of the previous ten years, Israel had been ruled by
fanatics determined to force through their beliefs or ideology at any
price.[26]

Yitzhak Rabin was not a charismatic leader. He was not endowed
with Ben-Gurion's prophetic fervor or with the warmth of Levi
Eshkol, who was Israel's prime minister when Rabin was serving as
IDF chief of staff. He did not have Golda Meir's engaging simplicity
or Menachem Begin's populist energy, to which the throngs in the
squares responded by chanting "Be-gin, Be-gin." Rabin's first term as
prime minister had ended in failure, and even during his second term
his government enjoyed only a slim majority in the Knesset. How,
then, did he reach the level of Israel's most celebrated leader after
Ben-Gurion?

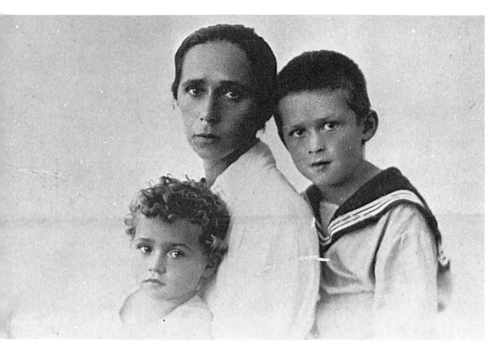

Six-year-old Yitzhak with his mother and his sister, Rachel. (Courtesy Israel Government Press Office)

Yitzhak with his father and his sister in 1940. (Courtesy Israel Government Press Office)

Right: Yitzhak in the year he graduated from Kadouri school. (Courtesy Israel Government Press Office)

Below: Yitzhak and Leah during the summer of 1948, the year they married. (Courtesy Israel Government Press Office)

Opposite, top: War of Independence. Rabin is second from right. (Courtesy Israel Government Press Office)

Opposite, bottom: Perched beside Chief of Operations Yigael Yadin as a member of the Israeli delegation to the Rhodes armistice talks with Egypt, February 1949. (Courtesy Israel Government Press Office)

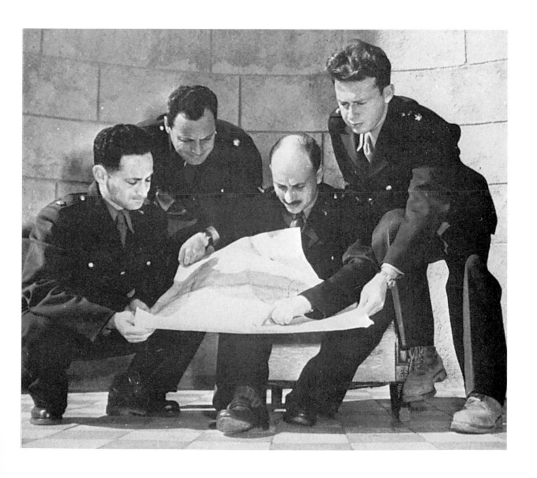

With former Prime Minister David Ben-Gurion, who promised Rabin he would become chief of staff. (Courtesy Israel Government Press Office)

With Prime Minister Levi Eshkol, who fulfilled that promise. (Courtesy Israel Government Press Office)

Chief of State Rabin (right) with GOC Northern Command David Elazar ("Dado," standing, center) and Chief of Operations Ezer Weizman (seated, left) as photographed by the Syrians during the rescue of an Israeli boat near the eastern shore of the Sea of Galilee. The photograph was discovered in Syrian intelligence files after the capture of the Golan Heights during the Six Day War. (Courtesy Israel Government Press Office)

Chief of Staff Rabin with his son, Yuval, and his daughter, Dalia. (Courtesy of Bamachaneh)

The IDF's three senior officers at the time of the Six Day War (from left): Deputy Chief of Staff Chaim Barlev, Chief of Staff Rabin, and Chief of Operations Ezer Weizman. (Courtesy Israel Government Press Office)

With GOC Northern Command, David Elazar, during the Six Day War.
(Courtesy Israel Government Press Office)

Speaking at the Hebrew University ceremony on Mount Scopus following the
Six Day War. (Courtesy Werner Braun)

From left: GOC Central Command Uzi Narkiss, Defense Minister Moshe Dayan, and Chief of Staff Rabin enter the Old City through the Lions' Gate hours after it was taken by the IDF. (Courtesy Israel Government Press Office)

Ambassador Rabin with President Lyndon Johnson, Secretary of State Dean
Rusk (seated, right, on couch), and American officials during a visit by Yigal
Allon (seated at Johnson's right). (Courtesy Israel Government Press Office)

With Hubert Humphrey. (Courtesy Israel Government Press Office)

With Assistant Secretary of State Joseph Sisco. (Courtesy Israel Government
Press Office)

Ambassador and Mrs. Rabin with Prime Minister Golda Meir and Dr. Henry
Kissinger during Mrs. Meir's first state visit to Washington in 1969. (Courtesy
Israel Government Press Office)

With President Richard Nixon and Zalman Shazar. (Courtesy Mel Cramowitz)

Prime Minister and Mrs. Rabin with President and Mrs. Jimmy Carter on the White House lawn. (Courtesy U.S. State Department)

With President Gerald Ford at a White House dinner. (Courtesy Israel
Government Press Office)

The grandfather. (Courtesy Israel Government Press Office)

With Yigal Allon, his commander in 1948 and his foreign minister in 1975.
(Courtesy Israel Government Press Office)

With Chancellor Helmut Schmidt during a visit to Germany in 1975.
(Courtesy Israel Government Press Office)

Discussing a point with Foreign Minister Yigal Allon (right) as Secretary of
State Kissinger, Defense Minister Shimon Peres, and Assistant Secretary of
State Sisco (in shirt sleeves) study the giant topographical map of Sinai during
the second round of negotiations toward an interim agreement with Egypt,
August 1975. (Courtesy Israel Government Press Office)

Above: Taking over from Prime Minister Shamir in July 1992. (Courtesy Israel Government Press Office)

Opposite, top: With President Bush, August 18, 1992. (Courtesy Israel Government Press Office)

Opposite, bottom: With Richard Nixon in New York, August 9, 1992. (Courtesy Israel Government Press Office)

Right: The weekly tennis game, August 1992. (Courtesy Israel Government Press Office)

Below: A close alliance, Rabin and President Clinton. (Courtesy Israel Government Press Office)

Opposite, top: The handshake. Signing the DOP in Washington, September 13, 1995. (Courtesy Israel Government Press Office)

Opposite, bottom: Signing the maps of the Olso 2 agreement with Arafat, September 28, 1995. (Courtesy Israel Government Press Office)

Receiving the Nobel Prize with Arafat and Peres, December 1994. (Courtesy Israel Government Press Office)

Ceremony of peace with King Hussein in Washington, July 1994. (Courtesy Israel Government Press Office)

With Hussein on the lake of Galilee, November 10, 1994. (Courtesy Israel Government Press Office)

The leaders of the Middle East Peace Camp, September 1995. Left to right: Arafat, Hussein, Mubarak, Rabin, Peres. (Courtesy Israel Government Press Office)

Above: Shir Hashalom, the "Song of Peace." The blood-stained copy Rabin used at the rally and had in his pocket when he was shot. (Courtesy Israel Government Press Office)

Opposite, top: In front of the grave. Leah Rabin, Dalia, Yuval, Presidents Clinton and Mubarak, Chancellor Kohl, Peres, Barak, and other dignitaries. (Courtesy Israel Government Press Office)

Opposite, bottom: "Shalom Friend." The wall in Tel Aviv square where Rabin was killed. (Courtesy Israel Government Press Office)

Prime Minister Yitzhak Rabin. (Courtesy Israel Government Press Office)

From a certain point of view, one might say that it was simply luck. If he had not obstinately hung on as an IDF general for years, after others had despaired of reaching the highest post, he would not have been appointed chief of staff. Had he left the army before 1967, or had there been no Six Day War, he would not have retired from the IDF as a decorated military commander and the liberator of Jerusalem. Had Yigal Allon and Moshe Dayan not worn out themselves and each other in a long drawn-out war of succession, and had Rabin not been free of involvement in any military or political post at the time of the Yom Kippur War, he would not have become prime minister in 1974. But were all of these happenstance? Can luck smile on a man so often and over such a long period of time?

Rabin did have something that made him a leader, a hard-to-define element. Sir Isaiah Berlin writes of Franklin Delano Roosevelt that he was accused of many weaknesses and failings, but that "he made up with his vast and irresistible public charm, and his astonishingly high spirits, for lack of other virtues, considered as more important qualities . . . the virtues of application, industry and responsibility."[27] In this sense, Rabin was the direct opposite of Roosevelt. He had no "magic," no pleasant manner. But he was diligent, persistent, responsible, and terribly serious. People were not at ease around him. When he entered a meeting room, all who were there would scrutinize themselves, to make sure they were okay, recounts one of his aides. Balanced and thoughtful, he would study every matter in which he was involved and immerse himself in the smallest details, not leaving anything unclear. And most of all, he was focused. His ability both to concentrate on one thing, obstinately immersing himself in it while ignoring people and their problems, and to see things sharply, in black and white with few shades of gray — this ability gave him the power to make the critical decisions required of the leadership positions that he held for so many years.

"From now on," he told his office staff when he assumed the post of prime minister, "no one here is to speak of 'the peace process,' but rather of 'making peace.' " This determination, cultivated as a young man on the battlefield, also characterized him in the game of politics. It may be that this trait was particularly necessary on the eve of Israel's entrance into the era of peace. After all, a very large segment of the population opposed his policy, and there were doubters even in the ranks of his own party. When asked why he did not accelerate the peace process, to run ahead of the pack, he replied, "A leader must go before the pack, but not too far ahead. Otherwise, when he looks back, he will find that there is no one behind him." This is why peace in the Middle East was perhaps delayed a few years. Yet the margins of Israeli history are strewn with any number of leaders tossed there because they went too fast, too far ahead of the pack.

And, indeed, in his appearance before the U.S. Congress on June 26, 1994, together with King Hussein, Rabin noted, "The debate goes on: Who shapes history — leaders or circumstances? My answer to you is: We all shape the face of history. We, the people. . . . And we, the leaders, hear their voices, and sense the deepest emotions and feelings of thousands and millions, and translate this into reality. If my people did not desire peace so strongly, I would not be standing here today."

People who worked with Rabin, even those who criticized him, said that he was smart and that he did his homework. However, did he have political intuition? The answer is less certain. But is that important? Bismarck once said that there was no such thing as political intuition: "Political genius consisted in the ability to hear the distant hoof-beat of the horse of history — and then by a super-human effort, to leap and catch the horseman by the coat-tails."[28] If so, then while Rabin's hearing was not bad, his ability to grab the rider and not let go, no matter what the difficulties, was superb. He stuck tenaciously to his objective — a practiced navigator upon whom one could rely. When a nation is entering a new era and is fearful of the unknown, the people will tend to depend on either those who are far above them, wreathed with sanctity, or those close to, resembling, or known to them — someone they can count on.

Rabin was like that. "By being a cautious engineer and a precise navigator," wrote author Amos Oz after the assassination, "he embodied the spirit of a new Israel, one that seeks not salvation, but rather solutions."[29] The seekers of salvation were, in fact, on the side of the assassin. And thus even his death, which at least for a time caused a

return to the political center, strengthened the hand of those seeking
practical solutions more than salvation, like Rabin himself.

Notes

Note: This afterword was based not only on the many conversations I had
with Yitzhak Rabin over the years but also on interviews with people who
knew him well and worked with him extensively, including ministers, senior
army personnel, Knesset members, journalists, and senior civil servants. For
reasons of confidentiality, the specific source is not given for each quotation.
Rabin's view of security issues is based on his statements in internal discussions, but reference is given only to sources that are not classified. Excerpts
from Rabin's autobiography were taken from the Hebrew version, which is
double the length of the translated English version.

1. Robert Slater, *Rabin: Biografiya* [Yitzhak Rabin: A Biography] (Tel
    Aviv: Edanim, 1993).
2. Yitzhak Rabin, *Pinkas Sherut* [Service Notebook] (Tel Aviv: Ma'ariv,
    1979), p. 477.
3. Yitzhak Rabin and Eitan Haber, *Yitzhak Rabin Mesocheach im Man-
    higim Verashey Medinot* [Conversations with Leaders and Heads of
    State] (Tel Aviv: Revivim, 1984), p. 37.
4. Ibid., p. 303.
5. *Ma'ariv*, October 3, 1976.
6. Uri Ben-Aliezer, *Derech Hakavenet, Hivatzruto Shel Hamilitarisn
    Ha'Israeli, 1936–1956* [The Emergence of Israeli Militarism, 1936–
    1956] (Tel Aviv: Dvir, 1995).
7. Arie Naor, *Memshala Memilchama* [A Government at War] (Tel Aviv:
    Lahav, 1986), p. 47.
8. Efraim Inbar, *Telfisat Hamilchama Shel Ha'elit Hapolitit Bishnot Ha-
    80* [The Perception of War of the Political Elite in the Eighties]
    (Jerusalem: Hebrew University, 1988).
9. Yehoshafat Harkabi, *Milchama Ve'estruglyu* [War and Strategy] (Tel
    Aviv: Ma'arachot, 1990).
10. Yitzhak Rabin, *Hamilchama Belevanon* [The War in Lebanon] (Tel
    Aviv: Am Oved, 1983), p. 45.
11. Ibid., p. 33.
12. Ibid., p. 214.
13. G. W. F. Hegel, *Philosophy of Right* (Oxford: Oxford University Press,
    1952), p. 43.
14. Rabin, *Hamilchama Belevanon*, p. 581.

15. Yitzhak Rabin, Discussion at the Efal Seminar about the Lebanon War, 1982.
16. Rabin, *Hamilchama Belevanon.*
17. Abraham Zohar, ed., *David Ben-Gurion: Medina, Tzava U'Tzvaiut* [David Ben-Gurion: State, Army, and the Military Way of Life] (Tel Aviv: Ma'arachot and Tel Aviv University, 1988), p. 55.
18. Rabin, *Pinkas Sherut,* p. 217.
19. Efraim Inbar, "Israel Small War: The Military Response to the Intifada," *Armed Forces and Society* 18, no. 1 (1991): 29–50.
20. Lewis B. Namier, *Personalities and Power* (London: H. Hamilton, 1955).
21. Frederick M. Powicke, *Modern Historians and the Study of History* (London: Odhams Press, 1956), p. 174.
22. Rabin, *Pinkas Sherut,* p. 486.
23. Micha Friedman, *Shelosha Perkim al Tikshoret* [Three Chapters on Communication], *Politika* 93 (1993): 32–41.
24. E. H. Carr, *What Is History?* (Harmondsworth, England: Penguin Books, 1966).
25. Rabin, *Pinkas Sherut,* p. 17.
26. Anthony Lewis, in *The New York Times,* June 22, 1992.
27. Isaiah Berlin, *Personal Impressions* (London: Hogarth Press, 1980), p. 25.
28. Ibid., p. 15.
29. Amos Oz, in *Asher Ahavta et Yitzhak* [As You Loved Isaac], ed. Zisi Stavi (Tel Aviv: Miskal, 1996), p. 26.

APPENDIXES

PASSAGE CENSORED FROM
THE FIRST EDITION

*The following passage, describing the forced eviction of Arabs from
Lod and Ramle during the 1948 War of Independence, was omitted
from the first edition of the* Memoirs. *It should follow the words "to
secure our gains around the road to Jerusalem" on page 35, line 3.*

While the fighting was still in progress, we had to grapple with a troublesome problem, for whose solution we could not draw upon any previous experience: the fate of the civilian population of Lod and Ramle,
numbering some 50,000. Not even Ben-Gurion could offer any solution, and during the discussions at operational headquarters, he
remained silent, as was his habit in such situations. Clearly, we could
not leave Lod's hostile and armed populace in our rear, where it could
endanger the supply route to Yiftach (another brigade), which was
advancing eastward. We walked outside, Ben-Gurion accompanying
us. Allon repeated his question: "What is to be done with the population?" B.G. waved his hand in a gesture which said, "Drive them out!"

Allon and I held a consultation. I agreed that it was essential to
drive the inhabitants out. We took them on foot toward the Bet
Horon Road, assuming that the legion would be obliged to look after
them, thereby shouldering logistic difficulties which could burden its
fighting capacity, making things easier for us.

"Driving out" is a term with a harsh ring. Psychologically, this was
one of the most difficult actions we undertook. The population of
Lod did not leave willingly. There was no way of avoiding the use of
force and warning shots in order to make the inhabitants march the
ten to fifteen miles to the point where they met up with the legion.
The inhabitants of Rami watched and learned the lesson. Their leaders agreed to evacuate voluntarily, on condition that the evacuation
was carried out by vehicles. Buses took them to Latrun, and from
there they were evacuated by the legion.

Great suffering was inflicted upon the men taking part in the eviction action. Soldiers of the Yiftach Brigade included youth-move-

ment graduates, who had been inculcated with values such as inter-national brotherhood and humanness. The eviction action went beyond the concepts they were used to. There were some fellows who refused to take part in the expulsion action. Prolonged propa-ganda activities were required after the action to remove the bitter-ness of these youth-movement groups and to explain why we were obliged to undertake such a harsh and cruel action.

NOT A PEACE PROCESS, BUT PEACEMAKING

ADDRESS TO THE KNESSET BY PRIME MINISTER YITZHAK RABIN INTRODUCING HIS GOVERNMENT

Jerusalem, 13 July 1992

Honorable Mr. President, Speaker of the Knesset, Members of the Knesset: The government that is today seeking the Thirteenth Knesset's confidence is keenly aware that the eyes of every one of Israel's citizens are focused upon it in prayer and with high hopes. Many people, both in Israel and abroad, are looking forward with expectations of embarking on a new path, gaining fresh momentum, and beginning a new page in the annals of the State of Israel. Attended by their blessings and their concern, we are this day setting out on a long and difficult journey.

Members of the Knesset: Please take note that this government is determined to muster all its strength to blaze new paths, to do everything necessary, everything possible, and more, for the sake of national and personal security, for the achievement of peace and the prevention of war, for the abolition of unemployment, for immigration and absorption of immigrants, for economic growth, to shore up the foundations of democracy and the rule of law, to ensure equality for all citizens, and to protect human rights.

We are going to change the nation's priorities. We know very well that obstacles will be put in our way. Crises will erupt; there will be disappointments, tears, and pain. But after all of that, having traversed this road, we shall have a strong state, a good state, a state where we are all partners in the great effort and whose citizens we are proud to be. "The concerted, tenacious, conscious effort of a thousand; will it succeed in rolling the stone from the mouth of the well?" asks the poet Rahel. It is up to us to provide our own answer. . . .

Mr. Speaker, Members of the Knesset: In the last decade of the twentieth century, the atlases and history and geography books no longer present an up-to-date picture of the situation. Walls of enmity have fallen, borders have been erased, great powers have crumbled and ideologies collapsed, states have been born and states have perished. And even the gates of immigration to Israel have opened. It is our duty, to ourselves and to our children, to see the new world as it is now — to discern its perils, explore its prospects, and do everything necessary for the integration of the State of Israel in this changing world. We are no longer of necessity "a people that dwelleth apart," and no longer is it true that "the whole world is against us." We must cast off the sense of isolation that has held us captive for nearly half a century. We must join in the international campaign for peace, reconciliation, and cooperation that is currently sweeping the globe. Otherwise we shall be left behind, all alone.

Accordingly, the new government has made it one of its central objectives to hasten the making of peace for Israel and to take vigorous steps toward ending the Arab-Israeli conflict. The basis for this action will be the recognition by the Arab states and the Palestinians of Israel as a sovereign state with a right to live in peace and security. We believe wholeheartedly that this is possible, that it is imperative, and that it will happen. "I will believe in the future," wrote the poet Shaul Tchernikovsky. "Even if it is far off, that day will come when peace and blessings are borne from nation to nation." I want to believe that that day is not far off.

The government will propose to the Arab states and the Palestinians that the peace talks continue according to protocols developed at the Madrid conference. As a first step toward a permanent solution, we shall discuss the implementation of autonomy in Judea, Samaria, and the Gaza Strip. We have no intention of losing precious time. The government's first directive to the negotiating teams will be to speed up the talks and to carry on continuous deliberations with the other side. We shall shortly resume the talks, so as to extinguish the flame of enmity between the Palestinians and the State of Israel.

As a first step, in order to give a concrete indication of our sincerity and good will, I wish to invite the Jordanian-Palestinian delegation to an informal discussion here in Jerusalem, in order to hear their views, make ours heard, and create the proper atmosphere for successful partnership.

I have something to say to you, the Palestinians in the territories, from this rostrum: We are fated to share this same plot of ground in the same land. We lead our lives along with you, alongside you, and against you. You have lost your wars against us. One hundred years of bloodshed and of your terrorism against us have caused you only suffering, pain, and bereavement. You have lost thousands of your sons and daughters, and you are losing ground all the time. For forty-four years and more you have been prey to illusions. Your leaders have guided you with lies and deceit. They have missed every opportunity, rejected all our proposals for a solution, and have led you to one disaster after another. You, the Palestinians in the territories, who live in the wretched poverty of Gaza and Khan Yunis and in the refugee camps of Nablus and Hebron, you who have not known even one day of freedom and joy in your lives — it would be advantageous to listen to us, if only this once. We are offering you the fairest and most viable proposal from our point of view today — autonomy, self-government — with all its advantages and limitations. You will not get everything you want. Perhaps we too will not get everything we want. Once and for all, take your destiny in your hands. Do not once more lose an opportunity that may never come again. Take our proposal with the seriousness it deserves — save yourselves from more suffering, more bereavement. Enough of tears and blood!

Today the new government is urging the Palestinians in the territories to give peace a chance — and to cease all violent and terrorist activity for the duration of the negotiations on autonomy. We are well aware that Palestinian society is not all of a piece, that there are deviants among them. But we urge the population, which has been suffering for years, and the perpetrators of riots in the territories to forswear the stone and the knife and to await the results of the talks that may well give rise to peace in the Middle East. If the Palestinians reject this proposal, we shall go on with the talks, but we shall treat the territories as if there were no deliberations going on between us. Instead of extending the hand of friendship, we shall employ every means at our disposal to prevent terrorism and violence. The choice is in the hands of the Palestinians.

We have lost our finest sons and daughters in the struggle over this land and in the war against the Arab armies. My comrades in the IDF [Israel Defense Forces], with whom I have come a long way, and I myself, as a former military man who took part in Israel's wars, lovingly cherish the memory of the fallen. We share the pain of the families, with their sleepless nights, for whom the whole year is one long Day of Remembrance. "Because only one who has lost his very best friend can understand us," [as Haim Guri's poem "Friendship" tells us]. Our hearts also go out to the disabled, upon whose bodies the scars of war and terrorism are engraved. Neither have we forgotten, on this ceremonial occasion, the IDF soldiers who are missing or prisoners. We shall continue to make every effort to bring them home. Our thoughts are with their families today, as always.

Members of the Knesset: We shall continue to fight for our right to live here in peace and tranquillity. No knife or stone, no Molotov cocktail or land mine will stop us. The government presented here today regards itself as being responsible for the security of every single citizen of Israel, Jew or Arab, in the State of Israel, Judea, Samaria, and the Gaza Strip. We shall strike hard, without flinching, at terrorists and their abettors. There will be no compromises in the war on terrorism. The IDF and other security forces will prove to those who would shed our blood that our lives are not free for the taking. We shall strive for the maximum reduction of hostile activity and maintenance of the personal security of the inhabitants of Israel and the territories, while scrupulously upholding the law and protecting the rights of the individual. . . .

Members of the Knesset: The plan to implement self-government for the Palestinians of Judea, Samaria, and Gaza — autonomy — based on the Camp David Accords, is a five-year interim arrangement. No later than three years after it is in place, deliberations on the permanent solution will begin. It is only natural for the very fact that talks are being held on this subject to arouse concern among those of us who have chosen to settle in Judea, Samaria, and the Gaza Strip. I hereby inform you that the government, through the IDF and other security forces, will be responsible for the security and welfare of the residents of Judea, Samaria, and the Gaza Strip. In any case, the government will avoid taking any steps or actions that would disrupt the proper conduct of the peace negotiations.

We see a need to stress that the government will continue to reinforce and strengthen Jewish settlement along the confrontation lines, because of its importance for security, and in metropolitan Jerusalem. This government, like all its predecessors, believes that there is no disagreement in this house concerning Jerusalem's being the eternal capital of Israel. Jerusalem, whole and unified, has been and forever will be the capital of the people of Israel under Israeli sovereignty, the focus of every Jew's dreams and longings. The government is firm in its resolve that Jerusalem is not a subject for bargaining. The coming years, also, will be marked by the extension of construction in greater Jerusalem. Every Jew, religious or secular, has vowed, "If I forget thee, O Jerusalem, may my right hand lose its cunning." This oath unites us all, and certainly applies to me as a native of Jerusalem.

The government will safeguard freedom of worship for followers of all the other religions in Jerusalem. It will rigorously maintain freedom of access to the holy places of all religions and all communities, and will ensure that both those who visit the city and those who reside there are able to enjoy an orderly life, free of inconvenience.

Members of the Knesset: The winds of peace have been blowing of late, from Moscow to Washington, Berlin to Beijing. The voluntary elimination of weapons of mass destruction and the dissolution of military alliances have reduced the risk of war in the Middle East, as well. And yet this region, with Syria and Jordan, Iraq and Lebanon, is still rife with danger. Thus, when it comes to security, we will not make the tiniest concession. From our point of view, security takes precedence even over peace. A number of countries in our region have recently augmented their efforts to develop and produce nuclear weapons. According to published reports, Iraq was very close to possessing nuclear arms. Fortunately for us, its nuclear capability was discovered in time and, according to various eyewitness reports, suffered damage both during and after the Gulf War. The possibility that nuclear armaments will be introduced into the Middle East in the next few years is a negative and extremely grave development from Israel's point of view. This government, from its very outset —

and possibly in collaboration with other countries — will address itself to precluding any possibility that one of Israel's enemies will gain possession of nuclear weaponry. Israel has long since readied itself to face the threat of nuclear arms. Nevertheless, this situation obliges us to give further thought to the urgent need for an end to the Arab-Israeli conflict and for peace with our neighbors.

From this moment on, the concept of a "peace process" is irrelevant. From now on we shall speak not of a "process" but of making peace. In that peacemaking we wish to call upon the aid of Egypt, whose late leader Anwar Sadat exhibited such courage and was able to bequeath to his people — and to us — the first peace agreement. The government will seek further ways of improving neighborly relations and developing closer ties with Egypt and its president, Hosni Mubarak.

I call upon the leaders of the Arab countries to follow the lead of Egypt and its president, and to take the step that will bring us — and them — peace. I invite the king of Jordan and the presidents of Syria and Lebanon to this rostrum in Israel's Knesset, here in Jerusalem, to come and talk peace. I am prepared to travel to Amman, Damascus, or Beirut, today or tomorrow, on a mission of peace, because there is no greater victory than the victory of peace. In war there are victors and vanquished; in peace all are victors.

Also sharing with us in the making of peace will be the United States, whose friendship and exceptional closeness we value and appreciate with all our hearts. We shall spare no effort to strengthen our special relationship with the world's sole superpower. We shall, of course, avail ourselves of its advice, but the decisions will be ours alone, those of Israel as a sovereign and independent state. We shall also take care to cultivate and strengthen our ties with the European Community. Even though we have not always seen eye to eye and have had our differences with the Europeans, we have no doubt that the road to peace will pass through Europe as well. We shall reinforce all possible ties with Russia and the other members of the Commonwealth of Independent States, with China, and with every country that responds to our outstretched hand.

Mr. Speaker, Members of the Knesset: Security is not only the tank, the plane, and the missile boat. Security is also, and perhaps above all, the person — the Israeli citizen. Security is also a person's education, his home, his school, his street and his neighborhood, the society in which he grew up. Security is also a person's hopes. It is the peace of mind and livelihood of the immigrant from Leningrad, the roof over the head of the immigrant from Gondar in Ethiopia, the factory that employs a demobilized soldier, a young native son. It is integration into our way of life and culture; that, too, is security.

You ask how we will ensure this security. We are going to change our national priorities with regard to the allocation of financial resources from the state budget and funds raised abroad. First and foremost, highest priority will be given to the war on unemployment and to the strengthening of the economic and social systems. Unemployment is "the mother of all evils." It deprives a person of dignity. It destroys the soul of the man who is unable to bring home even a loaf of bread, for there is no greater ignominy than hunger.

We intend to increase the rate of economic growth, to create jobs for the hundreds of thousands of new immigrants and natives of this country who will enter the workforce in the next few years. This we shall do by adapting our economy for "open" management, free of bureaucratic restrictions and excessive government intervention. There is too much paperwork and not enough productive work.

We shall go forward with the sale of government-owned enterprises — privatization — and do so in consultation with the workers, so that they do not get hurt. A free world demands a free economy. . . .

Members of the Knesset: It is proper to admit that for years we have erred in our treatment of Israel's Arab and Druze citizens. Today, almost forty-five years after the establishment of the state, there are substantial gaps between the Jewish and Arab communities in a number of spheres. On behalf of the new government, I see it fitting to promise the Arab, Druze, and Bedouin populations that we shall do everything possible to close those gaps. We shall try to make the great leap that will enhance the welfare of the minorities that have tied their fate to our own.

Members of the Knesset: Theodor Herzl once said, "All human achievements are based upon dreams." We have dreamed, we have fought, and we have established — despite all the difficulties, in spite of all the criticism — a safe haven for the Jewish people. This is the essence of Zionism. This is the fulfillment of the dream of generations:

In the last few years the gates of immigration to Israel have opened, and hundreds of thousands have arrived from the ends of the earth — particularly from Russia and the other countries of the Commonwealth of Independent States — to find and rebuild their lives as Jews among us. We are their home and family. No one is closer to us than they. We are obligated to be their guides, to absorb them in a spirit of Jewish solidarity.

In recent months the flow of immigrants has subsided, to our regret. The government will work for the resumption and increase of immigration, especially from Russia and the other countries of the CIS, and will persevere in its efforts to rescue Jews who are persecuted just for being Jewish. Without all of these efforts, we would not have the return to Zion. And we are all, after all, returnees to Zion.

In this small country dozens of diaspora communities, ethnic groups, and cultures have gathered. It is not easy to meld them all into a single nation, and in the interim we must cultivate tolerance and patience, to help bring people together.

The Jewish heritage has sustained the Jewish people throughout all their wanderings and dispersions, and we regard it as an obligation to ourselves to preserve the mutual ties between the government of Israel and the heritage of its people.

Preservation of the unity of the people requires the creation of conditions that will allow religious and secular people to live in mutual respect. We shall strive to prevent polarization and injury to the sensibilities of observant Jews. We shall see to it that all Jewish children are educated in accordance with Jewish values, continuing the inculcation of these values without deluding them.

The government will refrain from religious or antireligious coercion of any sort and will guarantee that the public religious needs of the residents of the country are met, regardless of political affiliation and without bowing to political influence. Special funding of certain religious institutions will be terminated. The minister of defense will appoint and head a team to investigate and determine the criteria for granting exemptions from military service to yeshiva students, so as to prevent the abuse of existing arrangements in this area.

I believe that these steps, along with full cooperation with the ultra-orthodox parties, will help alleviate the polarization of our nation and contribute to bringing its people closer together.

Members of the Knesset: There is still a long road ahead, and there is much work still to be done. We shall complete the promulgation of Basic Laws so that we can forge a constitution for the state. We shall take the reports of the state comptroller very seriously and root out any trace of corruption. We shall finally implement the law — already passed — for the direct election of the prime minister and a change in the method of elections to the Knesset. We shall pay particular attention to environmental quality and to the improvement of transportation and roads.

A few words to my friends in the opposition. We are well aware that we have been charged with great tasks. There is much to be done, and our efforts are liable to encounter difficulties. We shall concentrate on getting things done, and there can be no doing without errors. We look forward to your criticism, however penetrating, as long as it is constructive criticism, coming from concern for the future and fate of this people. . . .

This is our declaration of intent, our "identity card," these are the wishes that we want to turn into reality. Everything that I have said on behalf of the government and in my own name has been uttered in good faith and in eagerness to set out on a new path, to shake ourselves awake and to establish and maintain here a state that every Jew everywhere will regard as his home and the land of his dreams. Our entire policy can be summarized in one verse from the Book of Books: "May the Lord give his people strength, may the Lord bless his people with peace."

THE DAY WE YEARNED FOR WILL YET COME

ADDRESS AT THE AUSCHWITZ-BIRKENAU
EXTERMINATION CAMP

Auschwitz, 20 April 1993

Every plot of ground in this accursed place is drenched with the blood of the murdered. Every barracks in this terrible place has heard the screams of the tortured. Every wall here is the Wailing Wall. Every rusted barbed-wire fence in this city of death bore between its barbs the shriveled corpses of our brothers, and the wind here will forever carry on its wings the smoke of the crematoriums. Faced by starvation, faced by isolation, faced by humiliation, cold, torture — who could have behaved otherwise? They did not go as sheep to the slaughter. A deserted people, an abandoned people, an isolated people — here went to their death.

Fifty years later — and the screams still rend our ears even if the well of tears has long since dried up — we do not forget and we do not forgive. The fear-ravaged gaze of our brothers, who went from the land of the living without knowing why or wherefore; eyes wide with fright, searching for a salvation that tarried in coming; their screams and their tears and their silent weeping — cry out to us even today. All of our days, forever, will be overshadowed by the greatest crime in history. Everywhere we go in the State of Israel, the memory, burden, and lessons of the Holocaust go with us. We were not broken. In the face of the powerlessness here and in the presence of the terrible despair and the walk to the wall of death (the wall where the "selectzia" was carried), the hanging posts, gas chambers, and crematoriums — the people of Israel is alive. We rose from among the ashes of the victims and we established a people and a state of moral quality, of culture and intellect, of military might.

Fifty years later — today we have sufficient power and strength of spirit to stand up to the demands of the times, to repel enemies, to build a home, and to provide a shelter for the persecuted. And we also have the strength and the spirit to strike out at all who wish us ill — as well as the strength and the spirit to extend a hand in peace to our enemies. Our brothers, whose ashes call to us from within this accursed ground, we miss you, we miss your Jewish hearts, the mothers' love, the children's laughter. History has not been kind to you: for you, the founding of the State of Israel came too late. All we can do is fulfill your will — that which you whispered here on this ramp that led you to your end; that which is inscribed in your blood on the walls of these barracks; that which rose up from your screams in the gas chambers; that which went with you to the deathly silence of the crematoriums. So long as there is breath in our nostrils, so long as the people of Israel lives, never again will a disaster like this happen. We will defend every Jew in every place. Our blood will no longer be spilt in vain.

I speak here in the name of all citizens of the State of Israel. And standing here with me are the firebrands rescued from the flames, who reached home. I speak here in the name of the sons and daughters who arose in your place in your home, the home that you did not reach. In the name of the fighters of Israel, I salute the mute stones, your ashes, you — who did not have the good fortune to see us realize the dream of generations. "O land, do not cover their blood — do not muffle the echo for their cries."

Appendix D

WHAT KIND OF ISRAEL DO YOU WANT?

COMMENCEMENT EXERCISES AT THE NATIONAL SECURITY COLLEGE

G'lilot, 12 August 1993

Twenty-five years ago, the president of the United States and the prime minister of Israel held a meeting. On that occasion, Lyndon Johnson asked Levi Eshkol what kind of Israel he wanted. Today, forty-six years after the founding of the state, twenty-six years after the Six Day War, perhaps the time has come to repeat this question, "What kind of Israel do we want?" My answer is an all-encompassing one: We want a state of Jews, a Zionist state, a progressive democratic state, a strong state.

Commanders, Graduates: Jewish history has given the members of our generation privileges: I don't imagine that any generation before us has been privileged to have such powerful, bitter, and lovely experiences. We have been witnesses and participants in the most important, decisive, and thrilling period in the annals of the Jewish people since the destruction of the Temple. The past one hundred years will fill many important chapters in the history of the Jewish people, and we have taken part in the making of this history.

For me, as a native of this land, the Jew, in the collective sense, and the Diaspora were always represented by the image of the bent-over Jew possessed of meager bodily strength and immense mental powers. The Jews that we studied, about whom we read in Bialik's poems, in Shalom Aleichem's stories, were concerned mainly with survival. What do we remember from these poems, from these stories? Concepts and words like "exile," "riots," "pogroms," "ghettos." The most oft-quoted saying of that period was, "The sun was shining, the acacia was blooming — and the slaughterer was slaughtering."

It is true, however, that alongside ghetto life there was also a rich intellectual life. The Jewish people produced the highest-quality authors and poets, and to this day are represented among the top-ranking scientists, intellectuals, and moralists in the world. It is no coincidence that one quarter of all Nobel Prize laureates are members of our people. But the fact is that the picture of the world engraved upon the memory of members of our generation is of a Jew with fear in his eyes, a leaf being wafted about, "a straw subject to the spark of any evildoer" — in the words of the poet.

This picture changed totally in the middle of the twentieth century. The establishment of the State of Israel gave birth to the image of a new Jew — the sabra, a strong person, a fighter, standing upright, rooted, one who beats back all who rise up against him, a David who overcomes Goliath. And around the new Jew developed the image of the Israeli "superman," omnipotent, resourceful, sophisticated, victorious. This Israeli and Jew arose each morning anticipating a new Entebbe operation. . . .

It turns out that the image of the Israeli "superman" made an impression on the world in terms of military prowess. But the stronger we were, the more we were attacked. Perhaps it was envy; maybe the world was not used to the new Jew. Zionism was condemned; our international situation deteriorated. Markets were closed to us; we were boycotted. There was more than a grain of truth in the saying that dogged our footsteps for many long years: the whole world is against us.

I must say that Arab hostility and diplomatic isolation were damaging to us: We lost our trust in others. We were suspicious of everyone. We developed a siege mentality. We lived in a kind of political, economic, and mental ghetto. We secluded ourselves. We distanced ourselves. We became skeptical and harbored reservations. We developed patterns of obstinacy and of seeing the world in somber colors.

The truth is that there were advantages to the siege atmosphere. We drew out tremendous capabilities on our own. We brought miracles and wonders to pass. We achieved unbelievable feats. And all of this was done by a small, closed-in people, a people that felt it had its back to the wall.

Dramatic changes have taken place in the final decade of the twentieth century. Atlases from five years ago cannot serve as texts; the maps have changed, empires have dissolved, new states have arisen. New borders have been created; ideologies in which millions believed have collapsed, crumpling like a house of cards. Everything is on the move. The revolution that the world is going through today and the ideologies that have vanished have a price: some fifty armed conflicts are taking place at this moment in the world.

In face of the new reality of the changing world, we must forge a new dimension to the image of the Israeli. This is the hour for making changes: for opening up, for looking around us, for engaging in dialogue, for integrating, for making friends, for making peace. We must view this changing world through eyes informed by wisdom: now that it is no longer against us. Countries have established diplomatic ties with us. States that had never extended a hand to us, states that denounced us, that fought us, that aided and abetted our bitterest enemies — today regard us as worthy and respectable partners. Israel has become a lodestone; we also have strengthened the foundations of democracy in the only democratic state in this part of the world. This democracy is not to be taken for granted. Our fathers and forebears who arrived in the Land of Israel from Russia and Morocco, Poland and Yemen, were not born in, nor did they live in, democratic states, and they knew nothing of the democratic life. Our democracy here has its roots in the heritage of the Jewish people.

Commanders, Graduates: Alongside the great and increasing opportunities for peace, there exist risks to the security of Israel and its inhabitants — and these must not be ignored. Only a strong Israel will be capable of providing its leaders with the sense of security essential for the making of difficult and sometimes painful decisions for peace. Behind the words "a strong State of Israel" stand you and your comrades in the IDF and the other security forces. The fate of the State of Israel depends on you. The outcome of every war depends on you. There is no heavier responsibility than this.

Without false modesty, I say to you today: You are the best army in the world — there is no equal in terms of the level of professionalism, the quality of its commanders and soldiers, the morality of its battle, the willingness to sacrifice. Only in our own IDF do two medics dash to aid their wounded comrades — and to their death, as happened a month ago in Lebanon.

Commanders, Graduates: Our task, our objective is to bring peace. Your task is to be victorious in war and to defend peace if, God forbid, war is imposed upon us. In recent years you have had to contend daily with a complex reality: terrorism, a war against violence, the imposition of order, and preparedness for war. I monitor your doings in southern Lebanon, in the territories, in ongoing security activity, in multi-risk conditions, in maneuvers, and in the grueling, routine tasks that prepare you for the battlefield of tomorrow. And I say to you, the results are very good. The achievements are important, even if not all of them are readily apparent.

You are putting in motion long-term processes, whose consequences will become apparent in years to come. But that is not sufficient. As an army of the first quality, you, as commanders, must strive for excellence in all areas of endeavor, because you are the line separating the state — the Jewish, Zionist, democratic, strong State of Israel — from the dangers that lie in wait, even in an era of steps leading toward peace.

ON SIGNING THE ISRAELI-PALESTINIAN DECLARATION OF PRINCIPLES

Washington, 13 September 1993

President of the United States, Your Excellencies, Ladies and Gentlemen: This signing of the Israeli-Palestinian Declaration of Principles, here today, is not so easy — neither for myself, as a soldier in Israel's wars, nor for the people of Israel and the Jewish people in the Diaspora, who are watching us now with great hope, mixed with apprehension. It is certainly not easy for the families of the victims of terrorism and war, whose pain will never heal. For the many thousands who have defended our lives with their own, and have even sacrificed their lives for our own — this ceremony has come too late.

Today, on the eve of an opportunity for peace — and perhaps an end to violence and war — we remember each and every one of them with everlasting love.

We have come from Jerusalem, the ancient and eternal capital of the Jewish people. We have come from an anguished and grieving land. We have come from a people, a home, a family, that has known not a single year — not a single month — in which mothers have not wept for their sons. We have come to try and put an end to hostilities, so that our children and our children's children will no longer experience the painful cost of war, violence, and terror.

We have come to secure their lives, and to ease the sorrow and the painful memories of the past — to hope and pray for peace.

Let me say to you, the Palestinians: We are destined to live together, on the same soil in the same land. We, the soldiers who have returned from battle stained with blood, we who have seen our relatives and friends killed before our eyes, we who have attended their funerals and cannot look into the eyes of parents and orphans, we who have come from a land where parents bury their children, we who have fought against you, the Palestinians. We say to you today in a loud and clear voice; Enough of blood and tears. Enough. We harbor no hatred toward you. We have no desire for revenge. We, like you, are people who want to build a home, plant a tree, love, live side by side with you — in dignity, in empathy, as human beings, as free men. We are today giving peace a chance and saying to you: Enough. Let's pray that a day will come when we all will say: Farewell to arms.

We wish to open a new chapter in the sad book of our lives together — a chapter of mutual recognition, of good neighborliness, of mutual respect, of understanding. We hope to embark on a new era in the history of the Middle East.

Today, here in Washington, at the White House, we will begin a new reckoning in relations between peoples, between parents tired of war, between children who will not know war.

President of the United States, Ladies and Gentlemen: Our inner strength, our high moral values, have been derived for thousands of years from the Book of Books, in one of which, Ecclesiastes, we read:

> To every thing there is a season, and a time to every purpose
>   under the heaven:
> A time to be born, and a time to die;
> A time to kill, and a time to heal;
> A time to weep and a time to laugh;
> A time to love, and a time to hate;
> A time of war, and a time of peace

Ladies and Gentlemen: The time for peace has come.

In two days, the Jewish people will celebrate the beginning of a new year. I believe, I hope, I pray, that the New Year will bring a message of redemption for all peoples: a good year for you, for all of you. A good year for Israelis and Palestinians. A good year for all the peoples of the Middle East, for our American friends who so want peace and are helping to achieve it, for the presidents and members of previous administrations, for President Clinton and his staff, for all citizens of the world: may peace come to all your homes.

In the Jewish tradition, it is customary to conclude our prayers with "Amen." With your permission, men of peace, I shall conclude with words taken from the prayer recited by Jews daily, and I ask the entire audience to join me in saying "Amen."

May He who causes peace in the Heavens
Grant peace to us and to all Israel.

LET THE SUN RISE

ANNOUNCEMENT CONCERNING THE INTERIM
AGREEMENTS AS TO PALESTINIAN SELF-RULE AND
THE EXCHANGE OF OFFICIAL LETTERS WITH THE PLO

Special Session of the Knesset, Jerusalem, 21 September 1993

Honorable President of the State, Mr. Speaker, Honorable Knesset: Today the government has laid before you on the table of the Knesset the Declaration of Principles regarding the interim agreements pertaining to self-government for the Palestinians in the territories, as well as the letters exchanged by Israel and the PLO and the proposed schedule for negotiations between Israel and Jordan. All of the documents touching on this matter have been laid before the members of this house, and there are no additional secret agreements. Everything is in the open and on the table. The government will request the Knesset's approval and will regard the decision of the Knesset as an expression of confidence in the government and its decisions.

Honorable Knesset: Three days from now, every Jew everywhere will be enveloped in the holiness of Yom Kippur, the day for both national and personal spiritual stocktaking. That evening, at the hour of the closing prayer, millions of Jews in every corner of the globe, from Casablanca and Buenos Aires to Melbourne and Kiryat Shmonah, will recite: "Open a gate for us at the hour of gate-locking, because the day has turned." The government of Israel believes today that in the coming year, a gate is about to open, a gate of peace, of blessing. And we can already say, in the words of another prayer: "Grant peace, goodness and blessing, life, grace and benevolence, righteousness, and mercy unto us and unto all thy people, Israel." On the eve of the 5,754th Yom Kippur, the government of Israel is presenting the people of Israel with a chance of peace, and perhaps of an end to wars, violence, and terrorism.

During prayers on the High Holy Days we also say: "Who shall live and who shall die, who at the end of his days and who before his time, who by water, who by fire, and who by the sword." Twenty years ago, on this bitter day, we felt the "who by fire, and who by the sword" on our own flesh and bones. All of us, religious and secular, left and right, Jewish and non-Jewish citizens of Israel, lived through one of the most difficult hours in the annals of the state. In the sands of the Chinese Farm in the Sinai, on the cliffs of Mount Hermon in the Golan Heights, on the banks of the Suez Canal, IDF soldiers and reservists — some of our best sons — blocked with their bodies the waves of tanks and columns of soldiers threatening our existence.

In the battle against the Egyptian and Syrian armies, defending our lives and homes, 2,569 IDF soldiers and officers fell. Even today, twenty years later, we feel the pain of the death of those who were dear to us and we share the sorrow of the bereaved families, whose pain the passing years do not dull, nor do they heal the wounds inflicted by this tragedy. As Yom Kippur spreads its holiness around us, our hearts are with them, and thus shall it always be.

Honorable Knesset: The Yom Kippur War taught us and, pardon the comparison, our enemies as well, the limitations of military force — and the possibilities embodied in a political solution. Following the signing of the armistice agreements with Egypt and Syria, after signing the interim agreement with Egypt, after the withdrawal of IDF forces from deep inside Egypt and from the heart of Syria and right until this very day, we have known years of quiet and tranquility on those two fronts. Thanks to the determination and initiative of Prime Minister Menachem Begin, of blessed memory — and the honorable president of the state, who was a full partner in this and is sitting here with us — the government of Israel signed the first peace treaty with Egypt, an event of unrivaled importance, while on the border shared by Israel and Syria, quiet and security, enjoyed by the population of the Golan Heights, have already prevailed for twenty years.

Mr. Speaker, Honorable Knesset: For one hundred years and more, we have been seeking to build ourselves a home in the only place on Earth that ever was or ever will be our home, here in the land of Israel. For one hundred years and more, we have sought to live here in peace and tranquillity, to plant trees, to build roads. For one hundred years and more, we have desired to be good neighbors with those around us, living without fear or dread. For one hundred years and more, we have dreamed and fought. Over the one hundred years of our settlement, this land has known much suffering and blood. We, who returned home after two thousand years of exile, after a Holocaust that sent the best of the Jewish people to the crematoriums, we, who sought repose after the storm, a place to lay our heads, we extended our hand to our neighbors, and it was refused time after time, time after time. But our soul did not tire of seeking peace.

Our life in this tormented land has been accompanied by rounds of gunfire, by mines and grenades. We planted and they uprooted, we built and they destroyed. We defended — they attacked. Nearly every day we buried our dead. One hundred years of warfare and terrorism did us injury, but did not damage the dream. For one hundred years we dreamed of peace.

Honorable Knesset: This government, which took office over a year ago, has decided to attempt to put an end to the spiral of wars and terrorism, to try and build a new world in this state, in the homes and families that have not known even one year, even one month in their lives when mothers were not crying for their children. This government has decided to attempt to put an end to hatred, so that our children and grandchildren will no longer pay the painful price of war, terrorism, and violence. This government has decided to look out for their lives and their security, to dull the pain and the agonizing memories, to pray and to hope for peace. . . .

Fourteen months ago we brought a promise to the voters, to the people of Israel: We promised to try to bring peace to this land. In the time that has passed since then, we have left no door unopened, missed no opportunity, searched every crevasse, every clue; we did not stand in the way of a single chance to reach peace or interim agreements that would make normal lives possible for the two peoples in this land.

We carried on negotiations with Syrian, Lebanese, Jordanian, and Palestinian delegations. In the course of these negotiations — to tell the truth, from their beginning — it was clear that the only address for the decisions of the Palestinian delegation was PLO headquarters in Tunisia. It would have been possible to behave like ostriches. We could have hid our heads in the sand and lied to ourselves; we could have deceived ourselves and claimed that Faisal Husseini and Hannan Ashrawi and others [in the occupied territories] represented the inhabitants of the territories, and that we didn't know and didn't want to know who stood behind them. We decided not to do that. We well knew who stood behind them. The inhabitants of the State of Israel know this too. And we have no desire to deny: This is a terrorist organization that knew no mercy, an organization that visited upon us the killers of children in Avivim and Ma'alot, the gunmen who shot at guests at the Savoy Hotel in Tel Aviv, the men who attacked innocent passengers in the bloody bus on the Coast Highway; hundreds of acts of terrorism, murder, and sabotage. The hands of this organization spilled the blood of hundreds of our dear ones: the blood of the family of Semadar Haran in Nahariya, the blood of Ophra Tal, of the family of Abie Moses from Alfei-Menashe, the blood of innocents whose only crime was that they were Jews.

Members of the Knesset: We are able to choose neither our neighbors nor our enemies, not even the cruelest of them. We only have what there is — the PLO, who fought us and whom we fought. Today, with them, we are seeking a way to peace. We could lock the door, cut off any attempt at peace. Morally, we were entitled not to sit at the discussion table with the PLO, not to shake the hand that held a knife, not to shake the hand that pulled the trigger. It was within our power to reject the PLO's proposals in disgust, and then to be unwilling participants in the same circle that we have been compelled to live in up to now — war, terrorism, and violence.

But we chose a different route, one that gives a chance, that gives hope. We decided to recognize the PLO as the Palestinian people's representative to the peace negotiations. We knew then and we know now how heavy are the burdens of the past. We did this only after the PLO, in letters to the prime minister, took upon itself the following obligations: recognition of Israel's right to live in peace and security; the resolution of any future differences peacefully and through negotiations; the promise to renounce and cease terrorism and violence in Israel, in the occupied territories, and everywhere else.

I wish to report: since the signing of these agreements, the PLO has not carried out even one terrorist attack. It committed itself to enforce the halt to terrorism and violence as regards its members and to prosecute anyone who violates these commitments.

It also has committed itself to regard as null and void the articles in the Palestinian charter that are incompatible with Israel's right to exist and the peace process, and to bring about their official repeal. In Washington, Foreign Minister Shimon Peres signed an agreement, a Declaration of Principles, for the interim period only. In this agreement, which will allow the Palestinians to manage their own lives, the following assurances are made to Israel:

• Unified Jerusalem will remain under Israeli control, and the body that will be the administrative authority for Palestinians in the territories will have no authority there.
• The Israeli settlements in Judea, Samaria, and Gaza will remain under Israeli rule with no change in their status. The authority of the Palestinian council will not apply to any Israeli in the territories of Judea, Samaria, or Gaza. The IDF will continue to bear overall responsibility for the security of the Israeli settlements in the territories, for the security of every Israeli when present in the territories, and for external security. That is, defense of the present lines of confrontation along the Jordan River and the Egyptian border.

The IDF will be deployed throughout the territories of Judea, Samaria, and the Gaza Strip as required by these tasks. All issues pertaining to the permanent solution will be left for the negotiations that are to begin two years after the date stipulated in the agreement, while protecting the Israeli government's freedom to determine its positions as regards the shape of the permanent solution. That is, the Declaration of Principles leaves all of the options in this realm open to us.

The implementation of the interim agreement in Gaza and Jericho will precede the election of the Palestinian council, which will be the administrative authority for the Palestinians in Judea, Samaria, and Gaza. The council will be set up only after its structure, composition, and role are agreed upon between ourselves and the Palestinians. The target date for holding elections is nine months from the date that the Declaration of Principles comes into effect. Israel will regard the Gaza and Jericho stage first of all as a kind of test of the Palestinians' ability to live up to the Declaration of Principles.

Last week in Washington I said, and I wish to repeat my words here: We and the Palestinians "are destined to live together, on the same soil in the same land. We, the soldiers who have returned from battle stained with blood, we who have seen our relatives and friends killed before our eyes, we who have attended their funerals and cannot look into the eyes of their parents and orphans, we who have come from a land where parents bury their children, we who have fought against you, the Palestinians. We say to you today in a loud and clear voice: Enough of tears and blood. Enough. We harbor no hatred toward you. We have no desire for revenge. We, like you, are people who want to build a home, plant a tree, love, and live side by side with you — in dignity, in empathy, as human beings, as free men. We are today giving peace a chance and saying to you: Enough."

Mr. Speaker, Honorable Knesset: We have no intention or desire to hide the truth from the members of the Knesset and the people in Israel. Alongside the great benefits and the anticipated peace, there are also concealed risks for us. We have not hidden the risks from our sight, and we shall do all that is required to minimize them. In any event, we believe that these are calculated risks and that they are not capable of damaging the security or threatening the existence of the State of Israel any more than any existing dangers. In any case, the might of the IDF, the best army in the world, is at our disposal if and when we are, God forbid, put to the test.

Today we have turned our attention to the positive possibilities, to days free of worry and nights without anxiety, to a thriving economy and a society that knows not want. If and when the peace that we so wish for arrives, our lives will be completely changed. We will no longer live only by our swords. Today, on the threshold of a new year, after one hundred years of violence and terrorism, after wars and suffering, there is a good chance for a new paragraph in the annals of the State of Israel, there is hope for an end to the tears. New horizons are before us in the economy and in society. But most of all I want to say to you: This is a victory for Zionism, that it has won the recognition of its bitterest sworn enemies. There is a chance that we will enjoy good relations with our neighbors, an end to the bereavement that has haunted our homes, and the cessation of war.

I call upon every member of the house to give us a chance to get the most out of this great opportunity.

Members of the Knesset, "Let the sun rise."

Happy New Year to you and to all the people of Israel.

ON THE ROAD TO PEACE

December 1993

A great many people ask me: How did I feel, what did I think, when I shook Arafat's hand?

While I tend to keep my feelings to myself regarding those moments in Washington, I will share an experience that took place at the time of that momentous occasion:

On the day prior to my trip to Washington, I invited Semadar Haran to join me on my journey. Semadar Haran is a victim of a terrorist attack that took place several years ago in northern Israel. Terrorists broke into her home in Nahariya, abducted her husband and her infant daughter. Semadar hid in the attic of her home, with her second daughter close beside her, hearing the terrorists' voices, and the gunfire.

Her young daughter could not contain a muffled cry in that hiding place, just above the terrorists' gunshots, and Semadar feared that the cries would reveal them. We associate this kind of horror story with the time of our darkest hours in the Holocaust. Her daughter died in that attic hideaway. Her second daughter's infant head was smashed into a rock and crushed. Her husband was killed by the bullets.

I asked Semadar Haran if she would join me in Washington, in order to be with me for a special, and difficult, moment for the Jewish people, for the State of Israel, and for Semadar herself. I knew that for her, what I was asking was as difficult as parting the Red Sea. She would be sitting at the ceremony just meters away from the man who had given the orders to her family's murderers.

Semadar Haran agreed to come. She arrived at Ben-Gurion Airport just minutes before takeoff. I had great respect and tremendous admiration for her ability to respond positively. But Semadar did not accompany us on our flight. At the last moment, her memories overwhelmed her. She wished us luck, blessed us for our decision to pursue peace with the Palestinians, said that she would pray for us, and for us to return to Israel with peace. She said that she would support us publicly, that she would dream peace, and scream peace. . . . But she didn't come with us. "I wouldn't be able to bear it," she told me with her eyes filled with tears. "I can't shake his hand," she added, "but you, the prime minister, you are my messenger." We parted. Our plane rose into the sky on its way to Washington. Semadar remained in Israel. From the airport, she traveled directly to the cemetery, and laid olive branches on the grave of her husband, on the grave of her firstborn daughter, and on the grave of her second daughter.

In my youth I wanted to be a water engineer. Circumstances and the needs of the Jewish people led me on the path that had me spend much of my life in dealing with the security of Israel. I was a soldier for twenty-seven years. I commanded dozens, hundreds, thousands of soldiers. My life has held many experiences, both bitter and glorious. But as long as I live, I will never forget the rows of the bodies riddled by bullets, bodies that had once been my beloved friends, the brave fighters of the battalion near Kibbutz Kiriat Anavim in 1948. I remember the cars in flames on the road at Bab-el-Wad, whose drivers gave their lives trying to break the siege of Jerusalem. Night after night, we buried our dead from the battle for Jerusalem, and at dawn we returned to the fire, the fire that depleted our ranks further and further each day.

The cost of the wars and violence and terror was heavy and painful for us. From before 1949 until now, thousands of our sons and daughters have fallen in the battlefields against Egypt, Syria, Jordan, Lebanon, and Palestinian terror organizations. Since the rise of the State of Israel, hardly a single day has passed in which parents do not say Kaddish over the graves of their children.

We did not rejoice in battle. We wanted nothing to do with war. It was forced on us by countries and by organizations that wanted — and by some that still want — to destroy us. We ended every war as victors. We came out of every war wounded. There are no good wars, and no joyous victories. Our wars did not end on the day of the cease-fires. The scars of war stay with us.

Over the years we developed a special and unique military force, an armed forces that is one of a kind, that overtakes the enemy and destroys every obstacle in its path, but an army that has no hate in its heart. Even in the thick of battle, in the pilot's cockpit, in burning tanks, in the battlefield, we dreamed of peace. One of our military musical ensembles came out with one of Israel's most beautiful and popular songs, "Shir Ha Shalom, the Song of peace": "Let the sun arise to light up the morning."

All our lives in the Land of Israel, all our dreams, all our prayers were dominated by peace, in accordance with biblical command, "Seek peace and pursue it."

Most of you watched that ceremony on the White House lawn with mixed emotions, many of you grinding your teeth. I know that the hand outstretched to me from the far side of the podium was the same hand that held the knife, that held the gun, the hand that gave the order to shoot, to kill. Of all the hands in the world, it was not the hand that I wanted or dreamed of touching.

But it was not Yitzhak Rabin on that podium, the private citizen who lives on Rav Ashi Street in Tel Aviv; it was not the father of Dalia and of Yuval, who both completed their army service, or the grandfather of a soldier today, Yonatan, a grandfather who does not sleep too well at night and worries like all parents and grandparents in Israel.

I would have liked to sign a peace agreement with Holland, or Luxembourg, or New Zealand. But there was no need to. That is why, on that podium, on that world stage, I stood as the representative of a nation, as the emissary of a state that wants peace with the most bitter and odious of its foes, a state that is willing to give peace a chance. As I have said, one does not make peace with one's friends. One makes peace with one's enemy.

The world is turning upside down before our eyes: the globes and atlases in your homes have become archaeological findings. Your geography books are about to become collectors' items. The most unlikely events are unfolding before our very eyes. Ideologies that moved hundreds of millions vanished without a trace: ideas which brought about the death of millions died themselves overnight. Borders were erased, or were moved. New states came into being, others fell. Heads of state left center stage, while new leaders arose. Almost every day in recent years is more dramatic than the one before it. The great revolution in Moscow and in Berlin, in Kiev and in Johannesburg, in Bucharest and in Tiranë, is reaching Jerusalem, Tel Aviv, Beersheba, and Tiberias. We are undergoing the revolution of peace.

After this revolution, if and when it succeeds, we will find ourselves in another world, a world with new definitions, different concepts. Our lives will change, the economy will change, cultural life will change. The whole country will be changed.

There is one area in which there will be no change, no difference, and no innovation, in the most important area of all: the security of Israel. We believe that the Palestinians want peace, that the Jordanians want peace, that the Syrians want peace, and the Lebanese. But we put our trust in no one — but ourselves. In any agreement, in any situation and under any condition, the security of Israelis will be in the hands of Israelis. While we yearn for peace — our security comes first. Security for Israel, for every Israeli, for every Jew, no matter where they live.

We are witnessing a growing wave of bloody incidents in Israel and the territories by those who oppose peace: knifings and shootings inspired by the deranged teachings of Arab fanatics. Violent opposition to peace on the part of Hamas, Islamic Jihad, and other radical and extremist groups has not ceased. These groups are ideologically opposed to the mere existence of the State of Israel, let alone to peace with it. Their methods are clear and unequivocal: the murder of Jews and Israelis. But the wave of extremism is aimed not only at Israel, but at the entire free world. As our recent history teaches, what begins as a threat to the Jews is soon a menace to the entire world. It is but a short step between a knifing in Jerusalem and bombing the World Trade Center in New York. All of this has influenced the pattern of our position in the coming years. One hand we will outstretch in peace, the other we will keep poised on the trigger. We will live in peace but not with illusions. The danger has not passed. The hand of peace will, in time of need, pull that trigger.

There will be no change, no change whatsoever, in another matter, one that is the very heart of the Jewish people, and its very soul: Jerusalem. In whatever negotiation, we will be firm in our stand that Jerusalem is and will continue to be united and our eternal capital. From our perspective, Jerusalem of Gold, of Copper, and of Light — is ours.

The signing of the Declaration of Principles was without doubt one of the most important moments of my life. As a warrior, I have dreamed of peace all my life. As prime minister, I knew that I was in charge of achieving peace, for the sake of future generations.

ADDRESS TO THE U.S. CONGRESS
WITH THE KING OF JORDAN

Washington, 26 July 1994

Mr. Speaker; Mr. President; Distinguished Members of Congress; His Majesty, the King of Jordan: I start with the Jewish word — *Shalom*.

Each year, on Memorial Day for the fallen of Israel's wars, I go to the cemetery on Mount Herzl in Jerusalem. Facing me are the graves, the headstones, the colorful flowers blooming on them — and thousands of pairs of weeping eyes. I stand there, in front of that large silent crowd — and read in their eyes the words of "The Young Dead Soldiers" — as the famous American poet Archibald MacLeish entitled the poem from which I take these lines:

> They say:
> Whether our lives and our deaths
> were for peace and a new hope,
> or for nothing,
> we cannot say;
> it is you who must say this.

Mr. Speaker: We have come from Jerusalem to Washington because it is we who must say, and we are here to say: Peace is our goal. It is peace we desire.

With me here in this house today, are my partners in this great dream.

And allow me to refer to some Israelis who are with me, here with you:

• Amiram Kaplan, whose first brother was killed in an accident, whose second brother was killed in pursuit of terrorists, whose third brother was killed in war, and whose parents died of heartbreak. And today he is a seeker of peace.

• Moshe Sasson, who, together with his father, was an emissary to the talks with King Abdullah and to other missions of peace. Today he is also an emissary of peace.

• A classmate of mine from elementary school, Chana Rivlin of Kibbutz Gesher, which faces Jordan, who endured bitter fighting and lost a son in war. Today she looks out of her window onto Jordan and wants the dream of peace to come true.

• Avraham Daskal, almost ninety years old, who worked for the electric company in Trans-Jordan and was privileged to attend the celebrations marking King Hussein's birth. He is hoping for peace in his lifetime.

• And Dani Matt, who fought against Jordan in the War of Independence, was taken a prisoner of war, and devoted his life to the security of the State of Israel. He hopes that his grandchildren will never know war.

• And Mrs. Penina Herzog, whose husband wove the first threads of political ties with Jordan.

With us here in this hall are:

• The Mayor of Eilat, Mr. Gabi Kadosh, which touches on the frontier with Jordan and will be a focus of common tourism.

• And Mr. Shimon Cahaner, who fought against the Jordanians, memorializes his fallen comrades, and hopes that they will have been the last to fall.

• And Mr. Talal al-Krienawi, the mayor of a Bedouin town in Israel, whose residents look forward to renewing the friendship with their brothers in Jordan.

• And Mr. David Coren, a member of a kibbutz which was captured by the Jordanians in 1948, who awaits the day when the borders will be open.

• And Dr. Asher Susser, a scholar who has done research on Jordan throughout his adult life.

• And Dr. Sharon Regev, whose father was killed while pursuing terrorists in the Jordan Valley, and who yearns for peace with all his heart.

Here they are before you, people who never rejoiced in the victories of war, but whose hearts are now filled with the joy of peace.

I have come here today from Jerusalem on behalf of those thousands of bereaved families — though I haven't asked their permission. I stand here on behalf of the parents who have buried their children; of the children who have no fathers; and of the sons and daughters who are gone, but return to us in our dreams. I stand here today on behalf of those youngsters who wanted to live, to love, to build a home.

I have come from Jerusalem in the name of our children, who began their lives with great hope — and are now names on graves and memorial stones, old pictures in albums, fading clothes in closets. Each year as I stand before the parents whose lips are chanting Kaddish, the Jewish memorial prayer, ringing in my ears are the words of the same famous Archibald MacLeish, who echoes the plea of the young dead soldiers:

They say: We leave you our deaths,
Give them their meaning.

Let us give them meaning. Let us make an end to the bloodshed. Let us make true peace. Let us today be victorious in ending war.

Mr. Speaker: The debate goes on: Who shapes the face of history — leaders or circumstances?

My answer to you is: We all shape the face of history. We, the people. We the farmers behind our plows, the teachers in our classrooms, the doctors saving lives, the scientists at our computers, the workers on the assembly line, the builders on our scaffolds.

We, the mothers blinking back tears as our sons are drafted into the army; we, the fathers who stay awake at night worried and anxious for our children's safety. We, Jews and Arabs. We, Israelis and Jordanians. We, the people, we shape the face of history.

And we, the leaders, hear the voices, and sense the deepest emotions and feelings of thousands and millions, and translate them into reality.

If my people did not desire peace so strongly, I would not be standing here today. And I am sure that if the children of Amman, and the soldiers of Irbid, and the women of Salt and the citizens of Aqaba did not seek peace, our partner in this great quest, the King of Jordan, would not be here now, shaking hands, calling for peace.

We bear the responsibility. We have the power to decide. And we dare not miss this great opportunity. For it is the duty of the leaders to bring peace and well-being to their peoples. We are graced with the privilege of fulfilling this duty for our peoples. This is our responsibility.

The complex relations between Israel and Jordan have continued for a generation. Today, so many years later, we carry with us good memories of the special ties between your country, Your Majesty, and mine, and we carry with us the grim reminders of the times we found ourselves at war.

We remember the days of your grandfather, King Abdullah, who sought avenues of peace with the heads of the Jewish people and the leaders of the young State of Israel.

There is much work before us. We face psychological barriers. We face genuine practical problems. Walls of hostility have been built on the River Jordan, which runs between us. You in Amman, and we in Jerusalem, must bring down those barriers and walls, must solve those concrete problems. And I am sure that we will do it.

Yesterday we took a giant step toward a peace that will embrace it all: borders and water, security and economics, trade without boycotts, tourism, the environment, and diplomatic relations. We want a peace between countries, but above all between human beings.

Beyond the ceremonies, after the festivities, we will move on to the negotiations. They will not be easy. But when they are completed, a wonderful common future awaits us. The Middle East, the cradle of the great monotheistic civilizations — Judaism, Christianity, and Islam — the Middle east, which was a valley of the shadow of death, will be a place where it is a pleasure to live.

We live on the same stretch of land. The same rain nourishes our soil; the same hot wind parches our fields. We find shade under the same fig tree, and savor the fruit of the same green vine. We drink from the same well, and the laughter of a baby in Amman can wake the sleepy citizens of Jerusalem. Only a seventy-minute journey separates these cities, Jerusalem and Amman — and forty-six years. And just as we have been great enemies, so can we be good and friendly neighbors.

Since it is unprecedented that in this joint meeting two speakers will be invited, allow me to turn to His Majesty.

Your Majesty: We have both seen a lot in our lifetime. We have both seen too much suffering. What will you leave to your children? What will I leave to my grandchildren? I have only dreams: to build a better world — a world of understanding and harmony, a world in which it is a joy to live. This is not asking for too much.

In the Bible, our Book of Books, peace is mentioned, in its various idioms, two hundred thirty-seven times. In the Bible, from which we draw our values and our strength, in the Book of Jeremiah, we find a lamentation for Rachel the Matriarch. It reads: "Refrain your voice from weeping, and your eyes from tears: for their work shall be rewarded, says the Lord."

I will not refrain from weeping for those who are gone. But on this summer day in Washington, far from home, we sense that our work will be rewarded, as the prophet foretold.

The Jewish tradition calls for a blessing on every new tree, every new fruit, on every new season.

Let me conclude with the ancient Jewish blessing that has been with us in exile, and in Israel, for thousands of years; and allow me to do it in Hebrew: "Blessed are You, O Lord, who has preserved us, and sustained us, and enabled us to reach this time."

God, Bless the Peace.

ON RECEIVING THE NOBEL PEACE PRIZE

Oslo, 10 December 1994

Your Majesties; Esteemed Chairman and Members of the Norwegian Nobel Committee; The Honorable Prime Minister of Norway; My Fellow Laureates; Chairman Arafat and the Foreign Minister of Israel, Shimon Peres; Distinguished Guests: Since I don't believe that one person has ever received the Nobel Prize twice, allow me on this opportunity to attach to this prestigious award a personal touch.

At an age when most youngsters are struggling to unravel the secrets of mathematics and the mysteries of the Bible; at an age when first love blooms; at the tender age of sixteen, I was handed a rifle so that I could defend myself.

That was not my dream. I wanted to be a water engineer. I studied in an agricultural school, and I thought being a water engineer was an important profession in the parched Middle East. I still think so today. However, I was compelled to resort to the gun.

I served in the military for decades. Under my responsibility, young men and women who wanted to live, wanted to love, went to their death instead. They fell in the defense of our lives.

Ladies and Gentlemen: In my current position, I have ample opportunity to fly over the State of Israel, and lately over other parts of the Middle East as well. The view from the plane is breathtaking; deep blue seas and lakes, dark green fields, dune-colored deserts, stone-gray mountains, and the entire countryside peppered with whitewashed, red-roofed houses.

And also cemeteries. Graves as far as the eye can see.

Hundreds of cemeteries in our part of the world, in the Middle East — in our home in Israel — but also in Egypt, in Syria, Jordan, Lebanon. From the plane's window, from the thousands of feet above them, the countless tombstones are silent. But the sound of their outcry has carried from the Middle East throughout the world for decades.

Standing here today, I wish to salute our loved ones — and past foes. I wish to salute all of them — the fallen of all the countries in all the wars; the members of their families, who bear the enduring burden of bereavement; the disabled, whose scars will never heal. Tonight, I wish to pay tribute to each and every one of them, for this important prize is theirs.

Ladies and Gentlemen: I was a young man who has now grown fully in years, or as we say in Hebrew, *Na'ar Hayiti, VeGam Zakanti*. And of all the memories I have stored up in my seventy-two years, what I shall remember most, to my last day; are the silences.

The heavy silence of the moment after, and the terrifying silence of the moment before.

As a military man, as a commander, as a minister of defense, I ordered many military operations to be carried out. And together with the joy of victory and the grief of bereavement, I shall always remember the moment just after taking such decisions: the hush as senior officers or cabinet ministers slowly rise from their seats, the sight of their receding backs, the sound of the closing door, and then the silence in which I remain alone.

That is the moment you grasp that as a result of the decision just made, people may go to their death. People from my nation, people from other nations. And they still don't know it.

At that hour they are still laughing and weeping, still weaving plans and dreaming about love, still musing about planting a garden or building a house — and they have no idea these are their last hours on Earth. Which of them is fated to die? Whose picture will appear in the black frame in tomorrow's newspaper? Whose mother will soon be in mourning? Whose world will crumble under the weight of the loss?

As a former military man, I will also forever remember the silence of the moment before: the hush when the hands of the clock seem to be spinning forward, when time is running out and in another hour, another minute, the inferno will erupt.

In that moment of great tension just before the finger pulls the trigger, just before the fuse begins to burn; in the terrible quiet of the moment, there is still time to wonder, alone: Is it really imperative to act? Is there no other choice? No other way?

"God takes pity on kindergartners," wrote the poet Yehudah Amichai, who is here with us this evening — and I quote.

> God takes pity on kindergartners,
> Less so on the schoolchildren,
> And will no longer pity their elders,
> Leaving them to their own,
> And sometimes they will have to crawl on all fours,
> Through the burning sand,
> To reach the casualty station,
> Bleeding.

For decades, God has not taken pity on the kindergartners in the Middle East, or the schoolchildren, or their elders. There has been no pity in the Middle East for generations.

Ladies and Gentlemen: I was a young man who has now grown fully in years. And of all the memories I have stored up in my seventy-two years, I now recall the hopes.

Our peoples have chosen us to give them life. Terrible as it is to say, their lives are in our hands. Tonight, their eyes are upon us and their hearts are asking: How is the power vested in these men and women being used? What will they decide? Into what kind of morning will we rise tomorrow? A day of peace? Of war? Of laughter? Of tears?

A child is born into an utterly undemocratic world. He cannot choose his father and mother. He cannot pick his sex or color, his religion, nationality, or homeland. Whether he is born in a manor or a manger, whether he lives under a despotic or democratic regime is not his choice. From the moment he comes, close-fisted, into the world, his fate — to a large extent — is decided by his nation's leaders. It is they who will decide whether he lives in comfort or in despair, in security or in fear. His fate is given to us to resolve — to the governments of countries, democratic or otherwise.

Ladies and Gentlemen: Just as no two fingerprints are identical, so no two people are alike, and every country has its own laws and culture, traditions, and leaders. But there is one universal message which can embrace the entire world, one precept which can be common to different regimes, to races that bear no resemblance, to cultures that are alien to each other.

It is a message the Jewish people have carried for thousands of years, the message found in the Book of Books: *V'nishmartem me'od l'nafshoteichem* — "Therefore take good heed of yourselves" — or, in contemporary terms, the message of the Sanctity of Life.

The leaders of nations must provide their peoples with the conditions — the "infrastructure," if you will — which enables them to enjoy life: freedom of speech and movement, food and shelter, and most important of all, life itself. A man cannot enjoy his rights if he is not alive. And so every country must protect and preserve the key element in its national ethos: the lives of its citizens.

Only to defend those lives, we can call upon our citizens to enlist in the army. And to defend the lives of our citizens serving in the army, we invest huge sums in planes, and tanks, and other means. Yet despite it all, we fail to protect the lives of our citizens and soldiers. Military cemeteries in every corner of the world are silent testimony to the failure of national leaders to sanctify human life.

There is only one radical means for sanctifying human lives.

The one radical solution is a real peace.

Ladies and Gentlemen: The profession of soldiering embraces a certain paradox. We take the best and the bravest of our young men into the army. We supply them with equipment which costs a virtual fortune. We rigorously train them for the day when they must do their duty — and we expect them to do it well. Yet we fervently pray that that day will never come — that the planes will never take off, the tanks will never move forward, the soldiers will never mount the attacks for which they have been trained so well.

We pray that it will never happen because of the Sanctity of Life.

History as a whole, and modern history in particular, has known harrowing times when national leaders turned their citizens into cannon fodder in the name of wicked doctrines: vicious Fascism, terrible Nazism. Pictures of children marching to slaughter, photos of terrified women at the gates of the crematoriums must loom before the eyes of every leader in our generation, and the generations to come. They must serve as a warning to all who wield power.

Almost all regimes which did not place the Sanctity of Life at the heart of their worldview, all those regimes have collapsed and are no more. You can see it for yourselves in our own time.

Yet this is not the whole picture. To preserve the Sanctity of Life, we must sometimes risk it. Sometimes there is no other way to defend our citizens than to fight for their lives, for their safety and freedom. This is the creed of every democratic state.

In the State of Israel, from which I come today; in the Israel Defense Forces, which I have had the privilege to serve, we have always viewed the Sanctity of Life as a supreme value. We have never gone to war unless a war was forced on us.

The history of the State of Israel, the annals of the Israel Defense Forces, are filled with thousands of stories of soldiers who sacrificed themselves — who died while trying to save wounded comrades, who gave their lives to avoid causing harm to innocent people on their enemy's side.

In the coming days, a special commission of the Israel Defense Forces will finish drafting a Code of Conduct for our soldiers. The formulation regarding human life will read as follows, and I quote: "In recognition of its supreme importance, the soldier will preserve human life in every way possible and endanger himself, or others, only to the extent deemed necessary to fulfill this mission. The Sanctity of Life, in the point of view of the soldiers of the Israel Defense Forces, will find expression in all their actions."

For many years ahead — even if wars come to an end, after peace comes to our land — these words will remain a pillar of fire which goes before our camp, a guiding light for our people. And we take pride in that.

Ladies and Gentlemen: We are in the midst of building the peace. The architects and the engineers of this enterprise are engaged in their work even as we gather here tonight, building the peace layer by layer, brick by brick. The job is difficult, complex, trying. Mistakes could topple the whole structure and bring disaster down upon us.

And so we are determined to do the job well — despite the toll of murderous terrorism, despite the fanatic and cruel enemies of peace.

We will pursue the course of peace with determination and fortitude. We will not let up. We will not give in. Peace will triumph over all its enemies, because the alternative is grimmer for us all. And we will prevail.

We will prevail because we regard the building of peace as a great blessing for us, for our children after us. We regard it as a blessing for our neighbors on all sides, and for our partners in this enterprise — the United States, Russia, Norway — who did so much to bring about the agreement that was signed here, later on in Washington, later on in Cairo, which wrote a beginning of the solution to the longest and most difficult part of the Arab-Israeli conflict: the Palestinian-Israeli one. We thank others who have contributed to it too.

We wake up every morning, now, as different people. Peace is possible. We see the hope in our children's eyes. We see the light in our soldiers' faces, in the streets, in the buses, in the fields. We must not let them down. We will not let them down.

I stand here today, on this small rostrum in Oslo, I am not alone. I am here to speak in the name of generations of Israelis and Jews, of the shepherds of Israel (and you know that King David was a shepherd; he started to build Jerusalem about 3,000 years ago), of the herdsmen and dressers of sycamore trees, as the Prophet Amos was; of the rebels against the establishment, as the Prophet Jeremiah was; and of men who went down to the sea, like the Prophet Jonah.

I am here to speak in the name of the poets and of those who dreamed of an end to war, like the Prophet Isaiah.

I am also here to speak in the names of sons of the Jewish people like Albert Einstein and Baruch Spinoza, like Maimonides, Sigmund Freud, and Franz Kafka.

And I am the emissary of millions who perished in the Holocaust, among whom were surely many Einsteins and Freuds who were lost to us, and to humanity, in the flames of the crematoriums.

I am here as the emissary of Jerusalem, at whose gates I fought in the days of siege; Jerusalem, which has always been and is today the eternal capital of the State of Israel and the heart of the Jewish people, who pray toward Jerusalem three times a day.

And I am also the emissary of the children who drew their visions of peace, and of the immigrants from St. Petersburg and Addis Ababa.

I stand here mainly for the generations to come, so that we may all be deemed worthy of the medal you have bestowed on me and my colleagues today.

I stand here as the emissary today — if they will allow me — of our neighbors who were our enemies. I stand here as the emissary of the soaring hopes of a people who has endured the worst that history has to offer and nevertheless made its mark — not just on the chronicles of the Jewish people but on all mankind.

With me here are five million citizens of Israel — Jews, Arabs, Druze, and Circassians — five million hearts beating for peace — and five million pairs of eyes which look at us with such great expectations for peace.

Ladies and Gentlemen: I wish to thank, first and foremost, those citizens of the State of Israel, of all the generations, of all the political persuasions, whose sacrifices and relentless struggle for peace bring us steadily closer to our goal.

I wish to thank our partners — the Egyptians, the Jordanians, and the Palestinians, who are led by the Chairman of the Palestinian Liberation Organization, Mr. Yassir Arafat, with whom we share this Nobel Prize — who have chosen the path of peace and are writing a new page in the annals of the Middle East.

I wish to thank the members of the Israeli government, but above all my partner the foreign minister, Mr. Shimon Peres, whose energy and devotion to the cause of peace are an example to us all.

I wish to thank my family, who supported me all the long way that I have passed.

And, of course, I wish to thank the chairman, the members of the Nobel Prize committee, and the courageous Norwegian people for bestowing this illustrious honor on my colleagues and myself.

Ladies and Gentlemen: Allow me to close by sharing with you a traditional Jewish blessing which has been recited by my people, in good times and bad ones, as a token of their deepest longing: "The Lord will give strength to his people; the Lord will bless his people — and all of us — in peace."

THE LAST SPEECH

ADDRESS TO THE PEACE RALLY IN KINGS OF ISRAEL SQUARE

Tel Aviv, 4 November 1995

Permit me to say, I too am moved. I wish to thank each and every one of you who has stood up here against violence and for peace. This government, at whose head I have the privilege to stand, together with my friend Shimon Peres, decided to give peace a chance. A peace that will solve most of the problems of the State of Israel. I was a military man for twenty-seven years. I fought as long as there was no chance for peace. Today I believe that there is a chance for peace, a good chance. We must take advantage for it for the sake of those who are standing here, and for the sake of those who are not standing here. And they are many among our people.

I have always believed that the majority of the people want peace, are prepared to take risks for peace. And you here, by showing up for this rally, prove that — along with many who did not get here — that the people truly want peace and oppose violence. Violence is eating away at the foundations of Israeli democracy. It must be condemned, denounced, and isolated. It is not the way of the state of Israel. In a democracy there can be controversy, but the binding decision is by democratic elections, as happened in 1992, when we were given the mandate to do what we are doing and to continue to do so.

I wish to thank from here the president of Egypt, the king of Jordan, and the king of Morocco, whose representatives are here expressing their partnership with us in the march toward peace. But above all — the people of Israel, in this government's three years in office, have proven that it is possible to attain peace, a peace that will provide an opportunity for the development of the economy and a progressive society. Peace is first of all in our prayers, but not only in prayer. Peace is the aspiration of the Jewish people, a true aspiration.

Peace entails difficulties, even pain. For Israel there is no path without pain. But the path of peace is preferable to the path of war. I say this to you as one who was a military man and minister of defense, and saw the pain of the families of IDF soldiers. For their sake, for the sake of our children and our grandchildren, I want this government to extract every particle, to exhaust every possibility, to promote and to reach an inclusive peace.

This rally must send the message to the Israeli public, to the Jewish public throughout the world, and to many, many in the Arab world and the world at large, that the people of Israel want peace, that they support peace, and thank you very much for that.

INDEX

Abel, Elie, 127
Abu Ageila, 38, 40
Abu Rodeis oil fields, 247, 249, 251, 255, 257, 262, 264, 275
Agranat Commission, 238
airplane hijackings, 282; *see also* Entebbe airport operation
air strikes against Egypt (1970), 165–167, 173, 178
Allon, Yigal, 8, 19, 46, 123, 241, 253, 282, 308; Ben-Gurion's opinion of, 47
    POLITICAL ACTIVITIES OF: Six Day War, events prior to, 86, 92, 97; Syrian-Jordanian conflict, 187; War of Independence, 32–35
Alsop, Joseph, 126, 127, 167
Amin Dada, Idi, 283–285
Amit, Meir, 95
Amitai, Itiel, 30
Arab Israeli conflicts. *See* Israeli-Arab conflicts; Six Day War; War of Independence; war of 1956–57; Yom Kippur War
Arab Legion, 31, 32
Argov, Shlomo, 147, 167, 168
Assad, Hafez, 250, 260, 270, 318, 320
Atherton, Alfred, 200
Athlit rescue operation, 15
Avidar, Yosef, 14
Ayalon Valley, 23, 24

Bab el-Wad, 24, 28
Bank of Israel, 305
Barak, Aharon, 310

Barbour, Walworth, 177, 180
Barlev, Chaim, 85, 86, 90, 121 135, 136
Beersheba, 38
Begin, Menachem, 78, 96, 179, 285, 287, 298, 314, 316–318, 321, 324–325, 329, 332
Ben-Gurion, David, 5, 19, 20, 27, 32, 33, 36, 40, 46, 47, 53, 55–61, 73–76
Ben-Zvi, Yitzhak, 5
Bitan, Moshe, 123, 155
Black Panthers, 223, 224
Black Saturday (June 29, 1946), 18
Black September (1970), 186
Bloch, Dora, 288
Britain-Israeli Bank, 304
British aircraft incident, 41
British Mandate for Palestine, 10, 15, 26
Brookings report, 203 206
Brezhnev, Leonid, 204, 212, 250, 251
Brzezinski, Zbigniew, 144
Bull, Odd, 105
Bunch, Ralph, 42, 154
Burg, Yosef, 291

Cairo Summit Conference (1964), 62
Camp David accords, 326–328, 329
Camp David summit, 325–326, 327
Carter, Jimmy, 291, 292, 316, 317, 318, 319, 320, 325, 326
Ceauşescu, Nicolai, 302
classified information leaked to press, 308
Colorado, University of, 224

Cronkite, Walter, 321
Czechoslovakia, arms supplies to Arabs, 34

Daley, Richard J., 130
Dayan, Moshe, 10–12, 46, 73, 76, 78, 93, 94, 96–98, 136, 176, 183, 200, 201, 211, 212, 236–238, 321; Ben-Gurion's opinion of, 47
POLITICAL ACTIVITIES OF: chief of staff, 50–53; interim agreement (1975), 275; Rafi meeting (1965), 74; Six Day War, 106–108, 112–117; Syrian-Jordanian conflict, 187; Yom Kippur War, 235
de Gaulle, Charles, 90
demilitarized zones, friction over, 51, 52
Democratic Movement for Change, 291
Democratic National Convention (U.S. 1968), 129, 130
Din, Saif a-, 42
Dinitz, Simcha, 154, 265, 268
Dobrynin, Anatoly, 138, 147, 169, 176, 204, 205, 208, 210, 212, 214
Dori, Ya'akov, 11, 28, 45-48

early-warning system, 55, 268–271
Eban, Abba, 72, 79, 85–88, 90, 95, 97, 122, 123, 135, 145, 146, 154, 156, 159–161, 168, 175, 176, 195–197, 241, 242
Egypt: and peace negotiations and agreements with Israel (1978–79), 315–316, 318–319, 320–321, 326–331, 335; and Israel's War of Independence, 35, 37, 38, 40, 41, 43, 44; and Jarring questionnaire, 192–194; and Nasser's death, 190; and Rogers peace initiative, 176–178; Soviet aid to, 166, 167, 171, 174, 178; and Soviet cease-fire proposal (1970), 169, 170; expulsion of Soviets from, 214; and Suez Canal, 148, 191; three-stage war against Israel, Nasser's proclamation of, 143; violation of 1970 cease-fire, 183–185; Yom Kippur War, peace

quest following, 242, 243, 247–255, 272, 274
AND SIX DAY WAR: events leading to, 51, 56, 57, 67–71, 77, 85, 88, 93; military activities, 104, 106, 108, 113–115, 117; military strength, 100; quest for peace, 137, 140, 142, 149–151, 201
Eilat, 44
Eilts, Herman, 265
El Arish, 38, 40, 106, 108
El Arish–Ras Mohammed line, 254
Elazar, David ("Dado"), 106, 107, 112–117, 235, 238
Elitzur, Yuval, 232
Entebbe airport operation, Uganda, 283–289
Eran, Amos, 289
Eshkol, Levi, 61, 63, 64, 70, 73, 74, 78, 83–87, 91–97, 114, 122, 144
Etzel. See Irgun Zevai Leumi
Evron, Ephraim, 95

F-15 airplane, 290
Fahmy, Ismail, 259
Faluja pocket, Negev, 38, 43
Fatah, 62
Ford, Betty, 246
Ford, Gerald R., 168, 245, 246, 256, 261–263, 265, 268, 277, 298
fourteen-point program (U.S.), 149, 150
France: and airplane hijacking, 282; arms supplied to Israel, 54

Gadna troops, 28
Gahal party, 179, 183
Galili, Yisrael, 123, 282, 310
Gamasi, Abdel, 253
Gavish, Yishayahu ("Shayke"), 93–96
Gaza Strip, 51, 119, 316, 327, 328, 331, 332, 334
Gazit, Mordechai, 32
Geneva Peace Conference, 236, 250, 263, 267, 294, 297, 318–319, 320
Genscher, Hans-Dietrich, 269
Gidi Pass, 247, 249, 251, 254, 257, 262, 264–266, 268
Golan, Matti, 308

Golan Heights, 103, 116, 117, 153, 270, 280
Golani Brigade, 43, 44
Goldwater, Barry, 168
"Good Fence" policy, 281
Graham, Billy, 168
Gromyko, Andrei, 167
Gross, Peter, 168
Gur, Motta, 105, 106, 111, 112, 283, 284
Gush Emunim, 271, 308

Hadad, Wadia, 281
Haganah, 9–11, 13, 19
Haig, Alexander, 167, 168, 184
Ha'olam Hazeh, 305–306
Harel Brigade, 26, 28, 30
Harriman, Averell, 65, 144
Hebrew University, 119
Hercules plan. See Entebbe airport operation
Herut party, 325
Herzog, Ya'akov, 97
Histadrut housing company, 305
Histadrut Sick Fund, 304, 305
Hod, Motti, 79, 86, 98, 104
Humphrey, Hubert, 130, 131, 133, 134
Hussein, King, 105, 106, 186–188, 248, 249, 318, 333–334

IDF. See Israel Defense Forces
immigration to Israel (1940s–1950s), 49
interim agreement of 1975, 272–274
Iraq, 85, 100, 105
Irgun Zevai Leumi, 15
Ismail, Hafez, 214, 216
Ismailia Conference, 325
Israel: establishment of the state of, 29; see also Israeli- entries
Israel Corporation, 304
Israel Defense Forces, 35, 36, 45–66, 101, 102, 290, 301
Israeli-Arab conflicts: cease-fire (Aug. 7, 1970), 182, 191, 195; and Israeli-Egyptian peace agreements, 328–329; Israeli peace proposal (1971), 198, 199; Jarring questionnaire, 192, 193; Jordanian-Syrian con-

flict, Israel's role in, 187–189; Suez front activity (1968), 143, 148; water diversion scheme, 62; see also Six Day War; War of Independence; war of 1956–57; Yom Kippur War
Israeli-Egyptian armistice talks, Rhodes. See Rhodes armistice talks
Israeli-Egyptian peace negotiations and agreements (1978–79), 315–316, 318–319, 320–321, 326–331, 334–335
Israeli-Egyptian interim agreement (1975), 272–274
Israeli–United States' relations: agreement to disagree (1977), 317; arms deals, 54, 55, 64–66, 131–133, 141, 142, 151, 155, 156, 158, 163, 167–174, 177, 184, 186, 209, 216, 245, 246, 277, 290, 300; fourteen-point program (U.S.), 149, 150; Israel's policy, after Six Day War, 123, 124; Jordanian-Syrian conflict, 187–189; Liberty incident, 109–111; peace quest, 135, 138, 139, 146, 148, 156–164, 182, 193, 200, 245, 274; Six Day War, events leading to, 85–92, 95; U.S. reassessment of policy (1975), 261–263

Jabotinsky, Vladimir Ze'ev, 5
Jackson, Henry, 168, 229–233
Jackson amendment, 230, 231
Jarring, Gunnar, 137, 138, 146, 149, 155, 176, 179–181, 183, 192, 195, 197
Jarring questionnaire, 192–194
Jerusalem, 22, 23, 27, 29–32, 103, 105, 107, 108, 111, 112, 327
Jerusalem Brigade, 30, 106
Jewish Agency, 10, 17
Jewish vote (in U.S.), 131, 134
Johnson, Lyndon B., 64, 65, 77, 78, 85, 86, 90, 91, 95, 134, 135, 139, 141, 142, 144; and Liberty attack, 110; loss of credibility of, 127, 129
Jordan, 327, 333–334, 335; border question, 294; and quest for peace, 137, 159, 160, 248, 249; and Rogers peace initiative, 176, 177; conflict with Syria, 186–189; terrorists, 51,

186; and U.S. arms deal, 64, 65
AND SIX DAY WAR: events prior to,
93; military action, 104–106, 115;
military forces, 100
Jordanian-Palestinian state, proposed,
332–333
Jordan River diversion scheme, 62

Kadouri Agricultural School, 7, 8
Kahana, Karl, 301
Kastel Hill, 25
Keating, Kenneth, 249
Kennedy, Robert, 128
Kenya, 286
Kfir fighter planes, 216
Khaled, King, 318
Khartoum Conference (1967), 137, 145
Kibbutz Ginossar, 8
Kibbutz Ramat Yohanan, 9
King, Martin Luther, Jr., 127
Kissinger, Henry, 124, 144, 146, 155,
156, 158, 160–163, 223, 246, 258–
262, 264–274; and disengagement-
of-forces agreement (1974), 243;
and Dobrynin's peace plan, 204,
205; and Jackson amendment, 230,
231; and Jarring questionnaire,
195, 196; and Moscow summit, 212,
213; peace settlement, pursuit of,
199, 201–204, 207–212, 216–218,
245, 248–251, 253–257, 276; and
Rogers initiative, 181, 182; and
Soviet expulsion from Egypt, 214;
and Suez Canal opening, 191; and
Syrian-Jordanian conflict, 187–189;
transcripts of talks of, leaked to
press, 308; and U.S.-Israeli arms
deals, 169–171, 173, 186, 277
Komer, Robert, 65
Kook, Zvi Yehuda, 271
Kosygin, Aleksei, 90, 166, 213
Kuneitra, 103, 117, 118
Kvutzat Hasharon, 9

Labor Alignment, 293, 300
Labor party, 83, 235, 236, 238, 240,
291, 293, 302, 305–309, 314, 315,
332, 334
Laskov, Chaim, 46, 48, 53, 54, 57

Latrun, 23, 24, 27–29, 32, 33
Lavi, Naftali, 289
Lebanon, 279–281, 289, 295
Lehi. See Lohamei Herut Yisrael
Levavi, Aryeh, 90
Liberty (U.S. ship), 109–111
Libya, 215
Likud party, 236, 240, 275, 291, 294,
300, 325, 334
Lohamei Herut Yisrael, 15

McGovern, George, 232
Makleff, Mordechai, 50
Mapai party, 68, 123, 242
Mapam party, 293
Marcus, Mickey, 33, 34
Meany, George, 168
Meir, Golda, 6, 78, 123, 144, 174;
coalition government of, 236–238;
first visit to U.S. of, as prime minister, 152–156; and Jackson amendment, 230; peace settlement, pursuit of, 186, 203, 205–211, 215–218;
and Rogers peace plan, 158, 161,
177, 178, 180–183; and Syrian-Jordanian conflict, 187, 188; transcripts of talks of, leaked to press,
308
"Memorandum of Understanding"
(1975), 274
Ministerial Committee on Defense,
78, 96, 114, 115
Mitchell, John, 165, 233
Mitla Pass, 247, 249, 251, 254, 257,
262, 264–266, 268
Mondale, Walter, 299
Morocco, 320–321
Moscow summit (1972), 212–214, 232

Narkiss, Uzi, 111
Nasser, Gamal Abdel, 55–57, 67–70,
76, 77, 85, 103, 106, 107, 113, 117,
143, 166, 190
National Insurance Institute, 304
National Religious party, 80, 91, 237,
240, 241, 291
National Unity government, 135, 179
National Water Carrier, 60–62
Navon, Yitzhak, 287

Nazareth, 35
Negev, 37, 38, 43, 44, 102
Negev Brigade, 43, 44
Netanyahu, Yonatan, 288
Nixon, Richard M., 131–134, 143–
    163, 171–173, 175, 178, 179, 184,
    185, 208, 209, 217, 298; and Jack-
    son amendment, 230; and Jarring
    questionnaire, 195; and Moscow
    summit, 213; reelection of, 232,
    233; and Suez Canal reopening
    191; and Syrian-Jordanian conflict,
    189; visit to Israel of, 243, 244

O'Brien, Lawrence, 232
Ofer, Avraham, 305, 306
oil fields. See Abu Rodeis oil fields
O'Neill, Thomas ("Tip"), 295, 296
Operation Danny, 35
Operation Fact, 43
Operation Horev, 38, 41
Operation Nachshon, 25
Operation Rotem, 57
Operations Branch, IDF, 54
Operations Division, IDF, 49, 50
Operation Yoav, 37, 38

Palestine Liberation Army, 100
Palestine Liberation Organization,
    62, 248–250, 295–297, 318, 319, 324,
    332, 334
Palestine partition (1947), 20, 22
Palestinian problem, 316, 327, 329,
    331–334
Palestinian state, independent, 294,
    332–333
Palestinian terrorists, 186, 279–281
Palmach, 10–14, 19–20, 24, 26–28,
    31, 32, 35, 36, 45, 47, 48, 74, 75
Patton M-48 tanks, 64
Peled, Matti, 97
Peres, Shimon, 54, 55, 57, 59, 60, 236,
    237, 239, 241, 253, 258, 267, 277,
    278, 282, 285, 289, 291, 301, 307–
    309
Phantom fighter planes, 131, 133, 134,
    141, 142, 151, 167, 174, 178, 208–
    210
PLO. See Palestine Liberation Or-

ganization
Poalei Agudat Yisrael, 290
Police Mobile Force, British, 17
public mobilization exercise incident
    (1959), 53

Rabat Summit Conference (1974), 248,
    249, 333
Rabin, Dalia (daughter), 50, 125
Rabin, Leah (wife), 35, 50, 125, 310–
    313
Rabin, Yuval (son), 51, 125, 235
Rabinovich, Yehoshua, 303, 311
Rafael, Gideon, 123
Rafi faction, 74, 236, 241
"Red line," 280
Republican National Convention
    (U.S. 1968), 129
Resolution 242 (UN Security Coun-
    cil), 136–138, 140, 149, 176, 178,
    183, 213, 319
Rhodes armistice talks (1949), 41–43,
    154, 155
Riad, Mahmoud, 154
Ribicoff, Abraham, 130, 222
Richardson, Elliot, 156, 160, 161, 215
Riley, William, 42
Rimalt, Elimelech, 287
Rodman, Peter, 265
Rogers, William P., 146, 147, 153–
    155, 159, 164, 176, 177, 193, 194,
    197, 200
Rogers initiative (1970), 176–180, 183
Rogers Plan (1969), 157–164, 202–203,
    206, 207, 209, 211
Rosen, Meir, 259
Rostow, Walt, 95
Royal Staff College, Camberley, En-
    gland, 50
Rush, Kenneth, 215
Rusk, Dean, 88, 135, 138–141
"Rusk's seven points," 140, 142

Sadat, Anwar el-, 190, 193, 200, 201,
    214, 218, 248–251, 254, 255, 260–
    262, 275, 302; visits Jerusalem,
    321–324; and 1978–79 peace nego-
    tiations and agreements, 316, 318,
    319, 320

Sadeh, Yitzhak, 11, 14
Sa'ika terrorist organization, 279, 280
SAM missiles, 171–174
Sapir, Pinhas, 235, 239, 241
Sapir, Yosef, 96
Saudi Arabia, 100, 319
Schell, Walter, 269
Schmidt, Helmut, 269
School for Workers' Children, Tel
    Aviv, 6
Schutz, Klaus, 269
Sea of Galilee, 52
security versus sovereignty, principle
    of, 216, 217
Shaltiel, David, 30, 31
Shapira, Moshe Chaim, 80–82, 89, 90
Sharett, Moshe, 17
Sharm el-Sheikh, 102, 103, 107, 108,
    196, 216
Shazar, Zalman, 195
Sheba, Chaim, 18
Shikun Ovdim, 305
Sinai, 56, 106, 113, 216, 247, 253, 254,
    257, 272, 274, 324, 326–327, 329,
    335
Sinai Campaign, 51
Sisco, Joseph, 147–150, 156, 159, 164–
    167, 174–176, 178, 180, 181, 191,
    193–195, 199–201, 210, 265, 299
Six Day War, 100–121; events lead-
    ing to, 67–99; postwar problems,
    119; and quest for peace, 115, 118,
    135, 145–164, 182, 192
Skyhawk airplanes, 64, 66, 167, 174,
    209
Smith, Terrence, 289
Soviet Union. *See* Union of Soviet
    Socialist Republics
Springer, Axel, 269
Stanford University, 224
Stennis, John, 222
Straits of Tiran, 69–72, 77, 79, 139,
    213
Students for a Democratic Society
    (SDS), 223
Suez Canal, 113, 143, 148, 191, 213,
    274
Symington, Stuart, 232
Syria, 51, 52, 55, 57, 62–64, 67, 70, 85,
242–243, 248–250, 295, 318, 335;
    and conflict with Jordan, 186–189;
    and involvement in Lebanon, 279,
    280; and Resolution 242, 137; and
    Six Day War, 100, 105, 106, 112–
    118; and water diversion scheme,
    62; and Yom Kippur War, 237

Tal, Yisrael, 56, 63, 106
Tekoa, Yosef, 192
terrorist activities, 51, 62, 186, 242,
    281, 282
Thant, U, 70
Tohami, General, 321
Training Branch, IDF, 50
transit camps, 49

Um Hashiva early warning installa-
    tion, 255, 268–271
Umm Rashrash, 44
Union of Soviet Socialist Republics,
    67, 112, 113, 124, 148; arms sup-
    plies to Arab states, 54, 57, 132,
    171–174, 178; expulsion of advis-
    ers from Egypt, 214; and false "in-
    formation" passed to Arab states,
    55, 56, 67; Jews, struggles of, 229;
    Mediterranean fleet of, 109; Mid-
    dle East peace settlement, quest
    for, 138–141, 147, 150, 151, 164,
    166, 169, 170, 204–206; and Mos-
    cow summit, 213; joint commu-
    niqué with U.S. (Oct. 1977), 319–
    320, 321
United Arab Republic, 56, 57; *see
    also* Egypt
United Nations, 69–71; and Palestine
    partition, 20, 22; Middle East peace
    settlement, quest for, 113, 136–138,
    140
United States: campus unrest in,
    224–246; and Israel "agree to dis-
    agree" (1977), 317; Jewish commu-
    nity in, 227, 233; Jewish vote in,
    131, 134; Middle East peace set-
    tlement, quest for, 146–150, 156–
    164, 200; Middle East policy of,
    134, 135, 138–141, 261–263, 316,
    317–319, 324, 330; Rabin as am-

bassador to, 122–233; Rabin's bank account in, 310–313; Rabin visits, 261–267, 276–278; and events prior to Six Day War, 72, 77–79, 87–92, 95; joint communiqué with Soviet Union (Oct. 1977), 319–320, 321; conflict of, with Soviet Union, 166–168, 172, 176, 178; and Suez Canal, 191; and Syrian-Jordanian conflict, 187–189; and Vietnam War, 124–127; *see also* Israeli–United States' relations
USSR. *See* Union of Soviet Socialist Republics

Vance, Cyrus, 293–295, 297, 299, 318, 321
Vietnam War, 124–127, 223
Vornike, Paul, 141, 142

War of Independence, 22–44
war of 1956–57, 51
Washington Post, 232
Water Carrier. *See* National Water Carrier
Weizman, Ezer, 55–57, 77, 82–85, 90, 115, 116, 240
West Bank, 103, 106, 119, 249, 294, 316, 327, 328, 331, 332, 334
Western Wall, Jerusalem, 111–112
West Germany, Rabin's visit to, 268–269
White Paper (1939), 10
World War II, 9–14

Ya'akobi, Gad, 282
Yadin, Yigael, 28, 38, 41, 46, 49, 119; Ben-Gurion's opinion of, 47
Yadlin, Asher, 304, 305
Yariv, Aharon, 70, 71, 77, 84–86, 90, 92, 96, 174
Yishuv leadership, 10, 12, 15, 28, 34
Yom Kippur War, 235; disengagement-of-forces agreement, 242, 243; interim agreement, 247, 253, 272, 274

Zadok, Chaim, 282
Zion, Mount, 30–32
Zion Gate, Jerusalem, 32
Zur, Michael, 304
Zur, Zvi, 57–59, 220